LEARNING: THEORY AND PRACTICE

LEARNING: THEORY AND PRACTICE

Paul E. Johnson
University of Minnesota

WITHDRAWN

Thomas Y. Crowell Company   New York
Established 1834

195805

L. C. Card 78-136036
ISBN 0-690-48703-7

Designed by Virginia Smith

Manufactured in the United States of America

The theme of this book of readings is the nature of the interface between education and psychology. The essays were selected for the way they fit into a scheme of theoretical and empirical activity rather than for their specific content. Because there is no content thread running through the selections, it is important that we become acquainted early with some framework for relating activity in psychology to that in education. The framework proposed here is based on the concept of learning; the nature of this framework is discussed in the introductory essay.

Each of the five parts of the book is introduced with remarks that are designed to relate the selections in that part to the framework presented in the introduction. No attempt is made to analyze each essay. Instead, brief introductory comments suggest viewing them as prototypes of a range of thinking and scholarly activity concerned with the theory and practice of learning.

Part I, "Aspects of Schooling," is designed to represent a range of views on the phenomena upon which research and scholarship in educational psychology are based. These essays were selected to reflect historical flavor as well as present concerns.

Part II, "Psychology as Inquiry," is devoted to psychology per se. It attempts to illustrate the theoretical and methodological thinking from which current concepts of learning are derived. Because educational psychology overlaps with experimental psychology both in the sense of methodology or tools and in the sense of concepts, it is important to understand the nature of thinking within this domain of inquiry. The papers in this section represent views that range from whether it is necessary to formulate theories of learning at all, to the subtle and complex theories that have recently been proposed for the acquisition of language.

"The Psychology of School Learning," which is the title of Part III, presents a number of studies that share an effort to apply psychology, sometimes systematically but often intuitively, to problems in education. We have been remarkably unsuccessful, as teachers well know, in establishing a reliable datum upon which educational practice can be built. To understand why this is so, it is important to keep abreast of recent research on educational problems.

The articles in Part IV, entitled "Understanding, Meaning and Knowledge," **v** were chosen for two reasons. First, they illustrate the wide range of thinking from which problems in learning can be attacked. Second, learning defined as the acquisition of understanding, meaning, and knowledge is one way of identifying phenomena appropriate for study within the framework of educational psychology.

Finally, Part V, "Potpourri: Toward a Psychology of School Learning," presents some current empirical and theoretical directions in educational psychology based on issues raised in previous sections. While the essays in this section present a variety of viewpoints, they are all concerned with prescriptive statements about the ways in which behavioral change can be most effectively accomplished.

The emphasis of the book is on few rather than many articles to represent each section. Because of this, there are no doubt significant omissions with regard to both authors and topics. And, of course, the book could easily be much larger. It is hoped, however, that what has been included is sufficient to convey a manageable and useful perspective on a complex field to those who will study and shape its phenomena.

P. E. J.

University of Minnesota
May 1970

CONTENTS

LEARNING: THEORY AND PRACTICE

Introduction

Education is a very general term. It can mean the whole enterprise of schooling from the nursery school through the university, or, as interpreted by Henry Adams, it can mean virtually anything that influences a person throughout his life. But here we shall take the view of Alexander Bain, whose book, *Education as a Science*, states that education is the building up or acquiring of knowledge.

Within the process of education is a phenomenon called schooling. While this phenomenon is complex and properly subject to a variety of interpretations, we shall focus our attention on that aspect of schooling that is concerned with learning.

The experimental psychologist typically defines learning as a relatively permanent change in behavior that results from the repetition of some prescribed activity (i.e., practice). The term school learning, then, refers to the changing of behavior within the context of the school. As the subject of experimental investigation, school learning is the concern of the educational psychologist.

Because experimental and educational psychology overlap in their concern for learning, it is important to be clear about some of the similarities and differences between them. To begin with, experimental and educational psychology both have applied dimensions. The basis of applied experimental psychology is in statements (principles of training) of the conditions under which behavioral change can be brought about. In educational psychology, application is concerned with prescriptive statements (principles of instruction) about how this change can be accomplished in the context of the school.

Of course instruction is not limited to schools. We can have self-instruction by which individuals educate themselves outside of formal institutions. This means that the educational psychologist must sometimes be concerned with learning under more general conditions than those that define schooling. As applied educational psychology increases the generality of its prescriptive statements about behavior, 1 it overlaps with applied psychology. And, of course, this is as it should be, for educational and experimental psychology are not, in reality, separate disciplines. Each is concerned with developing and verifying concepts of behavior. What distinguishes them is simply the class of phenomena they attempt to explain.

Principles of instruction (or training) can be contrasted with principles of practice. These latter rules for changing behavior are developed by trial and error rather than from descriptive statements in laboratory psychology. They form the basis for most behavioral change in our society. The teacher, the parent, and the animal trainer have acquired such principles either, as stated above, by trial and error, or sometimes (especially in teaching) in the context of a master-apprentice relationship.

Principles of teaching, behavior modification (with human beings), and child-rearing are all principles of practice. In fact, in the sense in which we have been using the term here, our best developed principles of instruction are for animals. This is because our most rigorous descriptive statements about behavior come from studying animals, particularly through operant conditioning.

The major independent variable of school learning is the curriculum; the major dependent variable is achievement. The task of educational psychology is to describe conditions under which the curriculum can be manipulated so as to accomplish particular outcomes in achievement. Because we so often have little knowledge about the exact nature of these variables, however, we have very few formal principles of instruction.

The lack of useful principles of instruction for school learning can be traced back to the early history of psychology. Early work in experimental psychology was concerned with establishing precise control over the conditions under which well-defined behaviors occur. In educational psychology the major effort was directed toward problems of measurement and methods research. The emphasis upon experimental precision and methodology focused attention away from any serious concern with content. As a result, school learning situations were often characterized by vague definitions of both curriculum variables and achievement behaviors.

This is not to say that we have no useful principles of practice. The current emphasis on behavior modification in classrooms is one example of how psychological knowledge can influence school learning. In any school situation it is important that individuals learn to focus their attention on those things from which knowledge is to be acquired. If children are running around rooms, or in other ways not attending to the vehicle used to communicate knowledge, then in a very real sense that knowledge cannot be transmitted. Such is often the case in classrooms where children care little or nothing about schools as social institutions, and do not, therefore, produce the kinds of behaviors necessary for learning to occur. By using principles of behavior modification, we lead children to focus their attention on devices used to communicate knowledge, such as the teacher or the textbook.

Given our present state of knowledge about behavior, what can we offer individuals such as teachers, parents, and counselors who want to change behavior? On purely aesthetic grounds we can argue that individuals who deal with the behavior of others should know something about the determinants of behavioral change as these are defined by science. More to the point, however, is the argument that knowledge of psychology will provide the practitioner with a model for interpreting the behavior that confronts him. Because we are human beings we have prescientific models for behavior, but these models are typically limited to the situations in which they are constructed. The behavioral models of psychology are more general, and thus permit us to see our own models as instances of a more general case. The general case does not tell us what to do in a new situation where the models of practice do not apply. Rather, its value lies in providing some guidelines for what not to do. A general model for behavior makes the trial and error procedure of discovering new principles of practice more efficient and can prevent fruitless and sometimes hazardous hypotheses about what to do next. In other words, it is what we think the individual is that determines how we shall treat him when principles from the laboratory or from our intuitions do not seem to apply.

PART I   ASPECTS OF SCHOOLING

Although William James was a nineteenth-century psychologist, many of his ideas sound disturbingly familiar today. Nowhere is this more apparent than in his book *Talks to Teachers*, a portion of which comprises the first selection. James clearly viewed psychology as a science and teaching as an art. His principles of teaching are what we have called principles of practice, but they are useful, nevertheless, as instances of the intuitions of a brilliant psychologist about human behavior in practical situations.

Edward Thorndike was a student of William James and as an experimental psychologist he was responsible for a school of psychology called "Connectionism." A major component of Connectionism was the Law of Effect which can be intuitively stated as, "behavior is affected by its consequences." Thorndike wrote texts in educational psychology after he became a faculty member at Teachers College, Columbia University. In addition, he wrote on the psychology of subject matter, the psychology of arithmetic, and the psychology of algebra. Thorndike, like James, viewed problems in education largely as a matter of intuitions about behavior based on knowledge of principles of psychology.

B. F. Skinner, perhaps one of our most famous psychologists, incorporated Thorndike's Law of Effect into studies of operant conditioning that he conducted over a number of years at Harvard University. While James and Thorndike proposed principles of practice, Skinner formulated principles of instruction. The work done in operant conditioning by Skinner and others provided a reliable set of functional relationships that could be used to formulate prescriptive statements for optimizing behavior. Since most of this work was carried out on animals (especially pigeons and white rats), Skinner's principles of instruction are, strictly speaking, for animals. He has, however, developed principles of practice for human beings based on research with animals. Some of these principles appear in Selection 3, "The Science of Learning and the Art of Teaching." Skinner, like James and Thorndike, uses his intuition as a   **5** basis for formulating principles for practical situations involving human beings.

John Stephens is an educational psychologist who was a student of Thorndike at Columbia University. He is largely responsible for articulating the concept of schooling as a phenomenon in the study of education. The underlying motivation for Stephens's work was the methods research that demonstrated an abundance of "no difference" findings over a number of years. Stephens's theory of schooling was formulated in part as an attempt to account for these findings of "no difference."

The final essay in this section is by James Deese, an experimental psychologist. Deese asks if education can be a discipline like psychology, anthropology, or history. One argument for such a discipline is based on the premise that progress on problems in education may depend on whether phenomena of schooling can be viewed from a common perspective. If each academic discipline examines only those phenemona of schooling that are of interest to it, we may never establish a reliable datum from which principles of instruction can be formulated.

In his article Deese argues that people whose sentiments are toward problems in education but whose methods are based in existing academic disciplines, offer the greatest hope for understanding schooling.

1 PSYCHOLOGY AND THE TEACHING ART
William James

In the general activity and uprising of ideal interests which every one with an eye for fact can discern all about us in American life, there is perhaps no more promising feature than the fermentation which for a dozen years or more has been going on among the teachers. In whatever sphere of education their functions may lie, there is to be seen among them a really inspiring amount of searching of the heart about the highest concerns of their profession. The renovation of nations begins always at the top, among the reflective members of the State, and spreads slowly outward and downward. The teachers of this country, one may say, have its future in their hands. The earnestness which they at present show in striving to enlighten and strengthen themselves is an index of the nation's probabilities of advance in all ideal directions. The outward organization of education which we have in our United States is perhaps, on the whole, the best organization that exists in any country. The State school systems give a diversity and flexibility, an opportunity for experiment and keenness of competition, nowhere else to be found on such an important scale. The independence of so many of the colleges and universities; the give and take of students and instructors between them all; their emulation, and their happy organic relations to the lower schools; the traditions of instruction in them, evolved from the older American recitation-method (and so avoiding on the one hand the pure lecture-system prevalent in Germany and Scotland, which considers too little the individual student, and yet not involving the sacrifice of the instructor to the individual student, which the English tutorial system would seem too often to entail),—all these things (to say nothing of that coeducation of the sexes in whose benefits so many of us heartily believe), all these things, I say, are most happy features of our scholastic life, and from them the most sanguine auguries may be drawn.

Having so favorable an organization, all we need is to impregnate it with geniuses, to get superior men and women working more and more abundantly in it and for it and at it, and in a generation or two America may well lead the education of the world. I must say that I look forward with no little confidence to the day when that shall be an accomplished fact.

No one has profited more by the fermentation of which I speak, in pedagogical circles, than we psychologists. The desire of the school-teachers for a completer professional training, and their aspiration to-

SOURCE: William James, *Talks to Teachers* (New York: Henry Holt & Co., 1904), ch. 1, pp. 3–14.

ward the "professional" spirit in their work, have led them more and more to turn to us for light on fundamental principles. And in these few hours which we are to spend together you look to me, I am sure, for information concerning the mind's operations, which may enable you to labor more easily and effectively in the several schoolrooms over which you preside.

Far be it from me to disclaim for psychology all title to such hopes. Psychology ought certainly to give the teacher radical help. And yet I confess that, acquainted as I am with the height of some of your expectations, I feel a little anxious lest, at the end of these simple talks of mine, not a few of you may experience some disappointment at the net results. In other words, I am not sure that you may not be indulging fancies that are just a shade exaggerated. That would not be altogether astonishing, for we have been having something like a "boom" in psychology in this country. Laboratories and professorships have been founded, and reviews established. The air has been full of rumors. The editors of educational journals and the arrangers of conventions have had to show themselves enterprising and on a level with the novelties of the day. Some of the professors have not been unwilling to co-operate, and I am not sure even that the publishers have been entirely inert. "The new psychology" has thus become a term to conjure up portentous ideas withal; and you teachers, docile and receptive and aspiring as many of you are, have been plunged in an atmosphere of vague talk about our science, which to a great extent has been more mystifying than enlightening. Altogether it does seem as if there were a certain fatality of mystification laid upon the teachers of our day. The matter of their profession, compact enough in itself, has to be frothed up for them in journals and institutes, till its outlines often threaten to be lost in a kind of vast uncertainty. Where the disciples are not independent and critical-minded enough (and I think that, if you teachers in the earlier grades have any defect—the slightest touch of a defect in the world—it is that you are a mite too docile), we are pretty sure to miss accuracy and balance and measure in those who get a license to lay down the law to them from above.

As regards this subject of psychology, now, I wish at the very threshold to do what I can to dispel the mystification. So I say at once that in my humble opinion there *is* no "new psychology" worthy of the name. There is nothing but the old psychology which began in Locke's time, plus a little physiology of the brain and senses and theory of evolution, and a few refinements of introspective detail, for the most part without adaptation to the teacher's use. It is only the fundamental conceptions of psychology which are of real value to the teacher; and they, apart from the aforesaid theory of evolution, are very far from being new.—I trust that you will see better what I mean by this at the end of all these talks.

I say moreover that you make a great, a very great mistake, if you think that psychology, being the science of the mind's laws, is something from which you can deduce definite programmes and schemes and methods of instruction for immediate schoolroom use. Psychology is a science, and teaching is an art; and sciences never generate arts directly out of themselves. An intermediary inventive mind must make the application, by using its originality.

The science of logic never made a man reason rightly, and the science of ethics (if there be such a thing) never made a man behave rightly. The most such sciences can do is to help us to catch ourselves up and check ourselves, if we start to reason or to behave wrongly; and to criticise ourselves more articulately after we have made mistakes. A science only lays down lines within which the rules of the art must fall, laws which the follower of the art must not transgress; but what particular thing he shall positively do within those lines is left exclusively to his own genius. One genius will do his work well and succeed in one way, while another succeeds as well quite differently; yet neither will transgress the lines.

The art of teaching grew up in the schoolroom, out of inventiveness and sympathetic concrete observation. Even where (as in the case of Herbart) the advancer of the art was also a psychologist, the pedagogics and the psychology ran side by side, and the former was not derived in any sense from the latter. The two were congruent, but neither was subordinate. And so everywhere the teaching must *agree* with the psychology, but need not necessarily be the only kind of teaching that would so agree; for many diverse methods of teaching may equally well agree with psychological laws.

To know psychology, therefore, is absolutely no guarantee that we shall be good teachers. To advance to that result, we must have an additional endowment altogether, a happy tact and ingenuity to tell us what definite things to say and do when the pupil is before us. That ingenuity in meeting and pursuing the pupil, that tact for the concrete situation, though they are the alpha and omega of the teacher's art, are things to which psychology cannot help us in the least.

The science of psychology, and whatever science of general pedagogics may be based on it, are in fact much like the science of war. Nothing is simpler or more definite than the principles of either. In war, all you have to do is to work your enemy into a position from which the natural obstacles prevent him from escaping if he tries to; then to fall on him in numbers superior to his own, at a moment when you have led him to think you far away; and so, with a minimum of exposure of your own troops, to hack his force to pieces, and take the remainder prisoners. Just so, in teaching, you must simply work your pupil into such a state of interest in what you are going to teach him that every other object of attention is banished from his mind; then reveal it to him so impressively that he will remember the occasion to his dying day; and finally fill him with devouring curiosity to know what the next steps in connection with the subject are. The principles being so plain, there would be nothing but victories for the masters of the science, either on the battlefield or in the schoolroom, if they did not both have to make their application to an incalculable quantity in the shape of the mind of their opponent. The mind of your own enemy, the pupil, is working away from you as keenly and eagerly as is the mind of the commander on the other side from the scientific general. Just what the respective enemies want and think, and what they know and do not know, are as hard things for the teacher as for the general to find out. Divination and perception, not psychological pedagogies or theoretic strategy, are the only helpers here.

But, if the use of psychological principles thus be negative rather than positive, it does not follow that it may not be a great use, all the same. It certainly narrows the path for experiments and trials. We know in advance, if we are psychologists, that certain methods will be wrong, so our psychology saves us from mistakes. It makes us, moreover, more clear as to what we are about. We gain confidence in respect to any method which we are using as soon as we believe that it has theory as well as practice at its back. Most of all, it fructifies our independence, and it reanimates our interest, to see out subject at two different angles, —to get a stereoscopic view, so to speak, of the youthful organism who is our enemy, and, while handling him with all our concrete tact and divination, to be able, at the same time, to represent to ourselves the curious inner elements of his mental machine. Such a complete knowledge as this of the pupil, at once intuitive and analytic, is surely the knowledge at which every teacher ought to aim.

Fortunately for you teachers, the elements of the mental machine can be clearly apprehended, and their workings easily grasped. And, as the most general elements and workings are just those parts of psychology which the teacher finds most directly useful, it follows that the amount of this science which is necessary to all teachers need not be very great. Those who find themselves loving the subject may go as far as they please, and become possibly none the worse teachers for the fact, even though in some of them one might apprehend a little loss of balance from the tendency observable in all of us to overemphasize certain special parts of a subject when we are studying it intensely and abstractly. But for the great majority of you a general view is enough, provided it be a true one; and such a general view, one may say, might almost be written on the palm of one's hand.

Least of all need you, merely *as teachers*, deem it part of your duty to become contributors to psychological science or to make psychological observations in a methodical or responsible manner. I fear that some of the enthusiasts for child-study have thrown a certain burden on you in this way. By all means let child-study go on,—it is refreshing all our sense of the child's life. There are teachers who take a spontaneous delight in filling syllabuses, inscribing observations, compiling statistics, and computing the per cent. Child-study will certainly enrich their lives. And, if its results, as treated statistically, would seem on the whole to have but trifling value, yet the anecdotes and observations of which it in part consist do certainly acquaint us more intimately with our pupils. Our eyes and ears grow quickened to discern in the child before us processes similar to those we have read of as noted in the children,— processes of which we might otherwise have remained inobservant. But, for Heaven's sake, let the rank and file of teachers be passive readers if they so prefer, and feel free not to contribute to the accumulation. Let not the prosecution of it be preached as an imperative duty or imposed by regulation on those to whom it proves an exterminating bore, or who in any way whatever miss in themselves the appropriate vocation for it. I cannot too strongly agree with my colleague, Professor Münsterberg, when he says that the teacher's attitude toward the child, being concrete and ethical, is positively opposed to the psychological observer's, which is abstract and analytic. Although some of us may conjoin the attitudes successfully, in most of us they must conflict.

The worst thing that can happen to a good teacher is to get a bad conscience about her profession because she feels herself hopeless as a psychologist. Our teachers are overworked already. Every one who adds a jot or tittle of unnecessary weight to their burden is a foe of education. A bad conscience increases the weight of every other burden; yet I know that child-study, and other pieces of psychology as well, have been productive of bad conscience in many a really innocent pedagogic breast. I should indeed be glad if this passing word from me might tend to dispel such a bad conscience, if any of you have it; for it is certainly one of those fruits of more or less systematic mystification of which I have already complained. The best teacher may be the poorest contributor of child-study material, and the best contributor may be the poorest teacher. No fact is more palpable than this.

2 From THE PRINCIPLES OF TEACHING
Edward L. Thorndike

Introduction

THE TEACHER'S PROBLEM

The Aims, Materials and Methods of Education. The word Education is used with many meanings, but in all its usages it refers to *changes*. No one is educated who stays just as he was. We do not educate anybody if we do nothing that makes any difference or change in anybody. The need of education arises from the fact that *what is* is not what *ought to be.* Because we wish ourselves and others to become different from what we and they now are, we try to educate ourselves and them. In studying education, then, one studies always the existence, nature, causation or value of changes of some sort.

The teacher confronts two questions: "What changes to make?" and "How to make them?" The first question is commonly answered for the teacher by the higher school authorities for whom he or she works. The opinions of the educational leaders in the community decide what the schools shall try to do for their pupils. The program of studies is planned and the work which is to be done grade by grade is carefully outlined. The grammar-school teacher may think that changes in knowledge represented by the ability to read a modern language ought to be made in boys and girls before the high-school, but the decision is rarely his; the primary teacher may be obliged to teach arithmetic although her own judgment would postpone giving the knowledge of numbers until the fifth or sixth grade.

What changes should be made in human nature by primary, grammar and high schools and why these and not other changes should be the aim of the schools, are questions usually answered under the heading of "Principles of Education." How most efficiently to make such changes as educational aims recommend, is a question usually answered under the headings "Principles of Teaching," or "Methods of Teaching," or "Theory and Practice of Teaching," or "Educational Psychology." This book will try to answer this latter question,—to give a scientific basis for the art of actual teaching rather than for the selection of aims for the schools as a whole or of the subjects to be taught or of the general result to be gained from any subject. Not the *What* or the *Why* but the *How* is its topic.

SOURCE: Edward L. Thorndike, *Principles of Teaching Based upon Psychology* (New York: A. G. Seiler, 1906), pp. 1–10, 257–268.

It is not wise however to study the *How* of teaching without any reference to the *What* or the *Why*. If a teacher does not appreciate, at least crudely, the general aims of education, he will not fully appreciate the general aims of school education; if he does not appreciate the general aims of school education, he will not fully appreciate the aims of his special grade or of any one special subject; if he does not have fairly clear ideas of what the year's work as a whole or of what each subject as a whole ought to accomplish for the scholars, he will not know exactly what he is about in any particular day's work. The teacher must be something more than the carpenter who follows without reflection the architect's plan, or the nurse who merely administers the physician's prescriptions. His relation to the administration of the school system and the program of studies is more like that of the builder who is told to make the best house he can at a cost of ten thousand dollars, using three laborers, a derrick and such and such tools and providing especially for light, ventilation and protection against fire. Superior authorities say, "Make the best boys and girls you can, using arithmetic, geography, school regulations and so on, providing especially for knowledge, good habits of thought, worthy interests, bodily health, noble feelings and honest, unselfish conduct." The builder must often study how to dig a foundation, how to erect a frame, how to lay a floor and the like with reference to what is to be built; the teacher should often study how to utilize inborn tendencies, how to form habits, how to develop interests and the like with reference to what changes in intellect and character are to be made. The teacher should know about educational aims and values as well as about such principles of teaching as directly concern his own activities in the class-room.

The next three pages will accordingly outline the essential facts concerning the ideals which, in the opinion of the best qualified thinkers, should be followed in American education, and throughout the book due attention will be given to such facts about the ends the teacher should seek as he needs to know to improve his teaching.

The Aims of Education. Education as a whole should make human beings wish each other well, should increase the sum of human energy and happiness and decrease the sum of discomfort of the human beings that are or will be, and should foster the higher, impersonal pleasures. These aims of education in general—goodwill to men, useful and happy lives, and noble enjoyment—are the ultimate aims of school education in particular. Its proximate aims are to give boys and girls health in body and mind, information about the world of nature and men, worthy interests in knowledge and action, a multitude of habits of thought, feeling and behavior and ideas of efficiency, honor, duty, love and service. The special proximate aims of the first six years of school life are commonly taken to be to give physical training and protection against disease;

knowledge of the simple facts of nature and human life; the ability to gain knowledge and pleasure through reading and to express ideas and feelings through spoken and written language, music and other arts; interests in the concrete life of the world; habits of intelligent curiosity, purposive thinking, modesty, obedience, honesty, helpfulness, affection, courage and justice; and the ideals proper to childhood.

The special proximate aims of school life from twelve to eighteen are commonly taken to be physical health and skill; knowledge of the simpler general laws of nature and human life and of the opinions of the wisest and best; more effective use of the expressive arts; interests in the arts and sciences, and in human life both as directly experienced and as portrayed in literature; powers of self-control, accuracy, steadiness and logical thought, technical and executive abilities, cooperation and leadership; habits of self-restraint, honor, courage, justice, sympathy and reverence; and the ideals proper to youth.

With respect to the amount of emphasis upon different features of these general ideals, the best judgment of the present rates practical ability somewhat higher and culture of the semi-selfish sort somewhat lower than has been the case in the past. No sensible thinker about education now regards the ability to support oneself as a mean thing. Every one must gain power at school as well as at home to pull his own weight in the boat, to repay in useful labor what the world gives him in food and shelter. The cultured idler is as one-sided as the ignorant and clownish worker and may be even more of a danger to the world. The schools must prepare for efficiency in the serious business of life as well as for the refined enjoyment of its leisure.

The best judgment of the present gives much more weight than has been the case previously to health, to bodily skill and to the technical and industrial arts. The ideal of the scholar has given way to the ideal of the capable man,—capable in scholarship still, but also capable in physique and in the power to manipulate things.

Very recently thinkers about education have dwelt more and more upon the importance of aiming not only to prepare children for adult life and work but also to adapt them to the life of childhood itself. Aim more to make children succeed with the problems and duties of childhood and less to fit them for the problems and duties of twenty years after; let education adapt the child to his own environment as well as to some supposed work of his later years—such are the recommendations of present-day theories of education.

In actual practice aims often conflict. A gain in knowledge may mean a loss in health; to arouse ideals may mean less time for drill in correct habits; in zeal for the development of love of the beautiful the interest in the dry, cold facts of science may have to be neglected. The energy of any teacher, and of scholars as well, is limited. All that can be expected is that none of the aims of school education shall be wilfully violated and that energy should be distributed among them all in some reasonable way.

The degrees of emphasis on the different proximate aims vary (1) with the nature of the individual to be educated and (2) with the nature of the educational forces besides the school which are at work. Thus (1) the emphasis in a school for the feeble-minded is not the same as in an ordinary school; the emphasis in a high school representing a selection of the more ambitious, intellectual and energetic is not the same as in a school where the selection is simply on the basis of the ability of the parents to pay tuition. (2) The emphasis in a primary school attended by the children of recent immigrants will differ from that in a school in a suburb inhabited by American professional and business families. A high school in a farming community in the Southwest should not pattern its ideals after those proper to a school in New York City.

The Special Problem of the Teacher. It is the problem of the higher authorities of the schools to decide what the schools shall try to achieve and to arrange plans for school work which will attain the desired ends. Having decided what changes are to be made they entrust to the teachers the work of making them. The special problem of the teacher is to make these changes as economically and as surely as is possible under the conditions of school life. His is the task of giving certain information, forming certain habits, increasing certain powers, arousing certain interests and inspiring certain ideals.

The study of the best methods of doing so may be carried to almost any degree of detail. The principles of teaching may mean the general principles applicable to the formation of all habits or the highly specialized rules of procedure for forming the habit of correct use of *shall* and *will;* they include the laws valid for the acquisition of any knowledge and the discussion of the particular difficulties in teaching the spelling of *to, two* and *too.* But the problem is always fundamentally the same: —Given these children to be changed and this change to be made, how shall I proceed? Given this material for education and this aim of education, what means and methods shall I use?

PSYCHOLOGY AND THE ART OF TEACHING

The Scientific Basis of Teaching. The work of teaching is to produce and to prevent changes in human beings; to preserve and increase the desirable qualities of body, intellect and character and to get rid of the undesirable. To thus control human nature, the teacher needs to know it. To change what is into what ought to be, we need to know the laws by which the changes occur. Just as to make a plant grow well the gardener must act in accordance with the laws of botany which concern the growth of plants, or as to make a bridge well the architect must act in accordance with the facts of mechanics concerning stresses and strains, or as to change disease into health the physician must act in accordance with the laws of physiology and pathology, so to make human beings intelligent and useful and noble the teacher must act in accordance with the laws of the sciences of human nature.

The sciences of biology, especially human physiology and hygiene, give the laws of changes in bodily nature. The science of psychology gives the laws of changes in intellect and character. The teacher studies and learns to apply psychology to teaching for the same reason that the progressive farmer studies and learns to apply botany; the architect, mechanics; or the physician, physiology and pathology.

Stimulus and Response. Using psychological terms, the art of teaching may be defined as the art of giving and withholding stimuli with the result of producing or preventing certain responses. In this definition the term stimulus is used widely for any event which influences a person,—for a word spoken to him, a look, a sentence which he reads, the air he breathes, etc., etc. The term response is used for any reaction made by him,—a new thought, a feeling of interest, a bodily act, any mental or bodily condition resulting from the stimulus. The aim of the teacher is to produce desirable and prevent undesirable changes in human beings by producing and preventing certain responses. The means at the disposal of the teacher are the stimuli which can be brought to bear upon the pupil,—the teacher's words, gestures and appearance, the condition and appliances of the school room, the books to be used and objects to be seen, and so on through a long list of the things and events which the teacher can control. The responses of the pupil are all the infinite variety of thoughts and feelings and bodily movements occurring in all their possible connections.

The stimuli given by the teacher to arouse and guide the pupil's responses may be classified as:—

A. Stimuli under direct control.

The teacher's movements,[1]—speech, gestures, facial expression, etc.

B. Stimuli under indirect control.

The physical conditions of the school,—air, light, heat, etc.

The material equipment of the school,—books, apparatus, specimens, etc.

The social conditions of the school,—the acts (including spoken words) of the pupils and the spirit which these acts represent.

---

[1] The knowledge, love and tact of the teacher are, of course, of the highest importance as forces in teaching but their actual operation is in their expression in words, gestures or acts of some sort.

The general environment,—acts of parents, laws, libraries, etc.

The responses may be classified as:—

A. Physiological responses, such as deeper breathing, sounder sleep, vigorous exercise and the like.

B. Responses of knowledge,[2] such as connecting a sense stimulus with an appropriate percept, abstracting one element from a complex fact or making associations of ideas.

C. Responses of attitude, such as the connection of attention, interest, preference and belief with certain situations.

D. Responses of feeling, such as connecting sympathy, love, hate, etc., with certain situations.

E. Responses of action or of conduct and skill, connecting certain acts or movements with certain mental states.

The Value of Psychology. If there existed a perfect and complete knowledge of human nature,—a complete science of psychology,—it would tell the effect of every possible stimulus and the cause of every possible response in every possible human being. A teacher could then know just what the result of any act of his would be, could prophesy just what the effect of such and such a page read or punishment given or dress worn would be,—just how to get any particular response, of attention to this object, memory of this fact or comprehension of that principle.

Of course present knowledge of psychology is nearer to zero than to complete perfection, and its applications to teaching must therefore be often incomplete, indefinite and insecure. The application of psychology to teaching is more like that of botany and chemistry to farming than like that of physiology and pathology to medicine. Anyone of good sense can farm fairly well without science, and anyone of good sense can teach fairly well without knowing and applying psychology. Still, as the farmer with the knowledge of the applications of botany and chemistry to farming is, other things being equal, more successful than the farmer without it, so the teacher will, other things being equal, be the more successful who can apply psychology, the science of human nature, to the problems of the school.

The Scientific Study of Teaching

The efficiency of any profession depends in large measure upon the degree to which it becomes scientific. The profession of teaching will

---

[2] Knowledge is used here in a broad sense to include sensing objects, analyzing facts, feeling relationships and drawing inferences, as well as memory of facts or associations of ideas.

improve (1) in proportion as its members direct their daily work by the scientific spirit and methods, that is by honest, open-minded considera- tion of facts, by freedom from superstitions, fancies or unverified guesses,[3] and (2) in proportion as the leaders in education direct their choices of methods by the results of scientific investigation rather than by general opinion.

Throughout this book the student has been given training in thinking scientifically about teaching, and has been prepared to base his profes- sional work upon facts and to examine every act of teaching in the light of known laws of human nature. One thing more is essential to the proper intellectual attitude of a teacher toward class-room problems— the verification of results.

TESTING THE RESULTS OF TEACHING

The Importance of Tests. No matter how carefully one tries to follow the right principles of teaching, no matter how ingeniously one selects and how adroitly one arranges stimuli, it is advisable to test the result of one's effort,—to make sure that the knowledge or power or tendency ex- pected has really been acquired. Just as the scientist, though he has made his facts as accurate and his argument as logical as he can, still re- mains unsatisfied until he verifies his conclusion by testing it with new facts, so the teacher, after planning and executing a piece of work as well as he can, must "verify" his teaching by direct tests of its results and must consider uncertain any result that he cannot thus verify.

Their Difficulty. It is true that some of the most important results of teaching cannot be verified at all by the teacher himself. The perma- nence of interests, the effect of moral inspiration in childhood on adult behavior and the fortification of the pupil's heart against degrading forces that will assault it years after school is done, are of necessity not subject to full or accurate verification. The results of a teacher's work upon the life of the pupils out of school are also to a large extent inac- cessible to adequate observation. Finally certain changes in human in- tellect and character, such as nobler ideals, new ambitions and stronger powers, are hard to test even within the sphere of school and class-room life. The deeper ideals and ambitions are often cherished in secret and revealed only by some sudden access of intimacy or by unusual events. The strength of mental powers is not hard to test but the result is almost always the result of delayed capacity,—of mere inner growth,—as well as of the teacher's efforts; hence, the facts are hard to interpret.

In many cases, however, a teacher may not only hope and believe that

[3] The right intellectual attitude is, of course, not the sole factor in good teaching. A good will toward children, philanthropic devotion to the work, the zeal for perfec- tion that animates the true artist or craftsman and the personal qualities which work subtly by the force of imitation are also important.

a desired result has been obtained; he may know. In many cases he can do more than simply try the best plan he can devise; he can try, test the results, find the failures in them, and, with this new knowledge, devise a remedy. Such actual verification of the success of one's work is possible in the case of changes in knowledge, skill and all definite habits. One should be able to tell absolutely whether Johnny Smith gets ideas or only words when he reads, whether Mary Jones can sew well enough to be worth five dollars a week to a dress-maker, whether Fred Brown does or does not treat his class-mates with more justice than he did three months ago.

Their Value to the Teacher. Testing the results of one's teaching is useful not only because it gives a basis for improvements in one's methods, but also because it is one chief means of gaining knowledge of the mental content and special capacities of individuals. In applying the principle of apperception a teacher is constantly led to test the results of knowledge previously given as a preliminary to giving more. For the main thing in fitting stimuli to the mental make-up of pupils is not a host of ready-made devices to secure the cooperation of previous experience; it is rather constant readiness in testing for the presence of the essentials, in diagnosing the exact result of previous lessons.

Their Value to the Class. Testing the results of teaching is useful to the class as well as to the teacher, and to the class directly as well as indirectly through the betterment of future steps in teaching. Any scholar needs to know that he knows as well as to merely know; to be ignorant and know that you are so is far more promising than to be ignorant and not know it. By expression and use new ideas and habits get a double value; boys and girls in school need to know what progress their efforts have achieved and to guide their efforts by objective facts as well as by their own sense of progress.

It is a common opinion that examining a pupil, finding out "whether he knows his lesson" is the least part of teaching, is something that anyone can do. And it is fashionable amongst many teachers to spend the greater part of their time and still more of their energy in giving children opportunities to learn a great deal rather than in making sure that they learn something. The type of testing that uses the entire recitation simply to make sure that the pupil has studied certain pages of a book and remembered what he has learned is a small part of teaching and can be done by even a poor teacher. But the real verification of the work of teaching, that makes sure of just what the pupil knows and feels, that tests his comprehension and attitude as well as his memory, that prevents waste and prepares the way for better teaching of that pupil in the next topic and better teaching of that topic with the next class, is a most essential part of teaching and is one of the hardest things to do well. . . .

Summary

Testing the results of teaching and study is for the teacher what verification of theories is to the scientist,—the *sine qua non* of sure progress. It is a chief means to fitting teaching to the previous experience and individual capacities of pupils, and to arousing in them the instinct for achievement and the capacity for self-criticism. The test for knowledge, skill, appreciation and morality is in each case appropriate action. A valid test is one in which the response in question (knowledge or skill or ideal or whatever it may be) and only that response will produce a certain observable result.

TESTING THE GENERAL RESULTS OF SCHOOL WORK

The Importance of Tests of Methods. What the teacher should do with respect to each act of teaching each pupil, the leaders in education should do with respect to the general methods of teaching a subject recommended to all teachers. Expectations of results, even if based on right principles, must be corroborated by actual verification.

As a rule the best present judgment about the efficiency of a method of teaching will rest upon its harmony with the principles derived from the facts of human nature and upon its success or failure as measured by the opinion of those who try it. The best present judgment will not be mistaken very often or very much, but there could be safer tests of the worth of methods. For when a principle derived from the facts of human nature is applied under the peculiar conditions of school life it may need modification; and the opinions of even the best teachers concerning the value of a method may be shortsighted and partial. What is needed is the comparatively sure decision of that superior variety of opinion which is called science.

The Characteristics of Scientific Judgments of Methods. The judgments of science are distinguished from the judgments of opinion by being more impartial, more objective, more precise, more subject to verification by any competent observer, and by being made by those who by their nature and training should be better judges.

Science knows or should know no favorites and cares for nothing in its conclusions but their truth. Opinion is often misled by the "unconscious logic of its hopes and fears," by prepossessions for or against this or that book or method or result. Science pays no heed to anything but the facts which it has already made sure of; it puts nothing in the scales but objective evidence. Opinion trusts its personal impressions, bows to authority and follows the crowd. Anyone's opinion constantly favors the methods he is used to and is suspicious of new ideas except his own; it accepts without verification and rejects without a fair trial. Science seeks precise quantitative measures of facts by which changes and correspondences may be properly weighed; opinion is content to guess at amounts of difference and likeness, to talk in the vague terms of more or less, much and little, to rate a method as better or worse without taking the pains to find out just how much better or worse it is. Science reveals the sources of its evidence and the course of its arguments, so that any properly equipped thinker can verify for himself the facts asserted to be true. Opinion offers itself to be accepted or rejected, but not to be verified or intelligently criticised. Science is the work of minds specialized to search after truth and selected as fit for the work by their equals and superiors in it. Opinion is the occasional thought of those who, though important and capable people, are yet only amateurs in the work of getting truth.

Science would decide between two methods, say of teaching reading, by giving each an adequate trial, by measuring exactly the changes in bodily welfare, knowledge, interests, habits, powers and ideals caused by the two, and by comparing impartially the results in the two cases. It would, for instance, arrange that method A should be tried in ten or twenty classes and method B in ten or twenty other classes of equal ability and advantages taught by equally competent teachers. It would make sure that the two groups of teachers tried equally hard and that the two groups of classes were alike with respect to school-room equipment, the amount of time given to reading and the like. It would measure with precision the accomplishment of each pupil in reading itself, in spelling and writing, in knowledge of facts gained, in appreciation of good literature, in interest in reading, in such habits as might be influenced by the special training of reading, in power to learn new things and so on through the list of all the changes which instruction in reading may produce.

The Prospects of Scientific Investigations of Teaching. Obviously such a scientific basis for the professional work of teaching is in every way desirable. But for many reasons only a beginning has been made. The main reasons are perhaps, first that strictly scientific methods have only lately begun to be used in the case of facts of human activities and second that the complexity of the problems of teaching is so great as to make scientific treatment of them very intricate and laborious. There are a score of competent scientists engaged in the study of physical science for every one that is at work on the problems of social institutions. The task of knowing completely the facts and explanation of the mental and moral development of any one child is comparable to the study of the geology of an entire continent or the chemistry of all the metals.

The infrequency of the effort to investigate questions of teaching in the spirit and by the methods of science and the difficulty of the task itself are, however, no excuse for their neglect. The scientific study of teaching is at least as important as the scientific study of medicine and, though difficult, is in no way impossible. Even the subtle changes in powers, interests and aspirations can be measured; for sooner or later they must be manifested in actual facts. Even the remote influences of teaching on life after school can be known if the investigator has unlimited time and energy. The immediate influence of various sorts of teaching upon the knowledge and habits directly concerned, may be studied scientifically with much less difficulty and with promise of quick returns in knowledge. There should be no need to guess at the value of methods of teaching spelling or beginning reading or Latin grammar.

Such investigations lie beyond the scope of the activities of most teachers. The time, the training, the scientific frame of mind and the zeal which they require can only rarely be at the disposal of the teacher, who has so many other things to learn and to do. To advance scientific knowledge of education is a most worthy occupation for anyone who is able to succeed in it but it is not the duty of all or of many teachers. The burden of making exact measurements of children's attainments, of inquiring deeply into the what and why of the facts of school life and of feeling responsible for the verification or disproof of hypotheses about methods may be assumed voluntarily by the investigator, but it should not be imposed upon an already too busy teacher. Teachers should respect and encourage the labors of science but they should not feel bound to share them. The leaders in thought about education, on the other hand, *should* feel bound to study scientifically the field in which they claim to rank as experts. Since their opinions will be accepted by the profession as a whole, it is their duty to verify each opinion by a test of the results to which it leads.

3   THE SCIENCE OF LEARNING AND THE ART OF TEACHING
B. F. Skinner

Some promising advances have recently been made in the field of learning. Special techniques have been designed to arrange what are called "contingencies of reinforcement"—the relations which prevail between

SOURCE: B. F. Skinner, "The Science of Learning and the Art of Teaching," *Harvard Educational Review*, 24, no. 2 (Spring 1954), 86–97. Copyright © 1954 by the President and Fellows of Harvard College. Reprinted by permission of the *Harvard Educational Review*.

behavior on the one hand and the consequences of that behavior on the other—with the result that a much more effective control of behavior has been achieved. It has long been argued that an organism learns mainly by producing changes in its environment, but it is only recently that these changes have been carefully manipulated. In traditional devices for the study of learning—in the serial maze, for example, or in the T-maze, the problem box, or the familiar discrimination apparatus— the effects produced by the organism's behavior are left to many fluctuating circumstances. There is many a slip between the turn-to-the-right and the food-cup at the end of the alley. It is not surprising that techniques of this sort have yielded only very rough data from which the uniformities demanded by an experimental science can be extracted only by averaging many cases. In none of this work has the behavior of the individual organism been predicted in more than a statistical sense. The learning processes which are the presumed object of such research are reached only through a series of inferences. Current preoccupation with deductive systems reflects this state of the science.

Recent improvements in the conditions which control behavior in the field of learning are of two principal sorts. The Law of Effect has been taken seriously; we have made sure that effects *do* occur and that they occur under conditions which are optimal for producing the changes called learning. Once we have arranged the particular type of consequence called a reinforcement, our techniques permit us to shape up the behavior of an organism almost at will. It has become a routine exercise to demonstrate this in classes in elementary psychology by conditioning such an organism as a pigeon. Simply by presenting food to a hungry pigeon at the right time, it is possible to shape up three or four well-defined responses in a single demonstration period—such responses as turning around, pacing the floor in the pattern of a figure-8, standing still in a corner of the demonstration apparatus, stretching the neck, or stamping the foot. Extremely complex performances may be reached through successive stages in the shaping process, the contingencies of reinforcement being changed progressively in the direction of the required behavior. The results are often quite dramatic. In such a demonstration one can *see* learning take place. A significant change in behavior is often obvious as the result of a single reinforcement.

A second important advance in technique permits us to maintain behavior in given states of strength for long periods of time. Reinforcements continue to be important, of course, long after an organism has learned *how* to do something, long after it has acquired behavior. They are necessary to maintain the behavior in strength. Of special interest is the effect of various schedules of intermittent reinforcement. Charles B. Ferster and the author are currently preparing an extensive report of a five-year research program, sponsored by the Office of Naval Research, in which most of the important types of schedules have been investigated and in which the effects of schedules in general have been reduced to a few principles. On the theoretical side we now have a fairly good idea of why a given schedule produces its appropriate performance. On the practical side we have learned how to maintain any given level of activity for daily periods limited only by the physical exhaustion of the organism and from day to day without substantial change throughout its life. Many of these effects would be traditionally assigned to the field of motivation, although the principal operation is simply the arrangement of contingencies of reinforcement.[1]

These new methods of shaping behavior and of maintaining it in strength are a great improvement over the traditional practices of professional animal trainers, and it is not surprising that our laboratory results are already being applied to the production of performing animals for commercial purposes. In a more academic environment that have been used for demonstration purposes which extend far beyond an interest in learning as such. For example, it is not too difficult to arrange the complex contingencies which produce many types of social behavior. Competition is exemplified by two pigeons playing a modified game of ping-pong. The pigeons drive the ball back and forth across a small table by pecking at it. When the ball gets by one pigeon, the other is reinforced. The task of constructing such a "social relation" is probably completely out of reach of the traditional animal trainer. It requires a carefully designed program of gradually changing contingencies and the skillful use of schedules to maintain the behavior in strength. Each pigeon is separately prepared for its part in the total performance, and the "social relation" is then arbitrarily constructed. The sequence of events leading up to this stable state are excellent material for the study of the factors important in nonsynthetic social behavior. It is instructive to consider how a similar series of contingencies could arise in the case of the human organism through the evolution of cultural patterns.

Cooperation can also be set up, perhaps more easily than competition. We have trained two pigeons to coordinate their behavior in a cooperative endeavor with a precision which equals that of the most skillful human dancers. In a more serious vein these techniques have permitted us to explore the complexities of the individual organism and to analyze some of the serial or coordinate behaviors involved in attention, problem solving, various types of self-control, and the subsidiary systems of responses within a single organism called "personalities." Some of these are exemplified in what we call multiple schedules of reinforcement. In general a given schedule has an effect upon the rate at

---

[1] The reader may wish to review Dr. Skinner's article, "Some Contributions of an Experimental Analysis of Behavior to Psychology as a Whole," *The American Psychologist*, 1953, 8, 69–78. Ed.

which a response is emitted. Changes in the rate from moment to moment show a pattern typical of the schedule. The pattern may be as simple as a constant rate of responding at a given value, it may be a gradually accelerating rate between certain extremes, it may be an abrupt change from not responding at all to a given stable high rate, and so on. It has been shown that the performance characteristic of a given schedule can be brought under the control of a particular stimulus and that different performances can be brought under the control of different stimuli in the same organism. At a recent meeting of the American Psychological Association, Dr. Ferster and the author demonstrated a pigeon whose behavior showed the pattern typical of "fixed-interval" reinforcement in the presence of one stimulus and, alternately, the pattern typical of the very different schedule called "fixed ratio" in the presence of a second stimulus. In the laboratory we have been able to obtain performances appropriate to *nine* different schedules in the presence of appropriate stimuli in random alternation. When Stimulus 1 is present, the pigeon executes the performance appropriate to Schedule 1. When Stimulus 2 is present, the pigeon executes the performance appropriate to Schedule 2. And so on. This result is important because it makes the extrapolation of our laboratory results to daily life much more plausible. We are all constantly shifting from schedule to schedule as our immediate environment changes, but the dynamics of the control exercised by reinforcement remain essentially unchanged.

It is also possible to construct very complex *sequences* of schedules. It is not easy to describe these in a few words, but two or three examples may be mentioned. In one experiment the pigeon generates a performance appropriate to Schedule A where the reinforcement is simply the production of the stimulus characteristic of Schedule B, to which the pigeon then responds appropriately. Under a third stimulus, the bird yields a performance appropriate to Schedule C where the reinforcement in this case is simply the production of the stimulus characteristic of Schedule D, to which the bird then responds appropriately. In a special case, first investigated by L. B. Wyckoff, Jr., the organism responds to one stimulus where the reinforcement consists of the *clarification* of the stimulus controlling another response. The first response becomes, so to speak, an objective form of "paying attention" to the second stimulus. In one important version of this experiment, as yet unpublished, we could say that the pigeon is telling us whether it is "paying attention" to the *shape* of a spot of light or to its *color*.

One of the most dramatic applications of these techniques has recently been made in the Harvard Psychological Laboratories by Floyd Ratliff and Donald S. Blough, who have skillfully used multiple and serial schedules of reinforcement to study complex perceptual processes in the infrahuman organism. They have achieved a sort of psycho-physics without verbal instruction. In a recent experiment by Blough, for example, a pigeon draws a detailed dark-adaptation curve showing the characteristic breaks of rod and cone vision. The curve is recorded continuously in a single experimental period and is quite comparable with the curves of human subjects. The pigeon behaves in a way which, in the human case, we would not hesitate to describe by saying that it adjusts a very faint patch of light until it can just be seen.

In all this work, the species of the organism has made surprisingly little difference. It is true that the organisms studied have all been vertebrates, but they still cover a wide range. Comparable results have been obtained with pigeons, rats, dogs, monkeys, human children, and most recently, by the author in collaboration with Ogden R. Lindsley, human psychotic subjects. In spite of great phylogenetic differences, all these organisms show amazingly similar properties of the learning process. It should be emphasized that this has been achieved by analyzing the effects of reinforcement and by designing techniques which manipulate reinforcement with considerable precision. Only in this way can the behavior of the individual organism be brought under such precise control. It is also important to note that through a gradual advance to complex interrelations among responses, the same degree of rigor is being extended to behavior which would usually be assigned to such fields as perception, thinking, and personality dynamics.

From this exciting prospect of an advancing science of learning, it is a great shock to turn to that branch of technology which is most directly concerned with the learning process—education. Let us consider, for example, the teaching of arithmetic in the lower grades. The school is concerned with imparting to the child a large number of responses of a special sort. The responses are all verbal. They consist of speaking and writing certain words, figures, and signs which, to put it roughly, refer to numbers and to arithmetic operations. The first task is to shape up these responses—to get the child to pronounce and to write responses correctly, but the principal task is to bring this behavior under many sorts of stimulus control. This is what happens when the child learns to count, to recite tables, to count while ticking off the items in an assemblage of objects, to respond to spoken or written numbers by saying "odd," "even," "prime," and so on. Over and above this elaborate repertoire of numerical behavior, most of which is often dismissed as the product of rote learning, the teaching of arithmetic looks forward to those complex serial arrangements of responses involved in original mathematical thinking. The child must acquire responses of transposing, clearing fractions, and so on, which modify the order or pattern of the original material so that the response called a solution is eventually made possible.

Now, how is this extremely complicated verbal repertoire set up? In the first place, what reinforcements are used? Fifty years ago the answer would have been clear. At that time educational control was still frankly aversive. The child read numbers, copied numbers, memorized tables, and performed operations upon numbers to escape the threat of the birch rod or cane. Some positive reinforcements were perhaps eventually derived from the increased efficiency of the child in the field of arithmetic and in rare cases some automatic reinforcement may have resulted from the sheer manipulation of the medium—from the solution of problems or the discovery of the intricacies of the number system. But for the immediate purposes of education the child acted to avoid or escape punishment. It was part of the reform movement known as progressive education to make the positive consequences more immediately effective, but any one who visits the lower grades of the average school today will observe that a change has been made, not from aversive to positive control, but from one form of aversive stimulation to another. The child at his desk, filling in his workbook, is behaving primarily to escape from the threat of a series of minor aversive events—the teacher's displeasure, the criticism or ridicule of his classmates, an ignominious showing in a competition, low marks, a trip to the office "to be talked to" by the principal, or a word to the parent who may still resort to the birch rod. In this welter of aversive consequences, getting the right answer is in itself an insignificant event, any effect of which is lost amid the anxieties, the boredom, and the aggressions which are the inevitable by-products of aversive control.[2]

Secondly, we have to ask how the contingencies of reinforcement are arranged. When is a numerical operation reinforced as "right"? Eventually, of course, the pupil may be able to check his own answers and achieve some sort of automatic reinforcement, but in the early stages the reinforcement of being right is usually accorded by the teacher. The contingencies she provides are far from optimal. It can easily be demonstrated that, unless explicit mediating behavior has been set up, the lapse of only a few seconds between response and reinforcement destroys most of the effect. In a typical classroom, nevertheless, long periods of time customarily elapse. The teacher may walk up and down the aisle, for example, while the class is working on a sheet of problems, pausing here and there to say right or wrong. Many seconds or minutes intervene between the child's response and the teacher's reinforcement. In many cases—for example, when papers are taken home to be corrected—as much as 24 hours may intervene. It is surprising that this system has any effect whatsoever.

A third notable shortcoming is the lack of a skillful program which moves forward through a series of progressive approximations to the final complex behavior desired. A long series of contingencies is neces-

[2] Skinner, B. F. *Science and Human Behavior*, New York: Macmillan, 1953.

sary to bring the organism into the possession of mathematical behavior most efficiently. But the teacher is seldom able to reinforce at each step in such a series because she cannot deal with the pupil's responses one at a time. It is usually necessary to reinforce the behavior in blocks of responses—as in correcting a work sheet or page from a workbook. The responses within such a block must not be interrelated. The answer to one problem must not depend upon the answer to another. The number of stages through which one may progressively approach a complex pattern of behavior is therefore small, and the task so much the more difficult. Even the most modern workbook in beginning arithmetic is far from exemplifying an efficient program for shaping up mathematical behavior.

Perhaps the most serious criticism of the current classroom is the relative infrequency of reinforcement. Since the pupil is usually dependent upon the teacher for being right, and since many pupils are usually dependent upon the same teacher, the total number of contingencies which may be arranged during, say, the first four years, is of the order of only a few thousand. But a very rough estimate suggests that efficient mathematical behavior at this level requires something of the order of 25,000 contingencies. We may suppose that even in the brighter student a given contingency must be arranged several times to place the behavior well in hand. The responses to be set up are not simply the various items in tables of addition, subtraction, multiplication, and division; we have also to consider the alternative forms in which each item may be stated. To the learning of such material we should add hundreds of responses concerned with factoring, identifying primes, memorizing series, using short-cut techniques of calculation, constructing and using geometric representations or number forms, and so on. Over and above all this, the whole mathematical repertoire must be brought under the control of concrete problems of considerable variety. Perhaps 50,000 contingencies is a more conservative estimate. In this frame of reference the daily assignment in arithmetic seems pitifully meagre.

The result of all this is, of course, well known. Even our best schools are under criticism for their inefficiency in the teaching of drill subjects such as arithmetic. The condition in the average school is a matter of wide-spread national concern. Modern children simply do not learn arithmetic quickly or well. Nor is the result simply incompetence. The very subjects in which modern techniques are weakest are those in which failure is most conspicuous, and in the wake of an ever-growing incompetence come the anxieties, uncertainties, and aggressions which in their turn present other problems to the school. Most pupils soon claim the asylum of not being "ready" for arithmetic at a given level or, eventually, of not having a mathematical mind. Such explanations are readily seized upon by defensive teachers and parents. Few pupils ever reach the stage at which automatic reinforcements follow as the natural consequences of mathematical behavior. On the contrary, the figures and symbols of mathematics have become standard emotional stimuli. The glimpse of a column of figures, not to say an algebraic symbol or an integral sign, is likely to set off—not mathematical behavior—but a reaction of anxiety, guilt, or fear.

The teacher is usually no happier about this than the pupil. Denied the opportunity to control via the birch rod, quite at sea as to the mode of operation of the few techniques at her disposal, she spends as little time as possible on drill subjects and eagerly subscribes to philosophies of education which emphasize material of greater inherent interest. A confession of weakness is her extraordinary concern lest the child be taught something unnecessary. The repertoire to be imparted is carefully reduced to an essential minimum. In the field of spelling, for example, a great deal of time and energy has gone into discovering just those words which the young child is going to use, as if it were a crime to waste one's educational power in teaching an unnecessary word. Eventually, weakness of technique emerges in the disguise of a reformulation of the aims of education. Skills are minimized in favor of vague achievements —educating for democracy, educating the whole child, educating for life, and so on. And there the matter ends; for, unfortunately, these philosophies do not in turn suggest improvements in techniques. They offer little or no help in the design of better classroom practices.

There would be no point in urging these objections if improvement were impossible. But the advances which have recently been made in our control of the learning process suggest a thorough revision of classroom practices and, fortunately, they tell us how the revision can be brought about. This is not, of course, the first time that the results of an experimental science have been brought to bear upon the practical problems of education. The modern classroom does not, however, offer much evidence that research in the field of learning has been respected or used. This condition is no doubt partly due to the limitations of earlier research. But it has been encouraged by a too hasty conclusion that the laboratory study of learning is inherently limited because it cannot take into account the realities of the classroom. In the light of our increasing knowledge of the learning process we should, instead, insist upon dealing with those realities and forcing a substantial change in them. Education is perhaps the most important branch of scientific technology. It deeply affects the lives of all of us. We can no longer allow the exigencies of a practical situation to suppress the tremendous improvements which are within reach. The practical situation must be changed.

There are certain questions which have to be answered in turning to the study of any new organism. What behavior is to be set up? What reinforcers are at hand? What responses are available in embarking upon a program of progressive approximation which will lead to the final form of the behavior? How can reinforcements be most efficiently scheduled to maintain the behavior in strength? These questions are all relevant in considering the problem of the child in the lower grades.

In the first place, what reinforcements are available? What does the school have in its possession which will reinforce a child? We may look first to the material to be learned, for it is possible that this will provide considerable automatic reinforcement. Children play for hours with mechanical toys, paints, scissors and paper, noise-makers, puzzles—in short, with almost anything which feeds back significant changes in the environment and is reasonably free of aversive properties. The sheer control of nature is itself reinforcing. This effect is not evident in the modern school because it is masked by the emotional responses generated by aversive control. It is true that automatic reinforcement from the manipulation of the environment is probably only a mild reinforcer and may need to be carefully husbanded, but one of the most striking principles to emerge from recent research is that the *net* amount of reinforcement is of little significance. A very slight reinforcement may be tremendously effective in controlling behavior if it is wisely used.

If the natural reinforcement inherent in the subject matter is not enough, other reinforcers must be employed. Even in school the child is occasionally permitted to do "what he wants to do," and access to reinforcements of many sorts may be made contingent upon the more immediate consequences of the behavior to be established. Those who advocate competition as a useful social motive may wish to use the reinforcements which follow from excelling others, although there is the difficulty that in this case the reinforcement of one child is necessarily aversive to another. Next in order we might place the good will and affection of the teacher, and only when that has failed need we turn to the use of aversive stimulation.

In the second place, how are these reinforcements to be made contingent upon the desired behavior? There are two considerations here—the gradual elaboration of extremely complex patterns of behavior and the maintenance of the behavior in strength at each stage. The whole process of becoming competent in any field must be divided into a very large number of very small steps, and reinforcement must be contingent upon the accomplishment of each step. This solution to the problem of creating a complex repertoire of behavior also solves the problem of maintaining the behavior in strength. We could, of course, resort to the techniques of scheduling already developed in the study of other organisms but in the present state of our knowledge of educational practices, scheduling appears to be most effectively arranged through the design of the material to be learned. By making each successive step as small as possible, the frequency of reinforcement can be raised to a maximum, while the possibly aversive consequences of being wrong are reduced to a minimum. Other ways of designing material would yield other programs of reinforcement. Any supplementary reinforcement would probably have to be scheduled in the more traditional way.

These requirements are not excessive, but they are probably incompatible with the current realities of the classroom. In the experimental study of learning it has been found that the contingencies of reinforcement which are most efficient in controlling the organism cannot be arranged through the personal mediation of the experimenter. An organism is affected by subtle details of contingencies which are beyond the capacity of the human organism to arrange. Mechanical and electrical devices must be used. Mechanical help is also demanded by the sheer number of contingencies which may be used efficiently in a single experimental session. We have recorded many millions of responses from a single organism during thousands of experimental hours. Personal arrangement of the contingencies and personal observation of the results are quite unthinkable. Now, the human organism is, if anything, more sensitive to precise contingencies than the other organisms we have studied. We have every reason to expect, therefore, that the most effective control of human learning will require instrumental aid. The simple fact is that, as a mere reinforcing mechanism, the teacher is out of date. This would be true even if a single teacher devoted all her time to a single child, but her inadequacy is multiplied many-fold when she must serve as a reinforcing device to many children at once. If the teacher is to take advantage of recent advances in the study of learning, she must have the help of mechanical devices.

The technical problem of providing the necessary instrumental aid is not particularly difficult. There are many ways in which the necessary contingencies may be arranged, either mechanically or electrically. An inexpensive device which solves most of the principal problems has already been constructed. It is still in the experimental stage, but a description will suggest the kind of instrument which seems to be required. The device consists of a small box about the size of a small record player. On the top surface is a window through which a question or problem printed on a paper tape may be seen. The child answers the question by moving one or more sliders upon which the digits 0 through 9 are printed. The answer appears in square holes punched in the paper upon which the question is printed. When the answer has been set, the child turns a knob. The operation is as simple as adjusting a television set. If the answer is right, the knob turns freely and can be made to ring a bell or provide some other conditioned reinforcement. If the answer is wrong, the knob will not turn. A counter may be added to tally wrong answers. The knob must then be reversed slightly and a second attempt at a right answer made. (Unlike the flash-card, the device reports a wrong answer without giving the right answer.) When the answer is right, a further turn of the knob engages a clutch which moves the next problem into place in the window. This movement cannot be completed, however, until the sliders have been returned to zero.

The important features of the device are these: Reinforcement for the right answer is immediate. The mere manipulation of the device will probably be reinforcing enough to keep the average pupil at work for a suitable period each day, provided traces of earlier aversive control can be wiped out. A teacher may supervise an entire class at work on such devices at the same time, yet each child may progress at his own rate, completing as many problems as possible within the class period. If forced to be away from school, he may return to pick up where he left off. The gifted child will advance rapidly, but can be kept from getting too far ahead either by being excused from arithmetic for a time or by being given special sets of problems which take him into some of the interesting bypaths of mathematics.

The device makes it possible to present carefully designed material in which one problem can depend upon the answer to the preceding and where, therefore, the most efficient progress to an eventually complex repertoire can be made. Provision has been made for recording the commonest mistakes so that the tapes can be modified as experience dictates. Additional steps can be inserted where pupils tend to have trouble, and ultimately the material will reach a point at which the answers of the average child will almost always be right.

If the material itself proves not to be sufficiently reinforcing, other reinforcers in the possession of the teacher or school may be made contingent upon the operation of the device or upon progress through a series of problems. Supplemental reinforcement would not sacrifice the advantages gained from immediate reinforcement and from the possibility of constructing an optimal series of steps which approach the complex repertoire of mathematical behavior most efficiently.

A similar device in which the sliders carry the letters of the alphabet has been designed to teach spelling. In addition to the advantages which can be gained from precise reinforcement and careful programming, the device will teach reading at the same time. It can also be used to establish the large and important repertoire of verbal relationships encountered in logic and science. In short, it can teach verbal thinking. As to content instruction, the device can be operated as a multiple-choice self-rater.

Some objections to the use of such devices in the classroom can easily be foreseen. The cry will be raised that the child is being treated as a mere animal and that an essentially human intellectual achievement is being analyzed in unduly mechanistic terms. Mathematical behavior is usually regarded, not as a repertoire of responses involving numbers and numerical operations, but as evidences of mathematical ability or the exercise of the power of reason. It is true that the techniques which are emerging from the experimental study of learning are not designed to "develop the mind" or to further some vague "understanding" of mathematical relationships. They are designed, on the contrary, to establish the very behaviors which are taken to be the evidences of such mental states or processes. This is only a special case of the general change which is under way in the interpretation of human affairs. An advancing science continues to offer more and more convincing alternatives to traditional formulations. The behavior in terms of which human thinking must eventually be defined is worth treating in its own right as the substantial goal of education.

Of course the teacher has a more important function than to say right or wrong. The changes proposed would free her for the effective exercise of that function. Marking a set of papers in arithmetic—"Yes, nine and six *are* fifteen; no, nine and seven *are not* eighteen"—is beneath the dignity of any intelligent individual. There is more important work to be done—in which the teacher's relations to the pupil cannot be duplicated by a mechanical device. Instrumental help would merely improve these relations. One might say that the main trouble with education in the lower grades today is that the child is obviously not competent and *knows it* and that the teacher is unable to do anything about it and *knows that too*. If the advances which have recently been made in our control of behavior can give the child a genuine competence in reading, writing, spelling, and arithmetic, then the teacher may begin to function, not in lieu of a cheap machine, but through intellectual, cultural, and emotional contacts of that distinctive sort which testify to her status as a human being.

Another possible objection is that mechanized instruction will mean technological unemployment. We need not worry about this until there are enough teachers to go around and until the hours and energy demanded of the teacher are comparable to those in other fields of employment. Mechanical devices will eliminate the more tiresome labors of the teacher but they will not necessarily shorten the time during which she remains in contact with the pupil.

A more practical objection: Can we afford to mechanize our schools? The answer is clearly yes. The device I have just described could be produced as cheaply as a small radio or phonograph. There would need to be far fewer devices than pupils, for they could be used in rotation. But even if we suppose that the instrument eventually found to be most effective would cost several hundred dollars and that large numbers of them would be required, our economy should be able to stand the strain. Once we have accepted the possibility and the necessity of me-

chanical help in the classroom, the economic problem can easily be sur-
mounted. There is no reason why the school room should be any less
mechanized than, for example, the kitchen. A country which annually
produces millions of refrigerators, dish-washers, automatic washing-ma-
chines, automatic clothes-driers, and automatic garbage disposers can
certainly afford the equipment necessary to educate its citizens to high
standards of competence in the most effective way.

There is a simple job to be done. The task can be stated in concrete
terms. The necessary techniques are known. The equipment needed can
easily be provided. Nothing stands in the way but cultural inertia. But
what is more characteristic of America than an unwillingness to accept
the traditional as inevitable? We are on the threshold of an exciting and
revolutionary period, in which the scientific study of man will be put to
work in man's best interests. Education must play its part. It must accept the fact that a sweeping revision of educational practices is possible and inevitable. When it has done this, we may look forward with
confidence to a school system which is aware of the nature of its tasks,
secure in its methods, and generously supported by the informed and
effective citizens whom education itself will create.

4 NON-DELIBERATIVE FACTORS UNDERLYING
THE PHENOMENON OF SCHOOLING
J. M. Stephens

The Argument in Brief

The general phenomenon of schooling demands to be explained as well
as to be expedited. The general phenomenon of schooling is held to consist of the three-fold fact that schooling is widely prevalent; that it consists of a very definite kind of work, a work that has a loose but definite
relation to the interests of the home or other primitive agencies; and
that this specialized work of the schools has notable survival value. We
could imagine this three-fold phenomenon to be due to deliberate
human decisions and to deliberate efforts. We could also imagine it to
be due to some process whereby certain activities (in art or science) become ends in themselves and spontaneously elicit for themselves the at-

SOURCE: J. M. Stephens, "Non-Deliberative Factors Underlying the Phenomenon of
Schooling," *Educational Theory*, 6 (January 1956), 26–34. Reprinted by permission of the publisher and author.

tention of a cheering section or group of zealots. It is the contention of this paper, that, operating along with the mechanisms just mentioned, there have been powerful, automatic, primitive, unintelligent forces which have also helped to bring about the process of schooling and to keep that process directed into survival-favoring channels.

There is little need to develop the first assumption: namely that schooling is widely prevalent and has existed in some form for a considerable period of time. Schools or near schools have been found in many periods of history and may well have been in existence prior to the historical era. Schooling or something like it has also appeared in many different parts of the globe and in widely differing cultures.

In our second assumption we suggest that the work of the school has differed systematically from that of the home and of other primitive agencies and that this specialized work of the school has had survival value. Typically there has appeared to be a fairly reasonable division of labor between the school on the one hand, and the home and similar primitive agencies on the other. By accident or design, the activities of the home have guaranteed that children will have a rough competence in such matters as eating, avoiding the more prevalent physical dangers, and in wearing clothes, whereas the school has typically devoted more attention to such things as singing, ceremonial dancing, ritualistic knot tying, memorization of tribal legends, numerical relations, or the interpretation of written symbols. Consciously or unconsciously, the school has developed and nurtured those ways of behaving which many primitive agencies would tend to neglect, permitting them to be pushed aside by the more compelling claims of matters of immediate significance.

In fostering and nurturing these more decorative and less vital aspects of behavior, the school, unwittingly perhaps, has played a substantial part in the grim struggle for survival between one society and another. By concentrating on a vast number of these seemingly "useless" things, such as topology or electrostatics, and by inducing generation after generation to become familiar with the various nuances of the "scholastic" subjects, the school has helped develop a very few of the seemingly "useless" things to the point of tremendous practical return. In its fondness for the useless and decorative, the school has occasionally given its host society a terrific advantage over societies that refuse to tolerate dilletantism, or the pursuit of the impractical. Whatever its other virtues, the school has been a survival device which some societies evolved, or borrowed, or stumbled upon, or otherwise acquired during the remote past. In view of this long-term contribution to survival, it is not surprising to find some suggestion of schooling in many surviving societies.

Deliberate Planning as the Explanation of Schooling

It might seem at first glance that the coordination of the school's functions with those of the more primitive agencies, and its remarkable contribution to long-term survival, must have been the result of extraordinary social planning. It might even seem that some super-agency has had in mind the traits which should be developed in children, and has then parcelled them out, giving some traits or tendencies to the home, others to various incidental agencies, and still others to the school. Certainly, at a less fanciful level, we could easily imagine that the home and other primitive agencies, seeing the limitations of their own provisions, may have deliberately set up the schools to take care of the important traits that would otherwise be neglected. Or as an alternative possibility, it is easy to suppose that potential teachers or other groups with specialized interests, aware of the neglect of those interests, have set themselves up as the agency to make good the defect. Either of these deliberate arrangements, or a combination of such definite plans, would explain the loose but effective articulation between the work of the school and the home, and the definite direction of the former.

It is no more than common sense to suggest that deliberate human intention had much to do with the evolution of schools. It seems most unlikely, however, that all societies were clearly aware of this long-range survival factor when they developed or stumbled upon the process of schooling. It is probable, on the contrary, that any great amount of insight was the exception. It is probable that few people, either in the schools or out, had any clear awareness that they were developing tendencies which might come in handy several hundred years hence. It is probable that the activities of the schools had to be justified on other grounds, these justifications undoubtedly ranging from the utilitarian to the outright mystical.

The School as the Custodian of Important but Perishable "Goods"

Our stress on the considerable though remote survival value of certain seemingly useless tendencies must not mislead us into thinking that these tendencies were necessarily cherished on account of their survival value. Actually it would be very rare to find people contemplating the activities of the school and deliberately saying to themselves, "These activities, if further developed, may bring great dividends in the future. Therefore let us cultivate them carefully for the sake of generations yet to come." On the contrary, we find that, for the most part, when these activities are cultivated they are typically cultivated as ends in themselves. To the artist and his patrons, art is not just one of many activities that might happen to have practical value centuries from now. Art, to its devotees, has its own essential value, not derivable from its potential utility, and is to be cultivated for the satisfaction of intrinsic human needs. Similarly, disinterested science is often considered to be valuable for its own sake. Its pursuit and study bring intrinsic satisfaction which is good in its own right.

Not only is it a fact that "useless" activities bring rich and genuine satisfaction in their own right, quite apart from their survival value, but it is most helpful that they should do so. Activities which bring direct and powerful satisfactions in and of themselves are more likely to be carried on with zeal and efficiency than those which are undertaken merely from a sense of duty to future generations. The continuation of the species, for instance, is more likely to be guaranteed through procreative activities which are enjoyable or attractive in their own right than through a sheer sense of obligation to acquire progeny.

We could, if we wished, formulate a theory at this level. We have held that it is in the interests of survival that these "remote" tendencies should be cultivated. We have also held that it is in the interests of survival that the games, the art, the science, and the other activities which these tendencies engender should be attractive in their own right. If we accept these points, we could then merely proceed to study the school as an institution for cultivating this special class of activities which may lack practical usefulness, but which have acknowledged intrinsic value, and which bring satisfaction to important human needs.

This latter approach is quite legitimate and is, essentially, the approach which is developed in the classical residual theory of education. In that theory the school is considered as an agency for the cultivation of traits which are clearly important but which, in the hurly-burly of everyday life, are likely to be neglected by the home and by other agencies.

Schooling as the Automatic Outgrowth of Spontaneous Primitive Tendencies

As an alternative (or supplement) to the two theories discussed above, we now suggest that along with the deliberate or quasi-deliberate forces, there may have been other automatic, spontaneous, unintelligent forces which helped to bring about the device of schooling and to keep it directed to long-range survival needs.

Our attitude at this stage is not unlike the possible attitude of a visitor from Mars who is studying the procreative activities and is concentrating on the obvious survival function of those activities. Our Martian inquirer might find that these procreative activities are accompanied by elaborate but varying rationales. In one culture the procreative activities may be considered as a means of acquiring descendants who will worship at the shrine of the procreator. In another culture these same activities may be part of an invocation to the gods. The members of a third culture may cite the Biblical injunction to be fruitful and multiply. Still other groups may regard procreative activity as a means of exorcising a daemon that temporarily possesses the soul.

Our Martian investigator might well assume that deliberate intention does play some part in these matters. But he might be wise if he were to consider the possible existence of primitive, non-deliberative procreative tendencies that also play a part in guaranteeing the continuance of the race. Such primitive tendencies, although somewhat affected by various rationales, would still operate under many differing rationales and would operate, indeed, even when the people concerned could give no rational explanation of their behavior.

School activities, of course, have none of the crucial importance to survival that we can attribute to procreative activities. But the schools do have some long-range survival value, and we may well wonder if the continuation of these survival-favoring features has, in the past, depended *exclusively* on anything as precarious as human deliberation. Deliberate intellectual decisions, which are assumed to play so important a part in our current civilized life, are probably of very recent origin and, even now, are not very reassuring guarantees for the continuation of anything really vital to survival. If we are to explain the school's contribution to survival during the remote periods of the past, we should look for some of the responsible forces in a group of blind, primitive tendencies which operated to produce schools prior to the development of elaborate deliberation, and which have operated successfully under extremely diverse rationales. To provide a convincing explanation of the schools we must place some of our reliance on forces which will work when deliberation is inadequate or non-existent—which will work, indeed, even when deliberation is perversely obstructional.

Primitive Tendencies Underlying the Phenomenon of Schooling

It is held that schooling, or something like schooling, would automatically arise from the existence of a few clusters of primitive spontaneous tendencies. These postulated clusters are as follows:

1. A cluster of playful, manipulative tendencies whereby we are led to do many things that are usually of great interest but seldom

of immediate practical use. This cluster includes such widespread tendencies as doodling, making marks in the sand, exploiting an echo, dropping rocks in pools of water, rearranging ideas, playing with word patterns, and working out numerical relations. These tendencies are held to have genuine survival value but a survival value which is remote rather than immediate and which is seldom apparent to those in whom they operate.

2. A cluster of spontaneous tendencies leading us to talk about things that we know—about the story we have heard, about our children, our pets, our hobbies, our illnesses, our trips, our thoughts.

3. A cluster of tendencies by which we are led upon occasion to tolerate, to approve, or even to applaud the manipulative behavior of others. Such toleration or applause is often spontaneously directed to acrobatics, singing, magic, or linguistic fluency.

4. Closely related to item 3 is a *converse cluster of tendencies* by which we are led spontaneously to express disapproval of awkward, inappropriate, or incorrect manipulatory behavior. We may express this disapproval by a shudder or grimace, or by a formal protest, or by a demonstration of the proper behavior.

5. A combination of clusters 2 and 4 which would lead to a cluster of tendencies to "point the moral," to say, "See what happens when you rush into premature publication," or "See how much better things are when you clear the equation of fractions before transposing."

6. A cluster of tendencies that lead us to tolerate, and perhaps to encourage, those who are heavily endowed with the "communicative" tendencies listed in items 2, 3, 4 and 5.

Our main task, of course, is to show that, to some extent, schooling may arise from the blind, automatic operation of a group of non-deliberate, spontaneous tendencies such as those just postulated. It is now necessary to show (1) that the clusters of tendencies are fairly widespread, though, of course, much more pronounced in some people than in others; (2) that such tendencies will operate even without deliberate, conscious intention to help, or to instruct, or to improve; and (3) that such tendencies, even if unaided by deliberate intention, would bring about some sort of schooling.

Prevalence of the Postulated Tendencies

Tendencies to Manipulate. The frivolous, playful, result-getting tendencies are extremely widespread. They are found in our primate cousins and in human beings of all ages. The young child crumples papers and topples blocks with obvious relish. His older brother smashes light bulbs or sends rocks skimming over the surface of the pond. Other members of the species send balls soaring through space, or delight in the results to be obtained from manipulating lures near pools or streams. At a more "intellectual" level, many people rearrange the letters in words, do interesting mathematical puzzles, or develop ingenious theories on a wide variety of subjects.

Tendencies to Hold Forth. The tendency to hold forth on a variety of subjects is also very widespread, though this tendency also is much more pronounced in some people than in others. With little persuasion, most people will speak to some extent about themselves, about their family, their hobbies, or their views, and some people will speak interminably on such topics.

Tendencies to Approve or Applaud. The tendencies to tolerate, or approve, or applaud manipulative behavior in others are also fairly prevalent, and are probably very ancient. Most people are impressed by some form of manipulatory skill when they see it in others. The acrobat, the medicine man, and the storyteller have enjoyed prestige among many different groups. For some groups these tendencies may run chiefly to applause for very obvious forms of physical manipulation. For other groups, they may take the form of veneration for a mastery of the esoteric, or for linguistic prowess. But they are usually present in some degree.

The widespread presence of these applauding tendencies is probably no mere accident. The emergence of such tendencies represented a definite step in the evolutionary process. It probably took quite a bit of evolving before people came to tolerate the trifling, frivolous behavior of others. It would not be surprising, indeed, if many members of the early tribes took an exceedingly dim view of the manipulative activities of their colleagues. The hard-pressed primitive groups may well have questioned the social contribution of the curious one who amused himself throwing water on hot rocks, or who toyed with a ropelike vine when he could have been shaping flints or chasing rabbits. Not being seers, they could not foretell that the playful one was about to revolutionize the method of working rocks, or of snaring rabbits. Forbearance for triflers must have come hard to those sweating over the immediate tasks of the day. But such forbearance did come about in some species and it greatly helped such species to utilize the long-term survival value of these frivolous, manipulatory tendencies. Certainly, some toleration is quite prevalent in societies that survive at the moment.

Beyond mere tolerance, of course, comes the active approval and applause for manipulatory activities. The group which first carried its indulgent forbearance into spontaneous encouragement was also the first to take one more step toward the effective utilization of the survival value latent in these traits. The group who found themselves, for some strange reason, intrigued by the playful exploits of others, by the tales of the poet or the magic of the medicine man, would be more likely to survive than groups which gave mere grudging acceptance. This trait, too, is very widespread.

Tendencies to Correct. The tendency to express dismay, consternation, or disapproval at the awkward or incorrect manipulative behavior of others is also widespread and is also much more strongly entrenched in some people than in others. The prevalence of this tendency is perhaps shown by the deliberate efforts often applied to keep it in check. Rules and sanctions are continually enjoined to keep us from gasping at the overturned teacup, from commenting on our friend's inappropriate attire, or from correcting his faulty grammar.

The tendency to point the moral, to say, "I told you so", again, is frequently seen among us. Like some of the tendencies just mentioned, it is in fact so much a part of our makeup that many societies have erected taboos against it.

Tendency to Tolerate the Primitive Teacher. As has been suggested, toleration for the unusually "communicative" person is sometimes of a grudging nature. Typically we are not too happy when we ourselves must listen to a detailed account of our companion's esoteric hobbies, or when he comments on our own manipulatory deficiencies. or when he sharpens our insight into the reasons for our ineptitude. But we are more indulgent, or perhaps moderately enthusiastic, when the one who oozes information, corrections, or maxims applies himself to others, especially if those others stand in obvious need of the treatment being given. Presumably even in primitive groups there was some forbearance or perhaps support, for the oldster who took advantage of the more defenceless members of the group to tell them of the old days, to correct their off-key chant, or show how a violation of the tribal law brings its own retribution.

The Spontaneity of the Postulated Tendencies

Do these tendencies operate spontaneously? Would they function adequately in a group of people who lacked any conception of the survival value of such tendencies? Probably so. Probably, the boy who rattles the stick along the paling fence has no vision that this is one of the tendencies by which his species has fiddled and doodled its way into its present pre-eminence, and by which his descendants may achieve even more fantastic control of the environment. The man who is impelled to give you a detailed account of the book he has read is also probably completely oblivious of the fact that this urge has long-range survival value. The spectator who gazes in awe at the colored magic which the priest can induce in the camp-fire does not know that his appreciation or applause also pushes his species a little ahead of less effusive groups. The adult who feels impelled to correct the child's off-key chant probably does so as blindly as the rest. He merely feels uncomfortable in the presence of improper manipulation, and he acts. In so doing, he helps perpetuate manipulative tendencies which in some distant day may mean salvation for his descendants. But of this he probably knows nothing. The society which tolerates or encourages this primitive teacher also thereby adds to the long-time chances of survival, but again it probably does so with little realization that the encouragement has survival value.

It is not suggested, of course, that these activities are always completely lacking in deliberation. It is obvious that people may talk of their hobbies or their interests for the deliberate purpose of helping their hearers, or of accomplishing some other laudable aim. The man who tells you all about his operation, for instance, may believe that he can pass along some information that may be useful to you. But this is not always the case, or necessarily the case. Sometimes he just babbles. He is driven by some undeliberate, unintellectual tendency to talk, and he talks. He is sometimes the victim of that spontaneous unreasoning drive which leads the returning traveller, even as the gangplank falls, to look frantically for a pair of ears into which he can pour forth his experiences. He may merely belong to that group of people for whom an unshared experience is no experience at all. A story heard but untold leaves him in acute distress. It must be remembered, of course, that this spontaneous compulsion to tell others the things we know is much stronger in some people than in others. Most of us could sort our acquaintances into some rough ranking with respect to this trait. At the one extreme is the friend whom we avoid for some time after he has returned from his trip. We make a point not to lunch with him the day after he has been to the theater. We hope the book he has just read is interesting—and brief. At the other extreme, of course, is the unduly "secretive" person, the partaker of the solitary, intellectual delights. Most of us probably come somewhere between these two extremes.

The tendency to correct the mistakes of others may also, upon occasion, spring from a deliberate intention to help the erring one. But again this is not always true or necessarily true. In the margins of books no one else will ever see, we pen corrections to authors already dead. We correct spelling errors in examination books that will never be returned. Hearing the grammatical slip we mutter the correction but deliberately keep it under our breath. Many of our corrections that actually do reach the ears of others are probably equally devoid of deliberate, rational intention to help. Often there is absolutely nothing altruistic about them. We hear the mistake and, spontaneously—automatically—helplessly, wince, or supply the correct phrase, or shriek in outraged protest. Even when we feel that our comment may hurt rather than help, we are sometimes powerless to resist, and the spontaneous tendency to comment on the mistake wins out in the face of a deliberate resolve to mind our own business.

In this trait, as in the others, we may expect marked individual differences. At the one extreme are those we just can't keep quiet in the presence of error, irrespective of the harm or good that may follow from speaking out, and at the other extreme are those who can be aware of serious dereliction and feel no compulsion whatever to speak out or correct.

The Power of the Postulated Tendencies to Produce Schooling

If we grant the existence of these spontaneous tendencies, together with the individual differences that are also postulated, then something like schooling seems inevitable. From among those who are unusually endowed with manipulative tendencies, there would be some who are also strongly compelled to speak of what they know. Such people, of course, would tend to direct their efforts to any available audience. It would be amazing, however, if a disproportionate part of their hearers did not happen to be drawn from those too young or too timid to escape. Children constitute a natural captive audience of this kind especially if there is in the background the indulgent permission or blessing of parents (Postulate 6). The ancient mariner may well have "shared his experiences" with accessible 8-year olds if all the startled wedding guests had succeeded in giving him the slip.

Among the adults who are unthinkingly impelled to hold forth on "academic" matters, there would be some who, driven by similar blind, unreasoning compulsions, would also commend behavior that pleased them and correct those things that worried them. Many of these, in turn, would be spontaneously impelled to point the moral and to show why this result follows from that way of doing things.

The activities just outlined constitute a crude form of schooling. Here, for instance, we have the adult who, because of his own great interest in tribal history, talks to young people about tribal history. His remarks occasionally lead them to express themselves on the same subject. Some of their remarks he unthinkingly accepts and others he rejects. Such a one has taken a considerable step toward the teaching of tribal history, even though he may never have had the slightest intention to teach.

To the student of a social phenomenon, such as schooling, these powerful, primitive tendencies that motivate the snail watcher, the bore, and the compulsive "corrector" must not be taken lightly nor brushed aside as merely interesting or laughable human foibles. These tendencies, so prevalent and so characteristic of our species, have enabled our ancestors to develop a host of seemingly useless "academic" activities to the point where a very few of these tendencies have produced tremendous survival returns. It is claimed that these blind primitive forces are exceedingly dependable agencies for nurturing such academic matters and for capturing their sporadic, long-range survival value.

No attempt has been made to work out the detailed mechanisms by which these postulated tendencies have been handed on. *In general,* of course, our possession of these traits is adequately explained by the fact that the societies who happened to be endowed with these clusters of tendencies were able, in the exceedingly long run, to "out-compete" the societies who lacked such tendencies.

These clusters of primitive tendencies, so clearly prevalent in our day, and presumably prevalent in the past, would provide the basic forces necessary for a crude form of schooling. Those blind, undeliberate forces, at work in the past, would account for the continuity of schooling and for its prevalence in different cultures. These steady primitive tendencies, still functioning in our more elaborate schools, would also account for a certain constancy in the work of the school that has persisted in spite of widely differing rationales, justifications, or deliberate pressures.

Just as these unthinking, spontaneous tendencies played a part in producing the schools of the past, so they must still contribute a hidden, earthy substratum to the more elaborate schools of the present. Our many deliberate efforts to direct and refine the process of schooling must be imposed on these spontaneous tendencies that will continue to operate no matter which ideology may inspire our national decisions.

These primitive, spontaneous tendencies are charter members among the forces that lead to schooling. They deserve more serious study. At the very least we should seek to know how much scholastic growth would follow from these forces acting on their own and in the absence of any intention to teach. It would also help to know how much deliberate intervention is required to "trigger off" larger applications of these primitive forces, and to know the extent to which these forces are responsive to direction, facilitation, or attempts at inhibition. All in all it would seem that our deliberate efforts might be more intelligently applied if we had a clearer idea of the primitive, non-deliberative forces already at work.

5 THE NATURE AND THE USES OF THE STUDY OF EDUCATION
James Deese

Such important institutions of our society as law, finance, and religion are quite properly the sources of scholarly activity, research, and teaching. The teaching is necessary so that some of the formal knowledge useful to the managing of these institutions can be passed on to the young. The scholarly activity and research are part of the civilized interest in the study of man and his works. Thus, in modern society, money begets —in addition to evil—economics and graduate schools of business administration. Law begets lawyers but also legal and political theory. Religion produces both theology and seminarians.

The institution of education requires teachers and, in addition, places for the selection and training of those teachers. These places are the schools and colleges of education. Some of these are also centers for the study of schooling itself. It is this conjunction of teaching and research that provides the academic setting for the discipline of education.

This combination of teaching how to teach and research on teaching is a sensible arrangement despite its abuses, since it provides or should provide a meeting of new ideas about schooling and the teachers who will ultimately be concerned with the practical implications of those ideas. Thus, the school of education is a center of both pure and applied research, and a conjunction of the training of teachers and research upon schooling is the prevailing rule in such institutions.

It is not necessary, of course, that the study of any social institution be so directly associated with the training of the professional people who manage the institution. Many social institutions are studied in centers entirely divorced from teaching. The traditional place for the pure study of social institutions is the liberal arts faculty, whose students are not supposed to be trained for any particular profession or craft.

I hope to be able to show that the study of schooling is, at least in some important respects, a social science and that its study need not be ancillary to professional training of teachers. It is in many ways as pure a social science as the study of economics or psychology. In other respects it is not, and it is necessary to examine these in order to under-

SOURCE: James Deese, in *The Discipline of Education*, eds., John Walton and James Kuethe (Madison: The University of Wisconsin Press, 1965), ch. 8, pp. 163–83. Copyright © 1965 by the Regents of the University of Wisconsin. Reprinted by permission of the University of Wisconsin Press.

stand education's position within the social sciences. Because education is somewhat unusual as a social science and because of tradition, as well as practical demands, the study of schooling within the setting of the school of education is established, and I believe that it is not necessarily an evil arrangement. Because it is not widely accepted that schools of education should be places for pure research, some argument about the nature of education as a social science is necessary.

In a developed, urban, and overpopulated society such as ours, every aspect of human life is the subject of some learned inquiry. Even so prosaic an enterprise as poultry raising cannot be left to the vagaries of unaided nature. There are departments of poultry husbandry in the great state universities staffed by professors of poultry husbandry who do research on the problems of raising and marketing chickens, turkeys, and ducks.

Despite the good services provided by such departments, I think that it is reasonable to say that they do not constitute academic disciplines. This judgment does not imply that these departments are without value within the university. Most applied sciences have some role in society, and some disciplines that have traditionally been regarded as applied, such as education, make important contributions to pure knowledge. Society needs certain of the applied disciplines, and they are appropriate to the traditions and purposes of many American universities. Even among those critics of education who regard it, at best, as a purely applied study, I believe there are not many who would want to banish it altogether.

Part of the question of the nature of education is whether or not it is a pure or applied discipline. In order to separate the applied disciplines from the pure studies we need some criteria. These criteria should clearly designate such programs as poultry husbandry as applied, and they should tell us whether education is to be classed among the applied or among the pure disciplines. Or, since many subjects are mixed in character, education among these, these criteria should help us describe the ways in which the study of any subject is both pure and applied.

One criterion that differentiates the purely practical sciences from the academic disciplines is the extent to which inquiry contributes to the abstract understanding of some human, natural, or philosophic problem. This criterion would be met when the solution to some problem or the consideration of some idea has implications beyond the problem or the idea investigated. Many worthy scientific enterprises are not concerned with abstract questions or matters of pure knowledge, but concerned with rules of procedure designed to maximize the likelihood of some explicit outcome. A treatment of such a question as the economics of schooling could be a purely practical matter—the best procedure for the fiscal management of schools. Or, on the other hand, it could raise a general problem about the measurement of the utility of social services. In general, those problems which do not concern specific ends are the problems of pure inquiry, though as I shall mention later, applied problems sometimes raise general and abstract questions.

It is nevertheless evident that many of the problems which occupy the attention of persons in schools or departments of education are purely practical questions. This is necessarily the case. We cannot quarrel with such a necessity without endangering belief in some of the principles which give rise to the social support of schooling. We may quarrel with the competence of the investigation of particular practical problems in education, and we may even quarrel with the relative importance of some of the problems chosen for investigation, but not many of us would want to quarrel with the need for some practical study of educational problems.

Because so many of the investigations that have come out of the study of practical problems in education are trivial, there is no little temptation to class the study of education with the least significant and important of the practical sciences which find their way into the various curricula of American universities. Such a temptation should be avoided, since the study of education is in nearly all respects like the study of other important institutions of society. To ask questions about schooling is to ask questions about human nature, about social organization, and about values. The study of education raises questions of general intellectual importance.

It seems so evident to me that the study of schooling, of teaching and learning, is as fundamental as the study of money or law that it is almost unnecessary to raise any question about it. It is perhaps because of the cloud of criticism over the discipline of education that the question arises at all. Except among certain obscurantists, however, the main force of that criticism is seen to fall upon the competence of those who practice the study of education, not upon the discipline itself. The more fundamental study of education exists alongside of and sometimes as part of the study of the practical problems faced by the educators. This situation has created some confusion about the nature of education and is in part responsible for the widely held opinion that education is not a fundamental academic study. A word of comment on this situation is in order.

In the years following World War II it was fashionable to point out the difference between basic and applied science and to emphasize the really important scientific achievements that come out of basic research. At that time this point was made as an attempt to persuade the various governmental agencies responsible for the fiscal support of research to allot a greater share of the available funds to basic research. The distinction between the pure and the applied can be overdrawn, however. The criteria which differentiate the particulars of basic research from those of applied research vary from discipline to discipline. It is often very hard to tell what is basic and what is applied. Even when the most general criterion, generality itself, is applied, the distinction does not always seem to lead to the right results. Often, purely practical problems generate questions of great theoretical and general importance. Research upon applied problems does feed back to basic science, though not so spectacularly as in the reverse case. Often, we must admit, in the social sciences pure research is trivial because theories themselves are concerned with trivial questions.

A close interdependence between pure and applied research is characteristic of the social sciences. I think this is because of the great importance, at the present stage of development, of empirical investigation in the social sciences. Sound choice of empirical problems in the social sciences depends upon an intuitive, implicit knowledge on the part of the investigator of what is important of the number of things which are possible to investigate. The social scientist faces a very large number of problems to be investigated, and the importance of his research is probably more dependent upon the excellence of his choice among these than upon any other single factor.

Nowhere is the distinction between the purely basic and the purely applied more likely to lead to pernicious effects than in the study of education. Here, more than in other social sciences, the sound choice of a problem depends upon a close, firsthand knowledge of the conditions to be investigated. An insistence upon separation of pure and applied study leads to the emphasis, on the one hand, upon the trivial practical questions of the day and, on the other hand, to emphasis upon sterile academic problems generated from sterile academic theories. Academic questions in education are often sterile because they are of no general social importance and lead to no implications, practical or otherwise, except, perhaps, for further research upon sterile problems. I believe this state of affairs has been characteristic of much of the effort to study theories of learning in the educational context.

Education, in company with other social sciences, is by nature both a basic and applied discipline. Because there is mutual support and because the subject matter of education requires some concrete experience with the social realities of schooling, no strict line can profitably be drawn between the pure and applied aspects of the study. Suffice it to say that the nature of the subject matter insures opportunity for significant study uncontrolled by the demands for application.

There is another characteristic of the study of education which makes it a somewhat unusual social science. It is a characteristic typical of many disciplines that are largely applied in nature. Most basic disciplines have a body of method. Sometimes the method is well defined and specific, and sometimes it is only an intuitive knowledge of the way to proceed. Education, in company with most applied disciplines, does not have a unique body of method that serves to define its study. It relies on the methods in the traditions of other disciplines.

This may appear to be an astonishing statement in view of the frequency with which educators talk about "research methodology." There is, however, nothing unique about the methods of investigation employed by the educators. There are traditional techniques and methods of approach that have grown up as the result of special problems faced in the study of education. It is true that some important modifications of general principles of empirical investigation have come into prominence in the context of educational research. This is especially true in statistical analysis and experimental design. These principles, however, are as applicable to the study of agriculture or psychology as they are to education, and they are modifications of methods general to sciences which employ statistical analysis.

Within each discipline there is a tradition of method. These traditional methods differ as much from one another as the disciplines themselves differ. All intellectual enterprises make use of the common body of analytic technique and knowledge embodied in applied mathematics, logic, grammar, and the analysis of language. In addition, however, each special study is characterized by its own particular methods, and these methods define the unique contributions to knowledge made by that study.

Students of educational problems make use of the techniques and traditions of particular disciplines from which their studies derive. Thus, educational psychologists do about as many things as psychologists as a whole do. They use the technique of personality assessment and ability testing, and they rely for experimental techniques and hypotheses upon the body of psychological research at large. Educational psychologists contribute their share to the body of psychological knowledge, but they do so as psychologists, not as educators.

Much of contemporary theory of testing and the study of special abilities is in the hands of the educational psychologists. This, however, is an historical accident and by no means the result of particular skills developed by the study of education. The educational psychologist frequently publishes the results of his studies in journals devoted to larger areas of psychology. When he publishes in the more general educational journals, *The Harvard Educational Review* or *The Teachers College Record*, he is more likely to write as a psychologist talking to educators than as an educator among educators.

The dependency of educational psychology upon psychology as a whole can be seen by a casual inspection of the names of individuals who are Fellows of the Division on Educational Psychology of the American Psychological Association. A surprisingly large number of these individuals have appointments only in psychology departments. While their research activities are in educational psychology, they do not have appointments in schools or departments of education. A larger number, perhaps the majority of Fellows of this division, have joint appointments in psychology and education. Thus, educational psychologists are little more than psychologists with special interests. I doubt very much if one would find the reverse of this situation. That is to say, it would be hard to find individuals who were first and foremost educators in the psychology departments of the universities.

I do not know in any firsthand way, but I suspect that much the same would be true of educational sociology. I suspect that, in technique and ideas, educational sociologists are more sociologists than educators studying a particular problem. The methods and outlook of these individuals are sociological in nature, and they write as sociologists.

I think much the same must be true of the best efforts in educational history. I am not altogether certain that I know what precisely is meant by the phrase "historical method." One hears the phrase, however, and I am reasonably certain that it refers to something. The method of the historian is likely to be less formal, more intuitive, and less subject to textbook description, but nonetheless real. One has only to examine history written by a historian and compare it with history written by an educator or a psychologist to be convinced of the influence of historical method. Any satisfactory attempt to relate the institution of schooling to intellectual and social histories at large relies on the tradition and method of the professional historian.

The best histories of education are in the tradition of history, though they may be written by individuals whose primary university affiliations are with departments of education. They owe little or nothing beyond subject matter to the discipline of education. Thus in history, as in sociology and psychology, the study of schooling provides problems but no unique method nor any particular intellectual tradition.

Education is a discipline with a central object of study but with no unity of tradition or method. Perhaps it is this lack of unity of tradition that has produced the idols of scientism, professionalism, and obscurantism. In any event, when the professors of education contribute to the sum of human knowledge, they do so very often as practitioners of other traditions applied to the problems of schooling. In this sense education fails to meet the requirements of a basic discipline. It has no tradition or method and hence no intellectual viewpoint of its own. Because, however, the subject matter is a fundamental one, the study of education should not be left to those whose interests are solely in the practical and the immediate.

Because of the lack of a tradition in method, almost necessarily the study of basic problems in education is done by individuals whose backgrounds and academic preparation vary. In no small measure, educators depend for method upon the contributing disciplines upon which they draw. This fact implies that there should be a steady and large infusion of individuals from other fields into education. Historians, psychologists, philosophers, and linguists whose interests draw them to the topics of schooling need to be encouraged and rewarded for the study of education.

At the same time, the professors of education, the scholars who study the problems of schooling, should not be drawn entirely from the ranks of those who have their backgrounds in other fields. Nor should the study of education be left to fragmented efforts in other disciplines. Historians and sociologists who study education should know and understand each other. It is as important to relate the history of education to educational psychology as it is to relate the history of education to the history of technology. The problems which deserve attention from across disciplinary boundaries are exciting. I can think of no more worthwhile project for a historian of education than to tackle the question of transfer of training. To do so, however, such a historian must be steeped in education and social history and, in addition, know something about contemporary thought in educational psychology and the psychology of learning.

I do not intend to discuss the question of graduate training in education, but a word on this subject is necessary to avoid the possible implication that graduate work in education be entirely abandoned in favor of work in the other special fields. This should not be done for several reasons. For one thing, some students of education should have the first-hand intuitive knowledge that comes from actual work in the school systems. These people come to the scholarly study of eduation from direct experience with the subject. Second, there must be within the discipline of education a large body of individuals who can bring together and relate the methods and traditions of the special fields that contribute to the study of education. These are people who stand at the center of the field of inquiry, "generalists" in education, if you like. Third, some problems, problems in curriculum, administration, and the training of teachers are so close to applied studies that they cannot be considered in any other setting but education.

One implication of these views about education should be made explicit. It is that all students of education should have a thorough background in some one discipline useful to the study of education and a fair acquaintance with some of the other disciplines that contribute to education. This makes rigorous and difficult demands upon graduate students in education, but these are made by their chosen field of inquiry.

Though the study of education involves no unique tradition or method that serves to differentiate it from the other social sciences, its concern with an aspect of society so highly institutionalized makes the contributions of those who have worked in the schools useful. Those with some direct experience of teaching in the public schools serve to pull together the separate strands in the discipline of education. They are the individuals who can understand the jargon of special methods, who can see relationships between such things as the theory of transfer of training and the development of an industrial society, who, in a word, can contribute the problems of education.

I have implied that the study of education is primarily a social science. It is, of course, concerned with moral and philosophical problems often eschewed by social scientists. Most students of education, however, are concerned with the facts of schooling and theories about those facts. Thus an important issue in the study of education concerns the uses and limitations of empirical information about schooling. To deal with the nature of education, it is necessary to examine the kinds of factual information that can be gathered about learning and teaching and the uses to which these may be put.

There are two points of view from which we may look at the uses of the study of education, though one of these is by overwhelming use and importance the more usual one. We may, and usually do, consider the ends achieved by the society which supports academic inquiry into schooling. In addition, however, we may consider the ends achieved by those who are the students of education. This may seem to be a curious question to consider, but it is, I believe, an important determiner of the excellence of the study of education.

To some extent at least I hope that educators study their subject out of curiosity. At the same time I think that a curiosity about some aspect of schooling is not something that comes easily to the college student. It is very likely the result of some particular and quite specific experience with education. It may come sometimes from an interest in and study of one of the disciplines that lends its method to education, or it may come from direct experience with schooling, usually as a teacher, but surely on occasion at least, as a pupil.

Given the best motivation, an interest in ideas and in knowing, it is most certainly accidental contingencies and unique characteristics of personality that lead an academically bent individual into the study of education. Money, social origins and aspirations, job tenure have all been identified in empirical surveys as things which appear to push individuals into the study of education. These are not necessarily bad or damaging to the intellectual climate of the discipline. They are intellectually irrelevant, but they exert profound influence upon all academic disciplines, not the least upon the study of education. To the extent that education is a basic academic discipline, however, nothing further than curiosity need be relevant. The scholar and society generally agree in the broadest sense upon the ends of academic inquiry, and this is enough.

The goal of the study of any problem is to produce understanding of that problem. This is an easy enough principle to state (and to agree with), but an interpretation of exactly what it means leads to difficulties. There is not universal agreement on the criteria of understanding, nor should there be, given the variety of things into which the human mind inquires. Concern with the criteria of understanding has been a major philosophical activity of the past sixty years or so, and in the empirical social sciences that concern has led to some rather explicit methodological principles.

Many of the social sciences, particularly those in which investigators gather data in a form analogous to the methods of the natural sciences, have developed excellent and stringent, though by no means sufficient, criteria to apply to the achievement of understanding. These criteria have been variously stated, but in their baldest form they can be stated as the prediction of new events from principles derived from the study of past events, and the control of events by control over those variables that cause them. Prediction and control are objective criteria that tell us that some measure of understanding has been achieved.

These are powerful tests of understanding. They are so powerful that they have come to be regarded by many social scientists as the ends of knowledge. Sciences governed completely by these principles are applied sciences, sciences the ends of which are practical. Consequently, if there is any validity at all in the distinction between pure and applied study, prediction and control cannot be ends in themselves for pure inquiry.

Some of the questions examined by the students of education lend themselves to test by these criteria. Even in these cases, the criteria themselves need to be regarded only as tests of the degree to which some particular problem is understood. More than this is the province of the student of applied education. It is, however, difficult to apply these tests to all intellectual inquiry centering about schooling. They are difficult to apply to history or to the study of the individual personality. The study of personality or history is individualistic and intuitive. Predictive implications may be derived from such study, but only at the considerable risk of failure. Personality theory, more often than not, is a kind of attitude which orients one towards psychological problems, not a theory in the generally accepted scientific sense.

I use the study of personality as an example, and I mean it to illustrate the difficulty of applying so particular a criterion as prediction to the question of understanding. The function of the study of personality is to provide a background of experience against which we may judge and evaluate what is happening to individual human beings. We do not use the material of study to predict particular outcomes with a specified level of probability, but we can use such material to establish a range of possible outcomes. These let us know what the reasonable limits of expectation are.

I do not mean to imply that the lack of predictability in the study of the individual or in the study of certain aspects of social systems is something metaphysical or inherent in the freedom of the individual human mind or the human will. It is simply that the limitations of the methods available to us and the inherent difficulties in the subject matter do not allow us to apply the ordinary canons of induction with anything like a specifiable degree of accuracy. We may use historical material or case studies to predict outcomes with free abandon, but such prediction is intuitive, and it is usually based on preconception rather than inductive evidence. When it is inductive, it is based upon single instances which embody unique circumstances not likely to occur again.

The case method and the historical method provide poor foundation for inductive inference. Because the events that make up any considerable narrative about an individual or about a society are always but a part of the total possible narrative and because that narrative itself is a complicated causal chain, it can be nothing more than a description of a set of unique circumstances. We may know with some degree of accuracy the outcome of a relation between a pair of events in such a narrative, but we are usually reduced to ignorance when we try to examine all the possible interactions between these events and others that have occurred in the same narrative or before the narrative has begun. Any prediction is based upon the identification of some segment of the narrative with some events that have been studied by laboratory or other techniques outside of the narrative setting that makes up the case history. The use of such identification to make predictions is risky because the laboratory or controlled observations that gave rise to the prediction do not take into account the interactions with other events that occur in the narrative of the individual case.

One of the most successful and highly developed examples of the application of empirical study to individual histories occurs in psychological testing. All students of testing, however, are aware of the great discrepancies between the well-specified errors of measurement obtainable from normative information and the actual errors of measurement in individual cases. The outcome of a testing program may be used to establish, with specified limits of precision, what we are to expect from a population of individuals. Thus, the city of Baltimore can predict with considerable accuracy the distribution of abilities within its school system from year to year, and it may, by the use of social and ecological information, predict changes in these distributions from time to time and from area to area within the city. In theory the same knowledge about distributions should yield the limits of prediction for individual cases.

The results of even the best testing procedures must be used with "clinical judgment" in individual cases, however. If not, some information must be discarded. Clinical judgment means, I think, that the user of the test does not rely completely on the statistical information about the test but reserves the right to consider the statistical information in the light of individual facts known from the case history. It can be argued, of course, that the clinical judgment itself should be based upon inductive inference, and therefore, if we had the right information, it should be possible to outguess clinical judgment by statistical information. The fact is that we do not at present gather the right information, and—given the great range of possibilities in individual histories—it is unlikely that we can do so in the near future. The problem of prediction from any appreciable fraction of the range of individual circumstances is simply one of size. We cannot get enough statistical information about any particular combination of unique circumstances to make a distribution suitable for inductive inference. Even if the information were available, it would be impractical to process it by current techniques.

This example is meant to illustrate that the limitation in ways of gathering knowledge at the present time makes it impossible to apply the canons of inductive inference to all of the problems in so complicated a human system as the schools. It is not possible to experiment with histories, nor is it possible to compare histories which differ only in some particular detail as a means of testing out information about particular causal relations in complicated systems.

Even when it is possible to study parts of complicated systems experimentally, or by some other powerful empirical method, the great number of possible interactions between causative events makes the application of analytic empirical techniques difficult and liable to errors of oversimplification. Consider the problem of experimentally comparing the outcome of different procedures used by teachers in classrooms.

The effectiveness of any classroom procedure depends upon a large number of things, some of which are readily identifiable and others of which probably are not. Certainly a procedure depends upon the teacher who administers it. This is not an idle statement, but one which can be backed up by countless studies of educational practices, studies which show an interaction between method and teachers. In addition to the teacher, a classroom will have anywhere from twenty to fifty pupils (the number itself being an important variable), all of whom interact with each other and with the teacher. Each of these individuals provides a source of unique interaction with procedural differences. Thus, even though we may find an average difference between any particular procedures under study, we know by the results of our study that it will be modified to great degrees by the individuals who employ the procedures compared. Furthermore, these collections of twenty to fifty children will vary from locale to locale and from time to time in ways that will be relevant to the procedural differences.

Given this situation, it is not surprising that the literature on experimental variations in classroom procedures is disappointing. The mean effects are small and frequently applicable to particular situations only at the risk of destroying the small mean effect. I do not think that the experimental study of the classroom is hopeless or doomed to failure, but we ought not to expect too much from the traditional experimental comparisons. If we are to apply the outcomes of scientific studies of the individual and such collections of individuals as occur in the classroom, we must in most instances content ourselves with small average effects, and, in all probability, we must use some judgment in applying the information.

Information about average effects is necessary to the efficient management of large social institutions such as the schools or the military establishment. Thus, despite their limitations, the large objective testing programs of the schools are useful, and by now they are probably necessary. Such programs cannot be applied to individuals in the same way that they are applied in the mass, since the information available to us in single cases will lead us to modify the objective, statistical interpretation of results in the light of what else we know about the individual or particular school being considered.

Studies of procedural change and programs of testing have, in the past, been most efficient when the role of individual histories is minimized. Some new approaches give promise of much closer approximation to control over the factors responsible for individual histories and hence much greater control in individual cases. These are the approaches based upon the notion of programming, and the best known current examples are the teaching machines. Because programs are flexible, have large numbers of alternatives, and make decisions about alternatives in particular cases—decisions based upon the state of the individual at that moment—they can approximate the functions of the teacher or some other individual who makes decisions about what to do from moment to moment in the classroom. Furthermore, they can make these decisions upon some fixed, error-free criterion. Within some domains, the concept of programming will extend the uses of empirical information in education. At present, the teaching machines themselves appear to be most useful in the teaching of skills which have inherent logical structures, particularly hierarchical structures.

Prediction and control, then, are excellent criteria of understanding and they also provide us with some of the uses of understanding. They are not always easy to apply, however, and I think little is gained by pretending that they are. It is futile to issue promissory notes about the future applications of the scientific study of education. The scientific study of education can be justified on intrinsic grounds, on the return to the investigator himself and in terms of the gains to a society that places a value upon the understanding of social and natural problems. Indeed, I suspect that belief in utopian promises about the prediction and control of behavior has been in part responsible for some of the adverse criticism of the study of education and the social sciences generally. The scientific canons of prediction and control have led some people into the belief that all knowledge about a social system can and should be applied, and the sooner the better. Because any part of the social system studied scientifically is no more than a more or less arbitrary segment of the whole, the possible interactions of that part with other, unstudied parts of the whole are ignored. Furthermore, an easy reliance on scientific control leads us to neglect inquiry into the ends that are served by controlled change. I do not mean to imply that experimentalism and instrumentalism are bad, but I would like to suggest that we be a bit more tentative and skeptical in the application of the empirical information we have and that we be not so quick to demand that all information about man and his society meet the requirements of prediction and control.

What are the uses, then, of the study of education? I think we must answer that in some respects they are the same as the uses of any other academic discipline and, therefore, in important particulars should be distinguished from the uses of poultry husbandry or other applied disciplines. This is not to say, of course, that the study of education should not also be an applied study. The student of education, however, need not ask whether he is increasing the effectiveness of the schools or whether he is engaged in research designed to channel the activities of the schools into a more useful course. A study of education need not justify itself on the basis of any contribution it makes to the control over the outcomes of education, though this may be a useful by-product of that study.

It remains a basic supposition, I suppose, of the social support of any scholarly or scientific enterprise that study, investigation, and scholarship will, in the long run, increase our ability to adjust the human condition to the demands of the world in which we live and to do this by explicit and rational means. However vague this supposition may be, society does not support scholarly activity simply because of the intrinsic rewards to the scholar. It turns out, probably for social and psychological reasons that themselves deserve study, that society is best rewarded in the long run when the scholar is left to pursue his own basic interests. It is in this respect that the study of education has been a conspicuous failure. There are too few professional students of education who follow their own work untrammeled by the demands for specific results. Too often, the hardheaded criteria for empirical investigation, prediction and control, have agreed with the demands for quick returns in education. Educators, in company with many social scientists, have been too eager to see the results of their scholarly work embedded in social change.

The pressure for application is in good measure the result of the expectation that the study of education will, in the unelegant but singularly appropriate phrase, pay off. This pressure, accompanied by the scholar's own interests in further large-scale tests of his notions has resulted in a tendency to rush into action with some new device, principle, or method when a more leisurely consideration in the atmosphere of the ivory tower would be more appropriate.

In simple systems, the tendency to introduce specific and isolated change is not so objectionable. In physical systems, in which a localized set of events is controlled by a limited number of variables, there is little effect outside of the system when change is introduced, save, of course, when the effect is amplified by man's social structure. Thus, the consequences of change can be contained. No matter how carefully possible outside effects are considered, however, the study of an isolated social system necessarily neglects some conditions which function in a real society. It is impossible to effect a social change in isolation.

At one time I was convinced that a detailed and exhaustive study would show that the whole secondary educational system in the United States could be made more efficient by cutting off the twelfth year. Thus public school education would be terminated at the end of the eleventh grade. Suppose that a careful and thorough investigation, supported by an analysis of the aims of education in American society, were to suggest that such a scheme would be feasible and would result in correction of such diverse conditions as delinquency rates, failure rates in college, the excessive length of time in study for the learned professions, and so on. However carefully such a scheme would be considered, it is probable that unforeseen circumstances would appear in any application of the principle. Perhaps it would be in the form of an alarming increase in birth rate, or perhaps a decrease. One could go on enumerating such possibilities almost endlessly and still be sure that some were left unconsidered.

Such a scheme may indeed be useful to society; I do not mean to imply that we should cease all social action because we cannot foresee all outcomes. The more we know, however, the more consequences we can foresee. In a word, we know better what we are doing. Society, in the long run, is benefited by careful consideration of practical action as much as the social sciences suffer from hasty commitments to it.

The scholar should be the one to resist most firmly the pressure to precipitate action. I think one way that resistance may be stiffened is to make certain that scholarly activity is its own intrinsic reward. Intrinsic reward to scholarly or scientific work occurs less often in the study of education than it should. In education, the scholar is likely to yield to the pressure for application because of the emphasis upon results in the study of education; research is frequently bought and paid for on the basis of a specific problem. Moreover, I suspect that a lack of genuine intellectual curiosity about the subject matter results in many students of education substituting social action for the rewards of pure research. Finally, we all know that many Ph.D. dissertations are done (and not a few studies from mature scholars) not out of intrinsic interest but by extrinsic demands for publication and the accompanying notoriety. The inevitable result is a mass of busy-work.

I have tried to argue that education is a social science as well as an applied discipline. It is a somewhat unusual social science, though probably not absolutely unique, in that it has no unique tradition of method of its own. It makes use of a variety of traditions, traditions associated with psychology, philosophy, history, economics, and the study of social institutions. It provides a well-defined subject matter—schooling—which is a fundamental activity of civilized society and which, indeed, may be a direct outcome of human nature.

Because so much of the vitality of research and scholarly work on the subject of schooling depends upon traditions outside of the discipline of education, education cannot afford to be free of the other social sciences. There should, therefore, be a continuous infusion of individuals from other disciplines into the study of education. Since education has a central core of subject matter, however, it also needs an intellectual tradition, not of method but of firsthand acquaintance with the subject matter, a tradition that can be maintained by individuals whose training and career is entirely within the subject matter of education.

The study of education should satisfy both the demands of the society that supports the study and the needs of the scholar who pursues the investigation. Perhaps one of the great deficiencies of the study of education is the lack of intrinsic interest on the part of those who practice it. The extrinsic demands of society and the devotion to the concept of research—any kind of research—as a way of satisfying society's demands appear to be a substitute for intrinsic interest on the part of the student of education.

Scholarly activity is almost necessarily inefficient. No one can tell what kind of activity will in the long run be most satisfying to the investigator and those who support him. It is the inefficiency and uncertainty of scholarly work that makes the ivory tower so valuable a place. Educators are too often to be found in the marketplace selling their wares rather than in the ivory tower. They should be in the marketplace frequently enough as observers and perhaps as buyers, but not so often as sellers. The temptation provided by the rewards of action are many, and the current pressure on public education has increased them. If we cannot herd a large number of the educators into the ivory tower, perhaps we ought at least to press for such a sanctuary for those among the students of education who want one. One of the first steps in providing such a refuge is to recognize the claims of education as a pure discipline.

PART II   PSYCHOLOGY AS INQUIRY

Because we are concerned with behavioral change, we must come to grips with what the psychologist calls theories of learning. Hilgard describes the criteria that must be met in order for something to be called a theory of learning. Skinner argues, however, that theories of learning are actually unnecessary if one's goal is simply to accomplish behavioral change. Not all psychologists, of course, agree with this view. Moreover, Skinner's claim that an individual's behavior can be controlled by manipulating environmental events has become a general issue.

The principle mechanism used to accomplish behavioral change is the Law of Effect. Meehl addresses himself to the issue of circularity in the psychologists' definition of behavioral change attributed to the Law of Effect, and conditions that must be met in order for the law to be used effectively in practical as well as research settings.

Because behavior must be changed—the mentally ill must be helped, children must be taught, and animals must be trained—we cannot wait for results from the psychology laboratory to tell us what to do. Brody and Oppenheim present the case for using a personal one-to-one relationship as a means of discovering the stimuli that must be manipulated in order for an individual's behavior to be changed (indeed, this is done every day by successful teachers and clinicians).

Finally, we come to the heart of much recent psychological theorizing. Namely, that in order for any behavior to be studied psychologically, much less adequately understood, it must be described. In the case of language the linguist has constructed grammars that can be used as models for knowledge of language. Jenkins summarizes a conference addressed to problems of this sort. He describes the nature of some current linguistic models and the ways in which they can be used by the psychologist to further his understanding of verbal behavior.

6 From THE NATURE OF LEARNING THEORIES
Ernest R. Hilgard and Gordon H. Bower

The study of learning is shared by many disciplines. Physiologists, biochemists, and biophysicists have a legitimate interest in it; parents, teachers, industrial managers, rehabilitation workers, and others faced by the practical problems of the control of learning have their own needs which require that they understand the basic processes and how to manage them. Yet the scientific study of learning is carried on primarily by psychologists. Psychology's claim to the field was staked out in part by masterly pioneers such as Ebbinghaus (1885),[1] Bryan and Harter (1897, 1899), and Thorndike (1898). Those who have followed in their footsteps have been primarily psychologists. Professional educators have welcomed educational psychology as a foundation science upon which to build their practices, and studies of learning have gone on concurrently in laboratories of general psychology and laboratories of educational psychology, with interplay between the pure and applied fields. Under the circumstances, it is very natural for psychologists to feel that the study of learning belongs to them.

In addition to historical reasons, there is another basis on which to account for the psychologist's interest in learning. This is the centrality of learning in the more general systems of psychological theory. A scientist, along with the desire to satisfy his curiosity about the facts of nature, has a predilection for ordering his facts into systems of laws and theories. He is interested not only in verified facts and relationships, but in neat and parsimonious ways of summarizing these facts. Psychologists with a penchant for systems find a theory of learning essential because so much of man's diverse behavior is the result of learning. If the rich diversity of behavior is to be understood in accordance with a few principles, it is evident that some of these principles will have to do with the way in which learning comes about.

The Definition of Learning

WHAT LEARNING INCLUDES

There are many activities which everyone will agree count as illustrations of learning: acquiring a vocabulary, memorizing a poem, learning

---

[1] References cited can be found by author and date in the list at the end of the chapter.

SOURCE: Ernest R. Hilgard and Gordon H. Bower, *Theories of Learning*, 3d ed. (New York: Appleton-Century-Crofts, 1966), pp. 1–6. Copyright © 1966 by the Meredith Corporation. Reprinted by permission of Appleton-Century-Crofts.

to operate a typewriter. There are other activities, not quite as obviously learned, which are easily classified as learned once you have reflected upon them. Among these are the acquiring of prejudices and preferences and other social attitudes and ideals, including the many skills involved in the social interplay with other people. Finally there are a number of activities whose acquisition is not usually classifiable as a gain or improvement because their utility, if such there be, is not readily demonstrable. Among these are tics, mannerisms, and autistic gestures.

Such a pointing to illustrations of learning serves very well as a first approximation to a definition. It is, in fact, extremely difficult to write an entirely satisfactory definition. Although we are tempted to define learning as improvement with practice, or as profiting by experience, we know very well that some learning is not improvement, and other learning is not desirable in its consequences. To describe it alternatively as any change with repetition confuses it with growth, fatigue, and other changes which may take place with repetition. The following definition may be offered provisionally:

> Learning is the process by which an activity originates or is changed through reacting to an encountered situation, provided that the characteristics of the change in activity cannot be explained on the basis of native response tendencies, maturation, or temporary states of the organism (e.g., fatigue, drugs, etc.).

The definition is not formally satisfactory because of the many undefined terms in it, but it will do to call attention to the problems involved in any definition of learning. The definition must distinguish between (1) the kinds of changes, and their correlated antecedents, which are included as learning, and (2) the related kinds of changes, and their antecedents, which are not classified as learning. We can now go on to consider some of the changes that are excluded by our provisional definition.

NATIVE RESPONSE TENDENCIES VERSUS LEARNING

The older catalogs of innate behavior usually included among unlearned activities the reflexes (such as pupillary constriction to light), the tropisms (such as a moth's dashing into a flame), and the instincts (such as a bird's nest-building). We may continue to acknowledge such activities as characteristic of various species, and those more nearly idiosyncratic to one species as *species-specific.*

The concept of instinct has been the most controversial of these terms, partly because of a vagueness of connotation, partly because of a tendency to use the word as explanatory, hence as a cloak for ignorance. After a period of some years in which it was virtually taboo, the respectability of instinct was briefly revived by a group of European naturalists known as ethologists (e.g., Tinbergen, 1951; Thorpe, 1956) only to lead to so much controversy that its advocates have again abandoned it in favor or *species-specific behavior* (Hinde and Tinbergen, 1958).

The problem of what is naturally characteristic of a given species is not solved by attempting to classify some behavior as altogether innate, other behavior as altogether learned. The objections to the concept of instinct that come from finding much learning in so-called instinctive behavior (Beach, 1955), though useful in providing warning signs against overstating the case for instinct, do not meet the problem that some things are much easier for one organism to acquire than for another. Thus if learning is used exclusively in describing behavior, it ought to be possible to teach all birds to home as some pigeons do, or to teach an oriole to build a robin's nest. The in-between nature of behavior with large instinctive components is well illustrated by the experiments on imprinting (e.g., Lorenz, 1952; Hess, 1958). A young duckling, for example, is prepared instinctively to accept a certain range of mother-figures, characterized by size, movement, and vocalization. Once such a mother-figure has been accepted and followed about, only this *particular* mother can satisfy the instinctive demand. The selected mother (who may be Professor Lorenz crawling on hands and knees) has become imprinted, and is the only "mother" the duckling will follow. Imprinting is then a form of learning, but a form very closely allied to the instinctive propensities of a particular kind of organism of a particular age. (We lack at present clear evidence for imprinting except in fowls and other birds.) The problem of distinguishing between the instinctive and learned components of the behavior illustrated by imprinting is an experimental problem, depending for its clarification upon the ingenuity of the experimenter in designing appropriate control experiments.

MATURATION VERSUS LEARNING

Growth is learning's chief competitor as a modifier of behavior. If a behavior sequence matures through regular stages irrespective of intervening practice, the behavior is said to develop through maturation and not through learning. If training procedures do not speed up or modify the behavior, such procedures are not causally important and the changes do not classify as learning. Relatively pure cases such as the swimming of tadpoles and the flying of birds can be attributed primarily to maturation. Many activities are not as clear-cut, but develop through a complex interplay of maturation and learning. A convenient illustration is the development of language in the child. The child does not learn to talk until old enough, but the language which he learns is that which he hears. In such cases it is an experimental problem to isolate the effects of maturation and of learning. The ambiguity in such cases is one of fact, not of definition.

FATIGUE AND HABITUATION VERSUS LEARNING

When activities are repeated in rapid succession, there is often a loss in efficiency commonly attributed to fatigue. Such changes in performance are called *work decrements* in the experimental laboratory. The units of a work curve are like those of a practice curve: performance plotted against trials or repetitions. Hence the experimental arrangements in obtaining a work curve are essentially those of a learning procedure and, at first sight, it appears to be a form of question-begging to define the processes involved by the results obtained. It would be question-begging, however, only if we were to equate learning or fatigue with the change in performances, and it is permissible to make such inferences as the obtained performances require or suggest. Fatigue curves tend to show decreasing proficiency with repetition and recovery with rests. Learning curves ordinarily show gains with repetitions and forgetting over rests. These typical differences between learning effects and fatigue effects are evident enough, but the inferences from performance are made on somewhat more complex evidence. It is because of the complexity of these inferences that it is difficult to state a concise definition of learning which will conserve the learning inferences from performance while eliminating the fatigue inferences. The problem is logically the same as distinguishing changes due to maturation and to learning. But again the ambiguity is one of fact, not of definition.

Another kind of repeated situation that produces progressive changes in the direction of reduced responsiveness is known as *habituation*. This differs from fatigue in that little work is involved: what is reduced is responsiveness to a repeated stimulus. If you try to study (or to go to sleep) in a room with a loudly ticking clock this is at first very disrupting, but you soon "get used" to it, and it no longer bothers. This becoming accustomed is called habituation. While habituation has long been recognized as having some affiliations with learning (e.g., Humphrey, 1933; Thorpe, 1956), attention has again been called to it through the prominence given recently by Russian workers to the *orientation reflex* and its diminution with repetition (Sokolov, 1963). Some habituation may be due to sensory adaptation, as when the odor of a fish market or a laboratory is not detected by those who work there, but other effects are probably central, and more nearly related to learning and to that aspect of learning known as extinction. The effects of repeated habituation may be relatively enduring, so that later habituations are more rapid than earlier ones. Hence some learning is involved in habituation, but it is again a marginal case.

Learning must aways remain an inference from performance, and only confusion results if performance and learning are identified. A clear illustration is provided by performance under the influence of drugs or intoxicants. The fact that learned behavior fails when the organism is in such a state does not mean that forgetting has occurred. When the normal state has been restored, the performance may return to normal levels although there has been no intervening training.

LEARNING AND THE NERVOUS SYSTEM

Some definitions of learning avoid the problem of performance by defining learning as a change in the central nervous system. So long as this change in the nervous system persists, temporary changes in state, such as those in fatigue and intoxication, affect performance but not learning. This definition asserts that learning is an inference, but it goes on to make a particular sort of inference about the role of the nervous system in learning. In view of the lack of knowledge of what actually does take place inside the organism when learning occurs, it is preferable not to include hypothetical neural processes in the definition of learning. We know that learning takes place. We should therefore be able to define what we are talking about without reference to any speculation whatever. This position does not deny that what we are calling learning may be a function of nervous tissue. It asserts only that it is not necessary to know anything about the neural correlates of learning in order to know that learning occurs.

LEARNING, PROBLEM-SOLVING, AND REASONING

After you have learned, there are many things which you are able to do. If you can add and subtract, you can solve many novel problems without learning anything new. Where the solution of problems is relatively mechanical (as in addition and subtraction), the problem may be thought of as merely the exercise or utilization of a learned bit of behavior. When, however, there is greater novelty, more putting of things into relationship, as in reasoning or inventiveness, the process is interesting in its own light, and is not to be described simply as the running off of old habits.

The question has been raised, especially by Maier (1931), as to the appropriateness of including processes like reasoning within the same classification as other kinds of learning. Our preference is for including them. Leaving them in does not prejudge their explanation. There may be several kinds of learning from the simpler to the more complex, not all following the same principles. If so, we have no assurance that the only sharp break comes when "reasoning" appears. Leaving the doubtful processes in simply asserts that a complete theory of learning must have something to say about reasoning, creative imagination, and inventiveness, in addition to what may be said about memorizing and retaining or about the acquisition of skill.

DEFINITION NOT A MAJOR SOURCE OF DISAGREEMENT
BETWEEN THEORIES

While it is extremely difficult to formulate a satisfactory definition of learning so as to include all the activities and processes which we wish to include and eliminate all those which we wish to exclude, the difficulty does not prove to be embarrassing because it is not a source of controversy as between theories. The controversy is over fact and interpretation, not over definition. There are occasional confusions over definition, but such confusions may usually be resolved by resort to pointing, to denotation. For the most part it is satisfactory to continue to mean by learning that which conforms to the usual socially accepted meaning that is part of our common heritage. Where distinctions have to be made with greater precision, they can be made through carefully specified types of inference from experiments.

References

Beach, F. A. (1955) The descent of instinct. *Psychol. Rev.* 62, 401–410.

Bryan, W. L., & Harter, N. (1897) Studies in the physiology and psychology of the telegraphic language. *Psychol. Rev.* 4, 27–53.

Bryan, W. L., & Harter, N. (1899) Studies on the telegraphic language. The acquisition of a hierarchy of habits. *Psychol. Rev.*, 6, 345–375.

Ebbinghaus, H. (1885) *Memory.* Translated by H. A. Ruger and C. E. Bussenius. New York: Teachers College, 1913. Reissued as paperback, New York: Dover, 1964.

Hinde, R. A., and Tinbergen, N. (1958) The comparative study of species-specific behavior. In A. Roe, & G. G. Simpson (Editors), *Behavior and Evolution.* New Haven: Yale Univ. Press, 251–268.

Humphrey, G. (1933) *The Nature of Learning in Its Relation to the Living System.* New York: Harcourt Brace & World.

Hess, E. H. (1958) "Imprinting" in Animals. *Sci. American,* 198, March, 81–90.

Lorenz, K. Z. (1952) *King Solomon's Ring.* New York: Crowell.

Sokolov, E. M. (1963) Higher Nervous Functions: The Orienting Reflex. *Ann. Rev. Physiology,* 25, 545–580.

Thorpe, W. H. (1956) *Learning and Instinct in Animals.* London: Methuen.

Thorndike, E. L. (1898) Animal Intelligence: An Experimental Study of the Associative Processes in Animals. *Psychol. Rev., Monogr. Suppl.,* 2, No. 8.

Tinbergen, N. (1951) *The Study of Instinct.* London: Oxford Univ. Press.

7 ARE THEORIES OF LEARNING NECESSARY?
B. F. Skinner

Certain basic assumptions, essential to any scientific activity, are sometimes called theories. That nature is orderly rather than capricious is an
example. Certain statements are also theories simply to the extent that
they are not yet facts. A scientist may guess at the result of an experiment before the experiment is carried out. The prediction and the later
statement of result may be composed of the same terms in the same syntactic arrangement, the difference being in the degree of confidence. No
empirical statement is wholly nontheoretical in this sense, because evidence is never complete, nor is any prediction probably ever made
wholly without evidence. The term "theory" will not refer here to statements of these sorts but rather to any explanation of an observed fact
which appeals to events taking place somewhere else, at some other
level of observation, described in different terms, and measured, if at
all, in different dimensions.

Three types of theory in the field of learning satisfy this definition.
The most characteristic is to be found in the field of physiological psychology. We are all familiar with the changes that are supposed to take
place in the nervous system when an organism learns. Synaptic connections are made or broken, electrical fields are disrupted or reorganized,
concentrations of ions are built up or allowed to diffuse away, and so
on. In the science of neurophysiology statements of this sort are not necessarily theories in the present sense. But in a science of behavior, where
we are concerned with whether or not an organism secrets saliva when
a bell rings, or jumps toward a gray triangle, or says *bik* when a card
reads *tuz*, or loves someone who resembles his mother, all statements
about the nervous system are theories in the sense that they are not expressed in the same terms and could not be confirmed with the same
methods of observation as the facts for which they are said to account.

A second type of learning theory is in practice not far from the physiological, although there is less agreement about the method of direct observation. Theories of this type have always dominated the field of
human behavior. They consist of references to "mental" events, as in
saying that an organism learns to behave in a certain way because it
"finds something pleasant" or because it "expects something to happen."

SOURCE: B. F. Skinner, "Are Theories of Learning Necessary?" *Psychological Review*,
57, no. 4 (July 1950), 193–216. Copyright 1950 by the American Psychological
Association. Reprinted by permission of the publisher.

To the mentalistic psychologist these explanatory events are no more theoretical than synaptic connections to the neurophysiologist, but in a science of behavior they are theories because the methods and terms appropriate to the events to be explained differ from the methods and terms appropriate to the explaining events.

In a third type of learning theory the explanatory events are not directly observed. The writer's suggestion that the letters CNS be regarded as representing, not the Central Nervous System, but the Conceptual Nervous System (2, p. 421), seems to have been taken seriously. Many theorists point out that they are not talking about the nervous system as an actual structure undergoing physiological or bio-chemical changes but only as a system with a certain dynamic output. Theories of this sort are multiplying fast, and so are parallel operational versions of mental events. A purely behavioral definition of expectancy has the advantage that the problem of mental observation is avoided and with it the problem of how a mental event can cause a physical one. But such theories do not go so far as to assert that the explanatory events are identical with the behavioral facts which they purport to explain. A statement about behavior may support such a theory but will never resemble it in terms or syntax. Postulates are good examples. True postulates cannot become facts. Theorems may be deduced from them which, as tentative statements about behavior, may or may not be confirmed, but theorems are not theories in the present sense. Postulates remain theories until the end.

It is not the purpose of this paper to show that any of these theories cannot be put in good scientific order, or that the events to which they refer may not actually occur or be studied by appropriate sciences. It would be foolhardy to deny the achievements of theories of this sort in the history of science. The question of whether they are necessary, however, has other implications and is worth asking. If the answer is no, then it may be possible to argue effectively against theory in the field of learning. A science of behavior must eventually deal with behavior in its relation to certain manipulable variables. Theories—whether neural, mental, or conceptual—talk about intervening steps in these relationships. But instead of prompting us to search for and explore relevant variables, they frequently have quite the opposite effect. When we attribute behavior to a neural or mental event, real or conceptual, we are likely to forget that we still have the task of accounting for the neural or mental event. When we assert that an animal acts in a given way because it expects to receive food, then what began as the task of accounting for learned behavior becomes the task of accounting for expectancy. The problem is at least equally complex and probably more difficult. We are likely to close our eyes to it and to use the theory to give us answers in place of the answers we might find through further study. It might be argued that the principal function of learning theory to date has been, not to suggest appropriate research, but to create a false sense of security, an unwarranted satisfaction with the *status quo*.

Research designed with respect to theory is also likely to be wasteful. That a theory generates research does not prove its value unless the research is valuable. Much useless experimentation results from theories, and much energy and skill are absorbed by them. Most theories are eventually overthrown, and the greater part of the associated research is discarded. This could be justified if it were true that productive research requires a theory, as is, of course, often claimed. It is argued that research would be aimless and disorganized without a theory to guide it. The view is supported by psychological texts that take their cue from the logicians rather than empirical science and describe thinking as necessarily involving stages of hypothesis, deduction, experimental test, and confirmation. But this is not the way most scientists actually work. It is possible to design significant experiments for other reasons and the possibility to be examined is that such research will lead more directly to the kind of information that a science usually accumulates.

The alternatives are at least worth considering. How much can be done without theory? What other sorts of scientific activity are possible? And what light do alternative practices throw upon our present preoccupation with theory?

It would be inconsistent to try to answer these questions at a theoretical level. Let us therefore turn to some experimental material in three areas in which theories of learning now flourish and raise the question of the function of theory in a more concrete fashion.[1]

The Basic Datum in Learning

What actually happens when an organism learns is not an easy question. Those who are interested in a science of behavior will insist that learning is a change in behavior, but they tend to avoid explicit references to responses or acts as such. "Learning is adjustment, or adaptation to a situation." But of what stuff are adjustments and adaptations made? Are they data, or inferences from data? "Learning is improvement." But improvement in what? And from whose point of view? "Learning is restoration of equilibrium." But what is in equilibrium and how is it put there? "Learning is problem solving." But what are the

---

[1] Some of the material that follows was obtained in 1941–42 in a cooperative study on the behavior of the pigeon in which Keller Breland, Norman Guttman, and W. K. Estes collaborated. Some of it is selected from subsequent, as yet unpublished, work on the pigeon conducted by the author at Indiana University and Harvard University. Limitations of space make it impossible to report full details here.

physical dimensions of a problem—or of a solution? Definitions of this sort show an unwillingness to take what appears before the eyes in a learning experiment as a basic datum. Particular observations seem too trivial. An error score falls; but we are not ready to say that this is learning rather than merely the result of learning. An organism meets a criterion of ten successful trials; but an arbitrary criterion is at variance with our conception of the generality of the learning process.

This is where theory steps in. If it is not the time required to get out of a puzzle box that changes in learning, but rather the strength of a bond, or the conductivity of a neural pathway, or the excitatory potential of a habit, then problems seem to vanish. Getting out of a box faster and faster is not learning; it is merely performance. The learning goes on somewhere else, in a different dimensional system. And although the time required depends upon arbitrary conditions, often varies discontinuously, and is subject to reversals of magnitude, we feel sure that the learning process itself is continuous, orderly, and beyond the accidents of measurement. Nothing could better illustrate the use of theory as a refuge from the data.

But we must eventually get back to an observable datum. If learning is the process we suppose it to be, then it must appear so in the situations in which we study it. Even if the basic process belongs to some other dimensional system, our measures must have relevant and comparable properties. But productive experimental situations are hard to find, particularly if we accept certain plausible restrictions. To show an orderly change in the behavior of the *average* rat or ape or child is not enough, since learning is a process in the behavior of the individual. To record the beginning and end of learning or a few discrete steps will not suffice, since a series of cross-sections will not give complete coverage of a continuous process. The dimensions of the change must spring from the behavior itself; they must not be imposed by an external judgment of success or failure or an external criterion of completeness. But when we review the literature with these requirements in mind, we find little justification for the theoretical process in which we take so much comfort.

The energy level or work-output of behavior, for example, does not change in appropriate ways. In the sort of behavior adapted to the Pavlovian experiment (respondent behavior) there may be a progressive increase in the magnitude of response during learning. But we do not shout our responses louder and louder as we learn verbal material, nor does a rat press a lever harder and harder as conditioning proceeds. In operant behavior the energy or magnitude of response changes significantly only when some arbitrary value is differentially reinforced—when such a change is what is learned.

The emergence of a right response in competition with wrong responses is another datum frequently used in the study of learning. The maze and the discrimination box yield results which may be reduced to these terms. But a behavior-ratio of right *vs.* wrong cannot yield a continuously changing measure in a single experiment on a single organism. The point at which one response takes precedence over another cannot give us the whole history of the change in either response. Averaging curves for groups of trials or organisms will not solve this problem.

Increasing attention has recently been given to latency, the relevance of which, like that of energy level, is suggested by the properties of conditioned and unconditioned reflexes. But in operant behavior the relation to a stimulus is different. A measure of latency involves other considerations, as inspection of any case will show. Most operant responses may be emitted in the absence of what is regarded as a relevant stimulus. In such a case the response is likely to appear before the stimulus is presented. It is no solution to escape this embarrassment by locking a lever so that an organism cannot press it until the stimulus is presented, since we can scarcely be content with temporal relations that have been forced into compliance with our expectations. Runway latencies are subject to this objection. In a typical experiment the door of a starting box is opened and the time that elapses before a rat leaves the box is measured. Opening the door is not only a stimulus, it is a change in the situation that makes the response possible for the first time. The time measured is by no means as simple as a latency and requires another formulation. A great deal depends upon what the rat is doing at the moment the stimulus is presented. Some experimenters wait until the rat is facing the door, but to do so is to tamper with the measurement being taken. If, on the other hand, the door is opened without reference to what the rat is doing, the first major effect is the conditioning of favorable waiting behavior. The rat eventually stays near and facing the door. The resulting shorter starting-time is not due to a reduction in the latency of a response, but to the conditioning of favorable preliminary behavior.

Latencies in a single organism do not follow a simple learning process. Relevant data on his point were obtained as part of an extensive study of reaction time. A pigeon, enclosed in a box, is conditioned to peck at a recessed disc in one wall. Food is presented as reinforcement by exposing a hopper through a hold below the disc. If responses are reinforced only after a stimulus has been presented, responses at other times disappear. Very short reaction times are obtained by differentially reinforcing responses which occur very soon after the stimulus (4). But responses also come to be made very quickly without differential reinforcement. Inspection shows that this is due to the development of effective waiting. The bird comes to stand before the disc with its head in good striking position. Under optimal conditions, without differential reinforcement, the mean time between stimulus and response will be of the order of ⅓ sec. This is not a true reflex latency, since the stimulus is discriminative rather than eliciting, but it is a fair example of the latency used in the study of learning. The point is that this measure does not vary continuously or in an orderly fashion. By giving the bird more food, for example, we induce a condition in which it does not always respond. But the responses that occur show approximately the same temporal relation to the stimulus (Figure 1, middle curve). In extinction, of special interest here, there is a scattering of latencies because lack of reinforcement generates an emotional condition. Some responses occur sooner and others are delayed, but the commonest value remains unchanged (bottom curve in Figure 1). The longer latencies are easily ex-

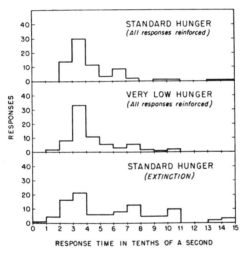

Figure 1

plained by inspection. Emotional behavior, of which examples will be mentioned later, is likely to be in progress when the ready-signal is presented. It is often not discontinued before the "go" signal is presented, and the result is a long starting-time. Cases also begin to appear in which the bird simply does not respond at all during a specified time. If we average a large number of readings, either from one bird or many, we may create what looks like a progressive lengthening of latency. But the data for an individual organism do not show a continuous process.

Another datum to be examined is the rate at which a response is emitted. Fortunately the story here is different. We study this rate by designing a situation in which a response may be freely repeated, choosing a response (for example, touching or pressing a small lever or key) that may be easily observed and counted. The responses may be recorded on a polygraph, but a more convenient form is a cumulative curve from which rate of responding is immediately read as slope. The rate at which a response is emitted in such a situation comes close to our pre-conception of the learning process. As the organism learns, the rate rises. As it unlearns (for example, in extinction) the rate falls. Various sorts of discriminative stimuli may be brought into control of the response with corresponding modifications of the rate. Motivational changes alter the rate in a sensitive way. So do those events which we speak of as generating emotion. The range through which the rate varies significantly may be as great as of the order of 1000:1. Changes in rate are satisfactorily smooth in the individual case, so that it is not necessary to average cases. A given value is often quite stable: in the pigeon a rate of four or five thousand responses per hour may be maintained without interruption for as long as fifteen hours.

Rate of responding appears to be the only datum that varies significantly and in the expected direction under conditions which are relevant to the "learning process." We may, therefore, be tempted to accept it as our long-sought-for measure of strength of bond, excitatory potential, etc. Once in possession of an effective datum, however, we may feel little need for any theoretical construct of this sort. Progress in a scientific field usually waits upon the discovery of a satisfactory dependent variable. Until such a variable has been discovered, we resort to theory. The entities which have figured so prominently in learning theory have served mainly as substitutes for a directly observable and productive datum. They have little reason to survive when such a datum has been found.

It is no accident that rate of responding is successful as a datum, because it is particularly appropriate to the fundamental task of a science of behavior. If we are to predict behavior (and possibly to control it), we must deal with *probability of response*. The business of a science of behavior is to evaluate this probability and explore the conditions that determine it. Strength of bond, expectancy, excitatory potential, and so on, carry the notion of probability in an easily imagined form, but the additional properties suggested by these terms have hindered the search for suitable measures. Rate of responding is not a "measure" of probability but it is the only appropriate datum in a formulation in these terms.

As other scientific disciplines can attest, probabilities are not easy to handle. We wish to make statements about the likelihood of occurrence of a single future response, but our data are in the form of frequencies of responses that have already occurred. These responses were presumably similar to each other and to the response to be predicted. But this raises the troublesome problem of response-instance *vs.* response-class. Precisely what responses are we to take into account in predicting a future instance? Certainly not the responses made by a population of different organisms, for such a statistical datum raises more problems than it solves. To consider the frequency of repeated responses in an individual demands something like the experimental situation just described.

This solution of the problem of a basic datum is based upon the view that operant behavior is essentially an emissive phenomenon. Latency and magnitude of response fail as measures because they do not take this into account. They are concepts appropriate to the field of the reflex, where the all but invariable control exercised by the eliciting stimulus makes the notion of probability of response trivial. Consider, for example, the case of latency. Because of our acquaintance with simple reflexes we infer that a response that is more likely to be emitted will be emitted more quickly. But is this true? What can the word "quickly" mean? Probability of response, as well as prediction of response, is concerned with the moment of emission. This is a point in time, but it does not have the temporal dimension of a latency. The execution may take time after the response has been initiated, but the moment of occurrence has no duration.[2] In recognizing the emissive character of operant behavior and the central position of probability of response as a datum, latency is seen to be irrelevant to our present task.

Various objections have been made to the use of rate of responding as a basic datum. For example, such a program may seem to bar us from dealing with many events which are unique occurrences in the life of the individual. A man does not decide upon a career, get married, make a million dollars, or get killed in an accident often enough to make a rate of response meaningful. But these activities are not responses. They are not simple unitary events lending themselves to prediction as such. If we are to predict marriage, success, accidents, and so on, in anything more than statistical terms, we must deal with the smaller units of behavior which lead to and compose these unitary episodes. If the units appear in repeatable form, the present analysis may be applied. In the

---

[2] It cannot, in fact, be shortened or lengthened. Where a latency appears to be forced toward a minimal value by differential reinforcement, another interpretation is called for. Although we may differentially reinforce more energetic behavior or the faster execution of behavior after it begins, it is meaningless to speak of differentially reinforcing responses with short or long latencies. What we actually reinforce differentially are (a) favorable waiting behavior and (b) more vigorous responses. When we ask a subject to respond "as soon as possible" in the human reaction-time experiment, we essentially ask him (a) to carry out as much of the response as possible without actually reaching the criterion of emission, (b) to do as little else as possible, and (c) to respond energetically after the stimulus has been given. This may yield a minimal measurable time between stimulus and response, but this time is not necessarily a basic datum nor have our instructions altered it as such. A parallel interpretation of the differential reinforcement of long "latencies" is required. This is easily established by inspection. In the experiments with pigeons previously cited, preliminary behavior is conditioned that postpones the response to the key until the proper time. Behavior that "marks time" is usually conspicuous.

field of learning a similar objection takes the form of asking how the present analysis may be extended to experimental situations in which it is impossible to observe frequencies. It does not follow that learning is not taking place in such situations. The notion of probability is usually extrapolated to cases in which a frequency analysis cannot be carried out. In the field of behavior we arrange a situation in which frequencies are available as data, but we use the notion of probability in analyzing and formulating instances or even types of behavior which are not susceptible to this analysis.

Another common objection is that a rate of response is just a set of latencies and hence not a new datum at all. This is easily shown to be wrong. When we measure the time elapsing between two responses, we are in no doubt as to what the organism was doing when we started our clock. We know that it was just executing a response. This is a natural zero—quite unlike the arbitrary point from which latencies are measured. The free repetition of a response yields a rhythmic or periodic datum very different from latency. Many periodic physical processes suggest parallels.

We do not choose rate of responding as a basic datum merely from an analysis of the fundamental task of a science of behavior. The ultimate appeal is to its success in an experimental science. The material which follows is offered as a sample of what can be done. It is not intended as a complete demonstration, but it should confirm the fact that when we are in possession of a datum which varies in a significant fashion, we are less likely to resort to theoretical entities carrying the notion of probability of response.

Why Learning Occurs

We may define learning as a change in probability of response but we must also specify the conditions under which it comes about. To do this we must survey some of the independent variables of which probability of response is a function. Here we meet another kind of learning theory.

An effective class-room demonstration of the Law of Effect may be arranged in the following way. A pigeon, reduced to 80 per cent of its *ad lib* weight, is habituated to a small, semi-circular amphitheatre and is fed there for several days from a food hopper, which the experimenter presents by closing a hand switch. The demonstration consists of establishing a selected response by suitable reinforcement with food. For example, by sighting across the amphitheatre at a scale on the opposite wall, it is possible to present the hopper whenever the top of the pigeon's head rises above a given mark. Higher and higher marks are chosen until, within a few minutes, the pigeon is walking about the cage with its head held as high as possible. In another demonstration the bird is conditioned to strike a marble placed on the floor of the amphitheatre. This may be done in a few minutes by reinforcing successive steps. Food is presented first when the bird is merely moving near the marble, later when it looks down in the direction of the marble, later still when it moves its head toward the marble, and finally when it pecks it. Anyone who has seen such a demonstration knows that the Law of Effect is no theory. It simply specifies a procedure for altering the probability of a chosen response.

But when we try to say *why* reinforcement has this effect, theories arise. Learning is said to take place because the reinforcement is pleasant, satisfying, tension reducing, and so on. The converse process of extinction is explained with comparable theories. If the rate of responding is first raised to a high point by reinforcement and reinforcement then withheld, the response is observed to occur less and less frequently thereafter. One common theory explains this by asserting that a state is built up which suppresses the behavior. This "experimental inhibition" or "reaction inhibition" must be assigned to a different dimensional system, since nothing at the level of behavior corresponds to opposed processes of excitation and inhibition. Rate of responding is simply increased by one operation and decreased by another. Certain effects commonly interpreted as showing release from a suppressing force may be interpreted in other ways. Disinhibition, for example, is not necessarily the uncovering of suppressed strength; it may be a sign of supplementary strength from an extraneous variable. The process of spontaneous recovery, often cited to support the notion of suppression, has an alternative explanation, to be noted in a moment.

Let us evaluate the question of why learning takes place by turning again to some data. Since conditioning is usually too rapid to be easily followed, the process of extinction will provide us with a more useful case. A number of different types of curves have been consistently obtained from rats and pigeons using various schedules of prior reinforcement. By considering some of the relevant conditions we may see what room is left for theoretical processes.

The mere passage of time between conditioning and extinction is a variable that has surprisingly little effect. The rat is too short-lived to make an extended experiment feasible, but the pigeon, which may live ten or fifteen years, is an ideal subject. More than five years ago, twenty pigeons were conditioned to strike a large translucent key upon which a complex visual pattern was projected. Reinforcement was contingent upon the maintenance of a high and steady rate of responding and upon striking a particular feature of the visual pattern. These birds were set aside in order to study retention. They were transferred to the usual living quarters, where they served as breeders. Small groups were tested

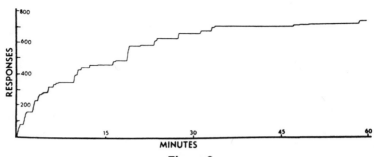

Figure 2

for extinction at the end of six months, one year, two years, and four years. Before the test each bird was transferred to a separate living cage. A controlled feeding schedule was used to reduce the weight to approximately 80 per cent of the *ad lib* weight. The bird was then fed in the dimly lighted experimental apparatus in the absence of the key for several days, during which emotional responses to the apparatus disappeared. On the day of the test the bird was placed in the darkened box. The translucent key was present but not lighted. No responses were made. When the pattern was projected upon the key, all four birds responded quickly and extensively. Figure 2 shows the largest curve obtained. This bird struck the key within two seconds after presentation of a visual pattern that it had not seen for four years, and at the precise spot upon which differential reinforcement had previously been based. It continued to respond for the next hour, emitting about 700 responses. This is of the order of one-half to one-quarter of the responses it would have emitted if extinction had not been delayed four years, but otherwise, the curve is fairly typical.

Level of motivation is another variable to be taken into account. An

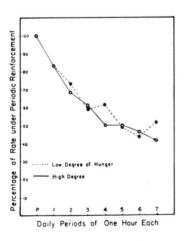

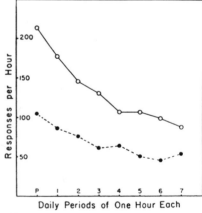

Figure 3

example of the effect of hunger has been reported elsewhere (3). The response of pressing a lever was established in eight rats with a schedule of periodic reinforcement. They were fed the main part of their ration on alternate days so that the rates of responding on successive days were alternately high and low. Two subgroups of four rats each were matched on the basis of the rate maintained under periodic reinforcement under these conditions. The response was then extinguished—in one group on alternate days when the hunger was high, in the other group on alternate days when the hunger was low. (The same amount of food was eaten on the nonexperimental days as before.) The result is shown in Figure 3. The upper graph gives the raw data. The levels of hunger are indicated by the points at P on the abscissa, the rates prevailing under periodic reinforcement. The subsequent points show the decline in extinction. If we multiply the lower curve through by a factor chosen to superimpose the points at P, the curves are reasonably closely superimposed, as shown in the lower graph. Several other experiments on both rats and pigeons have confirmed this general principle. If a given ratio of responding prevails under periodic reinforcement, the slopes of later extinction curves show the same ratio. Level of hunger determines the slope of the extinction curve but not its curvature.

Another variable, difficulty of response, is especially relevant because it has been used to test the theory of reaction inhibition (1), on the assumption that a response requiring considerable energy will build up more reaction inhibition than an easy response and lead, therefore, to faster extinction. The theory requires that the curvature of the extinction curve be altered, not merely its slope. Yet there is evidence that difficulty of response acts like level of hunger simply to alter the slope. Some data have been reported but not published (5). A pigeon is suspended in a jacket which confines its wings and legs but leaves its head and neck free to respond to a key and a food magazine. Its behavior in this situation is quantitatively much like that of a bird moving freely in an experimental box. But the use of the jacket has the advantage that the response to the key may be made easy or difficult by changing the distance the bird must reach. In one experiment these distances were expressed in seven equal but arbitrary units. At distance 7 the bird could barely reach the key, at 3 it could strike without appreciably extending its neck. Periodic reinforcement gave a straight base-line upon which it was possible to observe the effect of difficulty by quickly changing position during the experimental period. Each of the five records in Figure 4 covers a fifteen minute experimental period under periodic reinforcement. Distances of the bird from the key are indicated by numerals above the records. It will be observed that the rate of responding at distance 7 is generally quite low while that at distance 3 is high. Intermediate distances produce intermediate slopes. It should also be noted that the

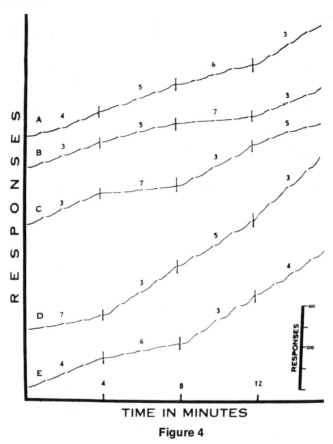

TIME IN MINUTES

Figure 4

change from one position to another is felt immediately. If repeated re-sponding in a difficult position were to build a considerable amount of reaction inhibition, we should expect the rate to be low for some little time after returning to an easy response. Contrariwise, if an easy re-sponse were to build little reaction inhibition, we should expect a fairly high rate of responding for some time after a difficult position is as-sumed. Nothing like this occurs. The "more rapid extinction" of a diffi-cult response is an ambiguous expression. The slope constant is affected and with it the number of responses in extinction to a criterion, but there may be no effect upon curvature.

One way of considering the question of why extinction curves are curved is to regard extinction as a process of exhaustion comparable to the loss of heat from source to sink or the fall in the level of a reservoir when an outlet is opened. Conditioning builds up a predisposition to respond—a "reserve"—which extinction exhausts. This is perhaps a de-fensible description at the level of behavior. The reserve is not neces-sarily a theory in the present sense, since it is not assigned to a different dimensional system. It could be operationally defined as a predicted extinction curve, even though, linguistically, it makes a statement about the momentary condition of a response. But it is not a particularly useful concept, nor does the view that extinction is a process of exhaustion add much to the observed fact that extinction curves are curved in a certain way.

There are, however, two variables that affect the rate, both of which operate during extinction to alter the curvature. One of these falls within the field of emotion. When we fail to reinforce a response that has previously been reinforced, we not only initiate a process of extinction, we set up an emotional response—perhaps what is often meant by frustration. The pigeon coos in an identifiable pattern, moves rapidly about the cage, defecates, or flaps its wings rapidly in a squatting position that suggests treading (mating) behavior. This competes with the response of striking a key and is perhaps enough to account for the decline in rate in early extinction. It is also possible that the probability of a response based upon food deprivation is directly reduced as part of such an emotional reaction. Whatever its nature, the effect of this variable is eliminated through adaptation. Repeated extinction curves become smoother, and in some of the schedules to be described shortly there is little or no evidence of an emotional modification of rate.

A second variable has a much more serious effect. Maximal responding during extinction is obtained only when the conditions under which the response was reinforced are precisely reproduced. A rat conditioned in the presence of a light will not extinguish fully in the absence of the light. It will begin to respond more rapidly when the light is again introduced. This is true for other kinds of stimuli, as the following classroom experiment illustrates. Nine pigeons were conditioned to strike a yellow triangle under intermittent reinforcement. In the session represented by Figure 5 the birds were first reinforced on this schedule for 30 minutes. The combined cumulative curve is essentially a straight line, showing more than 1100 responses per bird during this period. A red triangle was then substituted for the yellow and no responses were reinforced thereafter. The effect was a sharp drop in responding, with only a slight recovery during the next fifteen minutes. When the yellow triangle was replaced, rapid responding began immediately and the usual extinction curve followed. Similar experiments have shown that the pitch of an incidental tone, the shape of a pattern being struck, or the size of a pattern, if present during conditioning, will to some extent control the rate of responding during extinction. Some properties are more effective than others, and a quantitative evaluation is possible. By changing to several values of a stimulus in random order repeatedly during the extinction process, the gradient for stimulus generalization may be read directly in the rates of responding under each value.

Something very much like this must go on during extinction. Let us suppose that all responses to a key have been reinforced and that each has been followed by a short period of eating. When we extinguish the behavior, we create a situation in which responses are not reinforced, in which no eating takes place, and in which there are probably new emotional responses. The situation could easily be as novel as a red triangle after a yellow. If so, it could explain the decline in rate during extinction. We might have obtained a smooth curve, *shaped like an extinction curve,* between the vertical lines in Figure 5 by *gradually* changing the

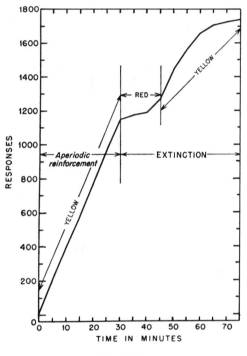

Figure 5

color of the triangle from yellow to red. This might have happened even though no other sort of extinction were taking place. The very conditions of extinction seem to presuppose a growing novelty in the experimental situation. Is this why the extinction curve is curved?

Some evidence comes from the data of "spontaneous recovery." Even after prolonged extinction an organism will often respond at a higher rate for at least a few moments at the beginning of another session. One theory contends that this shows spontaneous recovery from some sort of inhibition, but another explanation is possible. No matter how carefully an animal is handled, the stimulation coincident with the beginning of an experiment must be extensive and unlike anything occurring in the later part of an experimental period. Responses have been reinforced in the presence of, or shortly following, the organism is again placed in the experimental situation, the stimulation is this stimulation. In extinction it is present for only a few moments. When restored, further responses are emitted as in the case of the yellow triangle. The only way to achieve full extinction in the presence of the stimulation of starting an experiment is to start the experiment repeatedly.

Other evidence of the effect of novelty comes from the study of periodic reinforcement. The fact that intermittent reinforcement produces bigger extinction curves than continuous reinforcement is a troublesome difficulty for those who expect a simple relation between number of

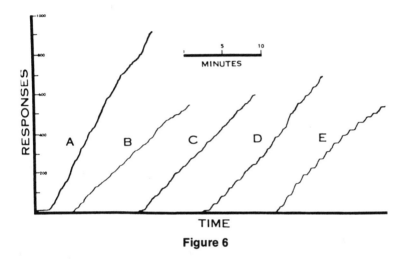

Figure 6

reinforcements and number of responses in extinction. But this relation is actually quite complex. One result of periodic reinforcement is that emotional changes adapt out. This may be responsible for the smoothness of subsequent extinction curves but probably not for their greater extent. The latter may be attributed to the lack of novelty in the extinction situation. Under periodic reinforcement many responses are made without reinforcement and when no eating has recently taken place. The situation in extinction is therefore not wholly novel.

Periodic reinforcement is not, however, a simple solution. If we reinforce on a regular schedule—say, every minute—the organism soon forms a discrimination. Little or no responding occurs just after reinforcement, since stimulation from eating is correlated with absence of subsequent reinforcement. How rapidly the discrimination may develop is shown in Figure 6, which reproduces the first five curves obtained from a pigeon under periodic reinforcement in experimental periods of fifteen minutes each. In the fifth period (or after about one hour of peri-

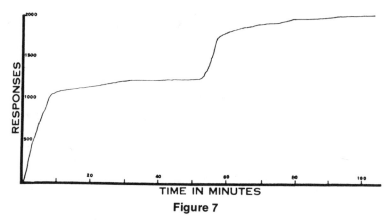

RESPONSES

TIME IN MINUTES

Figure 7

odic reinforcement) the discrimination yields a pause after each reinforcement, resulting in a markedly stepwise curve. As a result of this discrimination the bird is almost always responding rapidly when
reinforced. This is the basis for another discrimination. Rapid responding becomes a favorable stimulating condition. A good example of the
effect upon the subsequent extinction curve is shown in Figure 7. This
pigeon had been reinforced once every minute during daily experimental periods of fifteen minutes each for several weeks. In the extinction
curve shown, the bird begins to respond at the rate prevailing under the
preceding schedule. A quick positive acceleration at the start is lost in
the reduction of the record. The pigeon quickly reaches and sustains a
rate that is higher than the overall-rate during periodic reinforcement.
During this period the pigeon creates a stimulating condition previously
optimally correlated with reinforcement. Eventually, as some sort of exhaustion intervenes, the rate falls off rapidly to a much lower but fairly
stable value and then to practically zero. A condition then prevails
under which a response is not normally reinforced. The bird is therefore
not likely to begin to respond again. When it does respond, however,
the situation is slightly improved and, if it continues to respond, the

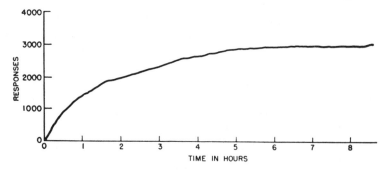

Figure 8

conditions rapidly become similar to those under which reinforcement has been received. Under this "autocatalysis" a high rate is quickly reached, and more than 500 responses are emitted in a second burst. The rate then declines quickly and fairly smoothly, again to nearly zero. This curve is not by any means disorderly. Most of the curvature is smooth. But the burst of responding at forty-five minutes shows a considerable residual strength which, if extinction were merely exhaustion, should have appeared earlier in the curve. The curve may be reasonably accounted for by assuming that the bird is largely controlled by the preceding spurious correlation between reinforcement and rapid responding.

This assumption may be checked by constructing a schedule of reinforcement in which a differential contingency between rate of responding and reinforcement is impossible. In one such schedule of what may be called "aperiodic reinforcement" one interval between successive reinforced responses is so short that no unreinforced responses intervene while the longest interval is about two minutes. Other intervals are distributed arithmetically between these values, the average remaining one minute. The intervals are roughly randomized to compose a program of reinforcement. Under this program the probability of reinforcement does not change with respect to previous reinforcements, and the curves never acquire the stepwise character of curve E in Figure 6. (Figure 9 shows curves from a similar program.) As a result no correlation between different rates of responding and different probabilities of reinforcement can develop.

An extinction curve following a brief exposure to aperiodic reinforcement is shown in Figure 8. It begins characteristically at the rate prevailing under aperiodic reinforcement and, unlike the curve following regular periodic reinforcement, does not accelerate to a higher overall rate. There is no evidence of the "autocatalytic" production of an optimal stimulating condition. Also characteristically, there are no significant discontinuities or sudden changes in rate in either direction. The curve extends over a period of eight hours, as against not quite two hours in Figure 7, and seems to represent a single orderly process. The total number of responses is higher, perhaps because of the greater time allowed for emission. All of this can be explained by the single fact that we have made it impossible for the pigeon to form a pair of discriminations based, first, upon stimulation from eating and, second, upon stimulation from rapid responding

Since the longest interval between reinforcement was only two minutes, a certain novelty must still have been introduced as time passed. Whether this explains the curvature in Figure 8 may be tested to some extent with other programs of reinforcement containing much longer intervals. A geometric progression was constructed by beginning with 10

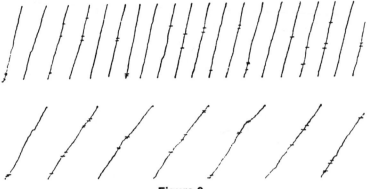

Figure 9

seconds as the shortest interval and repeatedly multiplying through by a
ratio of 1.54. This yielded a set of intervals averaging 5 minutes, the
longest of which was more than 21 minutes. Such a set was randomized
in a program of reinforcement repeated every hour. In changing to this
program from the arithmetic series, the rates first declined during the
longer intervals, but the pigeons were soon able to sustain a constant
rate of responding under it. Two records in the form in which they were
recorded are shown in Figure 9. (The pen resets to zero after every

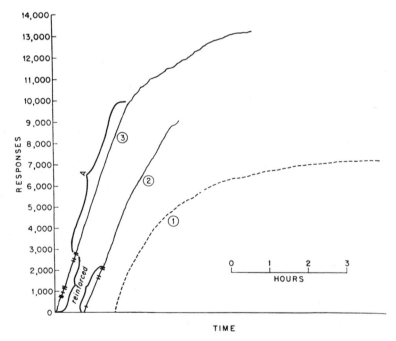

Figure 10

thousand responses. In order to obtain a single cumulative curve it would be necessary to cut the record and to piece the sections together to yield a continuous line. The raw form may be reproduced with less reduction.) Each reinforcement is represented by a horizontal dash. The time covered is about 3 hours. Records are shown for two pigeons that maintained different overall rates under this program of reinforcement.

Under such a schedule a constant rate of responding is sustained for at least 21 minutes without reinforcement, after which a reinforcement is received. Less novelty should therefore develop during succeeding extinction. In Curve 1 of Figure 10 the pigeon had been exposed to several sessions of several hours each with this geometric set of intervals. The number of responses emitted in extinction is about twice that of the curve in Figure 8 after the arithmetic set of intervals averaging one minute, but the curves are otherwise much alike. Further exposure to the geometric schedule builds up longer runs during which the rate does not change significantly. Curve 2 followed Curve 1 after two and one-half hours of further aperiodic reinforcement. On the day shown in Curve 2 a few aperiodic reinforcements were first given, as marked at the beginning of the curve. When reinforcement was discontinued, a fairly constant rate of responding prevailed for several thousand responses. After another experimental session of two and one-half hours with the geometric series, Curve 3 was recorded. This session also began with a short series of aperiodic reinforcements, followed by a sustained run of more than 6000 unreinforced responses with little change in rate (A). There seems to be no reason why other series averaging perhaps more than five minutes per interval and containing much longer exceptional intervals would not carry such a straight line much further.

In this attack upon the problem of extinction we create a schedule of reinforcement which is so much like the conditions that will prevail during extinction that no decline in rate takes place for a long time. In other words we generate extinction with no curvature. Eventually some kind of exhaustion sets in, but it is not approached gradually. The last part of Curve 3 (unfortunately much reduced in the figure) may possibly suggest exhaustion in the slight overall curvature, but it is a small part of the whole process. The record is composed mainly of runs of a few hundred responses each, most of them at approximately the same rate as that maintained under periodic reinforcement. The pigeon stops abruptly; when it starts to respond again, it quickly reaches the rate of responding under which it was reinforced. This recalls the spurious correlation between rapid responding and reinforcement under regular reinforcement. We have not, of course, entirely eliminated this correlation. Even though there is no longer a differential reinforcement of high against low rates, practically all reinforcements have occurred under a constant rate of responding.

Further study of reinforcing schedules may or may not answer the question of whether the novelty appearing in the extinction situation is entirely responsible for the curvature. It would appear to be necessary to make the conditions prevailing during extinction identical with the conditions prevailing during conditioning. This may be impossible, but in that case the question is academic. The hypothesis, meanwhile, is not a theory in the present sense, since it makes no statements about a parallel process in any other universe of discourse.[3]

The study of extinction after different schedules of aperiodic reinforcement is not addressed wholly to this hypothesis. The object is an economical description of the conditions prevailing during reinforcement and extinction and of the relations between them. In using rate of responding as a basic datum we may appeal to conditions that are observable and manipulable and we may express the relations between them in objective terms. To the extent that our datum makes this possible, it reduces the need for theory. When we observe a pigeon emitting 7000 responses at a constant rate without reinforcement, we are not likely to explain an extinction curve containing perhaps a few hundred responses by appeal to the piling up of reaction inhibition or any other fatigue product. Research which is conducted without commitment to theory is more likely to carry the study of extinction into new areas and new orders of magnitude. By hastening the accumulation of data, we speed the departure of theories. If the theories have played no part in the design of our experiments, we need not be sorry to see them go.

Complex Learning

A third type of learning theory is illustrated by terms like *preferring, choosing, discriminating*, and *matching*. An effort may be made to define these solely in terms of behavior, but in traditional practice they refer to processes in another dimensional system. A response to one of two available stimuli may be called choice, but it is commoner to say that it is the result of choice, meaning by the latter a theoretical pre-behavioral activity. The higher mental processes are the best examples of theories of this sort; neurological parallels have not been well worked out. The appeal to theory is encouraged by the fact that choosing (like discriminating, matching, and so on) is not a particular piece of behavior. It is not a response or an act with specified topography. The term characterizes a larger segment of behavior in relation to other variables

---

[3] It is true that it appeals to stimulation generated in part by the pigeon's own behavior. This may be difficult to specify or manipulate, but it is not theoretical in the present sense. So long as we are willing to assume a one-to-one correspondence between action and stimulation, a physical specification is possible.

or events. Can we formulate and study the behavior to which these terms would usually be applied without recourse to the theories which generally accompany them?

Discrimination is a relatively simple case. Suppose we find that the probability of emission of a given response is not significantly affected by changing from one of two stimuli to the other. We then make reinforcement of the response contingent upon the presence of one of them. The well-established result is that the probability of response remains high under this stimulus and reaches a very low point under the other. We say that the organism now discriminates between the stimuli. But discrimination is not itself an action, or necessarily even a unique process. Problems in the field of discrimination may be stated in other terms. How much induction obtains between stimuli of different magnitudes or classes? What are the smallest differences in stimuli that yield a difference in control? And so on. Questions of this sort do not presuppose theoretical activities in other dimensional systems.

A somewhat larger segment must be specified in dealing with the behavior of choosing one of two concurrent stimuli. This has been studied in the pigeon by examining responses to two keys differing in position (right or left) or in some property like color randomized with respect to position. By occasionally reinforcing a response on one key or the other without favoring either key, we obtain equal rates of responding on the two keys. The behavior approaches a simple alternation from one key to the other. This follows the rule that tendencies to respond eventually correspond to the probabilities of reinforcement. Given a system in which one key or the other is occasionally connected with the magazine by an external clock, then if the right key has just been struck, the probability of reinforcement *via* the left key is higher than that *via* the right since a greater interval of time has elapsed during which the clock may have closed the circuit to the left key. But the bird's behavior does not correspond to this probability merely out of respect for mathematics. The specific result of such a contingency of reinforcement is that changing-to-the-other-key-and-striking is more often reinforced than striking-the-same-key-a-second-time. We are no longer dealing with just two responses. In order to analyze "choice" we must consider a single final response, striking, without respect to the position or color of the key, and in addition the responses of changing from one key or color to the other.

Quantitative results are compatible with this analysis. If we periodically reinforce responses to the right key only, the rate of responding on the right will rise while that on the left will fall. The response of changing-from-right-to-left is never reinforced while the response of changing-from-left-to-right is occasionally so. When the bird is striking on the right, there is no great tendency to change keys; when it is striking on

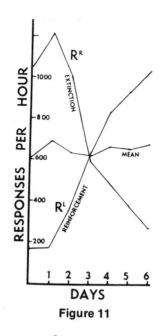

Figure 11

the left, there is a strong tendency to change. Many more responses come to be made to the right key. The need for considering the behavior of changing over is clearly shown if we now reverse these conditions and reinforce responses to the left key only. The ultimate result is a high rate of responding on the left key and a low rate on the right. By reversing the conditions again the high rate can be shifted back to the right key. In Figure 11 a group of eight curves have been averaged to follow this change during six experimental periods of 45 minutes each. Beginning on the second day in the graph responses to the right key (R^R) decline in extinction while responses to the left key (R^L) increase through periodic reinforcement. The mean rate shows no significant variation, since periodic reinforcement is continued on the same schedule. The mean rate shows the condition of strength of the response of striking a key regardless of position. The distribution of responses between right and left depends upon the relative strength of the responses of changing over. If this were simply a case of the extinction of one response and the concurrent reconditioning of another, the mean curve would not remain approximately horizontal since reconditioning occurs much more rapidly than extinction.[4]

The rate with which the bird changes from one key to the other depends upon the distance between the keys. This distance is a rough

---

[4] Two topographically independent responses, capable of emission at the same time and hence not requiring change-over, show separate processes of reconditioning and extinction, and the combined rate of responding varies.

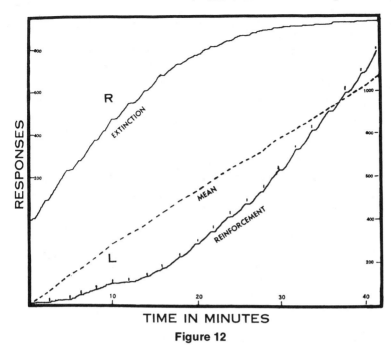

TIME IN MINUTES

Figure 12

measure of the stimulus-difference between the two keys. It also determines the scope of the response of changing-over, with an implied difference in sensory feed-back. It also modifies the spread of reinforcement to responses supposedly not reinforced, since if the keys are close together, a response reinforced on one side may occur sooner after a preceding response on the other side. In Figure 11 the two keys were about one inch apart. They were therefore fairly similar with respect to position in the experimental box. Changing from one to the other involved a minimum of sensory feedback, and reinforcement of a response to one key could follow very shortly upon a response to the other. When the keys are separated by as much as four inches, the change in strength is much more rapid. Figure 12 shows two curves recorded simultaneously from a single pigeon during one experimental period of about 40 minutes. A high rate to the right key and a low rate to the left had previously been established. In the figure no responses to the right were reinforced, but those to the left were reinforced every minute as indicated by the vertical dashes above curve L. The slope of R declines in a fairly smooth fashion while that of L increases, also fairly smoothly, to a value comparable to the initial value of R. The bird has conformed to the changed contingency within a single experimental period. The mean rate of responding is shown by a dotted line, which again shows no significant curvature.

What is called "preference" enters into this formulation. At any stage of the process shown in Figure 12 preference might be expressed in terms of the relative rates of responding to the two keys. This preference, however, is not in striking a key but in changing from one key to the other. The probability that the bird will strike a key regardless of its identifying properties behaves independently of the preferential response of changing from one key to the other. Several experiments have revealed an additional fact. A preference remains fixed if reinforcement is withheld. Figure 13 is an example. It shows simultaneous extinction curves from two keys during seven daily experimental periods of one hour each. Prior to extinction the relative strength of the responses of changing-to-R and changing-to-L yielded a "preference" of about 3 to 1 for R. The constancy of the rate throughout the process of extinction has

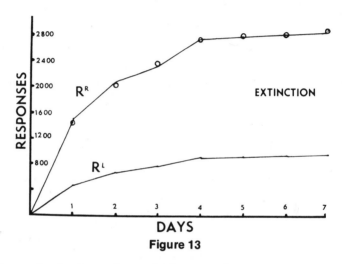

Figure 13

been shown in the figure by multiplying L through by a suitable constant and entering the points as small circles on R. If extinction altered the preference, the two curves could not be superimposed in this way.

These formulations of discrimination and choosing enable us to deal with what is generally regarded as a much more complex process— matching to sample. Suppose we arrange three translucent keys, each of which may be illuminated with red or green light. The middle key functions as the sample and we color it either red or green in random order. We color the two side keys one red and one green, also in random order. The "problem" is to strike the side key which corresponds in color to the middle key. There are only four three-key patterns in such a case, and it is possible that a pigeon could learn to make an appropriate response to each pattern. This does not happen, at least within the temporal span of the experiments to date. If we simply present a series of settings of the three colors and reinforce successful responses, the pigeon will strike the side keys without respect to color or pattern and be reinforced 50 per cent of the time. This is, in effect, a schedule of "fixed ratio" reinforcement which is adequate to maintain a high rate of responding.

Nevertheless it is possible to get a pigeon to match to sample by reinforcing the discriminative responses of striking-red-after-being-stimulated-by-red and striking-green-after-being-stimulated-by-green while extinguishing the other two possibilities. The difficulty is in arranging the proper stimulation at the time of the response. The sample might be made conspicuous—for example, by having the sample color in the general illumination of the experimental box. In such a case the pigeon would learn to strike red keys in a red light and green keys in a green light (assuming a neutral illumination of the background of the keys). But a procedure which holds more closely to the notion of matching is to induce the pigeon to "look at the sample" by means of a separate reinforcement. We may do this by presenting the color on the middle key first, leaving the side keys uncolored. A response to the middle key is then reinforced (secondarily) by illuminating the side keys. The pigeon learns to make two responses in quick succession—to the middle key and then to one side key. The response to the side key follows quickly upon the visual stimulation from the middle key, which is the requisite condition for a discrimination. Successful matching was readily established in all ten pigeons tested with this technique. Choosing the opposite is also easily set up. The discriminative response of striking-red-after-being-stimulated-by-red is apparently no easier to establish than striking-red-after-being-stimulated-by-green. When the response is to a key of the same color, however, generalization may make it possible for the bird to match a new color. This is an extension of the notion of matching that has not yet been studied with this method.

Even when matching behavior has been well established, the bird will not respond correctly if all three keys are now presented at the same time. The bird does not possess strong behavior if looking at the sample. The experimenter must maintain a separate reinforcement to keep this behavior in strength. In monkeys, apes, and human subjects the ultimate success in choosing is apparently sufficient to reinforce and maintain the behavior of looking at the sample. It is possible that this species difference is simply a difference in the temporal relations required for reinforcement.

The behavior of matching survives unchanged when all reinforcement is withheld. An intermediate case has been established in which the correct matching response is only periodically reinforced. In one experiment one color appeared on the middle key for one minute; it was then changed or not changed, at random, to the other color. A response to this key illuminated the side keys, one red and one green, in random order. A response to a side key cut off the illumination to both side keys, until the middle key had again been struck. The apparatus recorded all matching responses on one graph and all non-matching on another. Pigeons which have acquired matching behavior under continuous reinforcement have maintained this behavior when reinforced no oftener than once per minute on the average. They may make thousands of matching responses per hour while being reinforced for no more than sixty of them. This schedule will not necessarily develop matching behavior in a naive bird, for the problem can be solved in three ways. The bird will receive practically as many reinforcements if it responds to (1) only one key or (2) only one color, since the programming of the experiment makes any persistent response eventually the correct one.

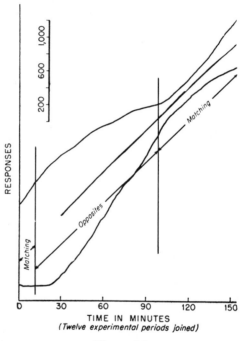

Figure 14

A sample of the data obtained in a complex experiment of this sort is given in Figure 14. Although this pigeon had learned to match color under continuous reinforcement, it changed to the spurious solution of a color preference under periodic reinforcement. Whenever the sample was red, it struck both the sample and the red side key and received all reinforcements. When the sample was green, it did not respond and the side keys were not illuminated. The result shown at the beginning of the graph in Figure 14 is a high rate of responding on the upper graph, which records matching responses. (The record is actually step-wise, following the presence or absence of the red sample, but this is lost in the reduction in the figure.) A color preference, however, is not a solution to the problem of opposites. By changing to this problem, it was possible to change the bird's behavior as shown between the two vertical lines in the figure. The upper curve between these lines shows the decline in matching responses which had resulted from the color preference. The lower curve between the same lines shows the development of responding to and matching the opposite color. At the second vertical line the reinforcement was again made contingent upon matching. The upper curve shows the reestablishment of matching behavior while the lower curve shows a decline in striking the opposite color. The result was a true solution: the pigeon struck the sample, no matter what its color, and then the corresponding side key. The lighter line connects the means of a series of points on the two curves. It seems to follow the same rule as in the case of choosing: changes in the distribution of responses between two keys do not involve the over-all rate of responding to a key. This mean rate will not remain constant under the spurious solution achieved with a color preference, as at the beginning of this figure.

These experiments on a few higher processes have necessarily been very briefly described. They are not offered as proving that theories of learning are not necessary, but they may suggest an alternative program in this difficult area. The data in the field of the higher mental processes transcend single responses or single stimulus-response relationships. But they appear to be susceptible to formulation in terms of the differentiation of concurrent responses, the discrimination of stimuli, the establishment of various sequences of responses, and so on. There seems to be no *a priori* reason why a complete account is not possible without appeal to theoretical processes in other dimensional systems.

Conclusion

Perhaps to do without theories altogether is a *tour de force* that is too much to expect as a general practice. Theories are fun. But it is possible that the most rapid progress toward an understanding of learning may be made by research that is not designed to test theories. An adequate impetus is supplied by the inclination to obtain data showing orderly changes characteristic of the learning process. An acceptable scientific program is to collect data of this sort and to relate them to manipulable variables, selected for study through a common sense exploration of the field.

This does not exclude the possibility of theory in another sense. Beyond the collection of uniform relationships lies the need for a formal representation of the data reduced to a minimal number of terms. A theoretical construction may yield greater generality than any assemblage of facts. But such a construction will not refer to another dimensional system and will not, therefore, fall within our present definition. It will not stand in the way of our search for functional relations because it will arise only after relevant variables have been found and studied. Through it may be difficult to understand, it will not be easily misunderstood, and it will have none of the objectionable effects of the theories here considered.

We do not seem to be ready for theory in this sense. At the moment we make little effective use of empirical, let alone rational, equations. A few of the present curves could have been fairly closely fitted. But the most elementary preliminary research shows that there are many relevant variables, and until their importance has been experimentally determined, an equation that allows for them will have so many arbitrary constants that a good fit will be a matter of course and a cause for very little satisfaction.

References

1. Mowrer, O. H., & Jones, H. M. Extinction and behavior variability as functions of effortfulness of task. *J. exp. Psychol.*, 1943, 33, 369–386.
2. Skinner, B. F. *The behavior of organisms.* New York: D. Appleton-Century Co., 1938.
3. ———. The nature of the operant reserve. *Psychol. Bull.*, 1940, 37, 423 (abstract).
4. ———. Differential reinforcement with respect to time. *Amer. Psychol.*, 1946, 1, 274–275 (abstract).
5. ———. The effect of the difficulty of a response upon its rate of emission. *Amer. Psychol.*, 1946, 1, 462 (abstract).

8   ON THE CIRCULARITY OF THE LAW OF EFFECT
Paul E. Meehl

In his recent review on "The History and Present Status of the Law of Effect," Postman (19) lays considerable emphasis on the problem of "circularity" which he sees as crucial in the formulation of the law. He says:

SOURCE: Paul E. Meehl, "On the Circularity of the Law of Effect," *Psychological Bulletin*, 47 (1950), 52–75. Copyright 1950 by the American Psychological Association. Reprinted by permission of the publisher.

Whereas some critics were most concerned with the mechanisms mediating effect, others focussed their attention on the nature of the satisfiers and annoyers to which reference is made in Thorndike's law. Although Spencer and Bain, in whose tradition Thorndike continued, frankly invoked pleasure and pain as agents responsible for the fixation and elimination of responses, Thorndike's law has been a law of *effect*, not *affect*. He carefully defines satisfiers and annoyers in terms independent of subjective experience and report. "By a satisfying state of affairs is meant one which the animal does nothing to avoid, often doing such things as to attain and preserve it. By a discomforting state of affairs is meant one which the animal avoids and abandons." Although admittedly free of hedonism, such a definition of satisfiers and annoyers has faced another serious difficulty: the danger of circularity. The critic may easily reword the definition to read: "The animal does what it does because it does it, and it does not do what it does not do because it does not do it." This *reductio ad adsurdum* is probably not entirely fair, but it points up the danger of the definition in the absence of an *independent* determination of the nature of satisfiers and annoyers. The satisfying or annoying nature of a state of affairs can usually be determined fully only in the course of a learning experiment and cannot then be invoked as a causal condition of learning without circularity. In their experimental work Thorndike and his associates have made no significant attempts to establish the satisfying or annoying nature of their rewards and punishments independently of the learning experiment (19, p. 496).

And a little later Postman says:

Stripped of virtually all defining properties and qualifications, the law does indeed have a very wide range of applicability but only at the expense of vagueness. The sum and substance of the argument now is that something happens in the organism (nervous system) after an act is performed. The fact that something happens influences further action. This something is, however, so little defined that it has almost no predictive efficiency. The O.K. reaction has no measurable properties, the conditions for its occurrence are so general as to embrace almost every conceivable situation. Hence the operation of O.K. reaction can be inferred only *ex post facto,* after learning has taken place. But here we are again impaled on the horns of the dilemma of circularity (19, p. 497).

And still further:

In attempting to evaluate the controversy which has raged around the definition of satisfiers one is struck by the key importance of the hedonistic issue. Certainly hedonism is an immediate ancestor of the law, and now that the principle of effect has reached an uneasy maturity it is clear that it cannot deny its origin without sacrificing much of its vigor. When the law is stripped of hedonistic implications, when effect is not identified with tension-reduction or pleasure (as by Thorndike), the law of effect can do no more than claim that the state of affairs resulting from a response in some way influences future responses. Such a statement is a truism and hardly lends itself to the rigorous deduction of hypotheses and experimental tests. If a neohedonistic position is frankly assumed (as, e.g., by Mowrer) the law becomes an important tool for research, provided "satisfaction" is independently defined and not merely inferred from the fact that learning has occurred (19, p. 501).

Throughout Postman's paper this problem is constantly lurking behind the scenes even when the author does not single it out for specific mention. I am in complete agreement with Postman's final remark that "at the present state of our knowledge the law of effect as a monistic principle explaining all learning has not been substantiated," and Postman performs a service by emphasizing this problem of circularity in his discussion of the "law." I am inclined, however, to think that he has settled the question of circularity somewhat too easily, and that his settlement of it has an effect upon much of his argumentation. I gather from the above quotations that Postman looks upon any definition of effect or reinforcement in terms of the resulting change in response strength as "circular," where that word has a pejorative sense. If he is right in this it is very serious. While the law of effect has many difficulties, I do not believe that "circularity" is among them. To show this is the aim of the present paper.

I shall consider the problem of circularity in the law of effect as identical with the problem of circularity in the definition of *reinforcement* in instrumental conditioning. I take it that Postman does the same, since in the first quotation above he cites a passage from Hilgard and Marquis' *Conditioning and Learning*, where the two problems are considered together and with free interchange of the two terminologies. These authors say:

> It is apparent that no definition of effect provides an independent measure of the strength of reinforcement. The degree of satisfaction, of complacency, or of tension reduction has not been objectively determined. The strength of reinforcement can be given comprehensive definition only in terms of the amount of learning resulting from it. This is, of course, a circular definition, if strength of reinforcement is to be used as a factor determining degree of learning. A partial escape from circularity is achieved by the fact that a stimulus such as food which is found to be reinforcing on one situation will also be reinforcing in other situations, and with other animals (9, p. 83).

Writing in 1948, however, Hilgard states concerning Thorndike's "operational" definition of satisfiers and annoyers:

> These definitions are not circular, so far as the law of effect is concerned. That is, the states of affairs characterized as satisfying and annoying are specified independently of their influence upon modifiable connections.

The law of effect then states what may be expected to happen to preceding modifiable connections which are followed by such specified states. The objection that Thorndike was lacking in objectivity in the statement of the law of effect is not a valid one (8, p. 24).

Hilgard is willing to let the concept of reinforcement (effect, satisfaction, reward) be introduced on the basis of behavior, but only because there are behavioral criteria of seeking and avoiding other than the effect of reinforcement upon *modifiable* connections. Whether this restriction is necessary needs to be considered carefully.

Skinner dismisses the whole problem in two sentences:

> A reinforcing stimulus is defined as such by its power to produce the resulting change. There is no circularity about this; some stimuli are found to produce the change, others not, and they are classified as reinforcing and nonreinforcing accordingly (22, p. 62).

Spence (23) takes essentially the same tack in his recent discussions of secondary reinforcement. The stimuli which impinge upon an organism may be divided, he says, into two classes: those which produce an increment in response strength, and those which do not. It seems from the several preceding quotations that there is a lack of agreement as to whether or not the law of effect or the principle of reinforcement involves an unavoidable circularity, or, if it does not, how circularity is to be avoided. In what follows, I make no claim to orginality, since the essence of my development is contained in the previous quotations, together with the work of Tolman. But I feel it worthwhile to bring the arguments together in one context, and to show that the problem merits somewhat more extended treatment than is usually given it. Without claiming to present a definitive solution, I shall indicate the general direction which I believe the solution might take, and in the process introduce certain distinctions and terminological proposals which I feel might clarify our discussion and experimentation.

The Meaning of Circularity

It must be pointed out that there are two meanings of the word "circular" in common use. We have on the one hand circularity in *definition*, in which an unfamiliar term is defined by using other terms which are (directly or ultimately) defined by the term in question. There is no question of circularity in this sense in a definition of the Skinner-Spence type. Let us accept as a crude preliminary formulation the following: "A reinforcing stimulus is one which increases the subsequent strength of responses which immediately precede it." The words *stimulus,*[1] *strength,*

---

[1] "Stimulus" will be used broadly to include "stimulus change," and stimulus configurations of all degrees of patterning and complexity.

increase and *response* are all definable without any reference to the fact or theory of reinforcement. The definitions of these terms, particularly the term "response," present terrible difficulties; but I do not know of anyone who maintains that they involve the notion of reinforcement. Words such as these are current in the vocabulary of many kinds of psychological theorists who do not accept the Law of Effect as a principle of learning and in the absence of any indications to the contrary, I shall assume that we can tell what we mean by them. We can determine empirically when the strength of a response has increased without knowing anything about reinforcing stimuli, drives, satisfactions, and the like. It seems clear that the definition of a reinforcing stimulus in terms of its effect on response strength does not involve circularity in *this* sense.

The other meaning of the word circularity refers not to meanings (definition of terms) but to the establishment of propositions. We speak of *proofs* as being circular if it can be shown that in the process of establishing (proving) a proposition we have made use of the probandum. I am not aware that any responsible theorist has attempted to "prove" the Law of Effect in this way. It is true that those who look upon the law as fundamental are skeptical when they hear of a case of increase of response strength which does not *seem* to involve any obvious reinforcing consequences so that they begin to invent hypotheses to explain the results. There is no harm in this so long as the proposed explanations are in principle confirmable on the basis of some other experimental consequences, however remote. If an animal learns a response sequence without being given food, water, or any of the usual rewards, I suspect most Hullians would begin to talk about secondary reinforcement present in the situation. One can, of course, be careless with this kind of explanation, but there is nothing intrinsic to the concept that entails non-confirmability. The establishment of secondary reinforcing effects as explanations of a given experimental result consists in combining the facts known about primary reinforcers with facts about the animal's life history, in terms of which we understand how certain stimuli have acquired their secondary reinforcing powers. People on both sides of the present controversy over reinforcement theory are performing many different sorts of experiments in order to confirm or disconfirm the Law of Effect. It would seem that if the law of effect *were* being treated by anyone as a consequence of definition, or established by some hidden assumption of its truth, the experiments would not be going on.

Can "Reinforcement" be Independently Defined?

Nonetheless, when I think about this definition we feel uncomfortable. I do not think we have in mind either a circularity in definition or a begging-the-question fallacy, but some sort of peculiar pseudo-circularity in which it seems to us vaguely that the law *could* be "derived" from the proposed definition, even though no one in fact seems to be trying to do it this way. The problem can be stated very simply: How can we introduce the concept of reinforcement in terms of effect upon strength, and still have a "law of effect" or "principle of reinforcement" which has the empirical content that everybody seems to be taking for granted in experimentation?

1. Suppose we reject the Thorndike-Skinner-Spence procedure of defining reinforcement in terms of response strength, and decide to define the term quite independently of the learning process. The first possibility, which we shall dismiss rather dogmatically, is to do it subjectivistically in terms of pleasure, experiences of satisfaction, and the like. Aside from the general behavioristic objections, and the specific problems of measurement created, this approach is not feasible because it leaves us without any basis for speaking of reinforcing value in the case of that very important class of motivations that are unconscious or at least inadequately verbalized in the human case; and it makes impossible the establishment of reinforcing value in the case of lower organisms. At the present time there are probably very few psychologists who would consider this alternative seriously.

2. Secondly, we might try to define reinforcers in terms of certain physical properties on the stimulus side. I shall attempt to show below that this is a procedure which *follows* the introduction of the generic notion of a reinforcer, and which at a later stage becomes very important. But no one wants to group together an arbitrary class of physical objects or stimuli and call them "reinforcers," since the aim of our concept formation is to make possible the statement of laws. The possibility of identifying common physical properties of that large class of stimuli already grouped together as "rewarding" seems very remote. Besides, we would set up these properties or sets of properties by examining the members of the reinforcing class, which we already have set apart on some basis or other; and the question is: How have we arrived at the members of that class?

3. A third possibility, seen in the work of Hull, is to define reinforcement ultimately in terms of drive reduction, that is, in terms of the inner physiological events involved. Here again, I do not suppose that anyone would be able to given even the vaguest specification of the defining property of all neural events which are reinforcing. Even for the so-called primary physiological needs such as hunger, the evidence as to their exact physiological basis is most incomplete. No psychologist today is willing to equate "hunger" with "stomach contractions," in the light of the experimentation on visceral denervations, specific sub-hungers, and the like. In other cases, we have practically no information on the neurophysiology, e.g., the neurophysiologic basis of the reinforcing effect of the presence of another organism, the turning off of a light in the Skinner box, or the going through of "exploratory" behavior on the other

side of a grill. There is some reason to suppose that certain stimuli retain their secondary reinforcing value in the absence of the primary drive (2, 16), which complicates the problem further.

These considerations force a return to the *effect* of stimuli as a basis for specifying that they are reinforcers, and this leads to the paradox. If we define a reinforcing agent by its effect upon learning, then it seems that whenever learning is effected, we know ("by definition") that we have given a reinforcement. For surely, when the organism behaves, some stimulus change occurs, if nothing else than the proprioceptive effects of responding. If the behavior increases in strength, then these stimulus changes, which were in fact preceded by the response, are reinforcers. Hence, it seems that a definition of reinforcement in terms of an increase of habit strength makes the law tautological and devoid of factual content. This train of thought, which I am sure is familiar to most readers, seems obvious and straightforward. But I believe it can be shown to be mistaken, once the law is stated *explicitly* in the way we all really think of it *implicitly* when we perform experiments or try to explain a given case of learning.

An Empirical Derivation of Reinforcement

Let us begin afresh by going to the behavior itself in a situation in which there is little or no disagreement as to what occurs. Consider a bright, inductively inclined Martian, who had never experienced any needs or satisfactions (except perhaps *n. Cognizance!*) and who was observing the behavior of a rat in successive runnings in a T-maze. For the moment we shall simply consider a "standard rat," neglecting the individual differences in parameters and the accidents of personal histories that generate special secondary reinforcing properties. These refinements need to be added later, but as is usually the case will have to be added by being integrated into the whole structure of reinforcement theory, since we cannot treat everything at once. At the beginning, the Martian observes that the organism turns to the right or left with, let us say, about equal frequency. With further trials, a change occurs until finally the rat is responding close to 100% of the time by turning to the right. A Martian could obviously discover this with no notion of rewards, pleasure and the like. If he is ingenious enough to think of the possibility that the strength of a response might be influenced by the events that follow it in time, he would then proceed to investigate the changes that are contingent on this right turning.[2] He notes that when

[2] Actually, no great ingenuity is involved here. Study of the events immediately *preceding* a run, e.g., the manner in which the experimenter handles the rat, what

the rat turns to the right he brings about the following states of affairs on the stimulus side which he does not bring about when he turns to the left: He ends up nearer to the right-hand wall, which is painted green; he twists his own body to the right in responding; he ends up in a wooden box having knots in the wood; he ends up nearer the North pole; and to a dynamo on the other side of the campus; and he comes into the presence of a cup of sunflower seeds. These are the stimuli (stimulus changes) which are contingent on right turns. Is it possible that the gradual strengthening of the right turning is dependent upon one, some, or all of these changes following it? Our scientist from Mars would proceed to study a series of standard rats in the situation, altering the above variables systematically by usual inductive procedures. As a matter of empirical fact, he would discover that, within certain very wide limits, alterations in the first five have no effect. The sixth, the sunflower seeds, have a tremendous effect. He finds that he can alter the geographical direction, the direction of the body twist required, the wall color approached, etc.—that he can introduce all manner of modifications in the other factors; and so long as the sunflower seeds are presented, the rat will tend to go to where they are. On the other hand, if the sunflower seeds are omitted, and nothing else put in their place, a preference fails to develop as a function of these remaining differences.

But we have already greatly over-simplified. Actually, the Martian would discover that the effect of finding sunflower seeds in some cases is almost too slight to be detected; furthermore, even after a preference has been acquired, it may on some occasions fail to show itself. Now, it has already been apparent that when he comes upon these sunflower seeds, the rat behaves toward them in a characteristic way, that is, he ingests them. In seeking to understand the variability in the development and manifestation of a preference, one would notice a correlation between the strengthening of a preference and the rate, strength, and consistency of ingestive responses in the presence of the food. Identifying the same rat on successive days, it is found that on those days on which a preference already established broke down, very frequently the ingestive response in the presence of the sunflower seeds was at a very low or even zero strength. Failing to find anything varying in the maze situation itself to account for these differences, one can study the experiences of the animals between runs. Here appears a very striking correlate of both preference strength *and* the ingestive response in the maze: that which a

---

orientation he gives its head in placing it in the entry box, etc., would fail to reveal any systematic factor related to the direction of a preference. Considering this, together with the fact that before any runs have been made no preference exists, the Martian would be led to ask whether it is something that happens *after* the run (or during it) that affects the probability of a similar choice in subsequent runs.

human experimenter would call the "feeding schedule." The Martian would observe that when sunflower seeds were made available to the rats in their cages, they behave with respect to them in the same way as they do when they come upon the sunflower seeds in the goal box: namely, with ingestive responses. He would discover, again by systematic variation in these conditions, that such matters as the chemical nature of the substance made available, the periodicity of its availability, the lapse of time between when it was last available and the maze run; the rate of ingestion manifested at the moment of beginning deprivation (i.e., how close the rat was to satiety when interrupted), and so on, all exert an effect upon the maze response. By far the most intimate correlate would be the lapse of time since feeding. To quote Skinner again,

> The problem of drive arises because much of the behavior of an organism shows an apparent variability. A rat does not always respond to food placed before it, and a factor called its "hunger" is invoked by way of explanation. The rat is said to eat only when it is hungry. It is because eating is not inevitable that we are led to hypothesize the internal state to which we may assign the variability. Where there is no variability, no state is needed. . . . In dealing with the kind of behavior that gives rise to the concept of hunger, we are concerned with the strength of a certain class of reflexes and with the two principal operations that affect it—feeding and fasting (22, pp. 341, 343).

For a considerable class of stimuli found to affect choice behavior in the maze, there is a fairly well demarcated class of events in the extra-maze activities which exert an effect. Food, water, a female rat, all depend for their efficacy upon a deprivation schedule of some sort. For other stimuli, the rest of the day's activities seem of less relevance. For example, the effects of turning off a light in the Skinner box upon the lever pressing response would not depend upon a schedule of extra box illumination in any such obvious way as the effects of a food pellet depend upon the extra maze operations of feeding and fasting. Even here, at the extremes, it is likely that the schedule has some effect. Although I know of no experimental material on the point, it would be surprising if rats raised and maintained in a dark or extremely bright living cage would show the same response to light-off as a reinforcing agent. In order to keep the discussion quite general, I shall refer to *schedule-reinforcer* combinations, which will be understood to include those combinations in which almost any life-maintaining schedule is adequate. Whether there are any such does not need to be settled here. The stimulus presented is a *reinforcer,* and the presentation of it (an "event") is a *reinforcement.*

We are now in possession of a rather simple set of empirical facts. A certain stimulus, for a rat which has been under a specified schedule, for instance the sunflower seeds for a rat who has not ingested anything for

23 hours, will exert a strengthening effect. We can formulate a "law" stated crudely as follows: "In a rat which has not recently ingested sunflower seeds, bran mash, Purina chow, etc., a response of turning in a given direction in the T-maze will be increased if the fairly immediate presentation of sunflower seeds, etc., is made contingent upon that response." Similarly, we would find such a specific law to hold for thirst and water, sex and a mate, and so on. The general form of such special laws would be: "On schedule M, the termination of response sequence R, in setting S, by stimulus S^1 is followed by an increment in the strength of S.R." Such a law may be called a *situational-reinforcement* law, where the "reinforcement" is understood to stand for "presentation-of-a-reinforcer-following-a-specified-maintenance-schedule," and the term "situational" covers "response R in situation S."

Actually, in any given case, M, R, S, S^1 are classes. This is indicated by the suspicious-looking "etc." in the first "law" above. There is nothing shady about this "etc.," inasmuch as what is actually involved here is a class of operations and effects which are ultimately to be specified by locating each instance with respect to a whole complex set of dimensions. For example, Guttman (6) shows a relation between concentration of sugar solution used as a reinforcing agent and the strength of the lever pressing response. Heron and Peake (7) have studied protein as a specific component of reinforcement. There is to be discovered a vast number of such rather special laws which are comparable to the myriads of laws in chemistry concerning the solubility of substance Y in substance X and the like.

The next thing to notice is that while the schedule, reinforcement, response, and situation are all classes showing certain relations to one another, in general the schedule and reinforcer are related to one another more intimately than either is to the situation or response. The strength of a response which is maintained by food reinforcement is heavily dependent upon the feeding-fasting schedule, whereas the effect of a food reinforcement upon a response is relatively independent of, say recency of copulatory activity, so that a given schedule-reinforcement pair are "tied" to one another. But the Martian observes that the strengthening effect of a given schedule-reinforcement combination is relatively (not wholly!) neutral with respect to the response we are trying to strengthen and the situation in which we are trying to strengthen it. For a hungry rat, right turning depends heavily upon finding food; for a satiated rat, it depends very little. So the feeding schedule is intimately related to the reinforcing agent's efficacy. However, this "hungry-food" schedule-reinforcement combination seems to be capable of strengthening chain-pulling, lever-pressing, wheel-turning, marble-rolling, gnawing-through-paper, and so on through a very wide range of behaviors differing greatly in their topography and in their stimulus conditions. This leads to the question, "Will a certain schedule-reinforcer combination increase the strength of *any* response, in *any* setting?" This question turns out empirically to be answered in the negative, since we find at least three limitations upon the generality of a schedule-reinforcer combination as response strengthener. Leaving out the trivial case in which the response is anatomically impossible, e.g., to teach an elephant to thread a needle, we find:

> 1. No situation-response sequences may involve stimulus dimensions which are not discriminable by the organism (Tolman's "discriminating capacities").
>
> 2. Some response sequences seem on the basis of their sequence, timing, or "complexity" not to be learnable by members of a given species, or subgroups within a species. It appears impossible to teach a rat a quintuple alternation problem, or to teach a human moron integral calculus.
>
> 3. There are cases in which the response we wish to strengthen is incompatible with responses at a very high (and relatively unmodifiable) strength under the schedule-stimulus combinations we are employing. For example, it would probably be next to impossible to teach a very hungry cat to carry a piece of fresh liver across the room, deposit it in a box, and return to receive food as a reinforcement. "Defensive" and "anxiety-related" responses are among the most important examples of this case.

How do we discover what responses have these characteristics? Experimentally, as we discover anything else. Let us call a situation-response combination having none of these properties *learnable*. A positive definition will be given below. What we find is that whereas learnable responses seem to differ somewhat in their "readiness" under different schedule-reinforcement combinations, this is a matter of parameters and does not invalidate the following tentative "law," which is stated qualitatively: "Any learnable response will be strengthened by sunflower seeds as a reinforcer." The general form of such a law is "the stimulus S^1 on schedule M will increase the strength of any learnable response." I shall call such a law a *trans-situational reinforcement* law. It must be noted carefully that such a law is still about a *particular* reinforcing agent, having, to be sure, a class character; but the particular reinforcing agent (and its associated necessary schedule, if any) is no longer tied to the response sequence first studied. The reinforcing property of sunflower seeds was noted first in the T-maze. The Martian will discover that white rats *can* learn to pull chains, press levers, and roll marbles. He finds that these learnable responses can also be strengthened by making the feeding of sunflower seeds contingent upon them. He makes the inductive generalization that sunflower seeds would exert this effect upon all learnable responses in the rat.

He now asks the obvious question: Are all schedule-reinforcer combinations like this? That is to say, when we study a new schedule-reinforcer combination and find it strengthens a response, can we assume that it will increase the strength of all learnable responses? Naturally our confidence in the general reinforcing power of any particular one will increase as we try it out on more and more learnable responses. But we do not know whether a higher-order inductive statement is justified, so long as we study sunflower seeds only or study several kinds of agents but in only one situation each.

Having found a particular reinforcer in a particular situation, we have discovered that it is trans-situational. Next we discover that all of the reinforcers that we have investigated have turned out to be trans-situational. The next induction is, "If a learnable response is followed by a stimulus which is known to be a reinforcer of learnable responses the strength will increase." A shorter way of saying this, having first defined a reinforcer as "a stimulus which will increase the strength of at least one learnable response," is simply: *all reinforcers are trans-situational.* Nothing is said as to the *amount* of strengthening. It is sufficient, in order to demonstrate the trans-situational character of a reinforcing agent, to show that it produces an increment in strength. If equal increments were required, it is probable that very few (if any) reinforcers would be trans-situational because of the varying behavior readinesses and different parameters of habit acquisitions from one drive to another and from one situation to another.

This assertion, that all reinforcers are trans-situational, I propose to call the *Weak Law of Effect*. It is not our problem in this paper to discuss whether the Weak Law of Effect holds or not. A "proof" of the Weak Law of Effect consists, as usual, of establishing inductively many instances of it in a variety of situations with our confidence increasing on the basis of the usual inductive canons. A "disproof" of the Weak Law of Effect would involve showing that a certain stimulus change acts as a reinforcing agent for one response, i.e., that the presentation of this stimulus following the response will increase the latter's strength; but that another response, previously established as learnable, cannot be strengthened by a presentation of this agent. A failure of the Weak Law of Effect to hold strictly would not be particularly serious, since one could (at the very least!) specify the exceptions and would hope to be able to generalize about them, that is, to discover empirically what are the kinds of reinforcers, or kinds of differences among situations, which reveal its invalidity. Actually, here again we have a case in which the law is stated in a qualitative all-or-none form; but the development of a science of behavior would eventually result in substituting a multiplicity of laws indicating the extent to which the reinforcing (strengthening) property generalized over various dimensions of the stimulus side, the reinforcing agent, and the "required" response properties. Assuming the Weak Law of Effect to have been established inductively, where are we now in our development? We have specific situation-reinforcer laws which state that a given stimulus is a reinforcing agent for a specified kind of response in a specified situation. As an example, we discover that for a standard rat, sunflower seeds will strengthen right turning in the T-maze. Having established several such specific situation-reinforcer laws, we find it convenient to introduce a definition, saying that a situational reinforcer is a stimulus which occurs as a term in such a specific situation-reinforcer law. Sunflower seeds are hence situational reinforcers. This definition is "arbitrary" or "conventional" in the usual sense, but clearly leads to no circularity. We cannot tell from the definition whether or not there is such a thing as a situational reinforcer, just as we cannot tell from the definition of a unicorn or of the phrase "King of France" whether such a thing exists. All we stipulate in the definition is that if a thing having certain properties turns out to exist, we will call it by this name. That there are situational reinforcers, that is to say, that we can find stimuli that do increase the strength of responses in a certain situation, is an empirical result. It is obvious that the specific situation-reinforcer laws have a perfectly good factual content (e.g., each such law could be false) in spite of the conventional character of the definition.

If our science contained nothing but a collection of such situational-reinforcer laws, we would still be in possession of valuable information. But we discover inductively that we can actually say more than this. For any given reinforcer, we discover that it can in fact be used to increase the strength of responses differing very greatly in topography from the one which originally led us to infer that it was a reinforcer, and in very different stimulating fields. It is true that there are a few special cases, as our cat with the liver, in which we cannot increase the strength of a *kind* of a response (carrying an object from one place to another) which we know from independent study this species is able to learn. But in all such cases we are able to specify an interfering response at such high strength that the behavior in question does not get a chance to be emitted, and hence cannot be reinforced. With this exception, we are able to say that a given reinforcer will increase the strength of all learnable responses of the species; although there will be quantitative differences which remain to be discovered and generalized about after much painstaking experimentation. We define a reinforcer which is of this sort as trans-situational, and from a study of numerous reinforcers we conclude that they are all of this type. The second order induction that all reinforcers are trans-situational (the Weak Law of Effect) is then made.

This last is certainly a very rich and powerful induction. It is true that to make predictions we must study at least one learnable response in order to find out whether a given stimulus change is reinforcing, and we must know for any contemplated response whether it is learnable. Experience with a given species need not be too extensive in order to get a general idea of the kinds of behavior which are possible and learnable; and once having this, we proceed to strengthen responses by means of reinforcing agents which have never been utilized before in connection with these responses. This is so commonplace that we are likely to underestimate its theoretical significance. So far as I know, no animal psychologist has the least hesitation in utilizing any of a very large class of reinforcing objects called "food" in experimentation upon practically any kind of behavior which he is interested in studying. Should he find a failure of response strength to increase, the chances of his asking what is wrong with the food are negligible. His inductive confidence in the Weak Law of Effect is such that he will immediately begin to investigate what is wrong with the stimulus field, or what requirements concerning the response properties he has imposed which transcend the powers of the organism. I am stressing this point because there is a tendency to say that since we have to study the effects upon strength in order to know whether an agent is reinforcing, we do not really "know anything" when we have enunciated the Law of Effect. I think it should be obvious from the diversity of both the class called learnable and the class of agents called reinforcing that to the extent that this law holds almost without exception, when we have enunciated it we have said a great deal.

The man from Mars might be tempted here to take a final step which would be suggested by the ubiquity of the manifestations of the Weak Law of Effect. It might occur to him that the great majority of the instances in which changes in response strength occur seem to involve the operation of the Weak Law, i.e., the presentation of a member of the reinforcing class. Perhaps it is not only true that any learnable response can be strengthened by the presentation of a trans-situational reinforcer but may it not be that this is the *only* way to increase the strength of responses (by learning)? Response strength may be increased by surgical and drug procedures, and also by maturation; but the demarcation of learning as a very general mode of response change, while it presents difficult problems, need not concern us here. Assuming that we have some satisfactory basis for distinguishing an increase in the strength which is based upon "experience" rather than upon interference with the reaction mechanism or biological growth determined by genetic factors given minimal (viable) environments, we may ask whether learning takes place on any *other* basis than the Weak Law of Effect. Certain apparent exceptions to this statement of reinforcement as a necessary condition would appear, but the Martian might ask whether these exceptions are more apparent than real. The formulation of such a law would run something like this: "Every learned increment in response strength requires the operation of a trans-situational reinforcer." I shall designate this rash inductive leap as the *Strong Law of Effect.*

It appears obvious that this also is a statement far from being experimentally empty or in any sense a consequence of definition. I have heard psychologists translate the statement "he learns because he was reinforced" as being tantamount to "he learns because he learns." Postman suggests the same kind of thing in the first quotation above. This is too easy. The expanded form which I suspect everyone has implicitly in mind when he talks about the Strong Law of Effect is: "He learns following the presentation of a stimulus change which for this species has the property of increasing response strength; and, other things being equal in the present setting, if this change had *not* occurred he would not have learned." Such a statement can clearly be false to fact, either because no such trans-situational reinforcer can be shown to have been present, or because the same learning can be shown to be producible without it in the present setting. The claim of the reinforcement theorist to explanation is (at this stage of our knowledge) of exactly the same character as "he developed these symptoms because he was invaded by the Koch bacillus, and we know that the Koch bacillus has these effects." This is not a very *detailed* explanation, because the intermediate or micro-details of the causal sequence are not given; but it is certainly neither factually empty nor trivial.

In our initial quotation from Postman, we find him saying, "The satisfying or annoying nature of a state of affairs can usually be determined fully only in the course of a learning experiment and cannot then be invoked as a causal condition of learning without circularity." The trouble with this remark lies in the ambiguity of the phrase "*a* learning experiment." That we cannot know what is reinforcing without having done *some* experimentation is obvious, and is just as it should be in an empirical science. But once having found that a certain state of affairs *is* reinforcing for a given species, there is no reason why a given case of learning cannot be explained by invoking the occurrence of this state of affairs as a causal condition. The definition of force does not entail the truth of Hooke's law. It is only by an experiment that we find out that strain is proportional to stress. Once having found it out, we are all quite comfortable in utilizing Hooke's law to account for the particular cases we come across. I am confident that Postman would not be disturbed if in answer to the question, "Why does that door close all the time?" someone were to reply, "Because it has a spring attached to it on the other side." There is no more "circularity" in this kind of causal accounting than in any other kind. It is perfectly true that this kind of "lowest-order" explanation is not very intellectually satisfying in some cases, although even here there is a considerable variability depending upon our familiarity with the situation. For a detailed consideration of these problems by more qualified persons I refer the reader to papers by Hospers (10), Feigl (4, 5), and Pratt (20).

I think it is obvious that this is the way we think of the Law of Effect, whatever we may think as to its truth. When an apparent case of learning in the absence of reinforcement occurs, those who are interested in preserving the status of the Law of Effect (in my terminology, in preserving the status of the *Strong* Law of Effect) begin to search for changes following the response which can be shown to be of the reinforcing sort. They do not simply look for *any* stimulus change and insist ("by definition") that it is a reinforcement. The statement that a given case of apparently non-reinforcement learning is actually based upon secondary reinforcement is essentially a claim that some stimulus change can be shown to have followed the strengthened response, and that this stimulus change has (still earlier) been put in temporal contiguity with a stimulus change of which we know, from a *diversity* of situations, that it exerts a reinforcing effect.

Abandoning the charge of circularity, a critic might offer a "practical" criticism, saying, "What good does it do to know that a reinforcer strengthens, when the only way to tell when something is a reinforcer is to see if it strengthens?" The trouble here lies in vagueness, since the *generality* is not indicated, and this failure to indicate generality neglects the usual advantages of induction. That a describable state of affairs *is* reinforcing can only be found out, to be sure, by experimenting on some organisms utilizing *some* learnable response. But it is not required (if the Weak Law of Effect is true) that we, so to speak, start afresh with each new organism of the species and each new response. As a matter of fact, after we have considerable experience with a given species, we can generalize about the physical properties of a stimulus class. So that finally "food" means many substances which may never yet have been tried in a learning situation, and may never have been presented in natural circumstances to the members of a particular species. Wild rats do not eat Purina Chow. Here we begin to approach inductively one of the previously rejected bases of defining reinforcement, namely, the physical character of the stimulus change itself. To ask for a definition of reinforcers which will tell us beforehand for a given species which objects or stimuli will exert the reinforcing effect is to ask that a definition should tell us what the world is like before we investigate it, which is not possible in any science. It happens that the psychologist is worse off than others, because species differences, individual hereditary differences, and differences of the reactional biography make a larger mass of facts necessary in order to know whether a given agent will reinforce a particular organism. But at worst the Weak Law of Effect in conjunction with its member laws is far from useless. When I know inductively that all non-toxic substances containing sugar will act as reinforcers for organisms from rat to man and therefore that I can almost certainly strengthen all responses learnable by any of these species on the basis of the presentation of any of these substances, I know a great deal and my science has a very considerable predictive power.

An Analogous Problem in Physics

It is instructive to consider a somewhat analogous problem in physics, in the definition of "force." Once mass has been defined by some such artifice as Mach's acceleration-ratio technique, and acceleration defined in terms of time and distance, Newton's second law is a *definition* of force. I neglect here other attempts to introduce the notion such as the "school of the thread" (18), utilizing Hooke's law in the form of a definition rather than a law, or its modern variants, e.g., Keenan's (13) recent effort. Force is "that which accelerates mass." Mach's introduction of the concept of mass was somewhat disturbing to certain of his contemporaries because of a suggested circularity. Mach saw that it was the *inertial* character of mass, rather than "weight" or "quantity of matter" which was crucial in setting up the definition of force. Accordingly, he proceeds as follows:

a. *Experimental Proposition.* Bodies set opposite each other induce in each other, under certain circumstances to be specified by experimental physics, contrary *accelerations* in the direction of their line of junction. (The principle of inertia is included in this.)

b. *Definition.* The mass-ratio of any two bodies is the negative inverse ratio of the mutually induced accelerations of those bodies.

c. *Experimental Proposition.* The mass-ratios of bodies are independent of the character of the physical states (of the bodies) that condition the mutual accelerations produced, be those states electrical, magnetic, or what not; and they remain, moreover, the same, whether they are mediately or immediately arrived at.

d. *Experimental Proposition.* The accelerations which any number of bodies A, B, C . . . induce in a body K, are independent of each other. (The principle of the parallelogram of forces follows immediately from this.)

e. *Definition.* Moving force is the product of the mass-value of a body into the acceleration induced in that body. Then the remaining arbitrary definitions of the algebraical expressions "momentum," "vis viva," and the like, might follow. But these are by no means indispensable. The propositions above set forth satisfy the requirements of simplicity and parsimony which on economico-scientific grounds, must be exacted of them. They are, moreover, obvious and clear; for no doubt can exist with respect to any one of them either concerning its meaning or its source; and we always know whether it asserts an experience or an arbitrary convention (17, pp. 243–244).

In the appendix to the second English edition, Mach replies to critics of this procedure as follows:

> A special difficulty seems to be still found in accepting my definition of mass. Streintz has remarked in criticism of it that it is based solely upon gravity, although this was expressly excluded in my first formulation of the definition (1868). Nevertheless, this criticism is again and again put forward, and quite recently even by Volkmann. My definition simply takes note of the fact that bodies in mutual relationship, whether it be that of action at a distance, so called, or whether rigid or elastic connexions be considered, determine in one another changes of velocity (accelerations). More than this, one does not need to know in order to be able to form a definition with perfect assurance and without the fear of building on sand. It is not correct as Höfler asserts, that this definition tacitly assumes *one and the same force* acting on both masses. It does not assume even the notion of force, since the latter is built up subsequently upon the notion of mass, and gives then the principle of action and reaction quite independently and without falling into Newton's logical error. In this arrangement one concept is not misplaced and made to rest on another which threatens to give way under it (17, pp. 558–559).

It is obvious that Mach defines mass in the way he does *so that* the definition of force by $F = ma$ will lead to the kinds of laws we want. That is, a previous "knowledge" of the law of gravity based upon a cruder notion of mass is involved historically in the formulation of such a definition. But the crucial point is that it is involved only in the context of discovery, not in the context of justification (21, pp. 6–7). There is nothing wrong with making use of any notions, including vague anthropomorphic experiences of pleasure, in deciding how we shall formulate definitions, since our aim is to erect concepts and constructs which will fit into the most convenient and powerful system of laws. The point is that we wish to come out with explicit notions that are free of this vagueness and which do not require any notions which cannot be finally introduced objectively. There is probably a remnant of hedonism in the thinking of the most sophisticated contemporary reinforcement theorists, and there is no reason why anybody should pretend that when he talks about rewards he does not have some faint component in his thinking which involves the projection of such pleasure-pain experiences. But this does not mean that these notions are made part of the scientific structure he erects, in the sense that either the definitions of terms or the establishment of the laws requires such associated imagery in his readers. I suggest that Thorndike's critics are in the same position as Mach's.

One might ask, why would a physicist be upset should he attend a spiritualist séance and find tumblers leaping off tables and floating through the air? If the concept of force is given simply by the relation $F = ma$, then, if a glass tumbler undergoes an acceleration, a force must act and his definition assures him that the physical world will not surprise him. I do not think the answer to this question is far to seek. While it is admittedly a question of decision, I doubt that most physicists would decide to say that an acceleration occurred in the absence of a force. If the genuineness of the phenomenon were satisfactorily established, I do not think there would be a re-definition of the *concept* of force, but rather that the existence of "forces" on other bases than those previously known would be assumed. That is, the physicist would not say "here is a case of acceleration without a force," but he would rather say "here is a case of force not arising from the usual mechanical, gravitational, or electro-magnetic situations which I have thought, up to now, were the sole bases on which forces came into being." It is certainly no criticism of a Newtonian definition of force (I leave out the fact that Newton, while he defined force in this way, apparently also treated his second law as one of empirical content) to say that having thus defined force you cannot know beforehand what are the conditions in the world under which forces will appear. The mechanical forces involved in direct contact, the force of gravity, and certain electrostatic and magnetic forces were known to Newton. There is nothing about his definition of force which tells us that a peculiarly directed force will exist between a wire carrying an electric current and a compass needle, nor that attracting or repelling forces will exist between parallel wires each of which carries a current. The discovery of these conditions under which forces exist was an empirical contribution of Oersted and Ampere.

Similarly, the psychologist defines what is meant by a reinforcer, and proceeds to search for the agents that fall under this definition. There are undoubtedly kinds of stimulus changes of which we are as yet unaware which will turn out to have the reinforcing property. Dr. Wilse Webb (personal communication) has found in preliminary experiments that at least in one kind of Skinner box the click produced by the operation of an empty magazine will exert a reinforcing effect in an animal whose experience has never given this stimulus an opportunity to acquire secondary reinforcing properties. This is surprising to us. What are the conditions under which this will occur? Suppose it should be found that almost *any* stimulus change within a fairly wide range (avoiding extreme intensities which are anxiety-producing) would exert a slight reinforcing effect in the Skinner box or in any similar apparatus in which there is a considerable stimulus restriction and a marked constancy in the homogeneity of the visual and auditory fields. It might be discovered that when a member of this species has remained in such a homogeneous field for a period of time, stimulus *changes* (not otherwise specified) exert a reinforcing effect. Maybe the rat is "bored" and just likes to make something happen! A difficult notion to nail down experimentally, to be sure. But its complexity and the number of things to be ruled out, does not take it out of the realm of the confirmable.

Let us consider a very extreme case. Suppose in the T-maze situation a systematic increase in the strength of the right turn should be discovered for a standard rat. Suppose that the most thoroughgoing, exhaustive manipulation of the external effect of right-turning should fail to reveal any condition necessary for the effect. "No member of the reinforcing class is to be found." I think that at this point we would begin reluctantly to consider a reinforcing property of the response itself. Perhaps turning to the right is inherently reinforcing to this species. It seems, for instance, that "fetching" behavior in certain species of dogs is self-reinforcing (or at least that it has a biologically replenished reserve). The only reason for calling right-turning "self-reinforcing" rather than simply saying that it is a response of innately high strength in the species is that a *change* in strength occurs with successive runs, otherwise "turning to the right" is simply a kind of tropism. Is the "self-reinforcing" idea factually empty? Although many people would disagree with me at this point, I do not think it is. But it has factual meaning only intradermally. There is no reason why we could not study the proprioceptive effects of a right turn and find out whether, if they are cut out, the increase in response strength continues to appear. In principle we could create the proprioceptive effects of a right turn by artificial means and on that basis strengthen a topographically different response such as lifting the fore paw, wiggling the whiskers, or the like. Here there are difficulties, but I would be prepared to argue that in principle the self-reinforcing effect of right-turning is an empirically meaningful notion.

An interesting side-light is that even the Strong Law of Effect is, as stated, compatible with the latent learning experiments. I am not interested in avoiding the consequences of those experiments by shrewd dialectics, but in the interests of clarity it should be pointed out that in, e.g., the Blodgett design, the big drop in errors *does* follow a reinforcement. So long as the Strong Law of Effect is stated qualitatively and does not explicitly mention amounts and times, it would be admittedly difficult to design an experiment in which it could be refuted. A neo-Hullian interested for some reason in preserving the Strong Law of Effect might simply add a quantitative postulate. He might assume that when a response undergoes an increment in strength on the basis of a minimally reinforcing agent (that is, one in which the asymptote of the acquisition of habit strength is relatively low), then, if subsequently a strong reinforcement is introduced, the parameter in the new growth function which determines the rate of approach to the new asymptote is greater than it would have been without the original learning. Since in the Blodgett design there is evidence of acquisition of differential habit strengths during the latent phase, such a postulate would lead to a preservation of the Strong Law of Effect. The main reason that we are concerned to deal with latent learning material of the Blodgett type is that in the reinforcement theory as now formulated, the effect of a reinforcer is implicitly assumed to operate immediately.

Relationship of Reinforcement to Drive

Perhaps a comment is needed on the way in which reinforcement has been treated here as the primary notion whereas drive, need, or demand is defined in terms of it. I do not mean to imply that need or drive is not the more "basic" factor, if by this is meant that what is a reinforcer or what acquires reinforcing properties depends upon a certain relevance to need. But this manner of speaking refers to the casual reconstruction of behavior, and reverses the epistemological order. The needs of an organism are inferred from changes in behavior strength as a function of certain states of affairs. That is to say, we "get a fix" on a need by being able to induce the chief defining properties of those states of affairs to which behavior is shown to tend. I do not see how there is any possibility in proceeding otherwise at the level of molar behavior. Whether it will be feasible or desirable to hypothesize a kind of state called need in the case of all reinforcers is a moot point at present. I gather that Hull would argue it will, whereas Skinner would argue it will not. One can consider a sort of continuum of reinforcing states of affairs at one end of which it is most easy and natural and obviously very useful to speak in terms of a need, e.g., the case of food or water; whereas at the other end, e.g., the reinforcing effects of hearing a click or turning off a light, the notion of needs seems relatively less appropriate. But the *casual* primacy of needs in our final reconstruction of behavior laws must not be confused with the epistemological status of needs, i.e., the operations by which we arrive at a conception of the needs. Whether the reduction of need is a necessary condition for learning is a question that is not involved in my formulation of either the Weak or the Strong Law of Effect since need-reduction is not equated to reinforcement. This independence of the notions of reinforcement and need-reduction is seen not only in the question of whether need-reduction is (for a sophisticated organism) a necessary condition for reinforcing effect, but it is the intention of these definitions to leave it an open question as to whether a kind of event called need-reduction is involved in reinforcing effects at any stage. The alternative to this is to exhaust completely the concept of need by defining an intervening variable via a class of reinforcing agents, i.e., the organism's "need" is not specified in any way except to say that it is "whatever state" within the organism is involved in the reinforcing effect of a stimulus change known experimentally to exert such an effect. In this case, of course, a rat may be said to have a "need" to keep the light off, to be with another rat, to hear a sound, etc. Whether this is a desirable way of speaking we need not consider here.

In the preceding developments, I have avoided consideration of refinements which would be necessary to complete the theoretical picture. The most important of these is the apparent exception to the Weak Law of Effect in which a change in strength does not occur in spite of the presentation of a known reinforcing agent because certain other dominant factors are at work. As an example, we may consider the "fixation" of a response which is followed by anxiety reduction to the point that an opposing response consistently reinforced with food fails to develop an increase in strength. In any particular situation it is the task of experimental analysis to show what the relations are; as a nice example of this I may refer to the recent work of Farber (3). Of course, if the response does not have sufficient opportunity to *occur*, be reinforced, and hence develop strength, the Weak Law of Effect is not violated. Those cases in which this is not an adequate explanation must be dealt with by considering the opposing forces, leaving open the question as to whether these opposing forces can themselves be satisfactorily subsumed under the Strong Law of Effect. The case here is not essentially different from the case in mechanics where we introduce the concept of force as a dynamic concept (that is, by accelerations produced) and subsequently apply the same notions to systems which are in equilibrium. In physics, one makes use of the laws about force which are based upon the dynamical notion of it in order to explain those cases in statics in which no motion results. Whereas the detailed reconstruction of the causal system remains as a task for the future, I do not believe there are any fundamental logical difficulties involved in the notion that a reinforcing state of affairs is initially defined by an increase in strength, and subsequently the failure of such a state of affairs to exert the effect is explained in terms of the occurrence of other operations or states which oppose it.

Summary

Let me conclude by summarizing the development, using Mach as a model. For convenience I neglect here the specification of a schedule:

> a. *Experimental Proposition:* In the rat, if turning to the right in the T-maze is followed by the presentation of sunflower seeds, the strength of the right-turning response will increase. (A situational-reinforcer law.)

   b. *Definition:* A stimulus or stimulus change which occurs as the strengthening condition in a situational-reinforcer law is a *reinforcer.*

This empirical law together with the above definition enables us now to assert (as an empirical statement) "sunflower seeds are a reinforcer." The empirical content of this is that there is at least one response which the presentation of sunflower seeds will strengthen.

   The presentation of a reinforcer is called *reinforcement.*

   c. *Definition:* If the strength of a response may be increased as a function of behavior in an exposure to a situation (rather than by surgical, drug, or maturational changes), such a response is *learnable* by the organism. No reference to reinforcement is made here; we simply require that response strength be shown to increase following "experience," of whatever sort.

   d. *Experimental Propositions:* Following suitable manipulation of their experiences, rats will show increases in the strength of pressing levers, pulling chains, rolling marbles, turning to the right at certain choice points, gnawing through paper, digging through sawdust, turning wheels, etc. (Expanded, this would consist simply in a long list of specific "laws" asserting the learnability of certain response classes.)

   e. *Experimental Propositions:* Sunflower seeds may be used to strengthen lever pressing, chain pulling, etc. In general, sunflower seeds may be used to strengthen all learnable responses in the rat. (This asserts the generality of the reinforcing effect of sunflower seeds and is what I am calling a trans-situational reinforcer law.)

   f. *Definition:* A trans-situational reinforcer is a stimulus which will strengthen all learnable responses. (We have already defined reinforcer so that it does not commit us to its generality, that is, a reinforcer is *at least* a situational reinforcer. If there are any reinforcers which exert the reinforcing effect upon all learnable responses, they are trans-situational.) This definition with the immediately preceding experimental propositions enables us to say, "Sunflower seeds are a trans-situational reinforcer."

Such a collection of specific empirical laws in combination with the above general definition leads to a large set of laws such as these last stated ones so that in the end we find the following:

   g. *Experimental Proposition:* All reinforcers are trans-situational. (The Weak Law of Effect.)

   h. *Experimental Proposition:* Every increment in strength involves a trans-situational reinforcer. (The Strong Law of Effect.)

It seems clear that in the above sequence both the definitional and the factual (empirical) elements are present, and in a simple, commonplace form. The definitional and conventional elements appear in the specification of the circumstances under which a stimulus is to be called "reinforcing." Such a stipulation, however, cannot tell us whether any such stimuli exist. That they do exist, which no one doubts, is an empirical finding; and the numerous statements about them constitute situational-reinforcer laws which are in a sense the special "sub-laws" of effect. These are related to the Weak Law of Effect somewhat in the same way that the particular empirical laws about the properties of bromine, fluorine, chlorine, and so on, are related to the Periodic Law. That the stimuli which occur in the situational-reinforcer laws have a generality of their reinforcing power is also an empirical finding, at present less well established (the Weak Law of Effect). That all cases of learning require certain time relationships to the presentation of such general reinforcers is yet a further factual claim, at present very much in dispute (the Strong Law of Effect).

I can see no reason why any theorist, whatever his position, should find the preceding treatment objectionable as an explication of the Law of Effect. I do not see any way in which the Strong Law of Effect, which is after all the big contemporary issue, has been surreptitiously put into the definitions in such a way that what is intended as an empirical proposition is effectively made a consequence of our use of words. The status of the Strong Law of Effect and even to some extent the Weak Law is presently in doubt. Further, some of the words used in these definitions, e.g., the word "response," are difficult to define in a way that makes them behave in the total system as we wish them to. I have not tried to deal with all these problems at once, but I hope that there are no difficulties springing from the problem of circularity which have not been met. That it is difficult to untangle the learning sequence which has given the reinforcing property to some states of affairs, particularly in the human organism, is admitted by everyone. That a large amount of detailed work of the "botanizing" type, not particularly ego-rewarding, needs to be done before the special sub-laws of effect are stated in terms of quantitative relations is quite clear. Finally, it would be very nice if in some magical way we could *know* before studying a given species exactly what stimulus changes would have the reinforcing property; but I have tried to indicate that this is an essentially irrational demand. In the light of the previous analysis I think the burden of proof is upon those who look upon a sophisticated formulation of the Law of Effect as circular, in either of the ordinary uses of that word.

Bibliography

1. Carr, H. A., *et al.* The Law of Effect: a roundtable discussion. *Psychol. Rev.,* 1938, 45, 191–218.
2. Estes, W. K. A study of motivating conditions necessary for secondary reinforcement. *Amer. Psychologist,* 1948, 3, 240–241. (Abstract.)
3. Farber, I. E. Response fixation under anxiety and non-anxiety conditions. *J. exp. Psychol.,* 1948, 38, 111–131.

4. Feigl, H. Operationism and scientific method. *Psychol. Rev.*, 1945, 52, 250–259.
5. Feigl, H. Some remarks on the meaning of scientific explanation. In H. Feigl & W. Sellars, *Readings in philosophical analysis.* New York: Appleton-Century-Crofts, 1949. Pp. 510–514.
6. Guttman, N. On the relationship between resistance to extinction of a bar-pressing response and concentration of reinforcing agent. Paper presented at the meeting of the Midwestern Psychological Association, Chicago, Ill., April 29, 1949.
7. Heron, W. T., & Peake, E. Qualitative food deficiency as a drive in a discrimination problem. *J. comp. physiol. Psychol.*, 1949, 42, 143–147.
8. Hilgard, E. R. *Theories of learning.* New York: Appleton-Century-Crofts, 1948.
9. Hilgard, E. R., & Marquis, D. G. *Conditioning and learning.* New York: Appleton-Century, 1940.
10. Hospers, J. On explanation. *J. Philos.*, 1946, 43, 337–356.
11. Hull, C. L. Thorndike's *Fundamentals of learning. Psychol. Bull.*, 1935, 32, 807–823.
12. Hull, C. L. *Principles of behavior.* New York: Appleton-Century, 1943.
13. Keenan, J. Definitions and principles of dynamics. *Sci. Mon., N. Y.*, 1948, 67, 406–414.
14. Lenzen, V. F. *The nature of physical theory.* New York: John Wiley, 1931.
15. Lindsay, R. B., & Margenau, H. *Foundations of physics.* New York: John Wiley, 1936.
16. MacCorquodale, K., & Meehl, P. E. "Cognitive" learning in the absence of competition of incentives. *J. comp. physiol. Psychol.*, 1949, 42, 383–390.
17. Mach, E. *The science of mechanics* (Transl. by T. J. McCormack). Second English Ed. Chicago: Open Court Publishing Co., 1902.
18. Poincaré, H. *The foundations of science.* New York: Science Press, 1913.
19. Postman, L. The history and present status of the Law of Effect. *Psychol. Bull.*, 1947, 44, 489–563.
20. Pratt, C. C. Operationism in psychology. *Psychol. Rev.*, 1945, 52, 262–269.
21. Reichenbach, H. *Experience and prediction.* Chicago: Univ. of Chicago Press, 1938.
22. Skinner, B. F. *The behavior of organisms.* New York: Appleton-Century, 1938.
23. Spence, K. W. Studies on secondary reinforcement. Address given to the Minnesota Chapter of Psi Chi, Minneapolis, April 22, 1948.
24. Taylor, L. W. *Physics, the pioneer science.* New York: Houghton, Mifflin, 1941.
25. Thorndike, E. L. *The fundamentals of learning.* New York: Teachers College, Columbia Univ., 1932.
26. Thorndike, E. L. *Animal intelligence.* New York: Macmillan, 1911.
27. Thorndike, E. L. *The original nature of man.* New York: Teachers College, 1913.
28. Thorndike, E. L. *The psychology of learning.* New York: Teachers College, 1913.
29. Tolman, E. C. *Purposive behavior in animals and men.* New York: Appleton-Century, 1932.

9 TENSIONS IN PSYCHOLOGY BETWEEN THE METHODS OF BEHAVIORISM AND PHENOMENOLOGY
Nathan Brody and Paul Oppenheim

> Only silence before the *Thou* . . . leaves the *Thou* free. . . . Every response binds up the *Thou* in the world of *It*. That is the melancholy of man, and his greatness. For that is how knowledge comes about. . . . He will, indeed, have to grasp as an object that which he has seen with the force of presence, he will have to compare it with objects, establish it in its order among classes of objects, describe and analyze it objectively. Only as *It* can it enter the structure of knowledge [Buber, 1958, pp. 39–40].

In this paper, methodological differences between behavioristic and phenomenological psychology are discussed. The plan of the paper is as follows: *First,* a brief definition of behaviorism and phenomenology will show how these terms are conceived here. *Second,* an analysis will be made of three loci of tension between behaviorism and phenomenology. *Third,* the question of rapprochement will be discussed.

Behaviorism and Phenomenology Defined

BEHAVIORISM

Behaviorism is conceived here in Bergmann's (1956) sense of methodological behaviorism. According to this position, the fundamental data of psychology are the publicly observable behaviors of organisms; these are conceived as being describable in an intersubjective observation language. For the behaviorist, private experiences per se are not admissible as data, but only their publicly observable symptoms, if any. Behaviorists differ as to whether it is necessary or at least advisable to assign to private experience any role at all in scientific psychology. Behaviorists who assign a role to private experiences would do so by referring to them by means of theoretical (as opposed to observational) terms (see Eriksen, 1962; Jessor, 1958).

If a behaviorist wanted to introduce into the vocabulary of psychol-

SOURCE: Nathan Brody and Paul Oppenheim, "Tensions in Psychology between the Methods of Behaviorism and Phenomenology," *Psychological Review*, 73, no. 4 (July 1966), 295–305. Copyright © by the American Psychological Association. Reprinted by permission of the publisher.

ogy theoretical terms referring to a person's private experience, it would be necessary for him to (a) define the terms by multiple convergent operations, that is, by several distinct operations which jointly determine the intended empirical meaning (see Garner, Hake, & Eriksen, 1956), (b) develop the theoretical relations between these terms and others, and (c) demonstrate the value of such terms for the explanation of behavior. These three conditions are not completely satisfied at present.

PHENOMENOLOGY

Phenomenology is conceived in this paper in a sense similar to MacLeod's (1964) interpretation (cf. Edie, 1964, for a more general discussion of phenomenology and its relation to Existential philosophy). We shall define pure phenomenological psychology (ppp) [1] by its subject matter and by its method of investigation. The subject matter of ppp is all of experience. It is the intent of the ppp to study that which is immediately given in experience. MacLeod (1964) states in this connection:

> . . . colors and sounds are data; so are impressions of distance and duration; so are feelings of attraction and repulsion; so are yearnings and fears, ecstasies and disillusionments; so are all the relations—ranging from the crude and obvious to the delicate and intangible—with which the world presents us [p. 51].

The ppp studies the data of experience by a method which involves the suspension of implicit and explicit assumptions. (This method is reminiscent of what is called by Husserl, in a more technical context, "phenomenological reduction" and the act of "bracketing"—1962, especially pp. 10, 12, 96–100.) That is, the ppp seeks to investigate experience freed, as far as possible, from the encumbrance of any preconceived theoretical ideas about that which is being investigated. This is sometimes referred to by Gestalt psychologists as naïve phenomenology (see Koffka, 1935, p. 73; Köhler, 1947). There is an attempt to investigate the immediate data given to the mind and not a theoretical construction or interpretation of these data. In the words of Lewis:

> There are in our cognitive experience two elements; the immediate data such as those of sense which are presented or given to the mind, and a form, construction, or interpretation, which represents the activity of thought. Recognition of this fact is one of the oldest and most universal of philosophic insights [1956, p. 38].

For a similar distinction made by phenomenologists between "fully reflexive categorical thought" and "prereflexive awareness," see Edie (1964). The subject matter of ppp is the former element.

---

[1] We shall use ppp to also stand for "pure phenomenological psychologist" and rely on the context to make clear which meaning is intended.

Carried to its logical extreme, the method of ppp demands the bracketing of all concepts since they arise out of the activity of thought. It is therefore appropriate to call the type of experience involved in the method of ppp *nonconceptualized experience,* that is, an experiece of the immediately given, sometimes referred to as "brute facts" (James, 1910) or "raw feels" (Feigl, 1958), not mediated by any concepts.

By characterizing ppp in this way, it is not implied that it is ever possible to have a purely nonconceptualized experience. But the method of ppp implies that one can approximate such an experience.

Three Loci of Tension Between ppp and Behaviorism

CONSTRUCTION AND EVALUATION OF PSYCHOLOGICAL THEORIES

The first locus of tension involves the *context of discovery* (Reichenbach, 1938) for psychology, that is, the considerations that govern the way in which psychological theories and hypotheses are discovered. We deal here with what is at least a stylistic difference between ppp and behaviorism. If we restrict ourselves to the context of discovery, there is no reason why a behaviorist should not have the option of letting his explanatory efforts be initially guided by a phenomenological analysis of experience. He could then continue his investigation by collecting behavioral data. On the other hand, for the ppp, the former starting point is considered indispensable. This stylistic difference can become the basis for the evaluation of theories and in this sense be extended into the *context of justification* (Reichenbach, 1938). Behavioristic theories which fail to represent some aspect of experience discovered by the method of ppp have been criticized by the latter as inadequate (see MacLeod, 1964).

Logical analysis of nonconceptualized experience. In order to evaluate such criticism, we shall present a logical analysis of nonconceptualized experience. This analysis is influenced in part by the writings of philosophers about what we call nonconceptualized experience (see Ayer, 1956; Black, 1954; Carnap, 1928, 1963; Lewis, 1946, 1956; Northrop, 1948, 1962). Also relevant are discussions of mysticism which can be considered a type of nonconceptualized experience (see Maslow, 1962; Stace, 1960; Zaecner, 1957).

What type of knowledge (the term knowledge is here understood in its usual conceptual sense) can be gained by an experiencer who has nonconceptualized experiences and who makes no attempt to introduce any hypothetical or theoretical construction into his discussion of his experiences? It is our contention that a person who restricts himself in such a way cannot have any knowledge at all.

In order for an experiencer to be able to claim that his experience has led to some sort of knowledge, he has to be able to give a description of the content of his experience for himself or others. Strictly speaking, any statement about a nonconceptualized experience involves an interpretation; this carries a conceptual element into the description. Let us examine more closely the types of inferences which are involved in such statements. Consider the statement "I saw red," or perhaps, "Redness was experienced by me," as an immediately given. We normally infer from such a statement that the experience of redness was not merely a figment of the experiencer's imagination. In addition, the statement is usually considered to imply that other persons, or the same person on another occasion, would experience redness if placed in the same situation. It is reasonably clear that such inferences would be logically excluded if one were restricted to reporting only what is immediately given in nonconceptualized experience. But can such a reporter legitimately affirm that he experienced redness? In order to assign properties such as red to an experience, it would be necessary to accept the division of the color continuum into the particular set of categories used in our everyday language. This classification carries a conceptual element into the description of the nonconceptualized experience (see Brown, 1965).

In general, whoever attempts to describe a nonconceptualized experience can do so only by a process of conceptualization which distorts and impoverishes the experience. Therefore, an experiencer who attempts to describe his nonconceptualized experience without such loss of content must in fact be speechless. In a similar vein, Black (1954) asserts that statements about the immediately given are not to be considered as descriptions but only as exclamations, as it were. Of course, a person can make a statement about his nonconceptualized experiences, but such statements are logically incommensurable with the experiences per se and can at best only be *correlated* with them, because statements per se involve the use of class concepts, whereas the idea of nonconceptualized experiences logically excludes the applicability of class concepts. Northrop (1962, especially pp. 154, 237, 238) calls the relation between such incommensurables "epistemic correlation" (see also Havens, 1961).

The discussion of nonconceptualized experiences will now be summarized and partially extended by the presentation of a list of characteristics, each of which is logically implied by the meaning of nonconceptualized experiences. The characteristics assigned to such experiences may not be independent of each other.

1. During a nonconceptualized experience, the experiencer is not capable of distinguishing himself conceptually as experiencer from that which he is experiencing and is in this sense in *union* with it.

2. During a nonconeptualized experience, the experiencer is not capable of assigning a locus to his experience in a public spatio-temporal coordinate system. Thus, the experience could only have a locus in a private frame of reference with respect to space and time. With respect to time, the experience is called a *specious present* (see James, 1890, Ch. 15).

3. Nonconceptualized experiences are *ineffable* in the sense that during and after the nonconceptualized experience the experiencer has not at his disposal words which could be used by him to describe for himself or others the content of his experience. A fortiori, they are *property-less*, since properties involving class terminology cannot be assigned to them. This implies that differences, if any, contained in the experience cannot be described; it remains in this sense an undifferentiated unity.

4. Nonconceptualized experiences are *solipsistic*. Since they cannot be verbally communicated to others, they have meaning, if any, only for the experiencer himself.

Two conclusions about the method of ppp. First, the advocates of ppp have criticized the method of analytic introspection, which had been used by the Structuralists, on the ground that their method was not a true investigation of experience, since the search for elements of experience leads to the introduction of elements where, in fact, the immediately givens are wholes. Thus, the method of investigation partially dictates its outcome (see Köhler, 1947; MacLeod, 1964). A similar argument can be made with respect to ppp: Its method emphasizes personal as distinguished from public time (see May, 1958, pp. 65–71). This is understandable as a logical consequence of its method (see Characteristic 2 above). In general, it will sometimes be difficult to know whether ppp has chosen a certain theme only as a logical consequence of its method of investigation, or in its own right because of its importance as an essential aspect of human experience, or as a result of confounding both elements.

Thus, paradoxically, the attempt to bracket all concepts in order not to bias the results of an investigation of experience introduces certain epistemic consequences which tend to influence the results of an investigation and creates a bias.

The second conclusion suggested by this analysis of nonconceptualized experiences is that these experiences do not provide the basis for the construction of any conceptual system. This conclusion follows directly from the ineffability of these experiences. Therefore, nonconceptualized experiences cannot be used as a basis for the criticism of any conceptual system. It is in this sense that we understand MacLeod's (1964) statement that ppp is only propaedeutic to the development of psychological theory.

DIFFERENCES IN TYPES OF EXPLANATION

The second locus of tension to be discussed here concerns the possibility of explanation in behaviorism and ppp. Explanation in science is generally thought to involve the use of some theory (Hempel & Oppenheim, 1948). Thus, strictly speaking, such a process of explanation is not compatible with the method of ppp.

Two possible alternatives can be adopted by the ppp: First, he can refuse to construct any explanatory system and rely rather on some kind of empathic or intuitive understanding which cannot be verbally communicated at all. Some Existential psychoanalysts have apparently used this approach. For example, Tymieniecka (1962, p. 69) mentions three fundamental "empirical" statements advanced by Jaspers. These are:

1. Man in his entirety cannot be objectively (conceptually) known;
2. Cognition is not limited to causal explanation;
3. There are essential aspects of mind which are by their very nature not accessible to experimental methods and cannot be rationally grasped.

Second, the ppp can at one time take the approach mentioned above. At another time, he can transcend the phenomenal world and construct a system which is conceptual and which is believed to preserve some of the intuitive insights obtained in nonconceptualized experience. But in such a case, ppp has only been a heuristic device limited to the context of discovery. It is not clear how the insights obtained by these methods can be carried over into the actual construction of theories.

METHODS OF TEST

The third locus of tension concerns the method of test. For the behaviorist, any psychological theory, law, or statement must be ultimately testable with reference to intersubjectively observable symptoms of phenomena. The advocates of ppp, in so far as they do not exclude any theoretical statements, may differ as to their agreement with this demand of the behaviorist. For example, Rogers (1964) would agree with this demand. But whoever accepts this demand becomes in effect a methodological behaviorist, since his conceptual system rests ultimately on a behavioristic base, and ppp is used only in the context of discovery. Other advocates of ppp would reject any such insistence.

What role, if any, can be assigned to nonconceptualized experiences in the testing process? At one time or another, several philosophers have suggested that nonconceptualized experiences provide the basis for testing all scientific statements (see Carnap, 1928, p. 273; Lewis, 1946, 1956; Russell, 1912, Ch. V; Schlick, 1934).

To our knowledge, no one has ever presented in sufficient detail a logical analysis of such a testing process. We shall discuss an approach by Schlick (1934) because he comes very close to this desideratum: He takes his point of departure from the idea that the test of a scientific statement always ultimately involves the derivation of some statement describing some observable phenomenon. Schlick, in common with other philosophers of science, calls the sentences in which the results of observations of this kind are reported "protocol sentences." Such a sentence may for example have the form: "John Doe perceived at that and that time, at that and that place, this and that." Protocol sentences may thus provide a basis for testing scientific statements, but not an absolutely certain one. They are hypothetical; it is conceivable that despite great care the sentence written down by an observer in the laboratory protocol is false.

Schlick, however, argues that there is another kind of sentence which provides a more suitable basis for the test of scientific sentences than protocol sentences. He calls them "Konstatierungen" and characterizes them as follows: They are descriptions of what is immediately experienced and always have the demonstrative form "here now this," for example, "here now blue," without any reference to an experiencer. Konstatierungen can be known with absolute certainty, though only in the fleeting moment of the occurrence of the experience mentioned in the Konstatierung. In addition, Konstatierungen and the certainty which attaches to them are private. A Konstatierung cannot be written down nor be communicated in words to others because, for lack of general definitions, the meaning of the words "here," "now," "this" can only be indicated by demonstrative gestures, like pointing, and not in words.

Thus, Schlick's Konstatierung can be understood as a description of a nonconceptualized experience by an experiencer during the moment of his experience. We shall revert presently to the difficulties of assigning any role to Konstatierungen in the testing process of scientific sentences. (For critical comments about Schlick's paper, see Ayer, 1953, especially pp. 10, 11, 90, 91; Nagel, 1954, p. 219.)

Despite the importance Schlick assigns to Konstatierungen in the testing process, they cannot, for him, be the basis for the construction of theories, because Konstatierungen are only momentary and have passed when one starts the construction.

A position similar to Schlick's, as to the role of nonconceptualized experiences in the testing process, has been taken by Lewis. He states that "without . . . apprehensions of direct and indubitable content of experience, there could be no basis for any empirical judgment, and no verification of one [1946, p. 182]." In his book, *Mind and the World Order*, Lewis (1956, Chs. 2–5) discusses this in detail. He calls the qualitative characteristics of an immediately given "qualia." They have no names as distinguished from the properties of objects. For Lewis, absorption in the immediately given transcends conceptual thinking altogether, whereas knowledge of objects involves conceptual interpretation. Though the experience of a quale is ineffable, Lewis (1956, p. 125) takes as an example the statement, "this is the same ineffable 'yellow' that I saw yesterday." Speaking in this way about the "ineffable yellow" seems like a contradiction in terms, and, interpreting it as the same as yesterday, contradicts, in our opinion, characteristics which Lewis assigns, as we do, to nonconceptualized experiences, namely, that they are not only ineffable, but propertyless and private as well.

Unless these contradictions are resolved, we do not see how Lewis is entitled to state that "without the correlation of concept and qualia no experience could verify or fail to verify anything [p. 144]."

The treatment of the testing process presented by both Schlick and Lewis is not compatible with the logical analysis presented in this paper: First, the question of the certainty of nonconceptualized experiences is a controversial one in philosophy (see Allport, 1960, p. 139; Ayer, 1956; Black, 1954; Born, 1924, pp. 4–5; Goodman, 1952; Tymieniecka, 1962, pp. 3–16; Weyl, 1949, p. 116). In addition, whatever position one takes about certainty, it is clear that in order to test a scientific statement by a nonconceptualized experience, or by a Konstatierung which purports to be a description of such an experience, the experiencer would have to abstract with reference to some relevant property of the experience. Otherwise, he could not know whether or not the content of his experience confirmed or disconfirmed the statement. Let us consider an example: Suppose an experiencer were to test a sentence referring to the occurrence of a coincidence, for example, between the pointer of an instrument and a mark on a scale. The experiencer might then have an experience which he might reasonably conceptualize, at a later time, as a coincidence. However, during the moment of his nonconceptualized experience, he cannot know whether what he is experiencing is or is not what, in the sentence, is meant by a coincidence, unless he makes a conceptual interpretation of his experience. If the experiencer, during his nonconceptualized experience, *could* know whether what he is experiencing is a coincidence, then he should be able to communicate his experience to others. Conversely, that which cannot be described to others cannot be described to oneself in terms which are clearly understandable to others. We do not see how Lewis or Schlick could overcome this objection. Thus, on the view presented here, nonconceptualized experiences per se cannot be used to test scientific statements.

As mentioned previously, ppp cannot be used as a basis for the construction of theories, nor, as we see now, for the purpose of testing any scientific statement, and ppp cannot even be used as a means of describing experience. Thus, on the view presented here, ppp is not relevant per se for scientific psychology. However, the analysis may have some relevance for understanding other important aspects of ppp.

As mentioned above, any conceptualization of nonconceptualized experience can lead to a feeling that the conceptual statement has impoverished and distorted the experience. The feeling can be particularly strong, for example, with respect to aesthetic experiences, where we may often feel the sheer inability of language to capture the subtlety of such an experience (see Schachtel, 1951). This feeling of impoverishment and distortion may be accompanied by a feeling of disunion between, or separation from, experiencer and that which is experienced. These feelings can become particularly acute when the object of our concern is another human being. Conceptualization, by assigning properties to a person, is sometimes even considered as a dehumanization. Such concerns are prevalent among Existential psychoanalysts and explain in part their rejection of Freud (see May, Angel, & Ellenberger, 1958).

We have quoted Buber at the beginning of this paper because it seems to us that he has clearly understood the advantages and disadvantages inherent in the act of conceptualization. Expressed in Buber's (1958) terminology, an experiencer has the following choice between two modes of relation: Either he may choose to have, in a receptive moment, a direct experience of another human being, a *Thou*, without separation by intervening concepts. But there can be no knowledge in the *I-Thou* relation. Or, he may choose to have knowledge, to describe, and analyze objectively. But in this *I-It* relation, man experiences another human being in separation from him.

A position similar to Buber's has been taken by Tillich (1960). He argues, in effect, that certain nonconceptualized experiences though not valuable for science at all are valuable in another way, namely, as a basis for religion. Similarly, on allegedly empirical grounds, Maslow (1962) has argued that peak experiences (a form of nonconceptualized experience) are valuable in that they promote psychological growth and health. What is maintained here is that any advantages inherent in nonconceptualized experiences are obtained at the price of their irrelevance per se for science. Also, the view presented here should not be interpreted as implying that one should not or cannot take nonconceptualized experiences as an object of scientific investigation. For example, the study of mysticism represents an interesting and legitimate scientific endeavor.

Question of Rapprochement

Despite the fact that the analysis presented here does not permit any role assignment to ppp in scientific psychology, it is of some interest to examine the difficulties confronted by various approaches to rapprochement which would be faced by those psychologists who would not entirely accept the logical analysis presented here.

COMPLEMENTARY ROLES FOR PPP AND BEHAVIORISM

A possible basis for rapprochement between ppp and behaviorism can be developed by assigning to them complementary roles in a unified psychology. We will examine two such possible bases for rapprochement.

A first basis would be afforded by the following two principles:

1(a). Only the methods of the behaviorist (and not those of the ppp) can be used to construct theoretical systems.

1(b). Only the methods of the ppp (and not those of the behaviorist) can be used to test theories. (Of course, 1b is contrary to the position taken in this paper.)

To our knowledge, such a basis for rapprochement has never been suggested by any psychologist. It is compatible with the position of such philosophers as Schlick and Lewis. It is not at all clear that the ppp would be satisfied with this abstention from theorizing as suggested by 1a above. As for condition 1b, most behaviorists would probably find this rather controversial. The behaviorists' insistence on an intersubjectively observable base for testing statements and their demand for observations which result in a high degree of intersubjective agreement tend to restrict the class of statements which could be directly tested to protocol sentences about publicly observable symptoms. No such restriction is implied by a method of test based on nonconceptualized experiences. In general, the class of statements which can be directly tested by nonconceptualized experiences appears to be larger than the class of statements which refers to experiences for which high degrees of intersubjective agreement can be obtained. Thus, if one can allegedly experience emotions as immediately given, then one could test directly statements about emotions. If one believes the mystics and accepts condition 1b, it would be possible to have a nonconceptualized experience of the divine, thus providing a basis for the direct test of statements about the divine. If nonconceptualized experiences are used as a means of testing statements instead of intersubjective tests by behavioristic symptoms, not only is the rational reconstruction of the testing process changed, but also the class of statements directly testable becomes larger. Of course, it is possible to add to condition 1b an arbitrary restriction which would vitiate the behaviorist's probable objection to the enlargement of the class of testable statements. Namely, it is possible to restrict the use of nonconceptualized experiences to the ultimate test of those statements which can be directly tested by behavioristic procedures, for example, to protocol sentences. If this is done, the class of statements which are directly testable is not enlarged. However, the addition of such a restriction would violate the intent of the ppp to study all of experience and to afford equal significance to all aspects of experience. Such a restriction would, in effect, divide the class of nonconceptualized experiences into two subclasses, one of which is assigned the role of testing scientific statements, and the other is not assigned any such role at all.

A second basis for rapprochement follows below:

2(a). Only the methods of ppp (and not those of the behaviorist) can be used to construct theoretical systems. (Of course, 2a is contrary to the position taken in this paper.)

2(b). Only the methods of the behaviorist (and not those of the ppp) can be used to test theoretical systems.

This is the basis of rapprochement suggested by Rogers (1964). The principal difficulty in connection with this basis for rapprochement involves the behaviorist's possible objection to condition 2a. Such a condition apparently restricts the theorist's ability to freely postulate theoretical concepts. Einstein (as cited by Holton, 1965 [2]) has expressed this idea as follows:

> Everything conceptualizable is constructive and not derivable in a logical manner from immediate experience. Therefore we are in principle completely free in the choice of those fundamental conceptions upon which we found our rendition of the world. Everything depends only on this: to what extent our construction is suitable for bringing order into the apparent chaos of the world of experience.

Condition 2a implies that the theorist is permitted to introduce only those concepts which somehow have a foundation in what is given.

TERMINOLOGICAL RAPPROCHEMENT

Any rapprochement between ppp and behaviorism would be dependent on agreement on terminology. There are surely terms in the vocabularies of ppp and behaviorism which could be successfully coordinated. Terms referring to certain sensory experiences, for example, "red," can be coordinated and assigned compatible meanings for both ppp and behaviorism. Other terms, the theoretical status of which has not been extensively developed and which are close to ordinary experiences, might also be assigned compatible meanings, for example, terms referring to

[2] This quote is an English translation by Gerald Holton contained in the paper presented by him at the 11th International Congress of the History of Science, Warsaw and Krakow, August 1965. The German text is contained in Einstein's unpublished papers.

emotional states, such as reverence. However, the fulfillment of this condition is dependent on the progress of psychological theory. As behavioristic psychology develops, terms which are used in a relatively atheoretical way, for example, "fear," acquire modified meanings by virtue of having entered into a network of theoretical laws and relations which serve to specify the meaning of the term. It is difficult to imagine how the modified meaning of such terms can be directly experienced or coordinated in any sense with an immediately given experience. A direct coordination and compatibility of meanings is possible only after their reduction to directly observable symptoms. Another obstacle to the fulfillment of a terminological rapprochement consists in the introduction of terms into a behavioristic psychology which have no counterpart at all in nonconceptualized experience, for example, terms contained in a highly formalistic mathematical model. Thus, as behavioristic psychology develops, the possibility of rapprochement between ppp and behaviorism may grow more remote in this respect. On the other hand, it can happen that theoretical psychology will develop in such a way that there will remain many aspects of nonconceptualized experience which have little counterpart in the terminology of behavioristic psychology, for example, the experience of disgust is at present without any extensively developed counterpart in the theoretical language of behavioristic psychology (see MacLeod, 1964).

There is one way in which future developments within behavioristic psychology might lead to a greater degree of terminological agreement between ppp and behaviorism. As Zener (1958) has pointed out, the insistence that science deals only with statements about intersubjectively valid observations must be qualified if it is to be properly understood. This statement should not be taken to imply that only statements about observations where the intersubjective agreement among a large class of observers is almost perfect should be considered as data in science. Since the degree of agreement with respect to protocol sentences is never perfect, each psychologist is faced with a somewhat arbitrary decision about the degree of agreement with regard to some observation that he will demand. Zener would, for example, have the psychologist study reports about aesthetic qualities of experience which might be based on a less than perfect agreement among a small group of individuals with refined aesthetic sensibilities. To the extent to which behavioristic psychology is open to reports about subtle qualities of experience and is willing to accept them as data to be explained, there should be an increased possibility of terminological agreement between ppp and behaviorism.

References

Allport, G. *The individual and his religion.* New York: Macmillan, 1960.

Ayer, A. J. *Language, truth and logic.* New York: Dover, 1953.

Ayer, A. J. *The problem of knowledge.* Harmondsworth, England: Penguin, 1956.

Bergmann, G. The contribution of John B. Watson. *Psychological Review*, 1956, 63, 265–276.

Black, M. The language of sense-data. In M. Black (Ed.), *Problems of analysis.* Ithaca: Cornell University Press, 1954. Pp. 58–79.

Born, M. *Einstein's theory of relativity.* London: Methuen, 1924.

Brown, R. *Social psychology.* New York: Free Press of Glencoe, 1965.

Buber, M. *I and thou.* New York: Scribners, 1958.

Carnap, R. *Der logische Aufbau der Welt.* Berlin, Germany: Im Weltkreis-Verlag, 1928. (Republished: *Logical reconstruction of the world and problem of appearance in philosophy.* Berkeley: University of California Press, 1966.)

Carnap, R. Nelson Goodman on "Der logische Aufbau der Welt." In P. A. Schlipp (Ed.), *The philosophy of Rudolf Carnap.* LaSalle, Ill.: Open Court, 1963. Pp. 944–947.

Edie, J. M., III. Recent work in phenomenology. *American Philosophical Quarterly*, 1964, 1, 115–128.

Eriksen, C. W. (Ed.), *Behavior and awareness.* Durham: Duke University Press, 1962.

Feigl, H. The "mental" and the "physical." In H. Feigl, M. Scriven, & G. Maxwell (Eds.), *Minnesota studies in the philosophy of science.* Vol. 2. Minneapolis: University of Minnesota Press, 1958. Pp. 370–497.

Garner, W. R., Hake, H. W., & Eriksen, C. W. Operationism and the concept of perception. *Psychological Review*, 1956, 63, 149–159.

Goodman, N. Sense and certainty. *Philosophical Review*, 1952, 61, 160–167.

Havens, J. The participants vs. the observer's frame of reference in the psychological study of religion. *Journal for the Scientific Study of Religion*, 1961, 1, 79–87.

Hempel, C. G., & Oppenheim, P. Studies in the logic of explanation. *Philosophy of Science*, 1948, 15, 135–175.

Husserl, E. *Ideas.* New York: Collier Books, 1962.

James, W. *The principles of psychology.* Vol. 1. New York: Holt, 1890.

James, W. *The meaning of truth.* New York: Longmans, Green, 1910.

Jessor, R. The problem of reductionism in psychology. *Psychological Review*, 1958, 65, 170–178.

Koffka, K. *Principles of gestalt psychology.* New York: Harcourt, Brace, 1935.

Köhler, W. *Gestalt psychology.* New York: Liveright, 1947.

Lewis, C. I. *Knowledge and valuation.* LaSalle, Ill.: Open Court, 1946.

Lewis, C. I. *Mind and the world order.* New York: Dover, 1956.

MacLeod, R. B. Phenomenology: A challenge to experimental psychology. In T. W. Wann (Ed.), *Behaviorism and phenomenology.* Chicago: University of Chicago Press, 1964. Pp. 47–78.

Maslow, A. H. *Toward a psychology of being.* Princeton: Van Nostrand, 1962.

May, R. Contributions of existential psychotherapy. In R. May, E. Angel, & H. F. Ellenberger (Eds.), *Existence.* New York: Basic Books, 1958. Pp. 37–91.

May R., Angel, E., & Ellenberger, E. F. (Eds.) *Existence.* New York: Basic Books, 1958.

Nagel, E. *Sovereign reason.* Glencoe, Ill.: Free Press, 1954.

Northrop, F. S. C. *The logic of the sciences and humanities*. New York: Macmillan, 1948.

Northrop, F. S. C. *Man, nature and God*. New York: Simon & Schuster, 1962.

Reichenbach, H. *Experience and prediction*. Chicago: University of Chicago Press, 1938.

Rogers, C. R. *Toward a science of the person*. In T. W. Wann (Ed.), *Behaviorism and phenomenology*. Chicago: University of Chicago Press, 1964. Pp. 109–140.

Russell, B. *The problem of philosophy*. London: Oxford University Press, 1912.

Schachtel, E. On memory. In P. Mullahy (Ed.), *A study of interpersonal relations; new contributions to psychiatry*. New York: Grove Press, 1951. Pp. 1–49.

Schlick, M. Ueber das Fundament der Erkenntnis. *Erkenntnis*, 1934, 4, 79–99.

Stace, W. T. *Mysticism and philosophy*. Philadelphia: Lippincott, 1960.

Tillich, P. The relationship today between science and religion. In J. A. Clark (Ed.), *The student seeks an answer*. Waterville: Colby College Press, 1960. Pp. 297–306.

Tymieniecka, A. T. *Phenomenology and science in contemporary European thought*. New York: Noonday Press, 1962.

Weyl, H. *Philosophy of mathematics and natural science*. Princeton: Princeton University Press, 1949.

Zaehner, R. C. *Mysticism sacred and profane*. London: Oxford University Press, 1957.

Zener, K. The significance of experience of the individual for the science of psychology. In H. Feigl, M. Scriven, & G. Maxwell (Eds.), *Minnesota studies in the philosophy of science*. Vol. 2. Minneapolis: University of Minnesota Press, 1958. Pp. 354–369.

10   THE CHALLENGE TO PSYCHOLOGICAL THEORISTS
James J. Jenkins

It is difficult to present some concluding note that will capture for the reader the excitement and irritation of the mealtime and evening arguments among the participants, the interest and intensity of the discussions, the positions explained informally, the changes of opinion and the new understandings generated by this conference.[1] Surely the record in this book, however, makes clear that clashes of opinion did occur and that both understandings and misunderstandings developed spirited debate.

---

[1] The conference referred to by Jenkins was held at the University of Kentucky in the Spring of 1966. The purpose of the conference was to have psychologists from a representative sample of specialities address themselves to the topic of verbal behavior theory and its relation to general stimulus-response theory.

SOURCE: James J. Jenkins, in *Verbal Behavior and General Behavior Theory*, eds., Theodore R. Dixon and David L. Horton (Englewood Cliffs, N.J.: Prentice-Hall, 1968), ch. 21, pp. 538–49. Copyright © 1968 by Prentice-Hall, Inc. Reprinted by permission of the publisher.

From the very outset of the conference the challenge to established positions in psychology was obvious. Proponents of "the establishment" felt that their positions were distorted and caricatured. Opponents felt that "the establishment" was being evasive and blind. Both groups, while trying to avoid doing so, came dangerously near the treacherous tactic of telling the other THE CORRECT WAY to conduct science. Since I feel quite strongly about the issues involved and especially strongly about telling someone else how to pursue his job, an appropriate focus for my remarks might be the recent histories of psychology and linguistics and the prescriptive tendencies of psychologists and linguists.

In the 1930's and '40's, psychology was shaken with furious debates about what was and what was not "scientific" in psychology. Advocates were outrageously prescriptive. It is easy to remember meetings at which distinguished psychologists, purple in the face, told other distinguished psychologists that what they were doing might be entertaining or clever but it was not and would never be scientific psychology. At many schools graduate students were given the "correct" view and carefully inoculated with the proper philosophical serum against the "incorrect" views. One must seriously question whether the cause of science was advanced by these battles.

During the same period the linguists were also impressed with a strong view about the philosophy of science, and Bloomfield firmly enjoined linguists not to have anything to do with mentalism and with psychologists.[2] As a result, linguists remained psychologically innocent except for naive behaviorism, and at the same time the psychologists

[2] L. Bloomfield, Language (New York: Holt, Rinehart and Winston, 1933), pp. 37–38. "A linguistic observer therefore can describe the speech-habits of a community without resorting to statistics. Needless to say, he must work conscientiously and, in particular, he must record every form he can find and not try to excuse himself from this task by appealing to the reader's common sense or to the structure of some other language or to some psychological theory, and, above all, he must not select or distort the facts according to his views of what the speakers out to be saying. Aside from its intrinsic value for the study of language, a relevant and unprejudiced description of this kind serves as a document of major importance for psychology. The danger here lies in mentalistic views of psychology, which may tempt the observer to appeal to purely spiritual standards instead of reporting the facts. To say, for instance, that combinations of words which are 'felt to be' compounds have only a single high stress (e.g., blackbird as opposed to black bird), is to tell exactly nothing, since we have no way of determining what the speakers may 'feel': the observer's task was to tell us, by some tangible criterion, or, if he found none, by a list, in which combinations of words are pronounced with a single high stress. A worker who accepts the materialistic hypothesis in psychology is under no such temptation; it may be stated as a principle that in all sciences like linguistics, which observe some specific type of human activity, the worker must proceed exactly as if he held the materialistic view. This practical effectiveness is one of the strongest considerations in favor of scientific materialism."

remained in ignorance of the concepts of linguistic structure. With few exceptions, psychologists at the beginning of this period treated language as a "word heap." Psychological theories of meaning were (and for the most part still are) theories about the reference relation—a kind of linkage between words and the world. With increasing sophistication, psychologists progressed toward models which considered language as consisting of strings of words (the "information theory" approach) or as composed of whole utterances which were relatively unanalyzed.

In the early 1950's the great meeting of the fields of linguistics and psychology took place under the gentle guidance of the Social Science Research Council (see Osgood and Sebeok, 1954). I remember quite well the fervor with which we were informed by some of the leading linguists of the day that linguistics was virtually a "closed book," "the most nearly complete of the social sciences," the "most objective of all behavioral disciplines." In a class on grammar one could hear the astonishing claim that in principle one could feed an appropriately programed computer the right phonetic transcription of a large corpus and the computer would produce the phonemics, morphemics, and syntax of the language. It was also explained that in practice "short cuts" (such as pair tests and knowledge of meanings) were used to achieve this result but that they could always be replaced by completely objective analysis that produced the correct set of concepts for the language. The psychologist, green with envy, confessed that he had not yet reached such a blessed state but felt that he was on the way. Surely we were encouraged by the obvious success of the simple, operational, positivistic approach of the linguist and determined to pursue the same tactics. The psychologist had a nice theory that made contiguity and succession the key ingredients, and the linguist had just the data to show that that was the right approach. All that remained was to bridge the gap between the linguists' putatively perfect analysis and the psychologists' entirely adequate theory. It turned out that bridging the gap was no great problem. Item-and-arrangement grammars and mediation theory were seen to be variations of the same line of thought. The linguist looks at distribution of an item in the corpus and if he finds another that has the same distribution, he knows that it is the same item (or belongs to the same class of items). To the psychologist, items which follow the same kinds of items or precede the same kinds of items are equivalent responses and equivalent stimuli; if they are not at the outset, they become so via mediation (see Jenkins and Palermo, 1964, and Jenkins, 1965). The only sad note in this little story is that by the time the bridge was completed, someone (namely Chomsky) dynamited the structure at the linguistic end.

Though many of us read *Syntactic Structures* when it first appeared, I think most of us failed to appreciate what was in store. We felt that transformations were appealing devices that we would have to give some thought to as soon as we had worked out the basic problem of the item and arrangement grammar. We failed to realize that a fundamentally new approach to grammar had been presented and that a "generative grammar" was a quite different kind of object from the old "descriptive grammar," exemplifying a different approach to science and making radically different claims.

As the consequences of the linguistic revolution became clearer, the psychologist's position became more and more painful. Having worked hard to build his bridge to linguistics, it was difficult (to say the least) to hear that the discipline was no longer there and that no one had really ever said that it was there anyway. Accompanying this was the consequent charge that the psychologist had been wasting his time by trying to do what he felt he had just done. The words "trivial" and "uninteresting" (even though used in their logical sense) are scarcely palatable. As one tries to understand what has happened, it is not helpful to be beaten about the ears or to be told that the thing that one does not understand is "obvious." If, in addition, the linguist has just been battling with his colleagues, he is in no mood for quiet explication. What the linguist was saying was that the new object he was describing was a fundamentally different kind of thing from what one thought it was and that it required a fundamentally different kind of machinery than the old system implied. In short, he was saying, no amount of revision, patching, or adding *neo*before the name was going to make it work.

Now, let us all agree that no one can tell another how to do his science. Philosophers of science in the main have quit trying to prescribe, and so, I think, must we. The job of the philosopher is to find out what it is that scientists do, especially when they are doing their science well or when the science is going wrong, and try to understand the process. One of the things that he should be able to do, however, is to answer questions about the formal properties of models that a science might employ. Essentially that is what happened here. We asked what a model, written in the surface language alone, might do, and when that question was answered, everyone said, "Don't tell me that! Tell me something different." I don't think that Fodor, Bever, Garrett, or McNeill care whether anyone says that they are being prescriptive or not. What I seem to hear them say is that if you want to know how they feel about a psychology of language and why they feel this is an answer. If you think you have a better way to handle language, you can try, but if you think you are going to use the old kind of machinery, you will be disappointed because there is a formal proof that this kind of machine won't do it.

You are free to try the rejoinder that Cofer has suggested. Lots of formal proofs seem wrong. Bumblebees *do* fly. But note that the "bumblebee proof" is telling you, not that bumblebees cannot fly, but rather that you cannot explain the flight of bumblebees. Bumblebees can *not* fly as other insects do. That is what the proof said. When one finds a new kind of stabilizer (vibrating rods with knobs on the end of them), one has in fact a different kind of machine. The assertion being made here is that if language depended on surface chains, it could not be the kind of language that it is. If flying depended only on gross body structure, weight, and wing shape, bumblebees could not fly.

The intuitive argument concerning the nature of language structure rests on a very simple set of notions having to do with many-to-one and one-to-many mappings. The purpose is to show in what way things that are said to be similar are similar and ways in which things that are different are said to be different. You have all seen such illustrations before; a typical complaint is that the same examples always come up over and over again. If the thing being illustrated is so important, why aren't there more examples of it? Or, as a distinguished psychologist recently said, "All the linguists go around with their little bags of sentences."

I think that psychologists need some coaching concerning the use of arguments by example and illustration. Each example is supposed to be an instance of a whole class of such behaviors. One is supposed to twist and turn and examine each such example until he is sure that he understands the implication. The same example may be used all the time because it serves as a familiar label for the distinction being made. I can say, "We are running a discrimination test on the 'growling of lions' versus 'raising of flowers' difference," and everybody who is in the club is supposed to know that means we are testing sentences that differ in the base though there is no difference in the derived sentence structure. Notice that the verbal learning fraternity can say, "I ran an $A–B$, $B–C$, $A–C$ paradigm against an $A–B$, $A–B'$." And within a very small club (a few Minnesotans) you can talk about "running paradigm I and III." But one does not conclude because of the labels that there is a single instance being examined. In fact, just the opposite is intended. Similarly, when I say that "The boy hit the ball" and "The ball was hit by the boy" are the same, implying that there is an abstract level at which the two sentences are represented in the same way, I also mean to imply that this relation holds for some indefinitely large number of pairs of sentences. The sentences are obviously different at the physical level, but the theory of the language must show the equivalence of active sentences to their appropriate passives at at least one abstract level.

In a different way the ambiguous sentence furnishes a compelling argument. The traditional references to "The shooting of the hunters was dreadful" or to "flying planes" or "cooking apples" serve to direct your attention to the fact that some sentences can be understood in more than one way. What does it mean to take a sentence in two ways? It presumably means that there are ways you can operate on that stimulus to see it as the outcome of two different derivations. The stimulus is *in some sense* two different things. Specifying exactly *in what sense* the stimulus is two different things demands levels of abstraction that can project overlapping or identical outcomes onto the surface level. How one recognizes this possibility when confronted with the surface level alone is indeed a formidable puzzle for the psychologist.

Another interesting variation is the case where, though the physical product is different, the sentences may be seen to be the same at a low level of abstraction. And, at still more abstract levels, they may be seen to be different again. Here the canonical examples are: "The growling of lions is unpleasant" and "The raising of flowers is difficult." Clearly the words are different and the messages are different. However, it is easy to see that the sequence of form classes is identical and at that level of abstraction the sentences are the same. Another and much deeper look, however, shows that the sentences must differ in some more fundamental sense. The illustration is intended to lead you to the conclusion that two vast sets of sentences differ in exactly the same way and that when you encountered the sentence "The shooting of the hunters was dreadful," you put first one of these derivations on it and then the other. The ambiguous case is the case where these two families of sentences fuse at the surface level.

Thus, sentence examples are used to indicate the unlimited numbers of cases where (1) the same structure of the obvious stimulus is mapped on different derivations, (2) different structures in the obvious stimuli map on to the same derivation, and (3) different structures in the obvious stimulus map on to the same abstract structure and then diverge again. The way to make clear what one is talking about is to specify exactly what is meant when one talks about these various abstract levels. And that, as Bever said more elegantly than I can, is a purpose of the grammar. When someone then asks about the nature of the stimulus, you can tell him at each level of representation what it is that you are talking about.

Now, surely, the psychologist working in his laboratory can choose one level and never move away from it. He need not concern himself with any other. And to some reasonable extent he can get away with it. But he must also, of course, be willing to be told that he is not studying all of language behavior. Language behavior is not at a particular level. It is the entire representation that is entailed at all levels of description. It can be *represented* at each of those levels but it cannot be identified with any one level.

Notice that the implications of this kind of thinking are far-reaching. This analysis implies that there are no simple ways to treat the surface level to make it yield up the deeper levels in some automatic fashion. If one takes the large corpus in a fine phonetic transcription and puts it in the computer for analysis, all one can expect to get now is confetti. If the psychologist picks one level and sticks to it, he will never see the rest of language behavior, and he is going to have to solve some very funny problems, like accounting for data that are the same when there is no reason to suppose that they should be the same and data that are different when there is no reason to suppose that they should be different. Such a decision puts one in the world of Alice's white knight in *Through the Looking Glass,* wandering about in a two-dimensional world and trying to explain the unfathomable events of the three-dimensional world that intersects his plane of observation. The notions of deep structure and abstract equivalence that the linguist is bringing to us are important notions for all psychologists, not just those interested in language. The ethologists are coming with the same message from a very different base. My feeling is that psychologists of this generation ought to give them very careful and attentive hearings.

Similarly, this conception of language has many important practical consequences. It helps explain, for example, why it is that we have failed to build a reading machine for the blind. As long as language is regarded as a collection of diverse, arbitrary sounds that have some simple invariance, it seems as if we should be able to get letters in a book to make distinctive sounds and we would have a bookreader that anyone could be trained to listen to. The newer conception of language suggests that the nature of language is different from that, and the research of the Haskins Laboratories shows that the notions of simple invariance have to be replaced with a variety of many-to-one and one-to-many mappings. The same set of reasons explain why it is that we do not yet have the voice typewriter that has so often been promised. And the prospect of high-quality, automatic machine translation of language has shifted from something that was to be achieved by next week to something that may well be impossible in our lifetimes.

One thing that psychologists also need to note is that the new viewpoint does not by any means "wipe out" or destroy the research that has been done. Clearly, what is known must be integrated with the more elaborate conception at the appropriate levels. We know that subjects can form point-to-point correspondences between colored figures and nonsense syllables. We know that such learning is tedious, slow, and difficult; but we also know that there are rules for manipulating these correspondences (e.g., giving a color syllable before a shape syllable) which subjects can learn with great speed. Learning new point-to-point correspondences is very hard; if we scramble the colors and names, we have a messy and difficult task; but if we change a manipulation rule (e.g., reverse the order of the color and form syllables), the new set of responses can be produced appropriately with amazing speed. This suggestion concerning the differences in the processes involved is very like the suggestions made by Lyle Bourne concerning the separation of rule learning from other learning in the concept formation domain. It does not imply that one kind of learning is better or worse or more important than another; it merely says that the task involves more than one kind of learning, that it has more than one level.

We psychologists have often shown our reluctance to study learning tasks that deviate from traditional procedures. We would like to have situations in which there is no question concerning the units that the subject is employing and the ways in which he employs them, but we also know that we have not been able to find such a case. Subjects seem to persist in trying to do more than we want them to do; and as a result we have to concern ourselves with response integration, stimulus differentiation, response differentiation, stimulus and response classes, selective fractionation of the stimulus, etc. If we present the subject with textual material, we face the problem that he may have perfect recall of the content but not of the form—i.e., he gives us a good paraphrase. Our inability to handle this kind of complexity drives us back to observations that we can call "more objective," but we must note that our retreat does not remove the importance or relevance of the original problem. It ought not act to redefine the field of acceptable problems. At this meeting, Dulany has shown us that one can use one's own knowledge of the meaning of a proposition to interpret the subject's verbal behavior and that this information can be used in objective fashion to describe the subject's other behaviors with great accuracy. In my eyes, this is a very important demonstration.

I believe that our experience in our own laboratories is pushing us in the directions that the linguist is arguing for. Tulving points out that subjects have units, that experimenters have units, and that they are not the same in the general case. Osgood pointed out long ago that subjects in one of Cofer's experiments could have been *generating* the lists they were supposed to be "learning" in the transfer stage of Cofer's experiment. In essence he was saying that the subject learned the first list one way and then learned to produce the second list in some other way. Surely something different was happening for the transfer lists. Just because it was not what the experimenter had in mind does not take it out of the domain of psychology or relieve us of the necessity of dealing with it. It does, however, argue against some kind of single principle, single process, single operation kind of psychology. Maltzman talks about an odd abstraction; a stimulus in which the critical property of a word is not what it is but whether it has been heard before in the experiment. This means, of course, that the first time the word appears in the experiment and the seond time it appears, it is a dramatically different stimulus. Surely this is a different level from the raw stimulus of acoustic disturbance. All of us who have worked in verbal learning have dealt with the many phenomena of integration of sequences. One begins with a behavior which is best seen as a series of elements, but during the course of the experiment the string becomes something different. It becomes a unit and a member of a pool or collection that is new.

I used to ask myself the question that someone asked here in the last few days, "What is *the* unit of language behavior?" I have folders full of notes on that question that never seem to get anywhere. I now believe that the reason these discussions never go anywhere is that this is the wrong kind of question to ask about complexly organized behavior. If we were omniscient and knew all that there was to know about language behavior all the way from the semantic structures down through the syntactics, the phrase structures, the transformations, down into the terminal strings and the mapping into symbols and the symbols into motor commands going on through the articulators and the effects of those on the air flow and the acoustic effects impinging on someone else's ear, etc., it would not occur to us to ask what *the* unit of behavior was supposed to be. We would know, I presume, that the behavior could be represented at any level, and at that level we would know what kinds of units or structures were appropriate to that representation; and, importantly, we would know how these were constrained by adjacent levels.

An example of linguistic constraint is found in our own invention—the nonsense syllables. If one talks about the meaningfulness of patterns of consonant-vowel-consonant in English, it is difficult to make sense of the data without taking "the right kind" of constraints into consideration. Raw frequency of letters or sounds is of little use. For example, one must attend to syllable boundaries and the differing effects of initial and final position. In the interpretation of a graphic symbol one must ask what the context is (e.g., C before O is /k/ but C before E is /s/; however, C in final position is /k/ in both cases). If one permits oneself to look both up and down the hierarchy, it is possible to make sense of the otherwise mystifying difference in C-V-C nonsense syllables.

Similarly, if we are interested in observing how a skilled reader reads a sentence, we find him responding to many cues that are not represented in any simple way in the material before him. We can *hear* parentheses or brackets or pauses in his sentences which he (and we) arrange to get in the right linguistic places, but we will not find much in the way of cues in the written material to explain this behavior. Similarly, he will be able to provide paraphrases and rereadings which must look for their explanation even further up the hierarchy of the sentence but are not present in any direct way in the surface structure or the symbols on the page. In these cases it is manifestly irrelevant to ask what is *the* unit of language.

If we grant that we must provide at least some levels of representation in language, it appears that we will find greatest agreement in making a division between syntax and semantics. It is the consensus of this group that the semantic problem is formidable. Indeed, all of psychology and linguistics must agree that this is a most important problem and one on which little progress has been made. The philosophers to whom we might turn for guidance seem to be in the same difficult position.

Deese and Osgood (and, long before them, Rogét) have a feeling that there ought to be some way to represent meaning by a set of distinctive features or dimensions. There is a persistent hope that we will be able to specify dimensions or domains which can systematically exhaust the varieties of meanings. Yet Deese, who has just completed such an effort, told us on the first day of the conference that he believes that it cannot be done in that fashion. At present, he can see no end to the number of dimensions one might have to employ; and that outcome is, of course, fatal to the approach. An infinite set of dimensions to describe meaning is no gain over no dimensions at all.

How, then, shall we consider this problem? Mandler proposes that we regard words as clustered in arrays and that we consider the arrays as being multi-dimensional; but he must wind up in the same situation. How many arrays do we need? How many relations between arrays will be required to specify all the interconnections? It seems to me that Mandler, too, fails to solve the problem; rather, his work suggests how great a problem we have.

Kjeldergaard offers help in the other direction. His work convinces him that the typical measures that we use in the laboratory (frequency, m, association value, semantic differential ratings, etc.) are all highly related. While one can find instances where the measures conflict (e.g., similar words that are associates $vs.$ similar words that are not associates), by and large, there is a component of psychological importance that is common to all of these measures and may be characterizable in some simple way. Osgood's position is similar to this, I think. While he will concede that there may be something to the notion that the dimensions of meaning are inexhaustible, he believes that there is a large core of meaning that we can isolate and that we ought to do that and try to get ahead with the task. While I have some sympathy with this pragmatic point of view, I cannot believe that it is going to be very useful in the long run in advancing psychological theory. In part, the commonalities we observe and the intercorrelations we find between measures are the consequence of our crude manipulations and our weak tests of equivalence. If one even approaches the question of the degree to which subjects can discriminate between meanings of words under the most favorable conditions (i.e., if one asks about competency), it is clear that we have not begun to touch the problem.

I feel with Deese that the need is for a device which can generate the dimensions of meaning we want for given purposes and given situations. What such a device might look like, I cannot imagine, but it is easy for me to believe that human beings have such a capacity and that the counting of observed dimensions is a never-ending task which perhaps indexes human needs more than human capacities.

This leads me naturally into the issue of instructions with which Dr. Postman has already treated. I only want to echo his remarks as strongly as possible. The investigator must ask himself what it is that he wants to know. If he is interested in what the subject *will do,* that is one kind of problem. The questions are phrased, "What does S do under conditions X, Y, and Z? " But, if you want to know what the subject *can do,* it should be clear that this is a different kind of question. One is presumbably trying to ask a question about the subject's capacity under the most favorable circumstances that can be provided.

In the research that we are trying to do in our laboratories at Minnesota, we are more interested in the second kind of question. We know that the subject brings all kinds of special instructions to the laboratory with him. If we want him to sort sentences into active and passive sentence types, we will have to wait for him to sort through all manner of semantic groupings (pleasant-unpleasant, animate-inanimate, happy-sad, common-uncommon, etc.) and obvious physical properties (order, length, position, etc.) before he arrives at grammatical sorts at all. However, if the experimenter keeps rejecting sorts that the subject makes he will, in over half the cases, eventually get to the one wanted—actives *vs.* passives. This kind of experiment is rich in information about what the subject *does do,* but that is not what we wanted to know about. We want to know whether he *can* sort active and passive sentences. A very simple thing to do is to ask him; it is surprising how fast one can cover the ground in that way.

As an aside, it is of some interest to note that many of our psychological friends regard this kind of experimentation as unethical, immoral, or simply nonscientific. They seem to believe that one must make the subject guess what the experimenter wants or that one must show that the behavior is some kind of automatic consequence of a reinforcement program to have the experiment "count" as real psychology. I think this is a direct result of confusing the two types of experimentation. An error on the other side is to assume that if one does not get the desired behavior under verbal instruction, it is not part of the capacity of the subject. This view is equally naive, of course. Many subjects make fine discriminations for which they have no verbal labels or even incorrect labels. To expect them to respond to the experimenter's words appropriately is wildly optimistic. In informal conversation, Dr. Postman furnished an excellent example of appropriate procedure. He was running subjects in successive three-stage mediation problems. He explained the relation between the lists on the first day. Subjects said that they understood. On the second day he repeated the entire procedure, and this time the subjects said, "Now I *really* understand." The instructions which seem to be understood are more thoroughly and deeply understood once the subject has actual experience with the situation.

Particularly with problems concerning the linguistic system, where so much of the subjects skill and knowledge is unconscious, the questions of what constitute appropriate and adequate instruction are thorny ones. An instance is furnished here by a study that we have recently completed (see Jenkins, Foss, and Greenberg, 1966). Subjects were presented with a six-pair paired-associate list to learn. The list was systematically structured from a linguistic point of view. The stimuli were unvoiced stops (PA, KA, TA, etc.), and the responses were the appropriately matched voiced stops (BA, GA, DA, etc.). If subjects are merely instructed to learn this set of pairs in the usual fashion, the systematic arrangement of the pairs confers no advantage over a list that is nonsystematically arranged. This shows that this variable *under these conditions* does not influence what a subject *does do*. If, however, we inject more information into the instructions by telling the subjects that there is a system in the arrangement, the learning is faster. If we also add that it has something to do with the way the syllables sound, however, there is no added advantage. If, on the other hand, we add, "Pay attention to what your mouth is doing" and omit reference to sound, subjects show markedly faster learning. Interestingly enough, though the instruction to "pay attention to your mouth" helps engage the appropriate system of regularities, many of the subjects report at the end that they were helped by the fact that the syllables "sounded alike." In this case it is clear that the capacity of the subject can be brought to bear on this problem by a specific instruction which at the end he may not even acknowledge that he used. In the various conditions of this experiment we have a series of lessons concerning the difference between can-do and does-do experiments and the tricky business of finding ways to instruct subjects which will, in fact, engage the capabilities that we believe can be brought to bear on the task.

Finally, I would like to add a brief word to the discussion of the job of science and the relative importance of description, prediction, and control on the one hand and explanation and understanding on the other. I do not think that it is wise to try to legislate another person's interests in the pursuit of science, but I do feel that we can try to understand what the other person is saying. As I see it, much of the argument hinges on whether one wants to do a psychology which at some point has a box labeled "organism" or "human being" or whether one wants to go ahead and analyze that portion of the system too. Surely, if one wishes to develop a technology to shape or control a piece of behavior, it should be possible. I care very much about this problem when I think of applications of psychology and most especially when I think of my children in school. However, when I ask myself what I want to know when I go to work in the laboratory, I find that I am interested in what goes on inside the organism. I really do want to know what goes on "in the head." I would hate to have to support an argument to the effect that this will necessarily lead to better control or better prediction. I must insist that these are not my immediate aims and that I am not at all crestfallen if I fail to show someone how to teach Freshman English better than it is now taught. Understanding and explanation themselves are adequate goals for me at this time. And though I will bet that in the very long run they will make better prediction and control possible, I do not think that makes much difference right now.

A charming and intriguing example of the difference between understanding and description is found in the persistent puzzle of the great English monument, Stonehenge.[3] In the last three years renewed attention has been given to these "rude, enormous monoliths" of Salisbury Plain. Stonehenge poses a set of disturbing questions: Why was it built? What is it supposed to be? How was it to be used? What is its purpose? None of the questions are answered, of course, in the straightforward description of the site as a physical object.

If one has some hypotheses, however, he can distinguish between relevant and accidental features of the monument with respect to that hypothesis and perhaps seek confirmation or disconfirmation of his notions by relating these features to other phenomena. The recent excitement was generated by a set of hypotheses concerning the function of Stonehenge as an astronomical observatory and computer. Confirmation of the hypotheses required the aid of ancillary sciences for describing the monument as it must have been originally, for dating purposes, for ascertaining the positions of astronomical objects and celestial events that one might assume to have been important, etc. In short, an elaborate theoretical and constructual net had to be built up to provide the basis for identifying confirmatory evidence if it did exist. Then a computer was set to work to compare relationships at the site to maximum and minimum elevations of the sun and moon and to the dating of events such as eclipses which were assumed to be of import to astronomical observers.

These studies yielded overwhelming evidence that this enormous device could have been used as a precise calendar, quartering the year with great exactness and providing counting points sufficient to keep

[3] For an account of the research and its related developments the reader is directed to *Stonehenge Decoded,* by Gerald S. Hawkins in collaboration with John B. White. The book provides not only an extensive account of the older and newer research but also reprints Hawkins' articles from *Nature* and *Science.*

track of events of importance between the quarters and to provide sufficient information to predict eclipses of the moon. Indeed, the very location of the monument can then be seen as determined since it makes possible regularities of the physical design features which would not have been possible in another latitude if the same celestial events were to be observed.

It is also interesting to note that this speculation is not without independent corroboration. If one addresses his attention to other, presumably related, stone circles of the same historical period in England, Scotland, and continental Europe, one should now be able to predict in what respects these other structures would be different from Stonehenge because of differences in latitude, given that the astronomical hypotheses are correct. If this proves possible, one must believe that Stonehenge is now understood and explained in a different, more elegant, and more beautiful way than it was when it was described only as a collection of physical properties.

I hope the point of the analogy is clear. The identification of important and relevant aspects of behavior to include in our descriptions is likely to be in large part dependent on our deeper understanding of the roots and sources of the behavior itself. When we understand the deep structures of behavior, our understanding of the relevant aspects of the surface structures should be greatly enriched.

References

Jenkins, J. J., "Mediation Theory and Grammatical Behavior," in S. Rosenberg, ed., *Directions in Psycholinguistics*. New York: The Macmillan Company, 1965.

——, D. J. Foss, and J. H. Greenberg, "Phonological Distinctive Features as Cues in Learning" (manuscript), 1966.

——, and D. S. Palermo, Mediation Processes and the Acquisition of Linguistic Structure," in U. Bellugi and R. W. Brown, eds., *The Acquisition of Language. Monographs of the Society for Research Child Development*, Vol. 29, No. 1, 1964, pp. 79–92.

Osgood, C. E., and T. A. Sebeok, "Psycholinguistics: A Survey of Theory and Research Problems," *Supplement to the Journal of Abnormal and Social Psychology*, 1954, pp. 203.

PART III THE PSYCHOLOGY OF SCHOOLING

The practitioner has not waited for results from the psychology laboratory in order to accomplish his work. Educational psychology, viewed as an applied field, has proceeded to engage the phenomenon of schooling and to effect it by manipulating a variety of environmental events.

The study by Rainey is a modern version of the traditional methods study. One factor that has served to modernize curriculum research is the interest of subject matter specialists such as Karplus, a physicist. Another factor is the work of psychologists such as Jensen and Keislar. In the essays included here Jensen explains how component processes in the analysis of laboratory learning can be used to account for such things as spelling behavior, while Keislar uses Skinnerian principles of practice to establish an understanding of arithmetic.

Knowledge cannot be acquired unless the learner attends to the stimuli used to communicate it. Recent work by Rothkopf is included to show how behaviors that govern the learning process can be manipulated by the context of written instruction.

The paper by Gardner and Johnson represents an attempt to assess achievement in terms of a specific curriculum model. A special feature of this study is that the testing instrument employed was primarily diagnostic rather than geared to specific skills or knowledges in the subject matter. We need to know much more about the role such instruments can play in evaluating learning outcomes.

11 THE EFFECTS OF DIRECTED VERSUS NON-DIRECTED LABORATORY WORK ON HIGH SCHOOL CHEMISTRY ACHIEVEMENT
Robert G. Rainey

Introduction

Within the last five years the National Science Foundation has sponsored major curriculum revision projects in the area of physics, chemistry, and biology. These have become known as PSSC physics, BSCS biology, and either CBA or CHEM Study chemistry.* The latter two present up-to-date subject matter chemistry, but present opposite approaches to the learning of laboratory techniques and procedures.

The Chemical Bond Approach (CBA) laboratory manual contains experiments designed to define the framework within which the student is to operate, but do not tell the student the sequence of steps he must go through or the other procedural details to which he must pay attention in order to arrive at a solution to the laboratory problem with which he is confronted. The Chemical Education Materials Study Course (CHEM Study) presents the student with an excellent sequence of experiments carefully designed to point out to the beginning student all the variables he must account for by listing for the student the kinds of things that he must do and not do, and by directing the student step by step through rather detailed experiments.

This study was not an attempt to measure the CBA program against the CHEM Study program. Rather, it was an attempt to evaluate the effectiveness of the kinds of laboratory approach the two courses offer.

Related Studies

In reviewing the studies relating to the role of the science laboratory, one finds that the use of the laboratory for problem solving has been done in all fields of science teaching. Kruglak,[1] Balcziak,[2] and Perlman [3]

---

* PPSC: Physical Science Study Committee, MIT, 1956–60. BSCS: Biological Sciences Curriculum Study, Colorado University, 1959–61. CBA: Chemical Bond Approach Committee, Earlham College, Richmond, Indiana, 1959–61. CHEMS: Chemical Education Materials Study, University of California at Berkeley, 1959–61.

SOURCE: Robert G. Rainey, "The Effects of Directed versus Non-Directed Laboratory Work on High School Chemistry Achievement," *Journal of Research in Science Teaching*, 3, no. 4 (December 1965), 286–92. Reprinted by permission of John Wiley & Sons, Inc.

in physics, Gunkle,[4] Thelen,[5] and Boeck [6] in chemistry, Mason,[7] Olson,[8] and Dearden [9] in biological science are just a few investigators examining the use of individual laboratory work in the various sciences. On the basis of evidence presented in these studies, one must conclude that the use of the inductive-deductive or problem-solving method in laboratory work was more effective than purely deductive or "traditional" methods. In this sense, the "traditional" method is taken to mean an approach directed toward verifying facts rather than solving a problem.

Several studies have been directed toward comparing individual laboratory work with lecture demonstration of the same material. (See references, 1 and 2.) Ward [10] and Novak,[11] among others, found that when students watched the teacher or someone else demonstrate the laboratory work, there were seldom any measurable differences in learning facts and principles.

The present study was concerned with presenting students with problem-solving situations in the high school chemistry laboratory, and examining the effects of this approach on the learning of facts and principles, the acquisition of the ability to use the problem-solving method, and the retention of facts learned after applying the problem-solving method.

The Problem

This study was designed to measure the effects on learning high school chemistry, of laboratory exercises with specific and detailed directions given in a directed way versus the same exercises presented in the form of problems without directions for their solution. With all other classwork kept equal, do students do as well in chemistry when their laboratory work is conducted in a directed as contrasted with a non-directed way?

Population

The students used in this study were enrolled in four classes of chemistry at South High School, Minneapolis, Minnesota. All students were seniors taking chemistry as an elective subject. In the year of this study, 324 students were graduated with 124, or 38%, having taken chemistry. They were distributed in four classes of 32, 31, 31, and 30 students each. These students had typically taken at least one year of algebra, and a year of some other science before their enrollment in chemistry as seniors.

Description of the Experimental Treatments

Under the assumptions that individual laboratory work contributes to student achievement and that the objectives of the high school chemistry course in this study would be measured by written tests, and a performance test, the two treatments under study were differentiated as follows:

THE NON-DIRECTED LABORATORY GROUP

One half of each class was randomly assigned to this group. When the instructor felt that enough background material had been discussed in the recitation-discussion sessions involving both groups together, this group went into the laboratory with a problem to solve and no directions as to procedure other than test material and notes from the discussions. Sixteen experiments, four during each nine-week quarter, were performed during the school term.

THE DIRECTED LABORATORY GROUP

One half of each class was randomly assigned to this group. The students of this treatment group waited in the classroom with text assignments to do while the non-directed groups completed their laboratory work. Upon entering the laboratory they picked up laboratory notebooks which outlined in detail what they were to do. This group also performed sixteen experiments during the school term. The experiments were concerned with the same problems as the non-directed group but detailed instructions and directions for performing the experiments were provided.

Elements common to both treatment groups include: (1) both groups were present when the recitation-discussion material was presented (every effort was made to keep this material constant for all classes); (2) notebook write-ups of the experiments were done by each treatment group (a regular format was followed, listing the problem, procedure, findings, calculations, and conclusions); (3) each treatment group waited in the classroom adjoining the laboratory when the other group was in the laboratory. Class work during this waiting time consisted of text assignments, problem assignments, and current discussion materials assignments. Since the non-directed groups took almost twice as long to do a given experiment, these non-directed groups had to use time outside of class to finish the assignments the directed group did in the classroom.

Experimental Design

The statistical design used in this study was a modification of a randomized block design. Each of the four classes represented a block, with the students within each class (block) randomly assigned to treatments. The blocks were then stratified into three ability levels on the basis of grade-point averages obtained over the previous two years of high school. The achievement level used to divide the blocks into ability groups was the same for all blocks.

This design was analyzed by means of a three-way analysis of variance and covariance, using the four classes, two treatments, and three student ability levels—high, middle, and low—as the three dimensions. The assumptions of normality and homogeneity of variance were tested and accepted for each analysis of variance, with two exceptions. The homogeneity of variance was rejected on two pre-tests. Examination of subgroup variances showed one high-ability subgroup from each treatment had significantly greater variance, suggesting a more variable background before entering chemistry than the other subgroups.

Measuring Instruments

Four examinations were used to evaluate the outcomes of this study. Two of the three achievement tests were commercially prepared; one was developed by the investigator. A fourth test, a performance test which consisted of a laboratory problem, was presented to a random sample of students selected from both treatment groups.

1. *The A.C.S.—N.S.T.A. High School Chemistry Test* (Form 1959) * was a test of 100 items relating to chemical principles and descriptive chemistry. It was divided into two parts, each requiring 40 minutes time.

2. The *Cooperative Chemistry Test* † was composed of 79 items, also relating to principles and the descriptive nature of chemistry. Test time was 45 minutes.

3. The written laboratory test consisted of 100 items, and was divided into four blocks of 25 questions. Each block represented questions on four experiments done by the students during a quarter of the school year. The first three tests were repeated at the end of the school year to give a measure of retention of each block of experiments.

° American Chemical Society, High School Chemistry Test, Form 1959, St. Louis University, 1402 South Grand Avenue, St. Louis 4, Missouri.
† Cooperative Chemistry Test, Form X, American Council on Education, Cooperative Test Service, 15 Amsterdam Avenue, New York 23, New York.

4. The performance test consisted of handling each student a problem which could be solved only through using laboratory procedures and apparatus. Three judges (third year graduate school Ph.D. candidates from the University of Minnesota chemistry department) evaluated the students as they worked. A random sample of 20 students, 10 from each group, was given a pre- and post-test (performance laboratory test) before the three judges. The three judges observed and talked with the students during the three and one-half hour laboratory performance test.

The validity of each of the written tests was established by experts in the field, and the reliabilities were computed using Hoyt's analysis of variance method from the data in this study. The written tests had reliability coefficients ranging from 0.80 to 0.83.

Findings and Conclusions

By means of t-tests of correlated measures, initial and final test scores were compared for each of the three written criterion tests. Significant gains were accepted if the t-values exceeded the 5% level of significance. The results as shown in Tables I, II, and III were as follows:

Table 1

t-Tests of the Means and Variances of Initial and Final Written Laboratory Test Scores[a]

Class	Treatment	$\overline{X}_1$	$\overline{X}_2$	t	Initial Variance	Final Variance	t
I	Non-directed	16.13	53.46	26.41[b]	13.55	39.74	2.33[c]
	Directed	15.70	47.73	11.17[b]	7.49	107.68	6.35[c]
II	Non-directed	13.57	47.16	10.69[b]	10.91	87.06	4.64[c]
	Directed	13.26	49.66	10.23[b]	7.95	196.42	8.63[c]
III	Non-directed	14.60	49.63	16.27[b]	6.25	74.82	5.70[c]
	Directed	13.38	54.93	13.63	8.13	169.20	8.51[b]
IV	Non-directed	13.53	52.66	17.50[b]	14.41	100.81	4.08[c]
	Directed	14.46	48.79	19.39[b]	9.70	73.02	4.28[c]

[a] $\alpha = 0.05$.
[b] Reject hypothesis of equal means.
[c] Reject hypothesis of equal variances.

1. Each treatment group gained significantly from pre- to post-test.
2. The t-tests of the variances showed that each treatment group significantly increased in variance from pre- to post-test.

From these results it seemed reasonable to conclude that the course offered was effective in increasing the students' knowledge of principles and facts of descriptive chemistry, as well as knowledge in the specifics of the 16 laboratory experiments performed. The results of the variance

Table II
t-Tests of the Means and Variances of Initial and Final Co-op Chemistry Test Scores[a]

Class	Treatment	$\overline{X}_1$	$\overline{X}_2$	t	Initial Variance	Final Variance	t
I	Non-directed	12.80	42.93	24.70[b]	16.31	30.64	1.15
	Directed	14.05	43.76	15.07[b]	26.31	109.94	3.01[c]
II	Non-directed	14.00	50.25	22.67[b]	10.93	60.73	3.61[c]
	Directed	13.53	54.00	15.48[b]	10.70	114.85	5.34[c]
III	Non-directed	12.93	35.86	15.68[b]	4.64	32.12	4.05[c]
	Directed	11.94	36.81	10.15[b]	5.53	110.03	7.94[c]
IV	Non-directed	14.80	45.86	9.64[b]	37.74	245.41	3.88[c]
	Directed	14.60	39.13	9.39[b]	11.68	126.12	5.37[c]

[a] $\alpha = 0.05$.
[b] Reject hypothesis of equal means.
[c] Reject hypothesis of equal variances.

Table III
t-Tests of the Means and Variances of Initial and Final A.C.S. Chemistry Test Scores[a]

Class	Treatment	$\overline{X}_1$	$\overline{X}_2$	t	Initial Variance	Final Variance	t
I	Non-directed	11.13	34.46	7.70[b]	13.84	158.41	5.55[c]
	Directed	13.17	40.58	6.88[b]	30.03	365.88	6.20[c]
II	Non-directed	12.50	40.25	8.59[b]	17.46	215.26	6.04[c]
	Directed	12.46	48.53	8.94[b]	14.27	291.12	7.71[c]
III	Non-directed	11.86	32.20	7.60[b]	14.12	109.31	4.36[c]
	Directed	12.12	36.81	6.83[b]	9.85	258.16	9.24[c]
IV	Non-directed	13.60	39.46	6.38[b]	61.40	389.84	3.82[c]
	Directed	13.33	35.33	5.94[b]	16.10	277.52	7.05[c]

[a] $\alpha = 0.05$.
[b] Reject hypothesis of equal means.
[c] Reject hypothesis of equal variances.

tests suggest that the course materials allowed students of both treatment groups to progress at a rate consistent with their abilities.

In comparing judges' scores of the students obtained from the final performance test, the non-directed group was significantly higher than the directed group. The results and analysis of the judges scores are shown in Table IV.

While this seemed to indicate the superiority of the non-directed group to carry through an experiment, upon examination of the data for the two groups randomly selected for the performance tests, it was found that the directed group mean was significantly higher than the non-directed group mean on two of the three final written tests. Thus it is not possi-

Table IV
t-Test Analysis of Final Scores—Final Performance Test

Non-directed Group	Directed Group	t-Test
168	210	
191	173	
130	162	
215	145	

$$t_0 = \cfrac{164.9 - 149.2}{\left[\left(\cfrac{11905.9 + 8622.6}{10 + 10 - 2} \right) \times \left(\cfrac{1}{10} + \cfrac{1}{10} \right) \right]^{\frac{1}{2}}}$$

199	144	$t_0 = 2.59$
173	129	
114	98	$0.01 < P < 0.02$
144	152	
118	118	
197	161	
1649	1492	

ble to say whether students of the same academic ability would also show this superiority. However, no significant difference between the groups was found on the performance laboratory pretest. Furthermore, the performance test was presented in the form of a problem with no procedural instructions, thereby favoring the non-directed group.

The analysis of variance and covariance results can be summarized by stating at the 5% level of significance:

Table V
Analysis of Covariance of the First Quarter Written Laboratory Re-Test with the First Quarter Initial Test as Covariate

Source of Variation	D.F.	Sum of Squares	Mean Squares	F-test	
Between classes	3	2.66	0.88	$F = .538$	$P > 0.05$
Between ability groups	2	18.98	9.49	$F = 5.80$	$P < 0.05$ [a]
Classes by ability groups interaction	6	9.97	1.66	$F = 1.01$	$P > 0.05$
Between treatments	1	5.62	5.62	$F = 3.43$	$P < 0.05$ [a]
Treatment by classes interaction	3	2.50	0.83	$F = .507$	$P > 0.05$
Treatment by ability group interaction	2	3.74	1.87	$F = 1.14$	$P > 0.05$
Treatment by class by ability group interaction	6	4.75	0.79	$F = .483$	$P > 0.05$
Error (adjusted)	99	161.88	1.63		

[a] Significant at 5% level.

1. Significant ability level differences were found with high, middle, and low ability students ranking in that order on all written criterion tests. Therefore, the course offered to each treatment group in this experiment did not affect any ability group differently than expected.

2. A significant difference was found on the laboratory re-test in favor of the non-directed group. This suggests that the non-directed group was able to recall the specifics about each laboratory experiment better than the directed group.

3. No significant treatment difference was noted on any of the other written tests, suggesting that the learning of principles and descriptive chemistry was not influenced by the treatments as described in this study.

An example of the variance-covariance analysis is shown in Table V, involving the results on the first quarter laboratory re-test.

Subjective Observations

In addition to the measurable factors, several less objectively measurable outcomes were observed during the course of the study. They include:

1. Students in the non-directed classes consistently produced better write-ups of experiments than the directed groups. A possible explanation might be that the students of the directed groups felt they were merely repeating the detailed directions in their write-ups.

2. Both treatment groups enjoyed the laboratory work, and both took reasonable interest in completely working through all experiments. However, the non-directed groups took longer to adjust to the laboratory work than the directed group.

At the start of the study, some students in the non-directed groups openly voiced their objection at having to determine their own laboratory procedures while the other part of the class had theirs all worked out for them. Later, some of these same students took great pride in being able to carry through an experiment on their own.

3. The non-directed groups were interesting to watch. At the start of the course, the students of these groups were very unsystematic and tended to look for shortcut methods of carrying out their laboratory work. After the results of each experiment were discussed with the group as a whole, they began to work more carefully, and by the end of the year it became necessary to hurry them along. On occasion they were spending extra laboratory periods checking results that could have been accepted without extra work.

On the basis of the findings of this study it is recommended that future research concern be directed toward seeking the best use of non-directed laboratory experiments, and of establishing the ratio of time spent in the classroom to that in the laboratory. If a teacher makes the decision to use non-directed laboratory experiments, he must be prepared to accept antagonism at first, but should be rewarded with student enthusiasm as the method is accepted later on.

Synopsis

Experimental and control groups of high school chemistry students attended the same class discussion, and class recitation sections, but had differing laboratory work. The experimental groups were presented with laboratory problems without specific directions, while the control groups worked through carefully planned and directed experiments involving the same general problems.

Initial resistance of the experimental groups gave way to acceptance of non-directed experiments, and finally to considerable pride in being able to carry through with this sort of procedure.

Slight, non-significant differences were noted between treatment groups on conventional tests, involved with the facts and principles of chemistry. On a performance test, a randomly selected group of experimental students scored significantly higher than a similar control group.

References

1. Kruglak, Haym, "Experimental Outcomes of Laboratory Instruction in Elementary College Physics," unpublished Ph.D. thesis, University of Minnesota, 1951.
2. Balcziak, Louis W., "The Role of the Laboratory and Demonstration in College Physical Science in Achieving the Objectives of General Education," unpublished Ph.D. thesis, University of Minnesota, 1953.
3. Perlman, James S., "An Historical vs. Contemporary Problem-Solving Use of the College Physical Science Laboratory Period for General Education," unpublished Ph.D. thesis, University of Minnesota, 1952.
4. Gunkle, Mennow, M., *J. Educ. Res.*, 46, 275–284 (1952).
5. Thelen, Herbert A., "An Appraisal of Two Methods for Teaching Scientific Thinking in General Chemistry," unpublished Ph.D. thesis, Chicago Graduate School, University of Chicago, 1944.
6. Boeck, Clarence H., "The Inductive Compared to the Deductive Approach to Teaching Secondary School Chemistry," unpublished Ph.D. thesis, University of Minnesota, 1950.
7. Mason, John M., "An Experimental Study in the Teaching of Scientific Thinking in Biological Science at the College Level," *Sci. Educ.*, 36, 270–284 (1952).
8. Olson, Kenneth V., "An Experimental Evaluation of a Student-Center Method and Teacher-Centered Method of Biological Instruction for General Education of Science Students," unpublished Ph.D. thesis, University of Minnesota, 1957.
9. Dearden, Douglas M., "An Evaluation of the Laboratory and Supplementary

Teaching Techniques Used in a College General Biology Course," unpublished Ph.D. thesis, University of Minnesota, 1959.

10. Ward, John N., "Group-Study vs. Lecture-Demonstration Method in Physical Science Instruction for General Education College Students," *J. Exper. Educ.*, 24, 197–210 (1956).

11. Novak, Joseph D., "An Experimental Comparison of a Conventional and Project-Centered Method of Teaching a College General Botany Course," *J. Exper. Educ.*, 26, 217–230 (1958).

12 BEGINNING A STUDY IN ELEMENTARY SCHOOL SCIENCE
Robert Karplus

Early in 1959 a group of natural scientists and educators at the University of California at Berkeley determined to establish a cooperative study for curriculum improvement in elementary science to meet what they felt was an urgent need in this area. With financial support from the National Science Foundation, they organized the Elementary School Science Project in July, 1959. The scientists, who had previously not been in close touch with elementary teaching, recognized that their professional competence nevertheless gave them a unique responsibility for formulating an elementary science program. They believed that their experience as university instructors, the assistance of the educators, and good will and patience would enable them to make the program usable in the public schools.

This article presents the author's view and interpretation of the first year of the project's activity, the academic year 1959–60. It is appropriate that we should begin by giving some background for our interest in the subject. The teaching of science (as contrasted with nature study) has been a part of the elementary school program for only about forty years. During this time many educators have contributed to the curriculum. Review studies have stressed the value of science teaching and described some general features that science courses should have.[1] Still, there appears to be an undercurrent of dissatisfaction with the present science program. Teachers' colleges have a weak science requirement for

---

[1] The 61st yearbook of the National Society for the Study of Education entitled "Rethinking Science Education" together with the 31st and 47th yearbooks give a picture of the development of science education in this country.

SOURCE: Robert Karplus, "Beginning a Study in Elementary School Science," *American Journal of Physics*, 30, no. 1 (January 1962), 1–9. Reprinted by permission of the publisher.

their students; the teachers themselves feel inadequately prepared to teach science; many school districts allot less than an hour a week to science instruction; and a few scientists have even called for the elimination of science as a poorly taught "frill" that competes for time with reading, writing, and arithmetic.

We, on the other hand, feel that there are strong reasons why science should be taught in the elementary school. That it should be taught in school at some stage will hardly be questioned today. Scientific knowledge is an essential part of our civilization. We owe it to our children to provide them with concepts that represent the modern outcome of the centuries long, worldwide process of scientific development. That the years from six to twelve should be used to begin formal instruction in science is our conclusion drawn from the results of Piaget[2] and others[3] and from our own observations of students in school and university. It appears that children begin in their first few years to organize their experiences into what may be called "informal sciences." These systems of knowledge and belief, partly confused, partly ordered, partly fluctuating, partly stable, consist of ideas and generalizations about the objects and phenomena that compose the world as perceived by the child. They guide the generally successful and adaptive behavior of children within their environment, but give rise also to fanciful descriptions and expectations that are often animistic and acausal. Unfortunately, it appears that the childish systems of knowledge are not used by children only; many of their components remain with an individual throughout his life. In our complex culture such remnants usually exist side by side with conflicting concepts, acquired later through education, which lack the power to replace the earlier ones in any but formal or academic situations.

It is possible, therefore, to postpone the introduction of science, a subject in which elementary school children are undergoing rapid untutored development, only at the expense of later long and difficult re-education. While we applaud the activity of many scientists who are involved in proposing reforms for high school and college science teaching, we nevertheless believe that such improvements only reach the fraction of the student body which is favorably disposed toward science because of earlier experience at home or in school; for the others it is too late. We are convinced that in this age of science and technology all citizens should have a positive attitude toward science and some understanding of scientific work. And for this an introduction to science on the intuitive level during the elementary school year is essential.[4] In

[2] Jean Piaget, *The Child's Conception of Physical Causality* (The Humanities Press, New York, 1951).

[3] K. Zietz, *Kind und Physische Welt* (Kösel Verlag, Munich, Germany, 1955).

[4] *The Process of Education*, edited by Jerome S. Bruner (Harvard University Press,

other words, the elementary school years are too precious to be used only for the teaching of certain skills; they must also be used to give children some of the knowledge and the inquiring critical attitude that make use of the skills meaningful and worthwhile.

The dissatisfaction with the present state of science teaching which we have mentioned earlier, and which we share in part, presented us with the challenge to show that science study in the elementary grades, taught by average schoolteachers, is indeed of value and can influence beneficially the approach to other subject matter. To introduce a new factor into the curriculum planning we enlisted the participation of research scientists who had so far not contributed significantly to elementary education. We hoped to reorganize the science program around those important and fundamental concepts, an understanding of which leads ultimately to an understanding of many diverse natural phenomena and to a feeling of familiarity with the natural environment. We meant to stress the concepts and methods of science, rather than the uses and usefulness of science that are stressed in present teaching practice. An additional item of concern to us was the failure of the existing elementary school science program to call on the pupils' skills in arthmetic. Not only is there lost an excellent opportunity for improving the pupils' numerical understanding, but their contact with science never reveals to them the fact that quantitative relationships are of central importance.

We may consider this difference in emphasis to be one consequence of a gulf that has developed over the years between academic specialists and those responsible for the public schools. In order to help bridge the gulf to the ultimate benefit of the school children, members of both groups participated in the project. The first year's activities of this unusual collaboration resulted in the preparation of three sample teaching units and associated material for use by teachers in their classrooms. Our guide in the work was not so much the desire to produce many "successful" units as the desire to learn—to explore what the teachers and their pupils could do or could not do. In this article we shall describe the participants of our cooperative endeavor, briefly review the units that were prepared and our experience with them, and finally mention some of the preliminary conclusions we have reached. The net effect of the year's activity has been to confirm our strong belief in the importance of science instruction in the elementary school and our conviction that scientists can make a substantial contribution to a reformulation of the science curriculum. At the same time we became more

---

Cambridge, 1960) is devoted to a consideration of the psychological aspects of the type of curriculum study we have undertaken. We are pleased to say that it gives elegant expression to views very close to our own. Unfortunately, it became available only after the work reported here was done.

aware of some of the difficulties that had been faced by earlier workers in this field, difficulties that we shall have to face as well.

Project Organization

To make clear the cooperative nature of the project, we shall briefly describe the participants. The project was guided by a steering committee which consisted of several scientist "principal investigators" and one educator. An essential feature of the project was that these faculty members did not confine themselves to an advisory role, but participated personally and actively by selecting topics, originating teaching approaches, and evaluating the pupils' progress. In this work they were assisted by a technical writer-engineer, who had a background in university teaching, and by three teaching consultants who had been highly effective as teachers in elementary schools but did not have a special background in science. The testing of the materials was carried out by eighteen teachers (we shall refer to them as laboratory teachers), one in each of the first six grades in each of three differing socio-economic areas. These teachers were partly volunteers, partly selected by their principals. The pupils numbered about 500 and ranged in intelligence from quite low to exceptionally high: their average intelligence was somewhat above the national average.

The four staff members did most of the detailed work that was neces- companied by the equipment and specimen for demonstrations, for tors into a form that could, hopefully, be used by teachers in self- contained classrooms. The result was rather lengthy manuals which contained a quite detailed description of the classroom procedure to be followed in presenting the lessons in each unit. These manuals were accompanied by the equipment and specimen for demonstrations, for group experiments, and for individual pupil experiments. A most informative activity was the conducting of experimental classes by principal investigators and staff members.[5] In them the pupils' reactions to a tentative teaching approach were observed directly by the authors of the unit who could then try to eliminate the most obvious sources of difficulty. We must add, though, that the pupils' reactions were often hard to interpret correctly.

The laboratory teachers were given some instruction and supervision during the testing of each unit. After they had had an opportunity to read a manual, they were introduced to the experimental equipment at a two-hour workshop at which they also had the opportunity to ask

[5] These were regular public school classes in which a project member replaced the classroom teacher for an hour or two a week. The classroom teacher remained as observer and consultant.

questions. The workshop was conducted by the principal investigators and staff members who had collaborated on the unit. Subsequently the teachers kept in contact with the project members who visited the schools to observe the teaching, answer questions, and encourage the teachers. This supervision, which took place only irregularly at the beginning of the year, was found so valuable that it was expanded until it occupied one teaching consultant full time in addition to occasional visits by the other project members. The results are being used to indicate the revisions needed in the teaching approach and in the teaching materials. Here also several interpretations were found possible.

The Experimental Units

The principal investigators chose the subjects to be included in the first year's program according to their interests and the general expectation that the topic would be appropriate for the elementary school with the only requirement that it deal with a fundamental aspect of nature. The construction of a conceptual framework for the entire science curriculum, one of our objectives, was postponed while we acquired experience as to what could be accomplished in the classroom. The three units that were prepared by the project and tested by the laboratory teachers were entitled "Coordinates," "Force," and "What Am I?" (human physiology and biochemistry). Near the end of the year experimental work was begun on two additional units, one concerned with the atomic structure of matter, the other with animal coloration and natural selection.

The first unit, "Coordinates," [6] was intended to serve as an introduction to the graphical representation of functional relationships. With this way of displaying an interdependence of two variables, we hoped to make the quantitative relationships in later units accessible to the children without the need for algebra. The first of its two major sections considered the coordinate system as a device for locating a point in a plane, while the second dealt with the graphing of linear functions, slopes, and equations, and descriptively with curves. Somewhat to their surprise, the teachers reported a very favorable response to the first section, which consisted mainly of exercises in which the children constructed pictures on graph paper by properly locating and connecting points whose coordinate values were provided by the teacher or by other children. (The first graders used numbered peg-boards and made

---

[6] The title seems to have been poorly chosen. Even though the noun "coordinates" is familiar to scientists and mathematicians, only the verb, with its quite different meaning, is known to most laymen. A much better title for the unit would have been "Graphs."

the pictures with pegs and yarn. It took them a little while to learn that they could locate desired points by reading the numbers stamped along the edge of the board rather than by counting holes.) The pupils in the upper grades were able to carry out some operations such as displacements, reflections, and scaling of figures. The second section, however, was obscure to the teachers, who were not accustomed to dealing with equations and graphs. This material could not be evaluated with any confidence, moreover, because the available time (a total of two months for the unit) enabled few classes to proceed far, and those that did set too fast a pace. A general reaction was that much of the material was too abstract. Later experimentation by project members with the ideas of the unit suggested that the straight line graph may have seemed a complicated way of representing a simple situation.[7] An attempt to use an algebraic approach to quantitative relationships supported our original judgment that the geometrical one was preferable, but that the two might be combined. We conclude that the children developed some facility in handling graph paper and locating points. The question of how the pupils can learn to use this skill to represent quantitative relationships graphically with some degree of self-confidence is still open. Granted that the concept of a functional relationship with its connotation of controlled variables is too abstract to be introduced at once, there appear to be two ways in which the unit can be revised. One is to improve the existing unit, but to retain its general approach. The other is to begin with a study of qualitative relationships between pairs of variables and use freehand graphs to indicate trends and tell stories. As the children become older the emphasis can become more quantitative until the pupils feel the need to draw precise graphs in order to convey accurately all the information in a given situation or experiment. We hope to explore both of these approaches.

The second unit, entitled "Force," was to serve as an introduction to Newton's laws of motion. The children's intuitive experience of pushes, pulls, and weight was used to introduce the word *force* and to establish the fact that two opposite forces are present at an interaction. In later lessons the relation between changes in motion and the action of forces was considered. The unit was issued in three parallel versions. An abbreviated one, which considered only the qualitative features of the subject, was prepared for use in the first grade. For the second, third, and fourth grades we made an attempt at a careful, systematic development in which forces acting in various situations were introduced through ex-

---

[7] Several examples, for instance, dealt with the time-distance relationship for a car moving at constant speed. Once a single number, the speed, is given, the complete behavior of the car is determined. The graph does not add any insight to the problem unless one contrasts it with the graph for an accelerating car, for which the result is not a straight line.

periments. Finally, the fifth and sixth grades covered much of the same material more quickly, but went on to a lesson on circular motion. All children except the first graders made scales by calibrating a rubber band or a spring. The fifth and sixth graders went on to do some quantitative experiments on Hooke's Law (with their spring scales), on the coefficient of friction, and on centripetal force. Graphs were used to display the results of measurements made in demonstrations and experiments.

The "Force" unit was initially received with greater enthusiasm than the "Coordinates" unit, for its motives appeared clearer to the teachers. The early lessons went smoothly, with the construction of the force-measuring scale being a high point. Some third and fourth graders were quite excited by the "discovery" that friction was a force in that it could slow down objects just as other forces could, and that gravity was a force in that it could speed up objects like other forces could. Paradoxically, the facts that friction could accelerate and that gravity could slow down were not appreciated.[8] It may therefore not be surprising that, as the teachers proceeded further into the unit, much of the material missed its mark. For instance, the "balanced forces" on a body at equilibrium were confused with the "equal, opposite forces" in Newton's third law, with the words "equal" and "balanced" being used interchangeably. Still, some of the vocabulary introduced in the unit turned up on the playground and at home, where the pupils apparently found it useful. The individual and group experiments were carried out quite well by the older children, even though the arithmetic required for the analysis did cause some difficulty. The possibilities of using graphs in this unit were not noted by teachers or pupils until they were pointed out by the project staff. Altogether, the performance of the pupils and of the teachers represented a substantial accomplishment on a difficult subject.

Just as was the case with "Coordinates," several ways have been suggested in which the unit should be revised and improved. One shortcoming was insufficient care in developing and reinforcing concepts which seemed "simple" to the scientists. For instance, the children distinguish so-called "active" forces from "passive" forces [9] (e.g., a person exerts an "active" force on the floor, the floor exerts a "passive" force on

[8] The experimental unit did not include explicitly a discussion of motion, speed, changes of speed, etc. With the benefit of hindsight, therefore, we are not really surprised that the pupils failed to grasp the element of change which is common to speeding up and slowing down, especially in an unusual context.

[9] The question of what we have called "passive forces" generated considerable debate between children who recognized their existence and children who did not. We tried to postpone a decision until it would become useful to have passive forces because they also could change the motion of an object (e.g., a ball bounces off the floor).

the person), while the physicist does not do so. Again, the physicist distinguishes between uniform and accelerated motion, a difference that seems very subtle to the children, who instead look at a state of rest with respect to the earth as a very special situation. The revision of the unit may therefore use the same conceptual approach as did the original, with more careful attention to details such as the ones mentioned. A radically different approach to the topic can be made through a consideration of the properties of moving objects and the introduction of momentum. Force then takes a secondary role and is used only as a special term in connection with the exchange of momentum. Still, to the children these approaches may not be so different as they seem to us. For instance, they meet linguistically in the words "push" and "pull": used as verbs, the two words are equivalent to "exert a force," while used as nouns they are equivalent to "momentum." [10]

An interesting impression we received from both "Coordinates" and "Force" was that children without special preparation have difficulty in envisaging an oversimplified, idealized situation as a limit of physical situations. In the first unit it was the strictly linear relationships, in the second unit it was the treatment of hard objects as perfectly rigid and "passive," that made the discussion unrealistic. In further experimental work we have had some success in avoiding the latter difficulty by an early introduction of the atomic structure of matter. Once it is recognized that all objects are deformed under stresses (even though some "hard" objects may be deformed only slightly), the distinction between "active" and "passive" forces becomes less sharp. Of course, the atomic structure is a powerful conceptual model for physical properties other than mechanical ones, and we hope to exploit it as such.

The third and last unit to be used in 1959–60 by the laboratory teachers associated with the project was entitled "What Am I?" (human physiology and biochemistry). It was intended to make the children aware of their own bodies as biologic units which consist of a number of interacting physiologic systems (skeletal, muscular, nervous, digestive, circulatory, and respiratory) that perform various physical and biochemical functions. Although the lessons necessarily included a good deal of descriptive matter, stress was placed on observation and experimentation, with the children serving as their own experimental subjects. A section on embryonic development was accompanied by the incubation of chicken eggs which were opened at regular intervals. For the fifth and sixth graders, additional material on body chemistry and on energy conversion in living systems was included.

The reaction of the teachers and the pupils to most of the unit was

[10] Compare, for instance, the statements "I push the chair" and "I give the chair a push." Some of our difficulties can be traced to the ambiguity of words like "push" and "pull."

very favorable, a fact that may be related to their familiarity with the material and to its largely descriptive and manipulative nature. Only the section on chemistry, though fascinating to the older children, was found difficult by the teachers because they lacked sufficient background information. The teaching was generally successful in arousing the children's curiosity about the human body and in bringing them to use simple experiments and analytical reasoning to better their understanding of its structure and functions. We were pleased that the children were able to look at themselves objectively even to the extent of discussing such functions as excretion without embarrassment. The comparison between the embryonic development of the chickens and human beings was very interesting to the children and particularly appreciated by the fifth and sixth graders. A highlight for pupils, teachers, and project staff was the hatching of the baby chicks.

The revised unit will consist of four main sections that can be used all in one year, but would more ideally be taught at different levels. A section on the skeletal and muscular systems is aimed at the first two grades, one on the nervous system, the senses, and the brain at the middle two grades, and one on metabolism and the circulatory system at the last two grades. The fourth section on embryology can be used at any time in the elementary school. The section on chemistry has been dropped. Summaries at the end of each section can be used for review purposes or as bases for accelerated coverage of the material. The instructions for experiments led in several instances to misunderstandings; the appropriate sections will be clarified in the revised unit. While this is not surprising, we mention it because it points up again that the difference in background between the laboratory teachers and the project staff makes necessary a very careful choice of expressions in the instructional material.

The Teaching Experience

It is difficult on the written page to communicate the alertness, interest, and enthusiasm with which children at all grade levels have responded to much of the experimental material that has been used. The teachers' and observers' reports confirmed our expectation that the pupils would be strongly motivated in the study of science and would find the combination of experiment and induction in our approach a stimulating challenge. While the more gifted pupils were, of course, quicker to learn the new material, the teachers also reported that some pupils who had displayed little interest in school subjects showed a positive response to the science course. Finally, a few observations taken from the author's own teaching experience may help to round out the picture.

In one lesson, as part of the instruction on "Force," first graders were given a number of similar small bar magnets, one of which had a colored spot on one end. They were asked to put a spot on each of the unmarked magnets in order to mark it "in the same way" as the sample magnet. Quite a few of the pupils systematically marked the poles that were repelled by the marked pole of the sample (rather than using attraction to define likeness) and were then able to arrange their magnets in a "train" in which the painted end of each "car" pointed to the front. Other pupils, of course, were less successful—some worked at random, some marked both ends, etc. In another lesson of the same series, the pupils were given a simple sketch of a table on the floor (later, other examples) and asked to draw different colored arrows that would distinguish the forces exerted by the table from the forces acting on the table. Again, some children were able to indicate the forces and make the distinction, some indicated the forces but did not recognize their direction, while a few drew miscellaneous arrows only. The first graders may be somewhat young for this kind of work, but they do not seem much too young.

Later, a class of second graders studying "graphs" plotted on the blackboard the age of one twin as a function of the other's age. It was simple for various members of the class to mark so many points (for integral and non-integral ages) that they appeared to form a line, and a few children, after considerable discussion, even suggested that one could draw a straight line with the ruler in response to the request for a short-cut method of showing all the points quickly. After a review of this conclusion in the lesson a few days later, an incident occurred that shed some light on the children's own attitude towards "discovery." The children who had "discovered" the straight line were invited to raise their hands so as to enhance their feeling of accomplishment. One little girl raised her hand even though she should not have done so. When asked whether she really had figured it out she replied, "I figured it out, too, but by watching." She obviously derived great satisfaction therefrom. Since it is almost impossible to have all pupils in a class achieve all insights independently, it is encouraging to know that the thrill of discovery can apparently be shared.

As part of the unit on "Force," the laboratory third and fourth grades made a rough scale by calibrating the extension of a strong rubber band in terms of a number of identical books suspended from it. When the teacher tabulated the extensions (measured in inches) produced by a certain number of books in the way that tables had been made for graphing figures in the "Coordinates" unit, many pupils suggested that the data be displayed on a graph. They also suggested an appropriate scale to be used when it turned out that representing one inch by one square would cover more space than available and representing one book by one square would leave a large part of the square blackboard unused. Apparently a good deal of the teaching of "Coordinates," which had taken place several months earlier, had been retained in a usable way.

Also as part of the "Force" unit, a laboratory fifth grade had studied and observed the force of friction exerted by the table top on a sliding block when the block was loaded with more and more identical blocks so as to increase the total weight. In response to questions they showed a good knowledge of the linear dependence of the frictional forces on the weight. When the author expressed skepticism about the linear relationhip and asked to be convinced of its validity, the class had no ready answer—at first, in fact, the pupils appeared surprised that the law of friction, which they had learned, needed demonstration. After some further discussion, however, one of the pupils did suggest as a last resort that the author take the blocks and do the experiment himself![11] In other words, the children may consider empirically obtained information as less sound than information given by the teacher or obtained from a book. It should be one goal of the science program to emphasize the source of the information, to bring this source as close to the children as possible, and to discuss the role of "authority" in science.

As a last example, we describe an experience in a sixth grade that had been studying organic chemistry as part of the physiology unit. Many pupils had made molecular models out of colored clay balls (atoms) connected by toothpicks (bonds). These models showed a partial understanding of valence, but seemed to be treated as display material that did not lead to further activity. To arouse some interest the author arranged the models according to the length of the carbon chain and introduced the Geneva convention for naming the hydrocarbons and the compounds derived by substitutions. Each model then became a challenge, for it had to be named, and new models had to be made to see whether they could be named, too. One boy opened a new avenue by "making" a cyclic compound. The hour was all too short for this! We mention this example not because we feel that organic chemistry should be studied so intensively, but because it shows how pleased the children are by the feeling of power that comes from the ability to master a new situation or problem. Such knowledge makes the children reach out for new questions that they can answer and for new understanding, on the endless road of learning.

Conclusions

We have already suggested that we looked upon the past year as an opportunity for learning, and in this respect our work was very reward-

[11] This was done, with the expected result, to the relief of the class.

ing. The novelty of the situation for both scientists and teachers was such that it made this outcome almost inevitable. There are also some conclusions that we have drawn, but they are subjective and mainly concern the identification of problems rather than the solutions thereof.

Most difficult of these problems is the determination of what the pupils are learning. Our attempts at evaluation made clear that the objective tests we have used have not been very informative. The classroom observation, on the other hand, while more informative, was incomplete and subjective and tended to focus on the active pupils. The laboratory teachers themselves were sensitive to pupil satisfaction and frustration, but were not sufficiently experienced in the material to be able to judge effectively the pupils' progress towards the goals set by the scientists. At the same time, the significance of the words used in the teaching and discussions depended on whether they were used by a scientist, by a teacher, or by a pupil.

The second problem is the programming of the learning experience so that a secure connection is achieved between the pupils' intuitive or "common sense" attitudes and the concepts that embody the modern scientific point of view. One difficulty here is that alert children generalize very rapidly and often in an invalid way on the basis of limited experience even in the face of contradictory evidence. The teaching program must take this possibility into account and help the children reshape the principles they have already inferred rather than merely trying to lead them to the desired conclusion. In this connection one must also remember that children apparently can consider at one time only a very small number of independent pieces of information in drawing a conclusion. Thus the sciences must be probed to uncover their structure of concepts, the scientist's language concerning these concepts must be confronted with the pupils' natural language and ideas (if any) about them, and finally, the components most directly accessible to direct experience at some stage of development must be selected as bases for the teaching program.

We have learned, moreover, that it is useful to distinguish between two levels of mental activity: one is observational, manipulative, descriptive, concerned with objects and skills; the other is analytical, abstract, concerned with relations and understanding. The illustrative and experimental material to which the children are exposed initially stimulates activity on the first of these levels. If we should like the children to grasp scientific principles, however, we are asking them to operate on the second level. We feel that the long-standing benefits of science education consist of an understanding of the fundamental generalizations of the various fields and of the practice in inductive and analytical thinking that construction or discovery of these generalizations entails. It is therefore the task of the teacher to introduce the materials in such a way that they will serve as a path to the ultimate conclusion rather than becoming and remaining ends in themselves. A fascinating question concerns the age at which and the way in which it might be possible to approach the children directly on the abstract level, rather than through the observational and manipulative as we have assumed necessary.

The third problem has to do with the teaching materials. The results of experimental work on the first two problems must be communicated to teachers in such a way that they can use it without, in effect, becoming scientists themselves. The information must, of course, go beyond the minimum required for the classroom presentation so that the teachers will have a reserve from which to draw in discussions, a reserve that is the basis for self-confidence in front of the class. They must also acquire a many-sided view of the subject so that they can link it to the pupils' experience in diverse ways. All this in addition to their other teaching obligations! The teaching materials bear the heavy burden of making the task a practical one.

The three units prepared during the past year enabled us to explore these problems somewhat. Even though we have been able to propose only imperfect solutions, our expectation that the scientists can and must make substantial contributions to the elementary school program has been borne out. At the same time, we remain convinced that the scientists must work closely with educators, school teachers, and psychologists if a satisfactory program is to be developed. Finally, we have an indication that it is possible to develop the pupils' powers of observation and discrimination, that they enjoy opportunities to "discover," that they can use their own perception and analysis as valuable instruments for learning, and that they will challenge "authority" in the domain of science if they feel that they have a good case.

Acknowledgments

During 1959–60 Professors Leo Brewer (chemistry), Nello Pace (physiology), Arthur Pardee (biochemistry), Lloyd Scott (education), and Robert Stebbins (zoology) were my colleague principal investigators. We were deeply saddened when Professor Brewer had to withdraw from the committee because of illness at the end of the academic year. Professors Stephen Diliberto (mathematics), Chester O'Konski (chemistry), Herbert Mason (botany), and Dr. Roger Wallace (physics) have joined the group since then. The staff was headed by Dr. David Ipsen, the project's technical writer; it consisted of Dr. Ipsen and three teaching consultants, Mrs. Gretchen Gillfillan, Mrs. Elizabeth Hansen, and Mrs. Phyllis Raabe. Mr. Theodore Kompanetz served as psychological consultant to the author toward the end of the year. I am particularly indebted to Professor Scott, to Dr. Ipsen, and to Mr. Kompanetz for assisting me in the preparation of this article. Other interested faculty members, with whom we enjoyed stimulating discussions, were Professors John McKee (psychology), Thomas Kuhn (history and philosophy of science), and David Russell (education). I should like to take this opportunity to thank publicly my colleagues for their generous participation in the project activities and to thank the project members and their spouses for unusual devotion to our work.

The Berkeley Unified School District, the San Leandro Unified School District, and the Orinda Union School District were most cooperative in permitting some of their teachers to conduct laboratory classes for the project. The participating teachers and their principals were the following:

Washington School, Berkeley (Dr. Harold Maves, Principal)—Miss Gibson, Mrs. Damgaard, Miss Peil, Miss Davidson, Mrs. Willett, Mr. Yoshida.

Madison School, San Leandro (Mr. Loyce McCormick, Principal)—Mrs. Wright, Mrs. Crestetto, Mrs. Bennett, Mrs. Campbell, Miss Potts, Mr. Howard.

Del Rey School, Orinda (Mr. Herman Nyland, Principal)—Mrs. McCormack, Mrs. Canty, Mrs. Cunningham, Mrs. Kisich, Miss Dewar, Mr. Robertson, Mrs. O'Dea.

Several other schools assisted graciously by allowing experimental teaching by project members to be conducted in selected classes. These were the Glorietta School and the Sleepy Hollow School, Orinda, the Thousand Oaks School, the LeConte School, and the Kensington School, Berkeley, and the Balboa School, Richmond.

Outside this area, across the nation, there are many groups engaged in curriculum study. We have especially benefited from contacts with Francis Friedman (Physical Science Study Committee—M.I.T.), Robert Davis (SMSG and Syracuse), Newton Hawley (Stanford), Fletcher Watson (Harvard), and Myron Atkin, David Page, and Richard Suchman (all at Illinois).

13 SPELLING ERRORS AND THE SERIAL-POSITION EFFECT
Arthur R. Jensen

Perusal of the research on spelling reveals that this subject has been traditionally dominated more by a linguistic than by a psychological orientation (Horn, 1960). Spelling difficulties have been analyzed largely in terms of phonetics, syllabication, parts of speech, and frequency of word usage. Spelling research is also predominantly characterized by a rather simple, unanalytical, correlational approach. Relationships have been found between measures of spelling ability and measures of reading, MA, IQ, achievement in various school subjects, and numerous other variables (Horn, 1960). Seldom, however, is spelling studied as a learning phenomenon or examined in terms of principles derived from the experimental psychology of learning. The investigator has conceived of what might be called a psychological theory of spelling based primarily on concepts in learning theory. The purpose of the present investigation is to examine only one aspect of the formulation, viz., the serial-position effect. The similarity of the distribution of spelling errors, when errors are plotted according to their position in the word, to the distribution of errors in serial rote learning—the so-called serial-position effect—has never before been noted. The correspondence between spelling and serial learning would seem to offer some clues concerning the nature of spelling errors.

When a series of words, nonsense syllables, symbols, or figures is learned, the errors made before mastery are distributed according to the position of each item in the series, producing the familiar, skewed, bow-shaped serial-position curve. Various theories have been proposed to account for this phenomenon (Jensen, 1962a; McGeoch & Irion, 1952, pp. 125–134). Since a word consists of a series of letters, and since spelling a word consists of putting each letter in its proper order, we might ask whether the serial-position effect, which is generally manifested in every form of serial learning investigated in the laboratory, is also manifested in spelling. If so, the distribution of spelling errors should be similar to the serial-position curves produced by the serial learning of other materials. That is to say, errors should generally be most frequent in the middle of a word, with fewest errors at the beginning and end of the word.

SOURCE: Arthur R. Jensen, "Spelling Errors and the Serial-Position Effect," *Journal of Educational Psychology*, 53, no. 3 (June 1962), 105–9. Copyright © 1962 by the American Psychological Association. Reprinted by permission of the publisher. **173**

That spelling errors occur more frequently in the middle of words has probably been noted before, but apparently not with sufficient precision to reveal the more subtle features of the serial-position effect.

Variations in the shape of the serial-position curve are mainly a function of the number of items in the series. The curve for a short series is markedly skewed, with the largest proportion of errors occurring well past the middle of the series. As the series become longer, the serial-position curve becomes more symmetrical (McGeoch & Irion, 1952, p. 123). It would be interesting indeed if this were found to be the case also for the distribution of spelling errors in words of different lengths. The present investigation was addressed to this question.

Method

SPELLING

So that word selection would be unbiased with respect to the purpose of the present study, every 7-letter, 9-letter, and 11-letter word of the Thorndike-Lorge word list (1944, pp. 1–208) was typed on a slip of paper. The slips were thoroughly shuffled to eliminate alphabetical order, and then 75 eight-item word lists were made up separately for 7-, 9-, and 11-letter words by drawing the words at random from the total word pool. Foreign words and proper nouns were eliminated.

In order to maximize spelling errors while at the same time presenting words that were reasonably familiar to the subjects, it was decided to give the 7-letter words only to the eighth graders ($N = 150$), the 9-letter words only to tenth graders ($N = 148$), and the 11-letter words only to junior college freshmen ($N = 89$).

The spelling tests were selected at random from all the eight-item spelling lists. Every eighth grader was given 24 7-letter words; every tenth grader was given 24 9-letter words, but different lists were used in different classes, so the total number of different 9-letter words was 96. Each of the junior college students was given 48 11-letter words.

The subjects had mimeographed forms on which to print the words. For a 7-letter word, for example, a row of seven adjacent squares was provided, with the instructions to put one letter in each square. Similar forms were used for 9- and 11-letter words. This procedure permitted the position of each spelling error to be easily tabulated.

For all groups of subjects, the words were read aloud by the regular classroom teacher in the fashion of the usual spelling test. Students were not given the words for study before the test. Neither the teachers nor the students knew the purpose of the test.

SERIAL LEARNING

To permit a detailed comparison between the position of errors in spelling and in serial rote learning, serial learning data were obtained.

Sixty subjects (college students) learned by the anticipation method a nine-item serial list composed of nine colored geometric forms: triangles, squares, and circles, colored red, blue, and yellow. The stimuli were projected automatically one at a time at a 3-second rate with a 6-second intertrial interval. (A detailed description of the apparatus is given elsewhere—Jensen, Collins, & Vreeland, 1962.) Never were figures of the same shape or color adjacent in the series. A green light of 3-seconds duration served as the signal for the subject to anticipate the first item in the series. Subjects responded by saying "red triangle, blue square," etc. All subjects learned to a criterion of one perfect trial. Two different orders of stimuli were used, with 30 subjects assigned to each order.

Results

All the serial-position curves are presented as the percentage of total errors that occur at each serial position, so that the area under all the curves is the same. This method of presentation was adopted since the interest here does not concern the absolute number of errors but only the relative shapes of the curves for serial learning errors and for spelling errors. For the color-form serial-learning data, the percentage of errors at each position was determined for each subject individually and then averaged over all subjects, in order to weight each subject equally in the group curve. A similar method was applied to the spelling data. Since some words were misspelled much more frequently than others, the percentage of errors at each position was determined for each word and these were averaged over all words so that every word is weighted equally in the final curve.

Figure 1 shows the distribution of errors as a function of letter position for 96 9-letter words and for the serial position of errors made by 60 subjects in learning the color-form series. Both curves evince the essential features of the serial-position effect, that is, a bowed curve with the greater proportion of errors occurring after the middle position. The intraclass correlation between the pairs of data points for the two curves may be regarded as an index of the degree of similarity in the shapes of the curves (Haggard, 1958). The intraclass r was .81 between the spelling and the color-form curves. When the curves produced by the two serial orders of the color-form test were intercorrelated, the r was .96, which may be regarded as an equivalent-forms reliability of the shape of the serial-position curve.

The error curves for 7- and 11-letter words are shown in Figure 2. These curves closely resemble serial-position curves found in the literature on serial learning (Jensen, 1962a; McGeoch & Irion, 1952, p. 123) with the degree of skewness varying as a function of the number of items in the series. The peak of errors for a 7-item list is generally at Po-

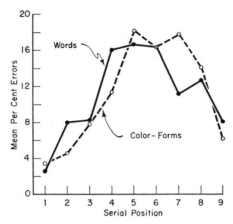

Figure 1 Serial-position curves for errors in nine-item color-form serial learning (60 subjects) and for spelling errors in nine-letter words. (The latter is based on a total of 3,864 spelling errors, i.e., incorrect letters, made on 96 words by 148 tenth graders.)

sition 5, and for an 11-item list it is at Position 7. The spelling errors conform perfectly to these expectations.

Since the usual method of learning to spell words is not the anticipation method generally used in serial learning experiments, but involves simultaneous viewing of all the letters in the word, one might ask if learning the color-forms by this method also evinces the serial-position effect. If it did not, it would be doubtful that the resemblance of the error curves for spelling to those of serial learning was indicative of a common psychological process underlying both forms of learning. To investigate this question, an additional 30 subjects (college students) were given a color-form test that involved simultaneous presentation of all the

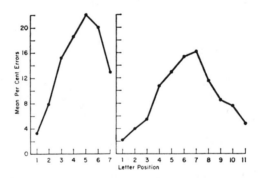

Figure 2 Serial-position curves for errors in 7- and 11-letter words. (The curve for 7-letter words is based on a total of 1,546 spelling errors made on 24 words by 150 eighth graders. The 11-letter curve is based on a total of 2,262 spelling errors made on 48 words by 89 junior college freshmen.

items in the series. Nine colored plastic forms (red triangle, green square, blue triangle, yellow diamond, red circle, yellow triangle, blue circle, pink square, and green diamond) were placed in a row before the subject. After the subject had studied the order of the objects for 10 seconds, the objects were disarranged haphazardly and the subject was asked to rearrange them in the proper order. This procedure was repeated, always with the same serial arrangement of the objects, until the subject learned to reconstruct their order perfectly. There was a different order for each subject.

Figure 3 shows the serial-position curve obtained by this method of si-

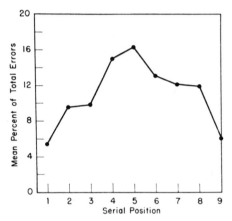

Figure 3 The serial-position curve for errors on a spatial serial learning task in which all nine items were presented simultaneously on each trial (30 subjects).

multaneous presentation. It may be regarded as a spatial, rather than the usual temporal, form of serial learning. The serial-position effect clearly is not limited to learning by the anticipation method (Jensen, 1962b). It should be noted that the curve in Figure 3 more closely resembles the curve for misspellings in words in Figure 1 than does the serial anticipation curve in Figure 1. In brief, the distribution of spelling errors more closely corresponds to the spatial serial-position effect than to the temporal. This is what we would expect, since the letters of words are viewed simultaneously as in the spatial serial learning procedure. The intraclass correlation between the words curve in Figure 1 and the curve in Figure 3 is .90, which indicates a degree of correspondence between these curves that is almost as high as the "reliability" of the curves would permit.

Discussion

A strictly linguistic, rather than psychological, interpretation of these findings is not readily apparent. The obvious linguistic explanation of these results is in terms of the relative easiness of spelling the common prefixes and suffixes in words, which would tend to make for fewer spelling errors at the beginnings and ends of words having these elements. This explanation is unconvincing for several reasons. If prefixes and suffixes, most of which are composed of two or three letters, are learned as units, and if these prefixes and suffixes account for the shape of the error curve, then we should expect quite a differently shaped curve than was actually found in the present study. Each of the first three and last three letter positions should have an almost uniformly small proportion of errors. Furthermore, the differences in the skewness of curves for words of different lengths would be difficult to explain by the prefix-suffix hypothesis. It is apparent that even if the first and last three positions of the error curves are ignored, the middle portion of the word still manifests the bowed serial-position effect. Note the curve for 11-letter words in Figure 2; even without the first and last three positions the errors are distributed in a fashion typical of serial-position curves. Furthermore, only a small proportion of the words used in this study had either suffixes or prefixes. Using as a criterion a list of 46 common Greek and Latin prefixes (McCrimmon, 1950, p. 186), it was found that only 16% of the 9-letter words had prefixes. The mean number of errors on the first three positions for these words was 5.60; for nonprefix words the mean number of errors was 6.80. This small difference, in addition to the fact that only 16% of the words had prefixes, could not account for the markedly bow-shaped error curves found in the present study.

It is not claimed that spelling errors are solely a function of serial position. Certainly some words are phonetically more difficult than others, and this factor is undoubtedly a large source of spelling errors. Each word has its own peculiar difficulties, and it appears that these difficulties can occur at any letter position in the word. It is only when the errors that are peculiar to individual words are "averaged out" by combining the position errors of a large number of words, as was done in the present experiment, that the distribution of errors associated with the serial-position effect becomes evident. Thus, a phonetically difficult element is probably more or less difficult according to its position in the word.

There is still another interesting point of correspondence between spelling and serial learning. A number of studies (reviewed by Horn, 1960, pp. 1346–1347) have found that emphasizing difficult parts of words, in presenting the words in a lesson, by underlining, writing the letters in capitals, using boldfaced type, etc., is of little or no value in increasing the probability that the word will be spelled correctly. Emphasis of particular letters in a word corresponds to the so-called von Restorff procedure in serial learning, in which an item in the series is perceptually emphasized in some manner. The emphasized item is usually learned more readily than would be a nonemphasized item in the same position, but the difficulty of learning the list as a whole remains the same as if no item had been emphasized (Jensen, 1962c; Newman & Saltz, 1958). When errors are reduced at one position, they are correspondingly increased at other positions, so that there is no overall advantage from emphasizing a particular element in the series. This seems to be true in spelling as well as in serial learning.

References

Haggard, E. A. *Intraclass correlation and the analysis of variance*. New York: Dryden, 1958.

Horn, E. S. In C. W. Harris (Ed.), *Encyclopedia of educational research*. New York: Macmillan, 1960. Pp. 1337–1354.

Jensen, A. R. An empirical theory of the serial-position effect. *J. Psychol.*, 1962, 53, 127–142. (a)

Jensen, A. R. Temporal and spatial serial-position effects. *Amer. J. Psychol.*, 1962, in press. (b)

Jensen, A. R. The von Restorff isolation effect with minimal response learning. *J. exp. Psychol.*, 1962, in press. (c)

Jensen, A. R., Collins, C. C., & Vreeland, R. W. A multiple S-R human learning apparatus. *Amer. J. Psychol.*, 1962, in press.

McCrimmon, J. M. *Writing with a purpose*. Boston: Houghton Mifflin, 1950.

McGeoch, J. A., & Irion, A. L. *The psychology of human learning*. New York: Longmans, Green, 1952.

Newman, S. E., & Saltz, E. Isolation effects: Stimulus and response generalization as explanatory concepts. *J. exp. Psychol.*, 1958, 55, 467–472.

Thorndike, E. L., & Lorge, I. *The teacher's word book of 30,000 words*. New York: Teachers College, Columbia University, Bureau of Publications, 1944.

14   THE DEVELOPMENT OF UNDERSTANDING IN ARITHMETIC BY A TEACHING MACHINE [1]
Evan R. Keislar

The use of teaching machines for the teaching of spelling and arithmetic combinations has already been shown to have merit (Skinner, 1954; Pressey, 1927). And studies have demonstrated that automated teaching can result in more than simple rote learning (Porter, 1957; Ferster and Sapon, 1958). In this study, the problem was to explore the possibility of using a multiple-choice method for the automated teaching of "understanding," specifically, an understanding of areas of rectangles. By *understanding* is meant the ability to answer a variety of questions different from those encountered during training but belonging to the same general class; the broader this class is, the greater is the understanding.

Essentially, the paper describes an attempt to devise a program for the teaching of understanding, together with the principles underlying its construction and weaknesses that were encountered in the use of the program. No information is available as to what a comparable group of pupils would have learned in regular classes. To have provided such information would have required a fairly large sample of teachers and classes. But more important is the fact that, at this writing, it is premature to compare the teaching machine approach with regular classroom instruction. Programs for use with such machines need improvement before such studies can have much meaning.

APPARATUS

The teaching machine used in this study was an extensive adaptation of the Film Rater used by the Navy for teaching aircraft identification. Multiple-choice items on a Kodachrome strip-film were projected in sequence upon a viewing plate. The learner responded to each item by pressing one of five buttons. If the answer was correct a green light was turned on and the next item could be brought into view by pressing a special button. But if this answer was wrong a red light came on; only

[1] Appreciation is expressed to the staff of the University Elementary School of the University of California, Los Angeles, and to Mrs. Pauline Bart for their cooperation in this study.

SOURCE: Evan R. Keislar, "The Development of Understanding in Arithmetic by a Teaching Machine," *Journal of Educational Psychology,* 50, no. 6 (December 1959), 247–53. Copyright © 1959 by the American Psychological Association. Reprinted by permission of the publisher.

after turning off this red light could the learner try again. To proceed to the next item the learner had to answer correctly.

A special device recorded a graph of all right and wrong answers for each item. If the wrong answer was given the pen moved to the right one-twentieth of an inch. For each correct answer the pen moved vertically an equal distance to a new line. Hence the subject's performance for any item could be read from the horizontal line on the graph corresponding to this item number.

THE ITEM SET

The total program consisted of 120 items, 10 of which instructed the learner how to operate the machine and informed him of the goal to be attained. The remaining 110 items were constructed to provide a sequence beginning with concepts of squares, rectangles, length, and width. Following items requiring the pupil to indicate the number of square units in rectangles, the concept of area was presented. Applications included paint coverage, rug size, and tile laying, followed by practical problems of adding and subtracting areas and finding the length or width of rectangles. The set concluded with items involving cost.[2]

PRINCIPLES OF PROGRAMMING

Several of the principles outlined by Skinner (1958) and illustrated in his completion-item set were applied to this multiple-choice approach. To illustrate the principles discussed below, a short sequence from the program, Items 18 through 29, is presented in Figure 1. The original program was in color.

1. The step from each item to the next in the sequence should be small enough so that the learner almost always gets each item right. Although Homme and Glaser (1958) and Coulson and Silberman (1959) found that smaller steps resulted in better learning and took less time per step than larger steps, definitive evidence on this issue has not yet been obtained. In this study it was assumed that if a pupil selected the wrong alternative to an item he did so either because he was improperly selected for the program or because of inadequate prior learning in the program itself. The programmer should make sure that a pupil learns enough before an item is presented so that generalization to this item is practically assured.

In opposition to this line of reasoning is the argument in favor of

---

[2] This program, consisting of a Kodachrome strip film of 120 frames, has been deposited with the American Documentation Institute. Order Document No. 6080, from ADI Auxiliary Publication Service, Library of Congress, Washington 25, D. C., remitting in advance $2.00 for microfilm, $16.25 for 35-mm. enlargement prints. Make checks payable to Chief, Photoduplication Service, Library of Congress.

18. Squares can be large or small. But if each side on a square is one foot long, this is called a square foot. Which figure is one square foot?

A. ☐ 4 ft. (4 ft.)

B. ☐ 5 ft. (5 ft.)

C. ☐ 1 ft.

D. ☐ 2 ft. / 1 ft.

E. ☐ 2 ft. / 1 ft.

19. Here are two squares; ☐ ☐
They are exactly the same size. Suppose I put the squares together side by side like this.

☐☐

What kind of a figure will the two squares together make if I leave out the middle line like this?

☐

A. Another bigger square.
B. A rectangle.

20. Here is a rectangle. It is 2 feet long and 1 foot wide.

1 ft. ☐ 1 ft. (2 ft.)

Suppose I draw a line in the middle, like this; I will make 2 squares. How long will each side of each square be?

1 ft. ☐ 1 ft. (2 ft.)

A. 1 ft.   B. 2 ft.   C. 3 ft.

21. Suppose you have a rectangle which is 3 feet long and 1 foot wide like this

1 ft. ☐ 1 ft. (3 ft.)

How many squares, 1 ft. long on each side, can I make out of this rectangle?

A. One   B. Two   C. Three

22. How many square feet are in a rectangle which is two feet high and one foot wide like this:

1 ft.
A. One
B. Two   ☐ 2 ft.
C. Three
D. Six
1 ft.

23. How many square feet are in a rectangle which is 2 feet wide and 4 feet long?

☐

A. Two   B. Four   C. Six   D. Eight

24. Each side of this square is one inch long. This is called one square inch. How many square inches are in this rectangle which is one inch wide and five inches long?

1 in. ☐ 1 in.

1 in. ☐ (5 in.)

A. One B. Two C. Three D. Four E. Five.

25. Here is a rectangle which is 2 inches wide and 4 inches long. How many square inches are there in this rectangle?

☐

There are 2 rows with 4 squares in each row. How can we write the total number of square inches?

A. 2 + 2   C. 2 + 4 + 2 + 4
B. 2 + 4   D. 4 + 4

26. This rectangle is 4 inches wide and 7 inches long. How many square inches are in this rectangle?

☐

A. There are 4 rows with 4 squares in each row.
B. There are 8 rows with 4 squares in each row.
C. There are 4 rows with 7 squares in each row.
D. There are 4 rows with 14 squares in each row.

27. This rectangle is 5 inches long and 3 inches wide.

3 in. ☐ (5 in.)

There are 3 rows of squares. In each row there are 5 square inches. How many square inches are there in the rectangle?

A. 5 + 5   B. 5 + 5 + 5   C. 5 + 5 + 5 + 5

28. Here is a rectangle which is 5 in. wide and 9 in. long. How many square inches are there in the rectangle?

☐

A. 9 + 9 + 9 + 9 + 9   B. 5 + 5 + 5 + 5 + 5
C. 9 + 5 + 9 + 5   D. 5 + 5 + 9 + 9 + 9

29. A rectangle which is 5 in. wide and 9 in. long contains 9 + 9 + 9 + 9 + 9 square inches. What is a quick way of finding how many square inches this is?

A. Add 9 and 5.
B. Add 9 and 9 and 9 and 9 and 9.
C. Multiply 9 by 5.
D. Divide 9 by 5.

Figure 1 A sample sequence of items, nos. 18–29, to illustrate programming principles

higher item difficulty that the learner is encouraged to "formulate his own hypotheses and try them out." This procedure may have merit if information is supplied to the student showing why the alternative is incorrect (Crowder, 1958) or if branching in the program permits special remedial instruction. But where, as in this study, the pupil is informed only that he is wrong when he makes an error, he is given no more information than when he gets the item correct. One fifth grade subject, after completing the program in this study, commented, "It's hard to know why you get something wrong. When I got it right, I knew it. When I got it wrong, I didn't know why." Since the absence of an explanation is likely to heighten the aversive consequences of failure, it appeared most desirable to adopt a minimum difficulty level for the items in this study. If it seemed helpful to emphasize that certain responses were wrong, instead of having the student learn this by "being wrong," special items were constructed for this purpose, e.g., "Which of the following figures is NOT a rectangle?"

2. Skinner's use of the vanishing stimulus and the prompt facilitates the occurrence of the correct response. For example, in Items 25 and 26 colored rows of squares encourage the right answer. In Item 27 these become merely dotted lines which vanish completely in Item 28. In Item 20 the correct answer "1 ft." is prompted by the dimension "1 ft." in the diagram.

3. To promote generalization within a broad class of items, a process necessary for understanding, the learner should acquire a variety of verbal responses which might later be used, through intraverbal associations, to evoke other appropriate responses. This is simply a process of mediated or secondary generalization, a complex example of which is found in Judd's theory of transfer through verbal principles. For instance, it was judged that if the pupil learned to group squares within a rectangle by rows, as in Items 25 through 28, he would acquire intraverbal associations which would promote the correct response in learning later in the program to multiply the length by the width to find the area and, still later, to divide the area by the length to find the width. In other words, with these items the pupil is being prepared to "gain insight into why" you multiply in one case and divide in the other. Appropriate intraverbal associations, such as verbal principles, definitions, or characteristics, should function to extend the pupil's learning to entirely new items which involve the same principle or concept. If this indeed can be accomplished, the use of multiple-choice items in automated teaching results in something more than "mere recognition" of the right answer.

4. Procedures or concepts which are not otherwise involved in the sequence of items should be reviewed periodically. For example, a review of the process of grouping squares into rows, originally presented in

Items 25–28, was provided later by six items occurring at intervals throughout the program.

5. Other techniques included the repetition of the correct answer on the succeeding item (as in Item 29), the irregular appearance of "interesting" colored pictures accompanying the item, and the use of a variety of forms of the multiple-choice item.

SUBJECTS

Fourteen experimental Ss and 14 controls, individually matched on the basis of intelligence, sex, reading ability, and pretest scores, were selected from the fifth and low sixth grades. All Ss showed competence in multiplication and division but little acquaintance with the topic of area. A fifteenth S who had completed the program was dropped from the study because of an automobile accident prior to the posttest. The control Ss were given no special instruction of any kind. They were used to control for the effects of incidental learning such as that which might result from the administration of the pretest.

PRETEST AND POSTTEST

Both of these tests were of the free-answer or essay type. The pretest consisted of 12 problems involving multiplication and division, in addition to 8 problems dealing with areas of rectangles. The posttest consisted of the same eight problems of the pretest on area plus another eight, most of which were more difficult. Sample problems on the posttest were:

1. A gallon of paint will cover an area of 200 sq. ft. How long a stretch of fence could you paint with 2 gallons if the fence is 5 feet high?

2. A sheet of cardboard is 3 feet long. It weighs exactly 4 ounces. What is the area of this cardboard if it is 2 feet wide?

3. A sheet of paper is 10 in. wide and 12 in. long. This sheet of paper is cut into strips. The strips are laid end to end and then joined with Scotch tape. This long strip now looks like this:

Can anyone tell what the area of this long strip is? . . . . . .
If so, what is it? . . . .

PROCEDURE

Experimental Ss operated the machine for two or three periods on successive days. The total time spent with the machine ranged from one hour and 30 minutes to slightly over two hours. The posttest was given the day following the end of such machine instruction to each experimental S and his control.

RESULTS

The mean score of the experimental group on the posttest was 12.4, with a standard deviation of 5.6. The corresponding control mean was 5.4, with a standard deviation of 3.7. Since the posttest scores for the experimental group showed a much greater variance than did the control, a sign test was used. All except one of the experimental Ss showed a higher posttest score than did their matched controls, a difference which is significant at the .01 level. Although the experimental group answered every item, except one, of the posttest better than the control group, most of these pupils missed several items which were similar to those presented in the program; they learned far less than what had been expected.

The total errors on the program ranged from 3 to 118 with a mean of 54. Jane's record, presented in Figure 2, was the poorest performance and indicates very little learning as measured by the posttest. Part of her problem may have been inadequate ability in computation, since her computation score was relatively low. Even for a typical student like Kenneth, whose record is shown in Figure 3, the program was too difficult; 40 mistakes is entirely too many according to the criterion adopted. The program appeared to be ideal for Byron, whose record appears in Figure 4. Although he showed little ability in the field of area on the pretest, Byron's performance on the posttest was outstanding. He was able to generalize from his training so well that on the posttest he solved completely new problems of obtaining the area of a parallelogram and a triangle.

The rank order correlation between total number of errors on the program and the gain on the posttest was $-.83$. While this of course supports the hypothesis that the optimum difficulty level of each item should be low, it does not permit, in itself, any such conclusion. The rank order correlation of mental age was .52 with gain on the posttest and $-.79$ with number of program errors. On the basis of this limited sample it appears that the program was more appropriate for the brighter children.

DESIRABLE REVISIONS IN THE PROGRAM

In the absence of definitive evidence on the question, it appears that the major weakness of this program was that it was too difficult for most of the pupils. Revisions should be made along the following lines:

1. Since the reading load was probably a major obstacle for many pupils, sentences should be shorter and the total amount of reading less for each item. Possibly several versions of the program, at different reading levels, would be desirable.

2. The steps in many if not most cases could be smaller. For example,

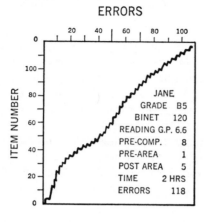

Figure 2 Graphic record of the poorest performance

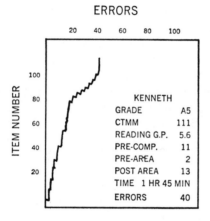

Figure 3 Graphic record of a typical pupil

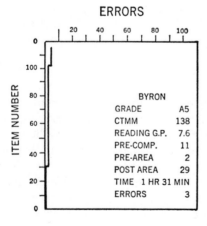

Figure 4 Graphic record of the best performance

Item 22, which was missed by three pupils, could be preceded by items analogous to 19 and 20. Item 24, also missed by three pupils, could be divided into two items, the first introducing the concept of square inch only. Item 25 could be rewritten as two or even three items.

The greatest misapplication of the principle of small steps occurred in the latter part of the program. For the group of 15 pupils who performed the item set, on the first 10 items there was a total of five errors on the first attempt (out of a possible 150). On succeeding sets of 10 items this number of first-attempt failures increased until it reached 66 for the last set of 10 items. The relatively high difficulty of the items in the latter part of the program appeared to result from the fact that these more complex items required a diversity of other understandings, abilities which were not tested for in the pretest. For example, although pupils were selected on the basis of their ability to divide, many failed to relate division to the process of successive subtraction. The program failed to provide adequate introduction or review of these concepts.

Faced with this type of problem a programmer can either use a more adequate pretest to provide for better selection or he can add the additional items as required. When a great variety of item sets in arithmetic become available, the problem largely disappears. The prerequisites to any item set can be stated in terms of the successful completion of previous item sets. Conversely, the record obtained for a pupil with one item set might be used diagnostically to indicate what the next set, remedial, optional, or otherwise, might be.

3. A wider variety of items should be used for each new process. For instance, Items 25–28 should be supplemented with items which provide verbal statements as alternatives and more familiar illustrations of the problem. As another example, on many of the posttest questions asking for an area, Ss wrote only the correct number failing to indicate the square units involved. Although six items had been presented in the program to reduce this kind of error, these items unfortunately were all stated in exactly the same way. The item stem called for an area and among the alternatives one distractor listed only the correct number. Although completion items may be necessary to teach this type of behavior, better results in this program could probably have been obtained if, instead of the single form, a variety of multiple-choice forms had been used, e.g., use of "none of these" as an alternative, asking "What is left out in this answer?" or asking for the appropriate rule.

CONCLUSION

The use of multiple-choice items in automated teaching appears to have some effectiveness under these conditions in teaching understanding, as herein defined, even though the criterion was a free-answer test. Although the average pupil did not show as high a degree of competence on the posttest as expected, the program was also far more difficult than intended. Since there appeared to be a strong relationship between success on the program and gains on the posttest, before the limitations and advantages of the multiple-choice method used in this study may be assessed, the program should be revised to include smaller steps and a greater variety of items. Whether the best performers on the present program would have learned more from such a longer and simpler revision remains to be determined; to accommodate individual differences in ability two or three versions of the program may be desirable.

Summary

Fourteen elementary school pupils responded individually to a set of 110 multiple-choice items in a teaching machine. The performance of each child was graphically recorded. Subjects performed significantly better on a test of understanding of areas of rectangles than did their matched controls who received no planned instruction on this topic. The principles of programming are discussed and illustrated. Suggestions given for the revision of the program, which appeared to be too difficult for most pupils, include the introduction of smaller steps and a greater variety of types of multiple-choice items.

References

Coulson, J. E., & Silberman, H. F. *Results of initial experiment in automated teaching.* Santa Monica, Calif.: System Development Corp., 1959.

Crowder, N. A. Automatic tutoring by means of intrinsic programming. Paper read at the Air Force Office of Scientific Research and the University of Pennsylvania Conference on the Automated Teaching of Verbal and Symbolic Skills. Philadelphia, December, 1958.

Ferster, C. B., & Sapon, S. M. An application of recent developments in psychology to the teaching of German. *Harv. educ. Rev.*, 1958, 28, 58–59.

Homme, L., & Glaser, R. Relationships between the programmed textbook and teaching machines. Paper read at the Air Force Office of Scientific Research and the University of Pennsylvania Conference on the Automated Teaching of Verbal and Symbolic Skills. Philadelphia, December, 1958.

Porter, D. A critical review of a portion of the literature on teaching devices. *Harv. educ. Rev.*, 1957, 27, 126–147.

Pressey, S. L. A machine for automatic teaching of drill material. *Sch. Soc.*, 1927, 25, 549–552.

Skinner, B. F. Science of learning and the art of teaching. *Harv. educ. Rev.*, 1954, 24, 86–97.

Skinner, B. F. Teaching Machines. *Science*, 1958, 128, 969–977.

15 LEARNING FROM WRITTEN INSTRUCTIVE MATERIALS: AN EXPLORATION OF THE CONTROL OF INSPECTION BEHAVIOR BY TEST-LIKE EVENTS
Ernst Z. Rothkopf [1]

The main purpose of the present experiment was to find out: (a) whether adjunct, test-like questions have generally facilitating effects on learning from written instructional materials and (b) whether it matters where the experimental questions are asked in the course of reading. Rothkopf (1963, 1965) has hypothesized that test-like events, such as questions, have a generally facilitating effect in learning from written material. These effects have been identified with a class of activities called inspection behavior.[2]

Hershberger and associates (Hershberger, 1963; Hershberger and Terry, 1965a, 1965b) has provided recent evidence that adjunct questions increase the amount learned from a written passage. However the experimental procedures used in these and in other related studies (see McKeachie, 1963, pp. 1154–1156), allow the possibility that the observed facilitated performance was due to specific instructive effects of the experimental questions rather than a generally facilitating learning set.

Test-like events with knowledge of results, e.g., the anticipation method in paired-associate learning, are well known to have direct instructive effects, and to produce improvement in recall performance on the material tested. Even without knowledge of results, test-like events have been observed to improve subsequent recall performance (Estes, 1960; Estes, Hopkins, and Crothers, 1960; Levine, Leitenberg, and Richter, 1964). As a consequence, it cannot be decided whether Hershberger's results were due to generally facilitating effects of test question because in his and in other related studies (see McKeachie, 1963, pp.

[1] Miss E. U. Coke made important contributions to the conduct of the experiment and analysis of the results. Mrs. C. K. Shefsky assisted in this effort.

[2] I actually prefer the term *mathemagenic* behavior or *mathemagenic responses* to *inspection behavior* because the last tends to be understood in an overly narrow sense. The roots of the new word are *mathema:* learning, that which is learned and *gignesthai:* to be born. This seems an appropriate reference to a class of responses which give birth to learning.

SOURCE: Ernst Z. Rothkopf, "Learning from Written Instructive Materials: An Exploration of the Control of Inspection Behavior by Test-Like Events," *American Educational Research Journal*, 3, no. 4 (November 1966), 241–49. Reprinted by permission of the author and the American Educational Research Association.

1154–1156), the subject matter on which Ss tested while reading was identical or closely related to the material on which the final criterion examination was based.

The present study attempts to evaluate the facilitative effects of adjunct questions under conditions when the direct instructive consequences of questions were eliminated. The logic of experimentation was to use adjunct test-like questions based on materials which had little or no transfer of training to the criterion examination. In this way any facilitative effects of testing could not be attributed to the specific training effects of the experimental test-like questions. Several conditions for using test questions were explored and compared with a control group which did not use the adjunct test.

Method

Materials. Subjects were asked to read a 5200 word selection from Rachel Carson's book *The Sea Around Us.*[3] It described marine life at the greater ocean depths. Although the content of the selection was topically related, adjacent paragraphs frequently deal with relatively independent factual domains.

The test was multilithed on 20 pages of approximately 260 words each. These materials were divided into seven sections. The first of these consisted of pages 1 and 2; the remainder of three successive pages each. Six questions were constructed from the material in each of four sections, and five questions from each of three sections, for a total of 39 questions. Questions were of the completion type requiring a one or two term answer. From the pool of 39 questions, two were chosen from every section. The resulting set of 14 questions (to be referred to as EQs—experimental questions) were used in the main experimental manipulations of this study. The EQs were selected so as to minimize transfer of training from the portions of text underlying these 14 questions to the material underlying the remaining 25 items.

The main experimental comparisons were based on two criterion tests which were administered after the completion of training. The first of these was the General Test (GT), intended to measure general facilitative effects of EQs. This test was composed of the 25 questions that were not used as EQs. Two forms of this test (A and B) differing only in question sequence, were used. The second criterion test was intended to measure specific learning which resulted from the EQs. This test, which

[3] Permission for the experimental use of these copyrighted materials was kindly granted by the publishers, Oxford University Press, 417 Fifth Avenue, New York 16, New York.

will be referred to as *EQRT* (*EQ* relevant test), consisted simply of all 14 *EQ*s bound in a booklet.

Treatments. Five experimental treatments and one control group were used. These differed mainly in the location of *EQ*s in the textual sequence and in whether knowledge of results (correct answers) were provided for *EQ*s. The experimental treatments were as follows:

SBA. (*EQ*s shortly before, with answers); just *before* starting on any section, S read the two *EQ*s for that section and was instructed to guess the correct answer for each. After writing his guess S obtained the correct answer by removing a mask from it. The general direction which accompanied this experimental condition and all other treatments in which *EQ*s were given prior to the readings stressed that the *EQ*s were samples of the kinds of questions which could be asked about the experimental materials.[4]

SB. (*EQ*s shortly before, no answers); same treatment as *SBA* except that the correct answers were not provided after S made his guess.

LBA. (All *EQ*s given before starting the chapter, with answers); just *before* starting to read the chapter, Ss were given all 14 *EQ*s *en bloc.* They were instructed to guess the answer to each EQ and write it into the appropriate space. The correct answer was then provided as in *SBA.*

SAA. (*EQ*s shortly *after* each section, with answers); immediately after reading each section, S was asked to respond to each of the two *EQ*s appropriate to the section he had just read. The correct answer was provided as soon as S responded to each question. The general directions which preceded this treatment and subsequently described SA stressed that the *EQ*s were samples of the kind of questions which could be asked about the experimental materials and also that they provide S with information about how much he was remembering about the material he was reading.

SA. (*EQ*s shortly after each section, no answers); same as *SAA* except that the correct answers were not provided after S responded to questions.

Control Group. No *EQ*s were given in this treatment and Ss were simply exposed to general directions which were composed of portions of those used in other treatments. These stressed that Ss should try to remember as much of the experimental chapter as they could and that they would be tested later.

Two additional groups of Ss were used for the purposes described below.

---

[4] Copies of the test questions and of the experimental directions used for each treatment have been deposited with the American Documentation Institute. Order Document No. 9018 remitting $1.75 for 35-mm microfilm or $2.50 for 6 by 8 in. photocopies.

Direction Reference Group (DRG). The purpose of this group was to provide a reference level which could be used to determine the relative magnitude of *EQ*-effects compared to hortatory care-inducing directions. This group was treated exactly as the *control* condition except that the general directions included statements that the reading material contained much detailed factual information and that the text should be read carefully and slowly.

Transfer Evaluation Group (TE). This group was used to assure that there was no transfer of specific training between *EQ* and *GT*. Group *TE* did not read the experimental text at all. Instead completed one form of *GT* and then studied the *EQs* and the correct answer to them by a modification of the anticipation method. When they could answer each *EQ* perfectly regardless of order of presentation, the Ss were again given the *GT* test but in an alternate form.

Procedure and Design. General directions, EQs when and where appropriate, and the experimental text were bound in looseleaf notebooks and given to each S without substantial additional directions. The Ss were brought into the experimental room individually and worked in one of seven booths which visually screened them from other Ss who were working in the room at the time. Each S worked through the book at his own rate. While reading through the textual material S recorded the time he started and finished reading each page directly on the page. A large digital clock, projected on a screen in the experimental room, served as time standard.

Each *EQ* was printed on the right half of a 5-7/16 x 8-3/8 in. sheet of paper which had notebook ring perforations along its left edge. Most of the left half of each of these sheets was obscured by a cardboard mask. This mask was also equipped with binding perforation and was bound into the notebook in a way that covered the left-hand portions of any *EQ* sheet until S tore the question sheet out of the notebook. For the *LBA*, *SBA*, and *SAA* treatments, the correct answer was printed close to the left edge of the *EQ* sheet. For the other treatments it was not given. After giving a response all Ss tore the question sheet out of the notebook. In this way the *LBA*, *SBA*, and *SAA* treatments obtained correct answers after responding while the other treatments did not. After use, the *EQ* sheets were placed into a slotted, ballot-type box.

The two final criterion tests were administered immediately after S had completed reading the chapter and the notebook had been collected. The 25-item *GT* test was administered first. Half of the Ss in each treatment were given Form A, and the remainder Form B. After the *GT* test, Ss were given the 14-item *EQRT*.

Subjects. Paid student volunteers ($N = 159$) from Fairleigh Dickinson University in Madison, N. J., served as Ss. All had stated that they had not read *The Sea Around Us* before. Only 12 Ss were used for *TE*. For each of the other treatments, $N = 21$.

One S was dropped from condition SAA because he did not follow directions. The first 12 Ss who participated in the experiment were not given in EQRT test.

Results

No Specific Transfer from EQ to GT. Data from the Transfer Evaluation Group (TE) verify that EQs were properly constructed and that no substantial, specific transfer of trainging exists between EQs and GT. Pretraining GT score for TE was 1.8 correct responses (7.2%). After mastery of EQs, this figure was 2.6 (10.4%). This gain of 3.2% in GT-performance as a function of learning EQs without reading the text is not reliable statistically. However, as an added safeguard against specific transfer which may have resulted from exposure to EQs, the four GT questions which were responsible for the slight gain in group TE were eliminated from all comparisons involving the GT test.[5] After removal of these four questions, mean correct responses on the pretest of posttest of the Control T group was 1.58 and 1.50 respectively.

General Facilitative Effects of EQs. Because of the evidence and measures described above, it is safe to assume that facilitated GT performance which is produced by EQs in the major experimental treatments, is the result of a general set-like factor rather than the direct instructive consequences of EQs. Performance on GT for the various treatments is shown in Table 1. The treatments in which EQs were administered im-

Table 1
Percentage Current Responses on the Two Final Tests and Mean and S. D. of Median Reading Times per Page for the Several Experimental Treatments

Treatment	GT	EQRT	Reading Time (Secs.)	S.D. of Reading Time *
Control	33.14	28.57	69.9	4.22
LBA	35.62	77.82	68.2	6.84
SB	30.10	65.36	69.0	8.16
SBA	34.67	77.82	71.6	6.62
SA	43.24	62.58	79.9	9.38
SAA	40.40	82.35	70.5	6.73
DRG	42.67	41.07	82.1	9.04

* Reading times for the first page were not included in the computations since they are considerably higher than any of the other pages.

[5] It should be noted that the elimination of these four items did not change the findings in any manner.

mediately after each section (i.e., *SAA, SA*) resulted in better general test (GT) performance than the *Control A* group. The Direction Reference Group (DRG) also exceeded the performance of the Control. The general facilitative effects due to *EQs* which were administered *after* each section, and that due to *DRG* direction, amounted to an approximately 10% rise in correct responses. An analysis of variance showed between-treatments effects to be significant ($F=2.44$, $d.f.=6{,}139$, $P<.05$). The *SA* treatment ($t=2.21$, $d.f.=139$, $P<.01$) and *DRG* ($t=2.09$, $d.f.=139$, $P<.05$) produced significantly higher *GT* scores than the Control Group. The difference between *SAA* and the control did not reach the conventional significance level ($t=1.59$, $P<.20$). All of the treatments which involved *EQs* administered prior to reading the relevant segment of text (i.e., *LBA, SBA, SB*) performed at about the same level as the control condition.

Specific Instructive Effects of EQs. Specific instructive effects of *EQs* can be estimated from performance on the *EQRT* test which is shown in Table 1. Analysis of variance indicated that differences due to treatment were significant beyond the .01 level ($F=28.62$, $d.f.=6{,}127$). All treatments involving previous exposure to *EQs* resulted in substantially higher performance than either group without these exposures, i.e., *Control A* ($t=10.54$, $P<.01$) or *DRG*. Subjects which obtained the correct answer after responding (*LBA, SBA, SAA*) responded correctly more often than those taking *EQs* without feedback of any kind (i.e., *SB, SA*; $t=4.54$, $P<.01$). No substantial changes in *EQRT* performance were found to be associated with location of the *EQs* in the text.

It should be noted that the performance on *EQRT* of *DRG* and the Control Group, neither of which had been exposed to *EQs* before, was at nearly the same respective level as on *GT*. The facilitating effect associated with the experimental directions in the *DRG* condition was of the same magnitude as before. It elevated the *EQRT* performance of *DRG* about 10 percent over *Control A* ($t=2.37$, $P<.02$).

Reading Time. Median reading time per page was determined for each condition. The means and standard deviation of these over all 20 pages are also shown in Table 1. Two treatments, *DRG* and *SA* resulted in markedly slower reading than the other conditions. These two treatments also result in the highest *GT* performance. It is not clear why the *SAA* treatment, which is like *DRG* and *SA* with respect to *GT* performance, differs so markedly from these two treatments with respect to reading time.

The change in reading speed over successive sections of the experimental passage is shown in Figure 1. The first section was read very slowly. The amount of time spent per page dropped sharply in the second section but the curves decelerate. The slower reading times found

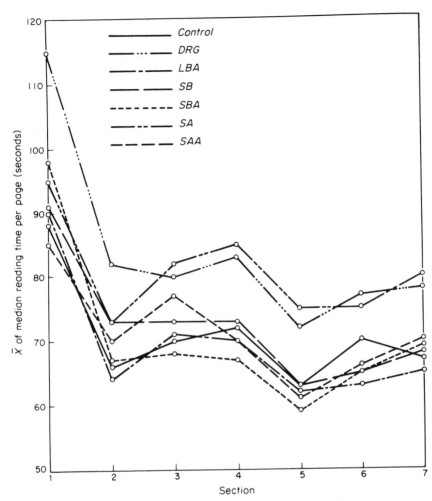

Figure 1 Means of the medial reading time per page for the seven sections of the experimental test. The first section contains two pages and the remaining sections three pages each.

in *DRG* and the *SA* treatment maintains itself throughout the experimental text. An analysis of individual page reading times gives some indication that pages which followed *EQ*s tended to have longer reading time and that increasingly less time was spent on the subsequent pages of the section. It is difficult to reach a definite conclusion in this matter, however, because the analysis is complicated by differences in reading speed between pages. It is notable, however, that the control group was observed to have less variability in reading time from page to page than the other treatments (see *S.D.*s in Table 1).

Discussion

Test-like questions, which are presented *after* reading the relevant text passage have apparently both specific and general facilitative effects on post-reading performance. The general facilitative effects were found to be of the same magnitude as those of specially prepared hortatory directions.

Test-like questions, which were presented *before* the relevant text passage was read produced only question-specific facilitative effects. These question-specific effects were greater when the correct answer was given to the student after he made his response than when no knowledge of results was available. However, even without knowledge of results, the specific trainings effects which resulted from exposure to EQs were very marked.

The fact that LBA, SBA, and SB treatments did not result in general facilitation effects could have been due to the distracting influence of EQs in the LBA, SBA, and SB treatments but the data does not support this view. According to this hypothesis, EQs which are administered prior to reading the material on which they are based resulted in greater attention to the EQ-specific materials in the experimental passage. As a consequence, less inspection activity was devoted to the material on which the general test questions were based. This however implies that the LBA, SBA, and SB treatments would perform better on the EQ-relevant test ($EQRT$) and this was not found to be the case.

The results of this experiment are consistent with the view that when a written passage is studied, Ss learn not only the specific content but also may acquire some general facilitative skills, namely inspection behaviors consistent with the training objectives (Rothkopf, 1963, 1965). The present experiment provides evidence that test-like questions on material which had just been read, which were self-administered approximately after every 1000 words of text are one of the environmental controls of these inspection behaviors. These short tests induced effective inspection behaviors even when correct answers were *not* supplied after the student made a response.

The directions used in DRG treatment resulted in GT performance improvements of the same order of magnitude as the 14 experimental questions (EQs) of the SA treatment. It must *not* be concluded, however, that this result argues for the practical advantage of admonitions over adjunct tests in promoting learning from written material. The data from the EQ relevant test ($EQRT$) clearly prove that EQs and other adjunct tests are in themselves instructive and that they are more so when correct answers are provided after responding. Hence, adjunct tests unlike hortatory directions not only may shape effective inspection behavior but are also useful in teaching specific skills.

References

Estes, William K. "Learning Theory and the New 'Mental Chemistry.' " *Psychological Review* 67: 207–23; 1960.

Estes, William K.; Hopkins, Billy L.; and Crothers, Edward J. "All-or-none and Conservation Effects in the Learning and Retention of Paired Associates." *Journal of Experimental Psychology* 60: 329–39; 1960.

Hershberger, Wayne A. *Learning via Programmed Reading and Cue versus Response in Programmed Reading.* American Institute for Research, Technical Report AIR-C28-7/63-TR, July 1963.

Hershberger, Wayne A., and Terry, Donald F. "Typographical Cueing in Conventional and Programmed Tests." *Journal of Applied Psychology* 49: 55–60; 1965. (a)

Hershberger, Wayne A., and Terry, Donald F. "Delay of Self-testing in Three Types of Programmed Test." *Journal of Educational Psychology* 56: 22–30; 1965. (b)

Levine, Marvin; Leitenberg, Harold; and Richter, Martin. "The Blank Trials Law. The Equivalence of Positive Reinforcement and Non-reinforcement." *Psychological Review* 71: 94–103; 1964.

McKeachie, Wilbert J. "Research on Teaching at the College and University Level." *Handbook of Research on Teaching.* (Edited by Nathaniel L. Gage.) Chicago: Rand McNally, 1963. pp. 1118–72.

Rothkopf, Ernst Z. "Some Conjectures about Inspection Behavior in Learning from Written Sentences and the Response Mode Problem in Programmed Self-instruction." *Journal of Programmed Instruction* 2: 31–46; 1963.

Rothkopf, Ernst Z. "Some Theoretical and Experimental Approaches to Problems in Written Instruction." *Learning and the Educational Process.* (Edited by J. D. Krumboltz.) Chicago: Rand McNally, 1965. pp. 193–221.

Rothkopf, Ernst Z., and Coke, Esther U. "Repetition Interval and Rehearsal Method in Learning Equivalences from Written Sentences." *Journal of Verbal Learning and Verbal Behavior* 2: 406–16; 1963.

16 EVALUATION OF LANGUAGE HABITS IN A BEHAVIORAL SCIENCE CURRICULUM [1]
William E. Gardner and Paul E. Johnson

Traditionally, curricula in the social studies have emphasized chronological history and descriptive political science and geography. New pro-

SOURCE: William E. Gardner and Paul E. Johnson, "Evaluation of Language Habits in a Behavioral Science Curriculum," *School Review,* 76, no. 4 (December 1968), 396–411. Copyright © 1968 by The University of Chicago. Reprinted by permission of the University of Chicago Press.

grams now being developed tend to shift the emphasis to the teaching of concepts from the behavioral sciences. The experimental curricula of the Project Social Studies Curriculum Development Centers, for instance, focus heavily upon the dynamic sciences which attempt to explain and predict man's behavior.[2]

In these projects and in the efforts of individual school districts to revise their social studies programs, special attention is devoted to the identification of "key" concepts in the various behavioral sciences and to the development of instructional materials which are built around the verbal representations of these concepts.

The current interest in teaching concepts taken from the behavioral sciences has its pedagogical base in the assumption that young people can learn sophisticated scientific concepts if only they are presented in appropriate form and through materials adequate to the task. The major intellectual support for this assumption appears to be Bruner's hypothesis that "any subject can be taught effectively in some intellectually honest form to any child at any stage of development." [3]

Exciting as this notion may be, it is far from being empirically established. Indeed, few data are available on even the most general questions related to the effects of teaching the behavioral sciences. Can young people deal with these ideas in any except a purely rote fashion? Will the introduction of concepts from the behavioral sciences into the early stages of the socialization process inject as well an unwanted ambivalence into the personality structure of the students? We do not know whether students can gain even a rudimentary knowledge of why men behave as they do. Nor do we have any completely reliable means for assessing the accuracy or the effects of the knowledge which a student may have of concepts such as "culture," "socialization," and "role," which serve as formal representations of man's behavior.

A major problem in assessing learning in behavioral science stems from a confusion concerning the nature of the relationship between the logical structure of the concepts within a discipline and the structures that appear among the verbal representations of these concepts in instruction. Certainly two of the most critical decisions involved in attempting to teach a subject matter are the manner in which its domain of concepts (i.e., its content) is to be sampled and how the concepts within a given sample are to be arranged for instructional purposes. Unfortunately, as Randall has pointed out,[4] nothing in the nature of a discipline speaks directly to the problem of how its subject matter should be taught. The structure of a behavioral science does not itself indicate how decisions concerning the sampling and arrangement of its concepts are to be made, and the nature of the relationship between the logical structure of a discipline and its representation in instruction is ultimately a psychological rather than a logical matter.

One form of psychological relationship which serves to relate the concepts in a discipline to their representation in instruction is derived from the order which a specialist in the discipline or a curriculum theorist imposes upon its subject matter when he attempts to describe or characterize how it is "done." [5] The relationships between groups of behaviors which have similar properties define the structure of the characterization and represent the central properties or "key" concepts around which the content of the subject matter is organized. This characterization, here termed a "subject-matter model," is descriptive rather than prescriptive with respect to instruction, and in its most complete form it constitutes a paradigm of the subject matter [6] in that it serves to differentiate doing the subject matter from not doing it and is presumably relevant to decisions concerning doing the subject matter well as against doing it badly.

Another form of psychological relationship which relates a subject matter of a discipline to its verbal representation in instruction is derived from the order which a specialist or curriculum theorist imposes upon the subject matter when he attempts to describe how it should be taught. This characterization, here termed a "teaching model," is based upon a subject-matter model and is prescriptive with respect to instruction. It involves assumptions about the learner, the teacher, the process of acquisition, and the activity of teaching.

Once instructional materials have been produced for teaching a discipline, a decision needs to be made concerning the behaviors that can be used to determine whether its content has been learned and the even more formidable problem of whether its content has been understood. The subject-matter model is a source of behaviors for testing acquisition. A sample of behaviors which the child has experienced in instruction can be used to see whether he has learned what he was taught, and a sample of behaviors which are different from but related to those used in instruction can be used to determine what he is able to do that he has not directly experienced.

The behaviors produced by the subject-matter specialist or curriculum theorist are a useful index of acquisition to the extent that they are appropriate to the knowledge which the child has of what he has been taught. If, however, the test behaviors are inappropriate to what the child has actually learned, we are left with little information except that he cannot perform them successfully. It is important to note that, whereas the specialist may be able to make explicit the interrelations among the "key" concepts which serve to define his subject matter for him, the child, especially in the early stages of acquisition, will very likely be unable to describe the rules which govern his behavior with respect to the content of instruction. Thus, a means is needed for indexing the interrelations among concepts which have been represented verbally in instruction which does not depend upon the child's awareness of the rules which apply to these concepts and which minimizes the distortion due to a "set" for such a rule system.

One means of indexing the interrelationships among concepts which have appeared in verbal behavior is the word-association test. The present paper is an attempt to describe the way in which language habits as indexed by verbal association are related to the representation of a subject matter in instruction when that subject matter is a behavioral science.

Method

The subjects in this investigation were from two classes of seventh-grade students at University High School, the laboratory school of the University of Minnesota. The students began a social studies course dealing with concepts in a behavioral science (sociology, primarily) in September, and their experience with the concepts examined in the experiment terminated in February of the same school year. The curriculum materials used in the instruction were constructed by the Project Social Studies Curriculum Development Center at the University of Minnesota.[7]

A packet of IBM cards was prepared for the word-association test together with a page of general instructions and a page of word-association instructions. The general instructions given to each subject were as follows:

> The following cards contain some test items designed to find out how people use words. There are a variety of items, none of which have anything to do with your ability in school, but which are intended to reveal facts about the usage of words not discoverable by more usual techniques. Treat each item as carefully as you can, even when the item calls for a judgment that seems almost impossible to make. Work rapidly, however, because we will learn most about how words are used if you give us the first response which occurs to you. You may open the packet and begin with the first page. Read the instructions carefully.

The twenty-five stimulus words used in the association test were selected as being representative of the subject-matter model around which the Project Social Studies Curriculum materials were constructed. The words are presented later in Tables 2, 3, and 4 ranked according to their importance in the subject matter as determined by the model used in constructing the curriculum materials.

Each of the twenty-five words on the association test was placed on an IBM card so that each subject received an independently randomized group of words. The randomization of the packet of cards was carried out by means of a computer.[8] The instructions given to each subject at the beginning of the association test were as follows:

> This is a test to see how quickly you can think of words. On each of the following cards you will find a word. You are to write next to each word the first word it makes you think of. It doesn't make any difference what word you write as long as the word on the card makes you think of it. There are no right or wrong answers. The purpose of the test is to see how quickly words will come to your mind. For example, suppose that *Coat* is the word you see. Your job is to write down the first word that *Coat* makes you think of. *Coat* might make you think of *Hat* or *Man* or *Wear* or *Big* or *Warm* or you might think of some other word. Whatever the first word is that you think of write it down next to *Coat*. You are to do the same thing for each word on each of the cards. Be sure to write clearly but don't worry if you are not sure how to spell a word. Spell it as best you can. This is a test of speed. When I tell you to start I want you to work straight through the packet of cards. When you finish a card, go right on to the next one. Write only one word on each card. Do not skip any cards. Be sure to write clearly.

The word-association test was administered to the subjects twice, once on the first day of classes in the fall and once when they had completed several units of study in the Project Social Studies course.

Results and Discussion

This investigation was conducted with a twofold purpose in mind: first, to obtain a measure of the change over time in the language habits of students who study a behavioral science and, second, to obtain data which might indicate how the instructional materials being taught were related to this change. The investigation was exploratory in nature with an emphasis upon acquiring data which would lead to future, more conclusive experimentation.

The distribution of responses to a word on an association test by a group of individuals constitutes the associative meaning of that word, and it has recently been shown that the associative meaning of the words which represent concepts in a subject matter reflect in part the structure of that subject matter.[9] In the present investigation responses to words on the association test were analyzed in terms of their similarity in associative meaning and in terms of categories of relation derived from the subject matter to which the concepts represented by the words belonged. In addition to words being associatively related in the sense that one word elicits another and vice versa, they may also be related to the sense that as stimulus words on an association test they have responses in common. Words with overlapping response distributions have associative meanings which are similar in some degree and should appear in the same verbal environments. The associations to verbal labels for the concepts in a subject matter such as sociology which comprise the associative meaning of those labels may be attributed to a structure acquired as a result of exposure to the subject matter as well as to the simple, contiguous occurrence of these labels in written and spoken instruction. The present data do not, however, indicate which of these alternatives is the case.

The percentage of responses in common was computed for each of the possible pairs of the twenty-five words on the association test. On the pretest ninety-eight pairs of words had 2 per cent or more responses in common, ten pairs of words had 10 per cent or more responses in common, and two pairs of words had 20 per cent or more responses in common. On the posttest ninety-eight pairs of words also had 2 per cent or more responses in common, fourteen pairs of words had 10 per cent or more responses in common, and three pairs of words had 20 per cent or more responses in common. The word pairs with 10 per cent or more of their responses in common on either the pretest or posttest are presented in Table 1 ranked according to percentage of responses in common on the pretest.

Table 1
Word Pairs with 10 Per Cent or More Responses in Common on Either the Pretest or Posttest

Word Pairs	Responses in Common (%)	
	Pretest	Posttest
Reflexes–instinct	33	21
Social control–identification	22	00
Social control–socialization	16	06
Intelligence–brain	14	17
Race–nationality	13	21
Social control–speech	11	00
Skin color–race	11	23
Skin color–nationality	11	17
Human beings–socialization	11	06
Personality–identification	10	06
Socialization–culture	09	15
Human beings–social control	08	10
Human beings–personality	08	12
Human beings–race	06	10
Human beings–identification	04	10
Role–behavior	04	15
Socialization–behavior	02	14
Social control–race	02	12
Role–expectations	00	10

Since a behavioral science contains many words which derive their associative meanings from outside as well as inside the domain of the subject matter, the associative organization among the twenty-five words on the association test as a group is not high. However, since the curriculum materials to which the students were exposed were constructed so as to establish certain patterns of relation among the concepts represented by these words, it is interesting that there was not more commonality among certain words on the posttest. For example, a linkage of common reference between "culture" and "behavior" could have been expected, yet only 8 per cent of the posttest responses to the two words were in common. While this lack of commonality is not, of course, an indictment of the curriculum materials, the consistent lack of associative commonality between such concept words needs further investigation.

The increase or decrease in common responses among words in Table 1 can be related to the course materials. For example, common responses to "culture" and "socialization" increased from 9 to 15 per cent, which is consistent with the subject-matter model employed in these curriculum materials, as is the decrease between "reflex" and "instinct." At the same time it is somewhat disturbing to note that the concept "race" was more commonly associated with both "nationality" and "skin color" on posttest data than in pretest results. If anything, the course content was designed to establish separate categories of associative meaning for these terms.

In order to determine the stability of the associative meaning of the twenty-five words on the association test, a comparison was made between the response distributions for each of the words on the two test occasions. The data presented in Table 2 show the percentage of responses in common for each stimulus word on the pretest and posttest for subjects in the two classes.

The twenty-five words in Table 2 were ranked according to the percentage of responses which they had in common on the two test occasions, and a rank-order correlation was computed between these rankings for the two classes. This correlation was .68 ($P<.01$).

In general, the percentage of response in common for a given word on the two test occasions varies from word to word Responses to the words "culture," "expectations," "role," and "socialization," for example, changed considerably from pretest to posttest in both classes. This is consistent both with the model employed in designing the curriculum materials and with unit tests and teacher feedback materials which were collected during the course of the experiment. On the other hand, the instruction did not seem to function toward the associative meanings of some words, such as "self," "human beings," and "nationality," so as to change the associative meanings of the words which represented these concepts. These results suggest that curriculum writers should examine

Table 2
Percentage of Responses in Common for Each Stimulus Word on the Two Test Occasions

Responses in Common (%)

Stimulus Word *	Class 1	Class 2
Culture	17	28
Socialization	31	20
Role	30	24
Behavior	54	36
Expectations	18	24
Needs	38	32
Theory	38	64
Social control	38	24
Human beings	62	68
Explanations	43	40
Identification	50	48
Self	81	60
Instincts	42	60
Intelligence	75	52
Race	46	56
Reflexes	26	48
Average	42	40
Personality	42	36
Speech	58	60
Growth	42	41
Biology	50	48
Skin color	64	68
Nationality	60	48
Brain	54	40
Time	62	64

* The stimulus words are listed in this table according to their importance in the subject-matter model, the most important concepts in this model being "culture" and the least important concept being "time."

carefully the materials designed to teach these particular concepts, since the representation given to the subject-matter model in written and spoken instruction may not adequately reflect the usage intended for the words serving as labels for the concepts.

To determine the relationship between the change in the associative meanings of concepts in the subject matter and the model employed in constructing the curriculum materials, the ranking of the concepts according to the number of responses in common on the pretest and posttest was compared for each class with the ranking according to importance in the subject-matter model as presented in Table 2. The rank-order correlation between these two rankings of the twenty-five words was .53 ($P<.01$) for Class 1 and .47 ($P<.01$) for Class 2. These results suggest that the importance of the concepts in the model employed in constructing the curriculum materials is reflected in the stability of the associative meanings of the words which label the concepts. That is to say, those concepts considered to be most important in the subject matter were the *least* stable (showed the greatest change in associative meaning) across experience in the subject matter.

To determine the role of language habits in establishing similarity of associative meaning among the verbal labels for concepts, as well as the usefulness of viewing such language habits as sources of information about the acquisition of curriculum content, the data from Class 1 were analyzed in terms of categories of intraverbal relation derived from the subject matter to which the concepts represented by the words belonged. Although the categories employed in the present investigation

Table 3
Percentage of Responses to Each Stimulus Word Which Were in Common with Responses to Other Stimulus Words

Response Categories

Stimulus Word	Stimulus List Word		Stimulus List with Suffix or Prefix		Stimulus List Synonyms		Other	
	Pre	Post	Pre	Post	Pre	Post	Pre	Post
Culture	9	25	26	29			17	29
Socialization		17	22	25	22	17	30	12
Role		12		21	8	33	12	4
Behavior		7	17	25	25	29	17	20
Expectations			21	17	12	17	12	
Needs				4	25	46	21	8
Theory	4		4	4	33	29	12	12
Social control	4	4	13	9	33	30	9	4
Human beings	4	4	4	21	67	62	17	8
Explanations			9	25	4	8	9	12
Identification			21	29	4	8	38	
Self				4	83	79		4
Instinct	30	42	17	8	9	8	17	26
Intelligence	12	21			71	67		4
Race	4	8		8	4	21	29	21
Reflexes		21	33	17	12	17		4
Average						12	13	12
Personality	8	8	17	38	21	21	25	8
Speech		4	4		67	42	4	
Growth			13	8	13	12	39	17
Biology			4	4		4	8	12
Skin color	21	33			4	4	29	38
Nationality	17	29	8		21	12	8	25
Brain	4		4		13	9	52	48
Time					4	4	8	4

are necessarily arbitrary and are only nominally grounded in the association process itself, they may be useful in establishing dimensions along which further analysis can take place. The percentage of responses given to each of the twenty-five words which occurred in each of these categories together with the category names appear in Tables 3 and 4.

The categories in Table 3 which contribute to responses in common among the twenty-five words and bear some relation to the stimulus list suggest the extent to which the associative concept represented by a word is constructed from among other prominent words in the unit. It is reasonable to suppose, for example, that an analysis of associative changes in terms of words within the curriculum material which represent important features of the subject matter employed in its construction will provide useful information concerning the role of these words in the acquisition of the concepts they represent. In particular, these categories may be useful in determining the extent to which students draw upon the semantic system which the subject matter employs in their thinking about these words and the extent to which they draw upon other categories of semantic relation derived from their everyday experience.

The data in Table 4 indicate that in many cases a considerable number of the responses given to a particular stimulus word did not occur to any of the other twenty-four words. Such responses were of two kinds, those responses which were unique to a single individual and those responses which, while unique to a particular word were nevertheless given as responses to that word by more than one subject. Responses in this latter category may deserve further analysis as sources of associative meaning outside the domain of sociology which contribute interference in the learning and retention of word usages within the more restricted verbal environment of the subject matter.

One way of interpreting the data in Tables 3 and 4 is in terms of words which show the greatest and least change from pretest to posttest in Table 2. Tables 3 and 4 show, for example, that 52 per cent (9+26+17) of the pretest responses to the word "culture" contributed to response commonality among the stimulus list words, 43 per cent (26+17) did not contribute to response commonality among these words, and 5 per cent were blank. On the posttest, 83 per cent of the responses to "culture" were in common with other stimulus words and only 17 per cent were not, suggesting a substantial increase in the relationship between "culture" and other prominent words in the subject matter. The change noted in Table 2 for this concept can thus be interpreted as being in the direction of more and better associations with other words from the subject matter.

A different pattern of relationship exists for the concept "expecta-

Table 4
Percentage of Responses to Each Stimulus Word Which Were Not in Common with Responses to Other Stimulus Words

	Response Categories					
	Multiple *		Unique †		Blanks	
Stimulus Word	Pre	Post	Pre	Post	Pre	Post
Culture	26	17	17		5	
Socialization	17	21		8	9	
Role	42		33	30	5	
Behavior	25	19	16			
Expectations	50	66			5	
Needs	33	33	21	8		
Theory	38	25	9	30		
Social control	37	35		18	4	
Human beings	8	5				
Explanations	35	21	39	34	4	
Identification	17	17	20	46		
Self	12	13			5	
Instinct	17	8	10	8		
Intelligence	8	8	9			
Race	25	33	38	9		
Reflexes	25	25	25	16	5	
Average	43	42	35	34		
Personality	21	25	8			
Speech	8	21	17	33		
Growth	17	29	18	34		
Biology	25	33	63	47		
Skin color	21	17	21	8	4	
Nationality	29	21	12	13	5	
Brain	13	26	14	17		
Time	42	39	46	53		

° Responses given by more than one subject to a single stimulus word.
† Responses given by a single subject to a single stimulus word.

tions." Forty-five per cent of the pretest responses are accounted for by intralist relationships, leaving 55 per cent in the unrelated category. On the posttest only 34 per cent of the responses were related to other words on the list, while 66 per cent had reference to words not in common among the stimuli. Thus the materials representing the subject matter were related, in this case, to an increase in the number of responses not related to the stimulus list. The materials designed to teach the subject matter attempted to relate the concept of "expectations" to other concepts, such as "role," "socialization," and "social control," yet associatively speaking this did not happen. These results indicate that careful attention may need to be given to the specific verbal materials designed to teach the concept of "expectation."

The concept words which changed the least between pretest and post-test ("self" and "intelligence") also exhibited slight change between the categories in Tables 3 and 4. The responses to "self" varied only slightly in type from pretest to posttest (83 per cent of the responses contributed to commonality on the pretest and 87 per cent on the posttest). The shift in the responses to the stimulus word "intelligence" was likewise relatively small. Thus the associative meanings of these words were relatively stable both with respect to the number of responses in common and with respect to the categories to which the common responses belonged.

Another way of discussing the data in Tables 3 and 4 is in terms of the importance of the words according to the subject-matter model. The five most important concepts in the subject matter were, in order, "culture," "socialization," "role," "behavior," and "expectations." The responses to "culture" and "expectations" (which, incidentally, showed considerable change between pretest and posttest in Table 1) have been previously discussed, and the responses to "behavior" and "role" showed similar effects. In general, the responses to these words changed substantially between pretest and posttest, and the course materials appear to have generated more responses of an intralist nature. In the case of "behavior," the proportion increased from 59 to 81 per cent, and for "role" from 20 to 70 per cent. Such results are consistent with the subject-matter model. The analysis of the data for "socialization," however, reveals no such pattern. Responses to this concept changed greatly from pretest to posttest, but the pattern of responses stayed about the same for categories contributing to response commonality among the stimulus words.

The five concepts considered to be least important in the subject matter were "biology," "skin color," "nationality," "brain," and "time." As Tables 3 and 4 show, the responses to the concepts "biology" and "nationality" moved slightly to the common response category from pretest to posttest, while the responses for "skin color" moved substantially in that direction. The responses to "brain" and "time" showed the opposite effect, although with the concept "time" the differences were slight.

The data in this paper suggest that an associative model may be useful in describing some of the capabilities which students have with respect to concepts from a behavioral science in the early stages of its acquisition. The language habits of children studying social-science concepts changed, in many cases substantially, in a direction which was appropriate to the subject-matter model employed in constructing the curriculum materials to which they were exposed. Moreover, substantial changes were common for concepts designated as important by the curriculum developers. On the other hand, the data raise questions regarding the materials employed for some of the concepts and suggest that careful revision may need to be done, taking into account the patterns of verbal relation revealed in this study.

The study, of course, has obvious limitations. The small sample and the lack of control groups constitute the most serious limitations, preventing broad inferences. Also, the major question of the "quality" with which seventh grade students could be said to know social-science concepts was not touched upon.

To the extent that the present paper is viewed from the traditional framework of evaluation, a word also needs to be said concerning the manner in which our effort departs from the usual sense in which this term is applied to curriculum materials. Rather than ask whether students learned what they were supposed to learn, or whether they learned what they had been taught, we have asked what students can do with various representations (in this case, verbal) of concepts taken from the subject matter to which they were exposed. To ask whether a student has learned what he was supposed to learn about these concepts presupposes that one has some notion of what the student could learn from the materials of the subject matter which represented them; and in the early stages of curriculum development, it is extremely difficult to be sure that what curriculum writers produce by way of a subject-matter model is in any sense a reasonable model of what students actually learn. It is our feeling that questions which have to do simply with a student's capabilities provide more information concerning the acquisition of various representations which may be given to a subject matter for purposes of instruction and also a better understanding of the psychological processes involved in the learning and understanding of its concepts.

Notes

1. This work was supported by the Minnesota National Laboratory, an adjunct of the Minnesota State Department of Education concerned with the evaluation of curriculum materials, and by the University of Minnesota Center for Research in Human Learning through grants from the National Science Foundation (65-541), the National Institute of Child Health and Human Development (HD-01136-01), and the Graduate School of the University of Minnesota.

2. A brief summary of the work of these centers is in Edwin Fenton and John M. Good, "Project Social Studies: A Progress Report," *Social Education*, XXIX (April, 1965), 206–8.

3. Jerome S. Bruner, *The Process of Education* (Cambridge: Harvard University Press, 1961), p. 33.

4. J. H. Randall, *Nature and Historical Experience* (New York: Columbia University Press, 1958).

5. Such a characterization is similar in some respects to the one suggested in Marc Belth, *Education as a Discipline* (Boston: Allyn & Bacon, 1965).

6. See, for example, T. S. Kuhn, *Structure of Scientific Revolutions* (Chicago: University of Chicago Press, 1962).

7. The program developed by the Project Social Studies Center at Minnesota is a sequential curriculum for grades kindergarten through twelfth. The seventh-grade course deals essentially with subject matter from sociology. Five basic units comprise the course: "The Physical Basis of Man's Behavior"; "The Social Basis of Man's Behavior"; "The Family"; "The School and Other Institutions"; and "Minority Problems in the United States."

8. The M orders of numbers between 1 and N were obtained by means of Multiplicative Pseudo-Random Number Generator, a program in the residence of the 1604 CDC computer of the Numerical Analysis Center of the University of Minnesota.

9. For an expanded discussion of associative meaning both in general and as it relates to subject-matter structure, see P. E. Johnson, "Some Psychological Aspects of Subject-Matter Structure," *Journal of Educational Psychology*, LVIII (1967), 58, 75–83, and J. Deese, *The Structure of Associations in Language and Thought* (Baltimore: Johns Hopkins Press, 1966).

PART IV   UNDERSTANDING, MEANING, AND KNOWLEDGE

The attempt by Skinner and others to use the techniques of operant conditioning to account for complex behavior has met with vigorous resistance. This resistance is represented in Chomsky's article reviewing Skinner's book, *Verbal Behavior*. Chomsky's argument is, in part, that in order for technology to be effectively applied to verbal behavior we need a better understanding of the nature of language.

A similar argument can be applied to conceptual behavior. In this case we assume concepts are not directly represented by stimuli but rather in relationships between stimulus events. To understand concepts in this sense, we need abstract descriptions of them. This is the subject of the essay by Jenkins. John Carroll makes a similar argument when he attempts to show how concepts are defined by the meanings of words.

Gagné's contribution is to provide a behavioral definition of knowledge. This definition consists of hierarchies of behaviors that can be assumed to represent what an individual who knows some principle or concept should be able to do. Gagné's analysis focuses upon the interdependencies between behaviors and the ways in which these are related to stimulus change.

Ausubel is concerned with structural rather than behavioral knowledge. Like Jenkins, he argues that it is the interrelations among events rather than among behaviors that are learned as one acquires knowledge. In the essay reprinted here, Ausubel tries to establish some terminology for a psychology of subject matter knowledge.

17 REVIEW OF *VERBAL BEHAVIOR* BY B. F. SKINNER
Noam Chomsky

1. A great many linguists and philosophers concerned with language have expressed the hope that their studies might ultimately be embedded in a framework provided by behaviorist psychology, and that refractory areas of investigation, particularly those in which meaning is involved, will in this way be opened up to fruitful exploration. Since this volume is the first large-scale attempt to incorporate the major aspects of linguistic behavior within a behaviorist framework, it merits and will undoubtedly receive careful attention. Skinner is noted for his contributions to the study of animal behavior. The book under review is the product of study of linguistic behavior extending over more than twenty years. Earlier versions of it have been fairly widely circulated, and there are quite a few references in the psychological literature to its major ideas.

The problem to which this book is addressed is that of giving a "functional analysis" of verbal behavior. By functional analysis, Skinner means identification of the variables that control this behavior and specification of how they interact to determine a particular verbal response. Furthermore, the controlling variables are to be described completely in terms of such notions as stimulus, reinforcement, deprivation, which have been given a reasonably clear meaning in animal experimentation. In other words, the goal of the book is to provide a way to predict and control verbal behavior by observing and manipulating the physical environment of the speaker.

Skinner feels that recent advances in the laboratory study of animal behavior permit us to approach this problem with a certain optimism, since "the basic processes and relations which give verbal behavior its special characteristics are now fairly well understood . . . the results [of this experimental work] have been surprisingly free of species restrictions. Recent work has shown that the methods can be extended to human behavior without serious modification." (3).[1]

---

[1] Skinner's confidence in recent achievements in the study of animal behavior and their applicability to complex human behavior does not appear to be widely shared. In many recent publications of confirmed behaviorists there is a prevailing note of skepticism with regard to the scope of these achievements. For representative comments, see the contributions to *Modern learning theory* (by Estes et al.; New York, 1954); Bugelski, *Psychology of learning* (New York, 1956); Koch, in *Nebraska symposium on motivation* 58 (Lincoln, 1956); Verplanck, Learned and

SOURCE: Noam Chomsky, "Review of *Verbal Behavior* by B. F. Skinner," *Language* 35, no. 1 (1959), 26–58. Reprinted by permission of the author and the Linguistic Society of America.

It is important to see clearly just what it is in Skinner's program and claims that makes them appear so bold and remarkable. It is not primarily the fact that he has set functional analysis as his problem, or that he limits himself to study of "observables," i.e. input-output relations. What is so surprising is the particular limitations he has imposed on the way in which the observables of behavior are to be studied, and, above all, the particularly simple nature of the "function" which, he claims, describes the causation of behavior. One would naturally expect that prediction of the behavior of a complex organism (or machine) would require, in addition to information about external stimulation, knowledge of the internal structure of the organism, the ways in which it processes input information and organizes its own behavior. These characteristics of the organism are in general a complicated product of inborn structure, the genetically determined course of maturation, and past experience. Insofar as independent neurophysiological evidence is not available, it is obvious that inferences concerning the structure of the organism are based on observation of behavior and outside events. Nevertheless, one's estimate of the relative importance of external factors and internal structure in the determination of behavior will have an important effect on the direction of research on linguistic (or any other) behavior, and on the kinds of analogies from animal behavior studies that will be considered relevant or suggestive.

Putting it differently, anyone who sets himself the problem of analyzing the causation of behavior will (in the absence of independent neurophysiological evidence) concern himself with the only data available, namely the record of inputs to the organism and the organism's present response, and will try to describe the function specifying the response in terms of the history of inputs. This is nothing more than the definition of his problem. There are no possible grounds for argument here, if one accepts the problem as legitimate, though Skinner has often advanced and defended this definition of a problem as if it were a thesis which other investigators reject. The differences that arise between those who affirm and those who deny the importance of the specific "contribution of the

---

innate behavior, *Psych. rev.* 52.139 (1955). Perhaps the strongest view is that of Harlow, who has asserted (Mice, monkeys, men, and motives, *Psych. rev.* 60.23–32 [1953]) that "a strong case can be made for the proposition that the importance of the psychological problems studied during the last 15 years has decreased as a negatively accelerated function approaching an asymptote of complete indifference." Tinbergen, a leading representative of a different approach to animal behavior studies (comparative ethology), concludes a discussion of "functional analysis" with the comment that "we may now draw the conclusion that the causation of behavior is immensely more complex than was assumed in the generalizations of the past. A number of internal and external factors act upon complex central nervous structures. Second, it will be obvious that the facts at our disposal are very fragmentary indeed"—*The study of instinct* 74 (Oxford, 1951).

organism" to learning and performance concern the particular character and complexity of this function, and the kinds of observations and research necessary for arriving at a precise specification of it. If the contribution of the organism is complex, the only hope of predicting behavior even in a gross way will be through a very indirect program of research that begins by studying the detailed character of the behavior itself and the particular capacities of the organism involved.

Skinner's thesis is that external factors consisting of present stimulation and the history of reinforcement (in particular the frequency, arrangement, and withholding of reinforcing stimuli) are of overwhelming importance, and that the general principles revealed in laboratory studies of these phenomena provide the basis for understanding the complexities of verbal behavior. He confidently and repeatedly voices his claim to have demonstrated that the contribution of the speaker is quite trivial and elementary, and that precise prediction of verbal behavior involves only specification of the few external factors that he has isolated experimentally with lower organisms.

Careful study of this book (and of the research on which it draws) reveals, however, that these astonishing claims are far from justified. It indicates, furthermore, that the insights that have been achieved in the laboratories of the reinforcement theorist, though quite genuine, can be applied to complex human behavior only in the most gross and superficial way, and that speculative attempts to discuss linguistic behavior in these terms alone omit from consideration factors of fundamental importance that are, no doubt, amenable to scientific study, although their specific character cannot at present be precisely formulated. Since Skinner's work is the most extensive attempt to accommodate human behavior involving higher mental faculties within a strict behaviorist schema of the type that has attracted many linguists and philosophers, as well as psychologists, a detailed documentation is of independent interest. The magnitude of the failure of this attempt to account for verbal behavior serves as a kind of measure of the importance of the factors omitted from consideration, and an indication of how little is really known about this remarkably complex phenomenon.

The force of Skinner's argument lies in the enormous wealth and range of examples for which he proposes a functional analysis. The only way to evaluate the success of his program and the correctness of his basic assumptions about verbal behavior is to review these examples in detail and to determine the precise character of the concepts in terms of which the functional analysis is presented. §2 of this review describes the experimental context with respect to which these concepts are originally defined. §§3–4 deal with the basic concepts "stimulus," "response," and "reinforcement," §§6–10 with the new descriptive machinery developed specifically for the description of verbal behavior. In §5 we consider the status of the fundamental claim, drawn from the laboratory, which serves as the basis for the analogic guesses about human behavior that have been proposed by many psychologists. The final section (§11) will consider some ways in which further linguistic work may play a part in clarifying some of these problems.

2. Although this book makes no direct reference to experimental work, it can be understood only in terms of the general framework that Skinner has developed for the description of behavior. Skinner divides the responses of the animal into two main categories. *Respondents* are purely reflex responses elicited by particular stimuli. *Operants* are emitted responses, for which no obvious stimulus can be discovered. Skinner has been concerned primarily with operant behavior. The experimental arrangement that he introduced consists basically of a box with a bar attached to one wall in such a way that when the bar is pressed, a food pellet is dropped into a tray (and the bar press is recorded). A rat placed in the box will soon press the bar, releasing a pellet into the tray. This state of affairs, resulting from the bar press, increases the *strength* of the bar-pressing operant. The food pellet is called a *reinforcer;* the event, a reinforcing event. The strength of an operant is defined by Skinner in terms of the rate of response during extinction (i.e. after the last reinforcement and before return to the preconditioning rate).

Suppose that release of the pellet is conditional on the flashing of a light. Then the rat will come to press the bar only when the light flashes. This is called *stimulus discrimination*. The response is called a *discriminated operant* and the light is called the *occasion* for its emission; this is to be distinguished from elicitation of a response by a stimulus in the case of the respondent.[2] Suppose that the apparatus is so arranged that bar-pressing of only a certain character (e.g. duration) will release the pellet. The rat will then come to press the bar in the required way This process is called *response differentiation*. By successive slight changes in the conditions under which the response will be reinforced it is possible to shape the response of a rat or a pigeon in very surprising ways in a very short time, so that rather complex behavior can be produced by a process of successive approximation.

A stimulus can become reinforcing by repeated association with an

[2] In *Behavior of organisms* (New York, 1938), Skinner remarks that "although a conditioned operant is the result of the correlation of the response with a particular reinforcement, a relation between it and a discriminative stimulus acting prior to the response is the almost universal rule" (178–9). Even emitted behavior is held to be produced by some sort of "originating force" (51) which, in the case of operant behavior is not under experimental control. The distinction between eliciting stimuli, discriminated stimuli, and "originating forces" has never been adequately clarified, and becomes even more confusing when private internal events are considered to be discriminated stimuli (see below).

already reinforcing stimulus. Such a stimulus is called a *secondary reinforcer*. Like many contemporary behaviorists, Skinner considers money, approval, and the like to be secondary reinforcers which have become reinforcing because of their association with food etc.[3] Secondary reinforcers can be *generalized* by associating them with a variety of different primary reinforcers.

Another variable that can affect the rate of the bar-pressing operant is drive, which Skinner defines operationally in terms of hours of deprivation. His major scientific book, *Behavior of organisms,* is a study of the effects of food-deprivation and conditioning on the strength of the bar-pressing response of healthy mature rats. Probably Skinner's most original contribution to animal behavior studies has been his investigation of the effects of intermittent reinforcement, arranged in various different ways, presented in *Behavior of organisms* and extended (with pecking of pigeons as the operant under investigation) in the recent *Schedules of reinforcement* by Ferster and Skinner (1957). It is apparently these studies that Skinner has in mind when he refers to the recent advances in the study of animal behavior.[4]

The notions "stimulus," "response," "reinforcement" are relatively well defined with respect to the bar-pressing experiments and others similarly restricted. Before we can extend them to real-life behavior, however,

[3] In a famous experiment, chimpanzees were taught to perform complex tasks to receive tokens which had become secondary reinforcers because of association with food. The idea that money, approval, prestige, etc. actually acquire their motivating effects on human behavior according to this paradigm is unproved, and not particularly plausible. Many psychologists within the behaviorist movement are quite skeptical about this (cf. fn. 23). As in the case of most aspects of human behavior, the evidence about secondary reinforcement is so fragmentary, conflicting, and complex that almost any view can find some support.

[4] Skinner's remark quoted above about the generality of his basic results must be understood in the light of the experimental limitations he has imposed. If it were true in any deep sense that the basic processes in language are well understood and free of species restrictions, it would be extremely odd that language is limited to man. With the exception of a few scattered observations (cf. his article, A case history in scientific method, *The American psychologist* 11.221–33 [1956]), Skinner is apparently basing his claim on the fact that qualitatively similar results are obtained with bar-pressing of rats and pecking of pigeons under special conditions of deprivation and various schedules of reinforcement. One immediately questions how much can be based on these facts, which are in part at least an artifact traceable to experimental design and the definition of "stimulus" and "response" in terms of "smooth dynamic curves" (see below). The dangers inherent in any attempt to "extrapolate" to complex behavior from the study of such simple responses as bar-pressing should be obvious, and have often been commented on (cf. e.g. Harlow, op. cit.). The generality of even the simplest results is open to serious question. Cf. in this connection Bitterman, Wodinsky, and Candland, Some comparative psychology, *Am. jour. of psych.* 71.94–110 (1958), where it is shown that there are important qualitative differences in solution of comparable elementary problems by rats and fish.

certain difficulties must be faced. We must decide, first of all, whether any physical event to which the organism is capable of reacting is to be called a stimulus on a given occasion, or only one to which the organism in fact reacts; and correspondingly, we must decide whether any part of behavior is to be called a response, or only one connected with stimuli in lawful ways. Questions of this sort pose something of a dilemma for the experimental psychologist. If he accepts the broad definitions, characterizing any physical event impinging on the organism as a stimulus and any part of the organism's behavior as a response, he must conclude that behavior has not been demonstrated to be lawful. In the present state of our knowledge, we must attribute an overwhelming influence on actual behavior to ill-defined factors of attention, set, volition, and caprice. If we accept the narrower definitions, then behavior is lawful by definition (if it consists of responses); but this fact is of limited significance, since most of what the animal does will simply not be considered behavior. Hence the psychologist either must admit that behavior is not lawful (or that he cannot at present show that it is—not at all a damaging admission for a developing science), or must restrict his attention to those highly limited areas in which it is lawful (e.g. with adequate controls, bar-pressing in rats; lawfulness of the observed behavior provides, for Skinner, an implicit definition of a good experiment).

Skinner does not consistently adopt either course. He utilizes the experimental results as evidence for the scientific character of his system of behavior, and analogic guesses (formulated in terms of a metaphoric extension of the technical vocabulary of the laboratory) as evidence for its scope. This creates the illusion of a rigorous scientific theory with a very broad scope, although in fact the terms used in the description of real-life and of laboratory behavior may be mere homonyms, with at most a vague similarity of meaning. To substantiate this evaluation, a critical account of his book must show that with a literal reading (where the terms of the descriptive system have something like the technical meanings given in Skinner's definitions) the book covers almost no aspect of linguistic behavior, and that with a metaphoric reading, it is no more scientific than the traditional approaches to this subject matter, and rarely as clear and careful.[5]

[5] An analogous argument, in connection with a different aspect of Skinner's thinking, is given by Scriven in *A study of radical behaviorism* = *Univ. of Minn. studies in philosophy of science,* Vol. 1. Cf. Verplanck's contribution to *Modern learning theory* (283–8) for more general discussion of the difficulties in formulating an adequate definition of "stimulus" and "response." He concludes, quite correctly, that in Skinner's sense of the word, stimuli are not objectively identifiable independently of the resulting behavior, nor are they manipulable. Verplanck presents a clear discussion of many other aspects of Skinner's system, commenting on the untestability of many of the so-called "laws of behavior" and the limited scope of many of the others, and the arbitrary and obscure character of Skinner's notion of

3. Consider first Skinner's use of the notions "stimulus" and "response." In *Behavior of organisms* (9) he commits himself to the narrow definitions for these terms. A part of the environment and a part of behavior are called stimulus (eliciting, discriminated, or reinforcing) and response, respectively, only if they are lawfully related; that is, if the "dynamic laws" relating them show smooth and reproducible curves. Evidently stimuli and responses, so defined, have not been shown to figure very widely in ordinary human behavior.[6] We can, in the face of presently available evidence, continue to maintain the lawfulness of the relation between stimulus and response only by depriving them of their objective character. A typical example of "stimulus control" for Skinner would be the response to a piece of music with the utterance *Mozart* or to a painting with the response *Dutch*. These responses are asserted to be "under the control of extremely subtle properties" of the physical object or event (108). Suppose instead of saying *Dutch* we had said *Clashes with the wallpaper, I thought you liked abstract work, Never saw it before, Tilted, Hanging too low, Beautiful, Hideous, Remember our camping trip last summer?*, or whatever else might come into our minds when looking at a picture (in Skinnerian translation, whatever other responses exist in sufficient strength). Skinner could only say that each of these responses is under the control of some other stimulus property of the physical object. If we look at a red chair and say *red*, the response is under the control of the stimulus "redness"; if we say *chair*, it is under the control of the collection of properties (for Skinner, the object) "chairness" (110), and similarly for any other response. This device is as simple as it is empty. Since properties are free for the asking (we have as many of them as we have nonsynonymous descriptive expressions in our language, whatever this means exactly), we can account for a wide class of responses in terms of Skinnerian functional analysis by identifying the "controlling stimuli." But the word "stimulus" has lost all objectivity in this usage. Stimuli are no longer part of the outside physical world; they are driven back into the organism. We identify the stimulus when we hear the response. It is clear from such examples, which abound, that the talk of "stimulus control" simply disguises a

---

"lawful relation"; and, at the same time, noting the importance of the experimental data that Skinner has accumulated.

[6] In *Behavior of organisms*, Skinner apparently was willing to accept this consequence. He insists (41–2) that the terms of casual description in the popular vocabulary are not validly descriptive until the defining properties of stimulus and response are specified, the correlation is demonstrated experimentally, and the dynamic changes in it are shown to be lawful. Thus, in describing a child as hiding from a dog, "it will not be enough to dignify the popular vocabulary by appealing to essential properties of 'dogness' or 'hidingness' and to suppose them intuitively known." But this is exactly what Skinner does in the book under review, as we will see directly.

complete retreat to mentalistic psychology. We cannot predict verbal behavior in terms of the stimuli in the speaker's environment, since we do not know what the current stimuli are until he responds. Furthermore, since we cannot control the property of a physical object to which an individual will respond, except in highly artificial cases, Skinner's claim that his system, as opposed to the traditional one, permits the practical control of verbal behavior [7] is quite false.

Other examples of "stimulus control" merely add to the general mystification. Thus a proper noun is held to be a response "under the control of a specific person or thing" (as controlling stimulus, 113). I have often used the words *Eisenhower* and *Moscow,* which I presume are proper nouns if anything is, but have never been "stimulated" by the corresponding objects. How can this fact be made compatible with this definition? Suppose that I use the name of a friend who is not present. Is this an instance of a proper noun under the control of the friend as stimulus? Elsewhere it is asserted that a stimulus controls a response in the sense that presence of the stimulus increases the probability of the response. But it is obviously untrue that the probability that a speaker will produce a full name is increased when its bearer faces the speaker. Furthermore, how can one's own name be a proper noun in this sense? A multitude of similar questions arise immediately. It appears that the word "control" here is merely a misleading paraphrase for the traditional "denote" or "refer." The assertion (115) that so far as the speaker is concerned, the relation of reference is "simply the probability that the speaker will emit a response of a given form in the presence of a stimulus having specified properties" is surely incorrect if we take the words "presence," "stimulus," and "probability" in their literal sense. That they are not intended to be taken literally is indicated by many examples, as when a response is said to be "controlled" by a situation or state of affairs as "stimulus." Thus, the expression *a needle in a haystack* "may be

---

[7] 253 f. and elsewhere, repeatedly. As an example of how well we can control behavior using the notions developed in this book, Skinner shows here how he would go about evoking the response *pencil.* The most effective way, he suggests, is to say to the subject, "Please say *pencil*" (our chances would, presumably, be even further improved by use of "aversive stimulation," e.g. holding a gun to his head). We can also "make sure that no pencil or writing instrument is available, then hand our subject a pad of paper appropriate to pencil sketching, and offer him a handsome reward for a recognizable picture of a cat." It would also be useful to have voices saying *pencil* or *pen and* . . . in the background; signs reading *pencil* or *pen and* . . . ; or to place a "large and unusual pencil in an unusual place clearly in sight." "Under such circumstances, it is highly probable that our subject will say *pencil.*" "The available techniques are all illustrated in this sample." These contributions of behavior theory to the practical control of human behavior are amply illustrated elsewhere in the book, as when Skinner shows (113–4) how we can evoke the response *red* (the device suggested is to hold a red object before the subject and say, "Tell me what color this is").

controlled as a unit by a particular type of situation" (116); the words in a single part of speech, e.g. all adjectives, are under the control of a single set of subtle properties of stimuli (121); "the sentence *The boy runs a store* is under the control of an extremely complex stimulus situation" (335); "*He is not at all well* may function as a standard response under the control of a state of affairs which might also control *He is ailing*" (325); when an envoy observes events in a foreign country and reports upon his return, his report is under "remote stimulus control" (416); the statement *This is war* may be a response to a "confusing international situation" (441); the suffix *-ed* is controlled by that "subtle property of stimuli which we speak of as action-in-the-past" (121) just as the *-s* in *The boy runs* is under the control of such specific features of the situation as its "currency" (332). No characterization of the notion "stimulus control" that is remotely related to the bar-pressing experiment (or that preserves the faintest objectivity) can be made to cover a set of examples like these, in which, for example, the "controlling stimulus" need not even impinge on the responding organism.

Consider now Skinner's use of the notion "response." The problem of identifying units in verbal behavior has of course been a primary concern of linguists, and it seems very likely that experimental psychologists should be able to provide much-needed assistance in clearing up the many remaining difficulties in systematic identification. Skinner recognizes (20) the fundamental character of the problem of identification of a unit of verbal behavior, but is satisfied with an answer so vague and subjective that it does not really contribute to its solution. The unit of verbal behavior—the verbal operant—is defined as a class of responses of identifiable form functionally related to one or more controlling variables. No method is suggested for determining in a particular instance what are the controlling variables, how many such units have occurred, or where their boundaries are in the total response. Nor is any attempt made to specify how much or what kind of similarity in form or "control" is required for two physical events to be considered instances of the same operant. In short, no answers are suggested for the most elementary questions that must be asked of anyone proposing a method for

In fairness, it must be mentioned that there are certain nontrivial applications of "operant conditioning" to the control of human behavior. A wide variety of experiments have shown that the number of plural nouns (for example) produced by a subject will increase if the experimenter says "right" or "good" when one is produced (similarly, positive attitudes on a certain issue, stories with particular content, etc.; cf. Krasner, Studies of the conditioning of verbal behavior, *Psych. bull.*, Vol. 55 [1958], for a survey of several dozen experiments of this kind, mostly with positive results). It is of some interest that the subject is usually unaware of the process. Just what insight this gives into normal verbal behavior is not obvious. Nevertheless, it is an example of positive and not totally expected results using the Skinnerian paradigm.

description of behavior. Skinner is content with what he calls an "extrapolation" of the concept of operant developed in the laboratory to the verbal field. In the typical Skinnerian experiment, the problem of identifying the unit of behavior is not too crucial. It is defined, by fiat, as a recorded peck or bar-press, and systematic variations in the rate of this operant and its resistance to extinction are studied as a function of deprivation and scheduling of reinforcement (pellets). The operant is thus defined with respect to a particular experimental procedure. This is perfectly reasonable, and has led to many interesting results. It is, however, completely meaningless to speak of extrapolating this concept of operant to ordinary verbal behavior. Such "extrapolation" leaves us with no way of justifying one or another decision about the units in the "verbal repertoire."

Skinner specifies "response strength" as the basic datum, the basic dependent variable in his functional analysis. In the bar-pressing experiment, response strength is defined in terms of rate of emission during extinction. Skinner has argued [8] that this is "the only datum that varies significantly and in the expected direction under conditions which are relevant to the 'learning process.'" In the book under review, response strength is defined as "probability of emission" (22). This definition provides a comforting impression of objectivity, which, however, is quickly dispelled when we look into the matter more closely. The term "probability" has some rather obscure meaning for Skinner in this book.[9] We are told, on the one hand, that "our evidence for the contribution of each variable [to response strength] is based on observation of frequencies alone" (28). At the same time, it appears that frequency is a very misleading measure of strength, since, for example, the frequency of a response may be "primarily attributable to the frequency of occurrence of controlling variables" (27). It is not clear how the frequency of a response can be attributable to anything BUT the frequency of occurrence of its controlling variables if we accept Skinner's view that the behavior occurring in a given situation is "fully determined" by the relevant con-

[8] Are theories of learning necessary?, *Psych. rev.* 57.193–216 (1950).

[9] And elsewhere. In his paper Are theories of learning necessary?, Skinner considers the problem how to extend his analysis of behavior to experimental situations in which it is impossible to observe frequencies, rate of response being the only valid datum. His answer is that "the notion of probability is usually extrapolated to cases in which a frequency analysis cannot be carried out. In the field of behavior we arrange a situation in which frequencies are available as data, but we use the notion of probability in analyzing or formulating instances of even types of behavior which are not susceptible to this analysis" (199). There are, of course, conceptions of probability not based directly on frequency, but I do not see how any of these apply to the cases that Skinner has in mind. I see no way of interpreting the quoted passage other than as signifying an intention to use the word "probability" in describing behavior quite independently of whether the notion of probability is at all relevant.

trolling variables (175, 228). Furthermore, although the evidence for the contribution of each variable to response strength is based on observation of frequencies alone, it turns out that "we base the notion of strength upon several kinds of evidence" (22), in particular (22–8): emission of the response (particularly in unusual circumstances), energy level (stress), pitch level, speed and delay of emission, size of letters etc. in writing, immediate repetition, and—a final factor, relevant but misleading—over-all frequency.

Of course, Skinner recognizes that these measures do not co-vary, because (among other reasons) pitch, stress, quantity, and reduplication may have internal linguistic functions.[10] However, he does not hold these conflicts to be very important, since the proposed factors indicative of strength are "fully understood by everyone" in the culture (27). For example, "if we are shown a prized work of art and exclaim *Beautiful!*, the speed and energy of the response will not be lost on the owner." It does not appear totally obvious that in this case the way to impress the owner is to shriek *Beautiful* in a loud, high-pitched voice, repeatedly, and with no delay (high response strength). It may be equally effective to look at the picture silently (long delay), and then to murmur *Beautiful* in a soft, low-pitched voice (by definition, very low response strength).

It is not unfair, I believe, to conclude from Skinner's discussion of response strength, the "basic datum" in functional analysis, that his "extrapolation" of the notion of probability can best be interpreted as, in effect, nothing more than a decision to use the word "probability," with its favorable connotations of objectivity, as a cover term to paraphrase such low-status words as "interest," "intention," "belief," and the like. This interpretation is fully justified by the way in which Skinner uses the terms "probability" and "strength." To cite just one example, Skinner defines the process of confirming an assertion in science as one of "generating additional variables to increase its probability" (425), and more generally, its strength (425–9). If we take this suggestion quite literally, the degree of confirmation of a scientific assertion can be measured as a simple function of the loudness, pitch, and frequency with which it is proclaimed, and a general procedure for increasing its degree of confirmation would be, for instance, to train machine guns on large crowds of people who have been instructed to shout it. A better indication of what Skinner probably has in mind here is given by his description of how the theory of evolution, as an example, is confirmed. This "single set of verbal responses . . . is made more plausible—is strengthened—by sev-

---

[10] Fortunately, "In English this presents no great difficulty" since, for example, "relative pitch levels . . . are not . . . important" (25). No reference is made to the numerous studies of the function of relative pitch levels and other intonational features in English.

eral types of construction based upon verbal responses in geology, paleontology, genetics, and so on" (427). We are no doubt to interpret the terms "strength" and "probability" in this context as paraphrases of more familiar locutions such as "justified belief" or "warranted assertability," or something of the sort. Similar latitude of interpretation is presumably expected when we read that "frequency of effective action accounts in turn for what we may call the listener's belief" (88) or that "our belief in what someone tells us is similarly a function of, or identical with, our tendency to act upon the verbal stimuli which he provides" (160).[11]

I think it is evident, then, that Skinner's use of the terms "stimulus," "control," "response," and "strength" justify the general conclusion stated in the last paragraph of §2 above. The way in which these terms are brought to bear on the actual data indicates that we must interpret them as mere paraphrases for the popular vocabulary commonly used to describe behavior, and as having no particular connection with the homonymous expressions used in the description of laboratory experiments. Naturally, this terminological revision adds no objectivity to the familiar "mentalistic" mode of description.

4. The other fundamental notion borrowed from the description of bar-pressing experiments is "reinforcement." It raises problems which are similar, and even more serious. In *Behavior of organisms*, "the operation of reinforcement is defined as the presentation of a certain kind of stimulus in a temporal relation with either a stimulus or response. A reinforcing stimulus is defined as such by its power to produce the resulting change [in strength]. There is no circularity about this: some stimuli are found to produce the change, others not, and they are classified as reinforcing and non-reinforcing accordingly" (62). This is a perfectly appropriate definition [12] for the study of schedules of reinforcement. It is

---

11 The vagueness of the word "tendency," as opposed to "frequency," saves the latter quotation from the obvious incorrectness of the former. Nevertheless, a good deal of stretching is necessary. If "tendency" has anything like its ordinary meaning, the remark is clearly false. One may believe strongly the assertion that Jupiter has four moons, that many of Sophocles' plays have been irretrievably lost, that the earth will burn to a crisp in ten million years, etc., without experiencing the slightest tendency to act upon these verbal stimuli. We may, of course, turn Skinner's assertion into a very unilluminating truth by defining "tendency to act" to include tendencies to answer questions in certain ways, under motivation to say what one believes is true.

12 One should add, however, that it is in general not the stimulus as such that is reinforcing, but the stimulus in a particular situational context. Depending on experimental arrangement, a particular physical event or object may be reinforcing, punishing, or unnoticed. Because Skinner limits himself to a particular, very simple experimental arrangement, it is not necessary for him to add this qualification, which would not be at all easy to formulate precisely. But it is of course necessary if he expects to extend his descriptive system to behavior in general.

perfectly useless, however, in the discussion of real-life behavior, unless we can somehow characterize the stimuli which are reinforcing (and the situations and conditions under which they are reinforcing). Consider first of all the status of the basic principle that Skinner calls the "law of conditioning" (law of effect). It reads: "if the occurrence of an operant is followed by presence of a reinforcing stimulus, the strength is increased" (*Behavior of organisms* 21). As "reinforcement" was defined, this law becomes a tautology.[13] For Skinner, learning is just change in response strength.[14] Although the statement that presence of reinforcement is a sufficient condition for learning and maintenance of behavior is vacuous, the claim that it is a necessary condition may have some content, depending on how the class of reinforcers (and appropriate situations) is characterized. Skinner does make it very clear that in his view reinforcement is a necessary condition for language learning and for the continued availability of linguistic responses in the adult.[15] However, the looseness of the term "reinforcement" as Skinner uses it in the book under review makes it entirely pointless to inquire into the truth or falsity of this claim. Examining the instances of what Skinner calls "reinforcement," we find that not even the requirement that a reinforcer be an identifiable stimulus is taken seriously. In fact, the term is used in such a way that the assertion that reinforcement is necessary for learning and continued availability of behavior is likewise empty.

To show this, we consider some example of "reinforcement." First of all, we find a heavy appeal to automatic self-reinforcement. Thus, "a man talks to himself . . . because of the reinforcement he receives" (163); "the child is reinforced automatically when he duplicates the sounds of airplanes, streetcars . . ." (164); "the young child alone in the nursery may automatically reinforce his own exploratory verbal behavior when he produces sounds which he has heard in the speech of others" (58); "the speaker who is also an accomplished listener 'knows when he has correctly echoed a response' and is reinforced thereby" (68); thinking is "behaving which automatically affects the behaver and is reinforcing because it does so" (438; cutting one's finger should thus be reinforcing, and an example of thinking); "the verbal fantasy, whether

---

[13] This has been frequently noted.

[14] See, for example, Are theories of learning necessary? 199. Elsewhere, he suggests that the term "learning" be restricted to complex situations, but these are not characterized.

[15] "A child acquires verbal behavior when relatively unpatterned vocalizations, selectively reinforced, gradually assume forms which produce appropriate consequences in a given verbal community" (31). "Differential reinforcement shapes up all verbal forms, and when a prior stimulus enters into the contingency, reinforcement is responsible for its resulting control. . . . The availability of behavior, its probability or strength, depends on whether reinforcements *continue* in effect and according to what schedules" (203–4). Elsewhere, frequently.

overt or covert, is automatically reinforcing to the speaker as listener. Just as the musician plays or composes what he is reinforced by hearing, or as the artist paints what reinforces him visually, so the speaker engaged in verbal fantasy says what he is reinforced by hearing or writes what he is reinforced by reading" (439); similarly, care in problem solving, and rationalization, are automatically self-reinforcing (442–3). We can also reinforce someone by emitting verbal behavior as such (since this rules out a class of aversive stimulations, 167), by not emitting verbal behavior (keeping silent and paying attention, 199), or by acting appropriately on some future occasion (152: "the strength of [the speaker's] behavior is determined mainly by the behavior which the listener will exhibit with respect to a given state of affairs"; this Skinner considers the general case of "communication" or "letting the listener know"). In most such cases, of course, the speaker is not present at the time when the reinforcement takes place, as when "the artist . . . is reinforced by the effects his works have upon . . . others" (224), or when the writer is reinforced by the fact that his "verbal behavior may reach over centuries or to thousands of listeners or readers at the same time. The writer may not be reinforced often or immediately, but his net reinforcement may be great" (206; this accounts for the great "strength" of his behavior). An individual may also find it reinforcing to injure someone by criticism or by bringing bad news, or to publish an experimental result which upsets the theory of a rival (154), to describe circumstances which would be reinforcing if they were to occur (165), to avoid repetition (222), to "hear" his own name though in fact it was not mentioned or to hear nonexistent words in his child's babbling (259), to clarify or otherwise intensify the effect of a stimulus which serves an important discriminative function (416), etc.

From this sample, it can be seen that the notion of reinforcement has totally lost whatever objective meaning it may ever have had. Running through these examples, we see that a person can be reinforced though he emits no response at all, and that the reinforcing "stimulus" need not impinge on the "reinforced person" or need not even exist (it is sufficient that it be imagined or hoped for). When we read that a person plays what music he likes (165), says what he likes (165), thinks what he likes (438–9), reads what books he likes (163), etc., BECAUSE he finds it reinforcing to do so, or that we write books or inform others of facts BECAUSE we are reinforced by what we hope will be the ultimate behavior of reader or listener, we can only conclude that the term "reinforcement" has a purely ritual function. The phrase "X is reinforced by Y (stimulus, state of affairs, event, etc.)" is being used as a cover term for "X wants Y," "X likes Y," "X wishes that Y were the case," etc. Invoking the term "reinforcement" has no explanatory force, and any idea that this paraphrase introduces any new clarity or objectivity into the description of wishing, liking, etc., is a serious delusion. The only effect is to obscure the important differences among the notions being paraphrased. Once we recognize the latitude with which the term "reinforcement" is being used, many rather startling comments lose their initial effect—for instance, that the behavior of the creative artist is "controlled entirely by the contingencies of reinforcement" (150). What has been hoped for from the psychologist is some indication how the casual and informal description of everyday behavior in the popular vocabulary can be explained or clarified in terms of the notions developed in careful experiment and observation, or perhaps replaced in terms of a better scheme. A mere terminological revision, in which a term borrowed from the laboratory is used with the full vagueness of the ordinary vocabulary, is of no conceivable interest.

It seems that Skinner's claim that all verbal behavior is acquired and maintained in "strength" through reinforcement is quite empty, because his notion of reinforcement has no clear content, functioning only as a cover term for any factor, detectable or not, related to acquisition or maintenance of verbal behavior.[16] Skinner's use of the term "conditioning" suffers from a similar difficulty. Pavlovian and operant conditioning are processes about which psychologists have developed real understanding. Instruction of human beings is not. The claim that instruction and imparting of information are simply matters of conditioning (357–66) is pointless. The claim is true, if we extend the term "conditioning" to cover these processes, but we know no more about them after having revised this term in such a way as to deprive it of its relatively clear and objective character. It is, as far as we know, quite false, if we use "conditioning" in its literal sense. Similarly, when we say that "it is the function of predication to facilitate the transfer of response from one term to another or from one object to another" (361), we have said nothing of any significance. In what sense is this true of the predication *Whales are mammals?* Or, to take Skinner's example, what point is there in saying that the effect of *The telephone is out of order* on the listener is to bring behavior formerly controlled by the stimulus *out of order* under control of the stimulus *telephone* (or the telephone itself) by a process of simple conditioning (362)? What laws of conditioning hold in this case? Furthermore, what behavior is "controlled" by the stimulus *out of order*, in the abstract? Depending on the object of which this is predicated, the present state of motivation of the listener, etc., the behavior may vary from rage to pleasure, from fixing the object to throwing it out, from simply not using it to trying to use it in the normal way (e.g. to see if it

---

[16] Talk of schedules of reinforcement here is entirely pointless. How are we to decide, for example, according to what schedules covert reinforcement is "arranged," as in thinking or verbal fantasy, or what the scheduling is of such factors as silence, speech, and appropriate future reactions to communicated information?

is really out of order), and so on. To speak of "conditioning" or "bringing previously available behavior under control of a new stimulus" in such a case is just a kind of play-acting at science. Cf. also footnote 43.

5. The claim that careful arrangement of contingencies of reinforcement by the verbal community is a necessary condition for language learning has appeared, in one form or another, in many places.[17] Since it is based not on actual observation, but on analogies to laboratory study of lower organisms, it is important to determine the status of the underlying assertion within experimental psychology proper. The most common characterization of reinforcement (one which Skinner explicitly rejects, incidentally) is in terms of drive reduction. This characterization can be given substance by defining drives in some way independently of what in fact is learned. If a drive is postulated on the basis of the fact that learning takes place, the claim that reinforcement is necessary for learning will again become as empty as it is in the Skinnerian framework. There is an extensive literature on the question of whether there can be learning without drive-reduction (latent learning). The "classical" experiment of Blodgett indicated that rats who had explored a maze without reward showed a marked drop in number of errors (as compared to a control group which had not explored the maze) upon introduction of a food reward, indicating that the rat had learned the structure of the maze without reduction of the hunger drive. Drive-reduction theorists countered with an exploratory drive which was reduced during the prereward learning, and claimed that a slight decrement in errors could be noted before food reward. A wide variety of experiments, with somewhat conflicting results, have been carried out with a similar design.[18] Few investigators still doubt the existence of the phenomenon. Hilgard, in his general review of learning theory,[19] concludes that "there is no longer any doubt but that, under appropriate circumstances, latent learning is demonstrable."

[17] See, for example, Miller and Dollard, _Social learning and imitation_ 82–3 (New York, 1941), for a discussion of the "meticulous training" that they seem to consider necessary for a child to learn the meanings of words and syntactic patterns. The same notion is implicit in Mowrer's speculative account of how language might be acquired, in _Learning theory and personality dynamics_, Chapter 23 (New York, 1950). Actually, the view appears to be quite general.

[18] For a general review and analysis of this literature, see Thistlethwaite, A critical review of latent learning and related experiments, _Psych. bull._ 48.97–129 (1951). MacCorquodale and Meehl, in their contribution to _Modern learning theory_, carry out a serious and considered attempt to handle the latent learning material from the standpoint of drive-reduction theory, with (as they point out) not entirely satisfactory results. Thorpe reviews the literature from the standpoint of the ethologist, adding also material on homing and topographical orientation (_Learning and instinct in animals_ [Cambridge, 1956]).

[19] _Theories of learning_ 214 (1956).

More recent work has shown that novelty and variety of stimulus are sufficient to arouse curiosity in the rat and to motivate it to explore (visually), and in fact, to learn (since on a presentation of two stimuli, one novel, one repeated, the rat will attend to the novel one); [20] that rats will learn to choose the arm of a single-choice maze that leads to a complex maze, running through this being their only "reward"; [21] that monkeys can learn object discriminations and maintain their performance at a high level of efficiency with visual exploration (looking out of a window for 30 seconds) as the only reward; [22] and, perhaps most strikingly of all, that monkeys and apes will solve rather complex manipulation problems that are simply placed in their cages, and will solve discrimination problems with only exploration and manipulation as incentives.[23] In these cases, solving the problem is apparently its own "reward." Results of this kind can be handled by reinforcement theorists only if they are willing to set up curiosity, exploration, and manipulation drives, or

[20] Berlyne, Novelty and curiosity as determinants of exploratory behavior, *Brit. jour. of psych.* 41.68–80 (1950); id., Perceptual curiosity in the rat, *Jour. of comp. physiol. psych.* 48.238–46 (1955); Thompson and Solomon, Spontaneous pattern discrimination in the rat, ibid. 47.104–7 (1954).

[21] Montgomery, The role of the exploratory drive in learning, ibid. 60–3. Many other papers in the same journal are designed to show that exploratory behavior is a relatively independent primary "drive" aroused by novel external stimulation.

[22] Butler, Discrimination learning by Rhesus monkeys to visual-exploration motivation, ibid. 46.95–8 (1953). Later experiments showed that this "drive" is highly persistent, as opposed to derived drives which rapidly extinguish.

[23] Harlow, Harlow, and Meyer, Learning motivated by a manipulation drive, *Jour. exp. psych.* 40.228–34 (1950), and later investigations initiated by Harlow, Harlow has been particularly insistent on maintaining the inadequacy of physiologically based drives and homeostatic need states for explaining the persistence of motivation and rapidity of learning in primates. He points out, in many papers, that curiosity, play, exploration, and manipulation are, for primates, often more potent drives than hunger and the like, and that they show none of the characteristics of acquired drives. Heb also presents behavioral and supporting neurological evidence in support of the view that in higher animals there is a positive attraction in work, risk, puzzle, intellectual activity, mild fear and frustration, etc. (Drives and the CNS, *Psych. rev.* 62.243–54 [1955]). He concludes that "we need not work out tortuous and improbable ways to explain why men work for money, why children learn without pain, why people dislike doing nothing."

In a brief note (Early recognition of the manipulative drive in monkeys, *British journal of animal behaviour* 3.71 2 [1955]), W. Dennis calls attention to the fact that early investigators (Romanes, 1882; Thorndike, 1901), whose "perception was relatively unaffected by learning theory, did note the intrinsically motivated behavior of monkeys," although, he asserts, no similar observations on monkeys have been made until Harlow's experiments. He quotes Romanes (*Animal intelligence* [1882]) as saying that "much the most striking feature in the psychology of this animal, and the one which is least like anything met with in other animals, was the tireless spirit of investigation." Analogous developments, in which genuine discoveries have blinded systematic investigators to the important insights of earlier work, are easily found within recent structural linguistics as well.

to speculate somehow about acquired drives [24] for which there is no evidence outside of the fact that learning takes place in these cases.

There is a variety of other kinds of evidence that has been offered to challenge the view that drive-reduction is necessary for learning. Results on sensory-preconditioning have been interpreted as demonstrating learning without drive-reduction.[25] Olds has reported reinforcement by direct stimulation of the brain, from which he concludes that reward need not satisfy a physiological need or withdraw a drive stimulus.[26] The phenomenon of imprinting, long observed by zoologists, is of particular interest in this connection. Some of the most complex patterns of behavior of birds, in particular, are directed towards objects and animals of the type to which they have been exposed at certain critical early periods of life.[27] Imprinting is the most striking evidence for the innate disposition of the animal to learn in a certain direction, and to react appropriately to patterns and objects of certain restricted types, often only long after the original learning has taken place. It is, consequently, unrewarded learning, though the resulting patterns of behavior may be refined through reinforcement. Acquisition of the typical songs of song birds is, in some cases, a type of imprinting. Thorpe reports studies that show "that some characteristics of the normal song have been learnt in the earliest youth, before the bird itself is able to produce any kind of full song." [28] The phenomenon of imprinting has recently been investigated under laboratory conditions and controls with positive results.[29]

Phenomena of this general type are certainly familiar from everyday experience. We recognize people and places to which we have given no particular attention. We can look up something in a book and learn it

[24] Thus J. S. Brown, in commenting on a paper of Harlow's in *Current theory and research in motivation* (Lincoln, 1953), argues that "in probably every instance [of the experiments cited by Harlow] an ingenious drive-reduction theorist could find some fragment of fear, insecurity, frustration, or whatever, that he could insist was reduced and hence was reinforcing" (53). The same sort of thing could be said for the ingenious phlogiston or ether theorist.

[25] Cf. Birch and Bitterman, Reinforcement and learning: The process of sensory integration, *Psych. rev.* 56.292–308 (1949).

[26] See, for example, his paper A physiological study of reward in McClelland (ed.), *Studies in motivation* 134–43 (New York, 1955).

[27] See Thorpe, op. cit., particularly 115–8 and 337–76, for an excellent discussion of this phenomenon, which has been brought to prominence particularly by the work of K. Lorenz (cf. Der Kumpan in der Umwelt des Vogels, parts of which are reprinted in English translation in Schiller (ed.), *Instinctive behavior* 83–128 (New York, 1957).

[28] Op. cit. 372.

[29] See e.g. Jaynes, Imprinting: Interaction of learned and innate behavior, *Jour. of comp. physiol. psych.* 49.201–6 (1956), where the conclusion is reached that "the experiments prove that without any observable reward young birds of this species follow a moving stimulus object and very rapidly come to prefer that object to others."

perfectly well with no other motive than to confute reinforcement theory, or out of boredom, or idle curiosity. Everyone engaged in research must have had the experience of working with feverish and prolonged intensity to write a paper which no one else will read or to solve a problem which no one else thinks important and which will bring no conceivable reward—which may only confirm a general opinion that the researcher is wasting his time on irrelevancies. The fact that rats and monkeys do likewise is interesting, and important to show in careful experiment. In fact, studies of behavior of the type mentioned above have an independent and positive significance that far outweighs their incidental importance in bringing into question the claim that learning is impossible without drive-reduction. It is not at all unlikely that insights arising from animal behavior studies with this broadened scope may have the kind of relevance to such complex activities as verbal behavior that reinforcement theory has, so far, failed to exhibit. In any event, in the light of presently available evidence, it is difficult to see how anyone can be willing to claim that reinforcement is necessary for learning, if reinforcement is taken seriously as something identifiable independently of the resulting change in behavior.

Similarly, it seems quite beyond question that children acquire a good deal of their verbal and nonverbal behavior by casual observation and imitation of adults and other children.[30] It is simply not true that children can learn language only through "meticulous care" on the part of adults who shape their verbal repertoire through careful differential reinforcement, though it may be that such care is often the custom in academic families. It is a common observation that a young child of immigrant parents may learn a second language in the streets, from other

---

[30] Of course it is perfectly possible to incorporate this fact within the Skinnerian framework. If, for example, a child watches an adult using a comb and then, with no instruction, tries to comb his own hair, we can explain this act by saying that he performs it because he finds it reinforcing to do so, or because of the reinforcement provided by behaving like a person who is "reinforcing" (cf. 164). Similarly, an automatic explanation is available for any other behavior. It seems strange at first that Skinner pays so little attention to the literature on latent learning and related topics, considering the tremendous reliance that he places on the notion of reinforcement; I have seen no reference to it in his writings. Similarly, Keller and Schoenfeld, in what appears to be the only text written under predominantly Skinnerian influence, *Principles of psychology* (New York, 1950), dismiss the latent-learning literature in one sentence as "beside the point," serving only "to obscure, rather than clarify, a fundamental principle" (the law of effect, 41). However, this neglect is perfectly appropriate in Skinner's case. To the drive-reductionist, or anyone else for whom the notion "reinforcement" has some substantive meaning, these experiments and observations are important (and often embarrassing). But in the Skinnerian sense of the word, neither these results nor any conceivable others can cast any doubt on the claim that reinforcement is essential for the acquisition and maintenance of behavior. Behavior certainly has some concomitant circumstances, and whatever they are, we can call them "reinforcement."

children, with amazing rapidity, and that his speech may be completely fluent and correct to the last allophone, while the subtleties that become second nature to the child may elude his parents despite high motivation and continued practice. A child may pick up a large part of his vocabulary and "feel" for sentence structure from television, from reading, from listening to adults, etc. Even a very young child who has not yet acquired a minimal repertoire from which to form new utterances may imitate a word quite well on an early try, with no attempt on the part of his parents to teach it to him. It is also perfectly obvious that, at a later stage, a child will be able to construct and understand utterances which are quite new, and are, at the same time, acceptable sentences in his language. Every time an adult reads a newspaper, he undoubtedly comes upon countless new sentences which are not at all similar, in a simple, physical sense, to any that he has heard before, and which he will recognize as sentences and understand; he will also be able to detect slight distortions or misprints. Talk of "stimulus generalization" in such a case simply perpetuates the mystery under a new title. These abilities indicate that there must be fundamental processes at work quite independently of "feedback" from the environment. I have been able to find no support whatsoever for the doctrine of Skinner and others that slow and careful shaping of verbal behavior through differential reinforcement is an absolute necessity. If reinforcement theory really requires the assumption that there be such meticulous care, it seems best to regard this simply as a reductio ad absurdum argument against this approach. It is also not easy to find any basis (or, for that matter, to attach very much content) to the claim that reinforcing contingencies set up by the verbal community are the single factor responsible for maintaining the strength of verbal behavior. The sources of the "strength" of this behavior are almost a total mystery at present. Reinforcement undoubtedly plays a significant role, but so do a variety of motivational factors about which nothing serious is known in the case of human beings.

As far as acquisition of language is concerned, it seems clear that reinforcement, casual observation, and natural inquisitiveness (coupled with a strong tendency to imitate) are important factors, as is the remarkable capacity of the child to generalize, hypothesize, and "process information" in a variety of very special and apparently highly complex ways which we cannot yet describe or begin to understand, and which may be largely innate, or may develop through some sort of learning or through maturation of the nervous system. The manner in which such factors operate and interact in language acquisition is completely unknown. It is clear that what is necessary in such a case is research, not dogmatic and perfectly arbitrary claims, based on analogies to that small part of the experimental literature in which one happens to be interested.

The pointlessness of these claims becomes clear when we consider the well-known difficulties in determining to what extent inborn structure, maturation, and learning are responsible for the particular form of a skilled or complex performance.[31] To take just one example,[32] the gaping response of a nestling thrush is at first released by jarring of the nest, and, at a later stage, by a moving object of specific size, shape, and position relative to the nestling. At this later stage the response is directed towards the part of the stimulus object corresponding to the parent's head, and characterized by a complex configuration of stimuli that can be precisely described. Knowing just this, it would be possible to construct a speculative, learning-theoretic account of how this sequence of behavior patterns might have developed through a process of differential reinforcement, and it would no doubt be possible to train rats to do something similar. However, there appears to be good evidence that these responses to fairly complex "sign stimuli" are genetically determined and mature without learning. Clearly, the possibility cannot be discounted. Consider now the comparable case of a child imitating new words. At an early stage we may find rather gross correspondences. At a later stage, we find that repetition is of course far from exact (i.e. it is not mimicry, a fact which itself is interesting), but that it reproduces the highly complex configuration of sound features that constitute the phonological structure of the language in question. Again, we can propose a speculative account of how this result might have been obtained through elaborate arrangement of reinforcing contingencies. Here too, however, it is possible that ability to select out of the complex auditory input those features that are phonologically relevant may develop largely independently of reinforcement, through genetically determined maturation. To the extent that this is true, an account of the development and causation of behavior that fails to consider the structure of the organism will provide no understanding of the real processes involved.

It is often argued that experience, rather than innate capacity to handle information in certain specific ways, must be the factor of overwhelming dominance in determining the specific character of language acquisition, since a child speaks the language of the group in which he lives. But this is a superficial argument. As long as we are speculating,

[31] Tinbergen (op. cit., Chapter VI) reviews some aspects of this problem, discussing the primary role of maturation in the development of many complex motor patterns (e.g. flying, swimming) in lower organisms, and the effect of an "innate disposition to learn" in certain specific ways and at certain specific times. Cf. also Schiller, *Instinctive behavior* 265–88, for a discussion of the role of maturing motor patterns in apparently insightful behavior in the chimpanzee.

Lenneberg (*Language, evolution, and purposive behavior*, unpublished) presents a very interesting discussion of the part that biological structure may play in the acquisition of language, and the dangers in neglecting this possibility.

[32] From among many cited by Tinbergen, op. cit. (this on page 85).

we may consider the possibility that the brain has evolved to the point where, given an input of observed Chinese sentences, it produces (by an "induction" of apparently fantastic complexity and suddenness) the "rules" of Chinese grammar, and given an input of observed English sentences, it produces (by, perhaps, exactly the same process of induction) the rules of English grammar; or that given an observed application of a term to certain instances it automatically predicts the extension to a class of complexly related instances. If clearly recognized as such, this speculation is neither unreasonable nor fantastic; nor, for that matter, is it beyond the bounds of possible study. There is of course no known neural structure capable of performing this task in the specific ways that observation of the resulting behavior might lead us to postulate; but for that matter, the structures capable of accounting for even the simplest kinds of learning have similarly defied detection.[33]

Summarizing this brief discussion, it seems that there is neither empirical evidence nor any known argument to support any SPECIFIC claim about the relative importance of "feedback" from the environment and the "independent contribution of the organism" in the process of language acquisition.

6. We now turn to the system that Skinner develops specifically for the description of verbal behavior. Since this system is based on the notions "stimulus," "response," and "reinforcement," we can conclude from the preceding sections that it will be vague and arbitrary. For reasons noted in §1, however, I think it is important to see in detail how far from the mark any analysis phrased solely in these terms must be and how completely this system fails to account for the facts of verbal behavior.

Consider first the term "verbal behavior" itself. This is defined as "behavior reinforced through the mediation of other persons" (2). The definition is clearly much too broad. It would include as "verbal behavior," for example, a rat pressing the bar in a Skinner-box, a child brushing his teeth, a boxer retreating before an opponent, and a mechanic repairing an automobile. Exactly how much of ordinary linguistic behavior is "verbal" in this sense, however, is something of a question: perhaps, as I have pointed out above, a fairly small fraction of it, if any substantive meaning is assigned to the term "reinforced." This definition is subse-

---

[33] Cf. Lashley, In search of the engram, *Symposium of the Society for Experimental Biology* 4.454–82 (1950). Sperry, On the neural basis of the conditioned response, *British journal of animal behaviour* 3.41–4 (1955), argues that to account for the experimental results of Lashley and others, and for other facts that he cites, it is necessary to assume that high-level cerebral activity of the type of insight, expectancy, etc. is involved even in simple conditioning. He states that "we still lack today a satisfactory picture of the underlying neural mechanism" of the conditioned response.

quently refined by the additional provision that the mediating response of the reinforcing person (the "listener") must itself "have been conditioned *precisely in order to reinforce* the behavior of the speaker" (225, italics his). This still covers the examples given above, if we can assume that the "reinforcing" behavior of the psychologist, the parent, the opposing boxer, and the paying customer are the result of appropriate training, which is perhaps not unreasonable. A significant part of the fragment of linguistic behavior covered by the earlier definition will no doubt be excluded by the refinement, however. Suppose, for example, that while crossing the street I hear someone shout *Watch out for the car* and jump out of the way. It can hardly be proposed that my jumping (the mediating, reinforcing response in Skinner's usage) was conditioned (that is, I was trained to jump) precisely in order to reinforce the behavior of the speaker. Similarly for a wide class of cases. Skinner's assertion that with this refined definition "we narrow our subject to what is traditionally recognized as the verbal field" (225) appears to be grossly in error.

7. Verbal operants are classified by Skinner in terms of their "functional" relation to discriminated stimulus, reinforcement, and other verbal responses. A *mand* is defined as "a verbal operant in which the response is reinforced by a characteristic consequence and is therefore under the functional control of relevant conditions of deprivation or aversive stimulation" (35). This is meant to include questions, commands, etc. Each of the terms in this definition raises a host of problems. A mand such as *Pass the salt* is a class of responses. We cannot tell by observing the form of a response whether it belongs to this class (Skinner is very clear about this), but only by identifying the controlling variables. This is generally impossible. Deprivation is defined in the bar-pressing experiment in terms of length of time that the animal has not been fed or permitted to drink. In the present context, however, it is quite a mysterious notion. No attempt is made here to describe a method for determining "relevant conditions of deprivation" independently of the "controlled" response. It is of no help at all to be told (32) that it can be characterized in terms of the operations of the experimenter. If we define deprivation in terms of elapsed time, then at any moment a person is in countless states of deprivation.[34] It appears that we must decide that the relevant condition of deprivation was (say) salt-deprivation, on the basis of the fact that the speaker asked for salt (the reinforcing com-

[34] Furthermore, the motivation of the speaker does not, except in the simplest cases, correspond in intensity to the duration of deprivation. An obvious counter-example is what Hebb has called the "salted-nut phenomenon" (*Organization of behavior* 199 [New York, 1949]). The difficulty is of course even more serious when we consider "deprivations" not related to physiological drives.

munity which "sets up" the mand is in a similar predicament). In this case, the assertion that a mand is under the control of relevant deprivation is empty, and we are (contrary to Skinner's intention) identifying the response as a mand completely in terms of form. The word "relevant" in the definition above conceals some rather serious complications.

In the case of the mand *Pass the salt*, the word "deprivation" is not out of place, though it appears to be of little use for functional analysis. Suppose however that the speaker says *Give me the book, Take me for a ride*, or *Let me fix it*. What kinds of deprivation can be associated with these mands? How do we determine or measure the relevant deprivation? I think we must conclude in this case, as before, either that the notion "deprivation" is relevant at most to a minute fragment of verbal behavior, or else that the statement "X is under Y-deprivation" is just an odd paraphrase for "X wants Y," bearing a misleading and unjustifiable connotation of objectivity.

The notion "aversive control" is just as confused. This is intended to cover threats, beating, and the like (33). The manner in which aversive stimulation functions is simply described. If a speaker has had a history of appropriate reinforcement (e.g. if a certain response was followed by "cessation of the threat of such injury—of events which have previously been followed by such injury and which are therefore conditioned aversive stimuli") then he will tend to give the proper response when the threat which had previously been followed by the injury is presented. It would appear to follow from this description that a speaker will not respond properly to the mand *Your money or your life* (38) unless he has a past history of being killed. But even if the difficulties in describing the mechanism of aversive control are somehow removed by a more careful analysis, it will be of little use for identifying operants for reasons similar to those mentioned in the case of deprivation.

It seems, then, that in Skinner's terms there is in most cases no way to decide whether a given response is an instance of a particular mand. Hence it is meaningless, within the terms of his system, to speak of the *characteristic* consequences of a mand, as in the definition above. Furthermore, even if we extend the system so that mands can somehow be identified, we will have to face the obvious fact that most of us are not fortunate enough to have our requests, commands, advice, and so on characteristically reinforced (they may nevertheless exist in considerable "strength"). These responses could therefore not be considered mands by Skinner. In fact, Skinner sets up a category of "magical mands" (48–9) to cover the case of "mands which cannot be accounted for by showing that they have ever had the effect specified or any similar effect upon similar occasions" (the word "ever" in this statement should be replaced by "characteristically"). In these pseudo mands, "the speaker simply describes the reinforcement appropriate to a given state of deprivation or aversive stimulation." In other words, given the meaning that we have been led to assign to "reinforcement" and "deprivation," the speaker asks for what he wants. The remark that "a speaker appears to create new mands on the analogy of old ones" is also not very helpful.

Skinner's claim that his new descriptive system is superior to the traditional one "because its terms can be defined with respect to experimental operations" (45) is, we see once again, an illusion. The statement "X wants Y" is not clarified by pointing out a relation between rate of bar-pressing and hours of food-deprivation; replacing "X wants Y" by "X is deprived of Y" adds no new objectivity to the description of behavior. His further claim for the superiority of the new analysis of mands is that it provides an objective basis for the traditional classification into requests, commands, etc. (38–41). The traditional classification is in terms of the intention of the speaker. But intention, Skinner holds, can be reduced to contingencies of reinforcement, and, correspondingly, we can explain the traditional classification in terms of the reinforcing behavior of the listener. Thus a question is a man which "specifies verbal action, and the behavior of the listener permits us to classify it as a request, a command, or a prayer" (39). It is a request if "the listener is independently motivated to reinforce the speaker"; a command if "the listener's behavior is . . . reinforced by reducing a threat"; a prayer if the mand "promotes reinforcement by generating an emotional disposition." The mand is advice if the listener is positively reinforced by the consequences of mediating the reinforcement of the speaker; it is a warning if "by carrying out the behavior specified by the speaker the listener escapes from aversive stimulation"; and so on. All this is obviously wrong if Skinner is using the words "request," "command," etc., in anything like the sense of the corresponding English words. The word "question" does not cover commands. *Please pass the salt* is a request (but not a question), whether or not the listener happens to be motivated to fulfill it; not everyone to whom a request is addressed is favorably disposed. A response does not cease to be a command if it is not followed; nor does a question become a command if the speaker answers it because of an implied or imagined threat. Not all advice is good advice, and a response does not cease to be advice if it is not followed. Similarly, a warning may be misguided; heeding it may cause aversive stimulation, and ignoring it might be positively reinforcing. In short, the entire classification is beside the point. A moment's thought is sufficient to demonstrate the impossibility of distinguishing between requests, commands, advice, etc., on the basis of the behavior or disposition of the particular listener. Nor can we do this on the basis of the typical behavior of all listeners. Some advice is never taken, is always bad, etc., and similarly with other kinds of mands. Skinner's evident satisfaction with this analysis of the traditional classification is extremely puzzling.

8. Mands are operants with no specified relation to a prior stimulus. A *tact*, on the other hand, is defined as "a verbal operant in which a response of given form is evoked (or at least strengthened) by a particular object or event or property of an object or event" (81). The examples quoted in the discussion of stimulus control (§3) are all tacts. The obscurity of the notion "stimulus control" makes the concept of the tact rather mystical. Since, however, the tact is "the most important of verbal operants," it is important to investigate the development of this concept in more detail.

We first ask why the verbal community "sets up" tacts in the child— that is, how the parent is reinforced by setting up the tact. The basic explanation for this behavior of the parent (85–6) is the reinforcement he obtains by the fact that his contact with the environment is extended; to use Skinner's example, the child may later be able to call him to the telephone. (It is difficult to see, then, how first children acquire tacts, since the parent does not have the appropriate history of reinforcement.) Reasoning in the same way, we may conclude that the parent induces the child to walk so that he can make some money delivering newspapers. Similarly, the parent sets up an "echoic repertoire" (e.g. a phonemic system) in the child because this makes it easier to teach him new vocabulary, and extending the child's vocabulary is ultimately useful to the parent. "In all these cases we explain the behavior of the reinforcing listener by pointing to an improvement in the possibility of controlling the speaker whom he reinforces" (56). Perhaps this provides the explanation for the behavior of the parent in inducing the child to walk: the parent is reinforced by the improvement in his control of the child when the child's mobility increases. Underlying these modes of explanation is a curious view that it is somehow more scientific to attribute to a parent a desire to control the child or enhance his own possibilities for action than a desire to see the child develop and extend his capacities. Needless to say, no evidence is offered to support this contention.

Consider now the problem of explaining the response of the listener to a tact. Suppose, for example, that B hears A say *fox* and reacts appropriately, looks around, runs away, aims his rifle, etc. How can we explain B's behavior? Skinner rightly rejects analyses of this offered by Watson and Bertrand Russell. His own equally inadequate analysis proceeds as follows (87–8). We assume (1) "that in the history of [B] the stimulus *fox* has been an occasion upon which looking around has been followed by seeing a fox" and (2) "that the listener has some current 'interest in seeing foxes'—that behavior which depends upon a seen fox for its execution is strong, and that the stimulus supplied by a fox is therefore reinforcing." B carries out the appropriate behavior, then, because "the heard stimulus *fox* is the occasion upon which turning and looking about is frequently followed by the reinforcement of seeing a fox"; i.e.

his behavior is a discriminated operant. This explanation is unconvincing. B may never have seen a fox and may have no current interest in seeing one, and yet may react appropriately to the stimulus *fox*.[35] Since exactly the same behavior may take place when neither of the assumptions is fulfilled, some other mechanism must be operative here.

Skinner remarks several times that his analysis of the tact in terms of stimulus control is an improvement over the traditional formulations in terms of reference and meaning. This is simply not true. His analysis is fundamentally the same as the traditional one, though much less carefully phrased. In particular, it differs only by indiscriminate paraphrase of such notions as denotation (reference) and connotation (meaning), which have been kept clearly apart in traditional formulations, in terms of the vague concept "stimulus control." In one traditional formulation a descriptive term is said to denote a set of entities and to connote or designate a certain property or condition that an entity must possess or fulfil if the term is to apply to it.[36] Thus the term *vertebrate* refers to (de-

[35] Just as he may have the appropriate reaction, both emotional and behavioral, to such utterances as *The volcano is erupting* or *There's a homicidal maniac in the next room* without any previous pairing of the verbal and the physical stimulus. Skinner's discussion of Pavlovian conditioning in language (154) is similarly unconvincing.

[36] Mill, *A system of logic* (1843). Carnap gives a recent reformulation in Meaning and synonymy in natural languages, *Phil. studies* 6.33–47 (1955), defining the meaning (intension) of a predicate "Q" for a speaker X as "the general condition which an object y must fulfill in order for X to be willing to ascribe the predicate 'Q' to y." The connotation of an expression is often said to constitute its "cognitive meaning" as opposed to its "emotive meaning," which is, essentially, the emotional reaction to the expression.

Whether or not this is the best way to approach meaning, it is clear that denotation, cognitive meaning, and emotive meaning are quite different things. The differences are often obscured in empirical studies of meaning, with much consequent confusion. Thus Osgood has set himself the task of accounting for the fact that a stimulus comes to be a sign for another stimulus (a buzzer becomes a sign for food, a word for a thing, etc.). This is clearly (for linguistic signs) a problem of denotation. The method that he actually develops for quantifying and measuring meaning (cf. Osgood, Suci, Tannenbaum. *The measurement of meaning* [Urbana, 1957]) applies, however, only to emotive meaning. Suppose, for example, that A hates both Hitler and science intensely, and considers both highly potent and "active," while B, agreeing with A about Hitler, likes science very much, although he considers it rather ineffective and not too important. Then A may assign to "Hitler" and "science" the same position on the semantic differential, while B will assign "Hitler" the same position as A did, but "science" a totally different position. Yet A does not think that "Hitler" and "science" are synonymous or that they have the same reference, and A and B may agree precisely on the cognitive meaning of "science." Clearly it is the attitude toward the things (the emotive meaning of the words) that is being measured here. There is a gradual shift in Osgood's account from denotation to cognitive meaning to emotive meaning. The confusion is caused, no doubt, by the fact that the term "meaning" is used in all three senses

notes, is true of) vertebrates and connotes the property "having a spine" or something of the sort. This connoted defining property is called the meaning of the term. Two terms may have the same reference but different meanings. Thus it is apparently true that the creatures with hearts are all and only the vertebrates. If so, then the term _creature with a heart_ refers to vertebrates and designates the property "having a heart." This is presumably a different property (a different general condition) from having a spine; hence the terms _vertebrate_ and _creature with a heart_ are said to have different meanings. This analysis is not incorrect (for at least one sense of meaning), but its many limitations have frequently been pointed out.[37] The major problem is that there is no good way to decide whether two descriptive terms designate the same property.[38] As we have just seen, it is not sufficient that they refer to the same objects. _Vertebrate_ and _creature with a spine_ would be said to designate the same property (distinct from that designated by _creature with a heart_). If we ask why this is so, the only answer appears to be that the terms are synonymous. The notion "property" thus seems somehow language-bound, and appeal to "defining properties" sheds little light on questions of meaning and synonymy.

Skinner accepts the traditional account in toto, as can be seen from his definition of a tact as a response under control of a property (stimulus) of some physical object or event. We have found that the notion "control" has no real substance, and is perhaps best understood as a paraphrase of "denote" or "connote" or, ambiguously, both. The only consequence of adopting the new term "stimulus control" is that the important differences between reference and meaning are obscured. It provides no new objectivity. The stimulus controlling the response is determined by the response itself; there is no independent and objective method of identification (see 3§ above). Consequently, when Skinner defines "synonymy" as the case in which "the same stimulus leads to quite different responses" (118), we can have no objection. The responses _chair_ and _red_ made alternatively to the same object are not synonymous, because the stimuli are called different. The responses _vertebrate_ and _creature with a spine_ would be considered synonymous because

---

(and others). [See Carroll's review of the book by Osgood, Suci, and Tannenbaum in his number of Language.]

[37] Most clearly by Quine. See _From a logical point of view_ (Cambridge, 1953), especially Chapters 2, 3, and 7.

[38] A method for characterizing synonymy in terms of reference is suggested by Goodman, On likeness of meaning, _Analysis_ 10.1–7 (1949). Difficulties are discussed by Goodman, On some differences about meaning, ibid. 13.90–6 (1953). Carnap (op. cit.) presents a very similar idea (§6), but somewhat misleadingly phrased, since he does not bring out the fact that only extensional (referential) notions are being used.

they are controlled by the same property of the object under investigation; in more traditional and no less scientific terms, they evoke the same concept. Similarly, when metaphorical extension is explained as due to "the control exercised by properties of the stimulus which, though present at reinforcement, do not enter into the contingency respected by the verbal community" (92; traditionally, accidental properties), no objection can be raised which has not already been levelled against the traditional account. Just as we could "explain" the response *Mozart* to a piece of music in terms of subtle properties of the controlling stimuli, we can, with equal facility, explain the appearance of the response *sun* when no sun is present, as in *Juliet is [like] the sun.* "We do so by noting that Juliet and the sun have common properties, at least in their effect on the speaker" (93). Since any two objects have indefinitely many properties in common, we can be certain that we will never be at a loss to explain a response of the form *A is like B*, for arbitrary A and B. It is clear, however, that Skinner's recurrent claim that his formulation is simpler and more scientific than the traditional account has no basis in fact.

Tacts under the control of private stimuli (Bloomfield's "displaced speech") form a large and important class (130–46), including not only such responses as *familiar* and *beautiful*, but also verbal responses referring to past, potential, or future events or behavior. For example, the response *There was an elephant at the zoo* "must be understood as a response to current stimuli, including events within the speaker himself" (143).[39] If we now ask ourselves what proportion of the tacts in actual life are responses to (descriptions of) actual current outside stimulation, we can see just how large a role must be attributed to private stimuli. A minute amount of verbal behavior, outside the nursery, consists of such remarks as *This is red* and *There is a man.* The fact that "functional analysis" must make such a heavy appeal to obscure internal stimuli is again a measure of its actual advance over traditional formulations.

[39] In general, the examples discussed here are badly handled, and the success of the proposed analyses is overstated. In each case, it is easy to see that the proposed analysis, which usually has an air of objectivity, is not equivalent to the analyzed expression. To take just one example, the response *I am looking for my glasses* is certainly not equivalent to the proposed paraphrases: "When I have behaved in this way in the past, I have found my glasses and have then stopped behaving in this way," or "Circumstances have arisen in which I am inclined to emit any behavior which in the past has led to the discovery of my glasses; such behavior includes the behavior of looking in which I am now engaged." One may look for one's glasses for the first time; or one may emit the same behavior in looking for one's glasses as in looking for one's watch, in which case *I am looking for my glasses* and *I am looking for my watch* are equivalent, under the Skinnerian paraphrase. The difficult questions of purposiveness cannot be handled in this superficial manner.

9. Responses under the control of prior verbal stimuli are considered under a different heading from the tact. An *echoic operant* is a response which "generates a sound pattern similar to that of the stimulus" (55). It covers only cases of immediate imitation.[40] No attempt is made to define the sense in which a child's echoic response is "similar" to the stimulus spoken in the father's bass voice; it seems, though there are no clear statements about this, that Skinner would not accept the account of the phonologist in this respect, but nothing else is offered. The development of an echoic repertoire is attributed completely to differential reinforcement. Since the speaker will do no more, according to Skinner, than what is demanded of him by the verbal community, the degree of accuracy insisted on by this community will determine the elements of the repertoire, whatever these may be (not necessarily phonemes). "In a verbal community which does not insist on a precise correspondence, an echoic repertoire may remain slack and will be less successfully applied to novel patterns." There is no discussion of such familiar phenomena as the accuracy with which a child will pick up a second language or a local dialect in the course of playing with other children, which seem sharply in conflict with these assertions. No anthropological evidence is cited to support the claim that an effective phonemic system does not develop (this is the substance of the quoted remark) in communities that do not insist on precise correspondence.

A verbal response to a written stimulus (reading) is called "textual behavior."

Other verbal responses to verbal stimuli are called "intraverbal operants." Paradigm instances are the response *four* to the stimulus *two plus*

[40] Skinner takes great pains, however, to deny the existence in human beings (or parrots) of any innate faculty or tendency to imitate. His only argument is that no one would suggest an innate tendency to read, yet reading and echoic behavior have similar "dynamic properties." This similarity, however, simply indicates the grossness of his descriptive categories.

In the case of parrots, Skinner claims that they have no instinctive capacity to imitate, but only to be reinforced by successful imitation (59). Given Skinner's use of the word "reinforcement," it is difficult to perceive any distinction here, since exactly the same thing could be said of any other instinctive behavior. For example, where another scientist would say that a certain bird instinctively builds a nest in a certain way, we could say in Skinner's terminology (equivalently) that the bird is instinctively reinforced by building the nest in this way. One is therefore inclined to dismiss this claim as another ritual introduction of the word "reinforce." Though there may, under some suitable clarification, be some truth in it, it is difficult to see how many of the cases reported by competent observers can be handled if "reinforcement" is given some substantive meaning. Cf. Thorpe, op. cit. 353 f.; Lorenz, *King Solomon's ring* 85–8 (New York, 1952); even Mowrer, who tries to show how imitation might develop through secondary reinforcement, cites a case, op. cit. 694, which he apparently believes, but where this could hardly be true. In young children, it seems most implausible to explain imitation in terms of secondary reinforcement.

two or the response *Paris* to the stimulus *capital of France*. Simple conditioning may be sufficient to account for the response *four* to *two plus two*,[41] but the notion of intraverbal response loses all meaning when we find it extended to cover most of the facts of history and many of the facts of science (72, 129); all word association and "flight of ideas" (73–6); all translations and paraphrase (77); reports of things seen, heard, or remembered (315); and, in general, large segments of scientific, mathematical, and literary discourse. Obviously the kind of explanation that might be proposed for a student's ability to respond with *Paris* to *capital of France*, after suitable practice, can hardly be seriously offered to account for his ability to make a judicious guess in answering the questions (to him new) *What is the seat of the French government?*, . . . *the source of the literary dialect?*, . . . *the chief target of the German blitzkrieg?*, etc., or his ability to prove a new theorem, translate a new passage, or paraphrase a remark for the first time or in a new way.

The process of "getting someone to see a point," to see something your way, or to understand a complex state of affairs (e.g. a difficult political situation or a mathematical proof) is, for Skinner, simply a matter of increasing the strength of the listener's already available behavior.[42] Since "the process is often exemplified by relatively intellectual scientific or philosophical discourse," Skinner considers it "all the more surprising that it may be reduced to echoic, textual, or intraverbal supplementation" (269). Again, it is only the vagueness and latitude with which the notions "strength" and "intraverbal response" are used that save this from absurdity. If we use these terms in their literal sense, it is clear that understanding a statement cannot be equated to shouting it frequently in a high-pitched voice (high response strength), and a clever and convincing argument cannot be accounted for on the basis of a history of pairings of verbal responses.[43]

---

[41] Though even this possibility is limited. If we were to take these paradigm instances seriously, it should follow that a child who knows how to count from one to 100 could learn an arbitrary 10×10 matrix with these numbers as entries as readily as the multiplication table.

[42] Similarly, "the universality of a literary work refers to the number of potential readers inclined to say the same thing" (275; i.e. the most "universal" work is a dictionary of clichés and greetings); a speaker is "stimulating" if he says what we are about to say ourselves (272); etc.

[43] Similarly, consider Skinner's contention (362–5) that communication of knowledge or facts is just the process of making a new response available to the speaker. Here the analogy to animal experiments is particularly weak. When we train a rat to carry out some peculiar act, it makes sense to consider this a matter of adding a response to his repertoire. In the case of human communication, however, it is very difficult to attach any meaning to this terminology. If A imparts to B the information (new to B) that the railroads face collapse, in what sense can the response *The railroads face collapse* be said to be now, but not previously, available

10. A final class of operants, called *autoclitics*, includes those that are involved in assertion, negation, quantification, qualification of responses, construction of sentences, and the "highly complex manipulations of verbal thinking." All these acts are to be explained "in terms of behavior which is evoked by or acts upon other behavior of the speaker" (313). Autoclitics are, then, responses to already given responses, or rather, as we find in reading through this section, they are responses to covert or incipient or potential verbal behavior. Among the autoclitics are listed such expressions as *I recall, I imagine, for example, assume, let X equal* . . . , the terms of negation, the *is* of predication and assertion, *all, some, if, then,* and, in general, all morphemes other than nouns, verbs, and adjectives, as well as grammatical processes of ordering and arrangement. Hardly a remark in this section can be accepted without serious qualification. To take just one example, consider Skinner's account of the autoclitic *all* in *All swans are white* (329). Obviously we cannot assume that this is a tact to all swans as stimulus. It is suggested, therefore, that we take *all* to be an autoclitic modifying the whole sentence *Swans are white*. *All* can then be taken as equivalent to *always*, or *always it is possible to say*. Notice, however, that the modified sentence *Swans are white* is just as general as *All swans are white*. Furthermore, the proposed translation of *all* is incorrect if taken literally. It is just as possible to say *Swans are green* as to say *Swans are white*. It is not always possible to say either (e.g. while you are saying something else or sleeping). Probably what Skinner means is that the sentence can be paraphrased "*X is white* is true, for each swan X." But this paraphrase cannot be given within his system, which has no place for *true*.

Skinner's account of grammar and syntax as autoclitic processes (Chapter 13) differs from a familiar traditional account mainly in the use of the pseudoscientific terms "control" or "evoke" in place of the traditional "refer." Thus in *The boy runs*, the final *s* of *runs* is a tact under control of such "subtle properties of a situation" as "the nature of running as an *activity* rather than an object or property of an object." [44] (Presumably, then, in *The attempt fails, The difficulty remains, His anxiety increases*, etc., we must also say that the *s* indicates that the object

---

to B? Surely B could have said it before (not knowing whether it was true), and known that it was a sentence (as opposed to *Collapse face railroads the*). Nor is there any reason to assume that the response has increased in strength, whatever this means exactly (e.g. B may have no interest in the fact, or he may want it suppressed). It is not clear how we can characterize this notion of "making a response available" without reducing Skinner's account of "imparting knowledge" to a triviality.

[44] 332. On the next page, however, the *s* in the same example indicates that "the object described as *the boy* possesses the property of running." The difficulty of even maintaining consistency with a conceptual scheme like this is easy to appreciate.

described as the attempt is carrying out the activity of failing, etc.) In *the boy's gun,* however, the *s* denotes possession (as, presumably, in *the boy's arrival, . . . story, . . . age,* etc.) and is under the control of this "relational aspect of the situation" (336). The "relational autoclitic of order" (whatever it may mean to call the order of a set of responses a response to them) in *The boy runs the store* is under the control of an "extremely complex stimulus situation," namely, that the boy is running the store (335). *And* in *the hat and the shoe* is under the control of the property "pair." *Through* in *the dog went through the hedge* is under the control of the "relation between the going dog and the hedge" (342). In general, nouns are evoked by objects, verbs by actions, and so on.

Skinner considers a sentence to be a set of key responses (nouns, verbs, adjectives) on a skeletal frame (346). If we are concerned with the fact that Sam rented a leaky boat, the raw responses to the situation are *rent, boat, leak,* and *Sam.* Autoclitics (including order) which qualify these responses, express relations between them, and the like, are then added by a process called "composition" and the result is a grammatical sentence, one of many alternatives among which selection is rather arbitrary. The idea that sentences consist of lexical items placed in a grammatical frame is of course a traditional one, within both philosophy and linguistics. Skinner adds to it only the very implausible speculation that in the internal process of composition, the nouns, verbs, and adjectives are chosen first and then are arranged, qualified, etc., by autoclitic responses to these internal activities.[45]

This view of sentence structure, whether phrased in terms of autoclitics syncategorematic expressions, or grammatical and lexical morphemes, is inadequate. *Sheep provide wool* has no (physical) frame at all, but no other arrangement of these words is an English sentence. The sequences *furiously sleep ideas green colorless* and *friendly young dogs seem harmless* have the same frames, but only one is a sentence of English (similarly, only one of the sequences formed by reading these from back to front). *Struggling artists can be a nuisance* has the same frame as *marking papers can be a nuisance,* but is quite different in sentence structure, as can be seen by replacing *can be* by *is* or *are* in both cases. There are many other similar and equally simple examples. It is evident that more is involved in sentence structure than insertion of lexical

---

[45] One might just as well argue that exactly the opposite is true. The study of hesitation pauses has shown that these tend to occur before the large categories—noun, verb, adjective; this finding is usually described by the statement that the pauses occur where there is maximum uncertainty or information. Insofar as hesitation indicates on-going composition (if it does at all), it would appear that the "key responses" are chosen only after the "grammatical frame." Cf. C. E. Osgood, unpublished paper; Goldman-Eisler, Speech analysis and mental processes, *Language and speech* 1.67 (1958).

items in grammatical frames; no approach to language that fails to take these deeper processes into account can possibly achieve much success in accounting for actual linguistic behavior.

11. The preceding discussion covers all the major notions that Skinner introduces in his descriptive system. My purpose in discussing the concepts one by one was to show that in each case, if we take his terms in their literal meaning, the description covers almost no aspect of verbal behavior, and if we take them metaphorically, the description offers no improvement over various traditional formulations. The terms borrowed from experimental psychology simply lose their objective meaning with this extension, and take over the full vagueness of ordinary language. Since Skinner limits himself to such a small set of terms for paraphrase, many important distinctions are obscured. I think that this analysis supports the view expressed in §1 above, that elimination of the independent contribution of the speaker and learner (a result which Skinner considers of great importance, cf. 311–2) can be achieved only at the cost of eliminating all significance from the descriptive system, which then operates at a level so gross and crude that no answers are suggested to the most elementary questions.[46] The questions to which Skinner has addressed his speculations are hopelessly premature. It is futile to inquire into the causation of verbal behavior until much more is known about the specific character of this behavior; and there is little point in speculating about the process of acquisition without much better understanding of what is acquired.

Anyone who seriously approaches the study of linguistic behavior,

[46] E.g. what are in fact the actual units of verbal behavior? Under what conditions will a physical event capture the attention (be a stimulus) or be a reinforcer? How do we decide what stimuli are in "control" in a specific case? When are stimuli "similar"? and so on. (It is not interesting to be told e.g. that we say *Stop* to an automobile or billiard ball because they are sufficiently similar to reinforcing people [46].)

The use of unanalyzed notions like "similar" and "generalization" is particularly disturbing, since it indicates an apparent lack of interest in every significant aspect of the learning or the use of language in new situations. No one has ever doubted that in some sense, language is learned by generalization, or that novel utterances and situations are in some way similar to familiar ones. The only matter of serious interest is the specific "similarity." Skinner has, apparently, no interest in this. Keller and Schoenfeld (op. cit.) proceed to incorporate these notions (which they identify) into their Skinnerian "modern objective psychology" by defining two stimuli to be similar when "we make the same sort of *response* to them" (124; but when are responses of the "same sort?"). They do not seem to notice that this definition converts their "principle of generalization" (116), under any reasonable interpretation of this, into a tautology. It is obvious that such a definition will not be of much help in the study of language learning or construction of new responses in appropriate situations.

whether linguist, psychologist, or philosopher, must quickly become aware of the enormous difficulty of stating a problem which will define the area of his investigations, and which will not be either completely trivial or hopelessly beyond the range of present-day understanding and technique. In selecting functional analysis as his problem, Skinner has set himself a task of the latter type. In an extremely interesting and insightful paper,[47] K. S. Lashley has implicitly delimited a class of problems which can be approached in a fruitful way by the linguist and psychologist, and which are clearly preliminary to those with which Skinner is concerned. Lashley recognizes, as anyone must who seriously considers the data, that the composition and production of an utterance is not simply a matter of stringing together a sequence of responses under the control of outside stimulation and intraverbal association, and that the syntactic organization of an utterance is not something directly represented in any simple way in the physical structure of the utterance itself. A variety of observations lead him to conclude that syntactic structure is "a generalized pattern imposed on the specific acts as they occur," and that "a consideration of the structure of the sentence and other motor sequences will show . . . that there are, behind the overtly expressed sequences, a multiplicity of integrative processes which can only be inferred from the final results of their activity." He also comments on the great difficulty of determining the "selective mechanisms" used in the actual construction of a particular utterance.

Although present-day linguistics cannot provide a precise account of these integrative processes, imposed patterns, and selective mechanisms, it can at least set itself the problem of characterizing these completely. It is reasonable to regard the grammar of a language L ideally as a mechanism that provides an enumeration of the sentences of L in something like the way in which a deductive theory gives an enumeration of a set of theorems. ("Grammar," in this sense of the word, includes phonology.) Furthermore, the theory of language can be regarded as a study of the formal properties of such grammars, and, with a precise enough formulation, this general theory can provide a uniform method for determining, from the process of generation of a given sentence, a structural description which can give a good deal of insight into how this sentence is used and understood. In short, it should be possible to derive from a properly formulated grammar a statement of the integrative processes and generalized patterns imposed on the specific acts that constitute an utterance. The rules of a grammar of the appropriate form can be subdivided into the two types, optional and obligatory; only the latter must be applied in generating an utterance. The optional rules of the grammar can be viewed, then, as the selective mechanisms involved in the production of a particular utterance. The problem of specifying these in-

[47] The problem of serial order in behavior, in Jeffress (ed.), *Hixon symposium on cerebral mechanisms in behavior* (New York, 1951).

tegrative processes and selective mechanisms is nontrivial and not beyond the range of possible investigation. The results of such a study might, as Lashley suggests, be of independent interest for psychology and neurology (and conversely). Although such a study, even if successful, would by no means answer the major problems involved in the investigation of meaning and the causation of behavior, it surely will not be unrelated to these. It is at least possible, furthermore, that such notions as "semantic generalization," to which such heavy appeal is made in all approaches to language in use, conceal complexities and specific structure of inference not far different from those that can be studied and exhibited in the case of syntax, and that consequently the general character of the results of syntactic investigations may be a corrective to oversimplified approaches to the theory of meaning.

The behavior of the speaker, listener, and learner of language constitutes, of course, the actual data for any study of language. The construction of a grammar which enumerates sentences in such a way that a meaningful structural description can be determined for each sentence does not in itself provide an account of this actual behavior. It merely characterizes abstractly the ability of one who has mastered the language to distinguish sentences from nonsentences, to understand new sentences (in part), to note certain ambiguities, etc. These are very remarkable abilities. We constantly read and hear new sequences of words, recognize them as sentences, and understand them. It is easy to show that the new events that we accept and understand as sentences are not related to those with which we are familiar by any simple notion of formal (or semantic or statistical) similarity or identity of grammatical frame. Talk of generalization in this case is entirely pointless and empty. It appears that we recognize a new item as a sentence not because it matches some familiar item in any simple way, but because it is generated by the grammar that each individual has somehow and in some form internalized. And we understand a new sentence, in part, because we are somehow capable of determining the process by which this sentence is derived in this grammar.

Suppose that we manage to construct grammars having the properties outlined above. We can then attempt to describe and study the achievement of the speaker, listener, and learner. The speaker and the listener, we must assume, have already acquired the capacities characterized abstractly by the grammar. The speaker's task is to select a particular compatible set of optional rules. If we know, from grammatical study, what choices are available to him and what conditions of compatibility the choices must meet, we can proceed meaningfully to investigate the factors that lead him to make one or another choice. The listener (or reader) must determine, from an exhibited utterance, what optional rules were chosen in the construction of the utterance. It must be admitted that the ability of a human being to do this far surpasses our present understanding. The child who learns a language has in some sense constructed the grammar for himself on the basis of his observation of sentences and nonsentences (i.e. corrections by the verbal community). Study of the actual observed ability of a speaker to distinguish sentences from nonsentences, detect ambiguities, etc., apparently forces us to the conclusion that this grammar is of an extremely complex and abstract character, and that the young child has succeeded in carrying out what from the formal point of view, at least, seems to be a remarkable type of theory construction. Furthermore, this task is accomplished in an astonishingly short time, to a large extent independently of intelligence, and in a comparable way by all children. Any theory of learning must cope with these facts.

It is not easy to accept the view that a child is capable of constructing an extremely complex mechanism for generating a set of sentences, some of which he has heard, or that an adult can instantaneously determine whether (and if so, how) a particular item is generated by this mechanism, which has many of the properties of an abstract deductive theory. Yet this appears to be a fair description of the performance of the speaker, listener, and learner. If this is correct, we can predict that a direct attempt to account for the actual behavior of speaker, listener, and learner, not based on a prior understanding of the structure of grammars, will achieve very limited success. The grammar must be regarded as a component in the behavior of the speaker and listener which can only be inferred, as Lashley has put it, from the resulting physical acts. The fact that all normal children acquire essentially comparable grammars of great complexity with remarkable rapidity suggests that human beings are somehow specially designed to do this, with data-handling or "hypothesis-formulating" ability of unknown character and complexity.[48]

---

[48] There is nothing essentially mysterious about this. Complex innate behavior patterns and innate "tendencies to learn in specific ways" have been carefully studied in lower organisms. Many psychologists have been inclined to believe that such biological structure will not have an important effect on acquisition of complex behavior in higher organisms, but I have not been able to find any serious justification for this attitude. Some recent studies have stressed the necessity for carefully analyzing the strategies available to the organism, regarded as a complex "information-processing system" (cf. Bruner, Goodnow, and Austin, *A study of thinking* [New York, 1956]; Newell, Shaw, and Simon, Elements of a theory of human problem solving, *Psych. rev.* 65.151–66 [1958]), if anything significant is to be said about the character of human learning. These may be largely innate, or developed by early learning processes about which very little is yet known. (But see Harlow, The formation of learning sets, *Psych. rev.* 56.51 65 [1949], and many later papers, where striking shifts in the character of learning are shown as a result of early training; also Hebb, *Organization of behavior* 109 ff.) They are undoubtedly quite complex. Cf. Lenneberg, op. cit., and Lees, review of Chomsky's *Syntactic structures* in *Lg.* 33.406 f. (1957), for discussion of the topics mentioned in this section.

The study of linguistic structure may ultimately lead to some significant insights into this matter. At the moment the question cannot be seriously posed, but in principle it may be possible to study the problem of determining what the built-in structure of an information-processing (hypothesis-forming) system must be to enable it to arrive at the grammar of a language from the available data in the available time. At any rate, just as the attempt to eliminate the contribution of the speaker leads to a "mentalistic" descriptive system that succeeds only in blurring important traditional distinctions, a refusal to study the contribution of the child to language learning permits only a superficial account of language acquisition, with a vast and unanalyzed contribution attributed to a step called "generalization" which in fact includes just about everything of interest in this process. If the study of language is limited in these ways, it seems inevitable that major aspects of verbal behavior will remain a mystery.

18 MEANINGFULNESS AND CONCEPTS; CONCEPTS AND MEANINGFULNESS
James J. Jenkins

I was originally asked to write on "the role of meaningfulness in the learning of concepts." I took this to imply concern with the number of associates given to particular stimuli and the role of relevant and irrelevant associates in achieving or delaying concept formation or identification. Such ground has already been well covered by Dr. Archer and Dr. Underwood in their excellent chapters (3 and 4) and they have suggested appropriate directions of attack. Fortunately, for the sake of the reader, I reread the suggestions for discussion that accompanied the topic and decided that my first reading was in error. The questions included "What are the most promising methods of assessing the *meaningfulness of concepts?*" and "To what extent are there differences in the *meaningfulness of concepts?*"

At this point the task became much simpler and much harder. It became much simpler because I think one must argue that "meaningfulness" is *not* a property of concepts. It became harder because it was clear that I would have to make that argument and try to spell out its

SOURCE: James L. Jenkins in *Analyses of Concept Learning*, eds., Herbert J. Klausmeier and Chester W. Harris (New York: Academic Press, 1966), ch. 5, pp. 65–79. Reprinted by permission of the author and the publisher.

consequences. In the course of the writing it seemed to me that the basic issue was somehow inverted—that meaningfulness had no direct relation to concepts but that concepts might have a powerful relation to meaningfulness. This idea, I shall attempt to illustrate later.

Concepts, Stimuli, and Meaningfulness

Let us first consider why it is that concepts cannot be said to have "meaningfulness." Meaningfulness is a venerable term in the verbal learning tradition and one with which a writer would tamper only under great provocation. It is ordinarily held to be measured by indices such as the number of subjects reporting an association in the presence of the stimulus, the number of associations to a stimulus per unit time, and the subjective appraisal of associative richness by a subject, objectified by a rating scale. All these measures appeal to responses of subjects in the presence of the stimulus when the subjects have a particular set of instructions. It is obvious that all these operations require a stimulus to be responded to and it is to the stimulus that the meaningfulness attaches. I want it to be painfully clear that I am going to insist that *a concept is not a stimulus*. A concept is, rather, a construct, in every sense equivalent to constructs in scientific theory and no more directly available than such constructs usually are.

Consider the construct "a word in English." How shall I define its meaningfulness? No matter what procedure I choose, I must have a word or a set of words to be rated, and it will be those particular ratings of those particular stimuli rather than "the concept" that is summarized in the meaningfulness measure.

Alternatively, I might seek the meaningfulness of more traditional concepts such as those Heidbreder used in her classic experiment. Any particular instance I choose can be appraised—say I choose the card showing six birds—and the meaningfulness of the stimulus will be specified by that appraisal but the meaningfulness of the concept "six" is beyond my reach. It must be presented in particularized form. If I present the word "six" instead of six items, I only appear to solve the problem. An association to "six" such as "bricks" makes clear the fact that the word, too, is a particular stimulus with properties of its own which affect the associative distribution.

It may be helpful to approach this problem from still another point of view. Elementary textbooks sometimes talk of concepts as being represented in stimuli or being identifiable in different sets of stimuli. The concept *a red patch* is presumably represented in every red patch but it is clear that it is not identical with any particular one of them nor could it be. The issue here is readily seen to be the same as that involved in the older discussions of "images." "What triangle is *the image* of triangle?" The answer, of course, had to be that no particular image could serve, precisely because it *was* particular and, therefore, could not be the image that was "matched" when one said some other stimulus was a triangle. The fruitlessness of the debate on images should suggest to us that this is the wrong way to approach the problem. Surely, we must consider more complex notions of what a concept is than the notion that it is some stimulus invariant, isolated as a cue by some process that stores a family of instances and then somehow identifies what is common to the physical display of all of them.

To say that the concept is in some way "available" or identifiable in the stimulus attributes of any particular exemplar is false, I suspect, not only in special cases but in the usual and general case. When I see a colleague, I may say that he is an example of a *bearded man*. This chooses an intersection of concepts each of which is more or less identifiable on the basis of physical properties (although we may have a terrible time specifying what the sets of stimulus cues are supposed to be). In addition, I have chosen classes or concepts which are supposed to combine in a known and unambiguous fashion (note that I might not be sure what was meant by "bearded lion" or "lion man"). This is the kind of example that encourages one to continue with the struggle of assigning physical attributes to the delineation of a concept. But the inappropriateness of the approach can be immediately sensed when I go on to point out that he is a psychologist, a Unitarian, a father, a musician, or, indeed, as I said at the outset, a colleague. These kinds of concepts are not to be identified in the stimulus but rather in *my knowledge* of the stimulus person.

At this point it is fashionable to say that I ought not to talk in this careless fashion, that I should not say "my knowledge of the stimulus" but rather I should say that the important properties are not in the stimulus but rather in my "responses to the stimulus." This is, of course, the approach taken by all mediation theories and to the extent that any theory deals with "concepts" currently it must *at least* be mediational. But even here there is disappointment. It must also be clear that it is the "potential response" rather than the actual response that identifies an instance of a concept. In the case of my colleague, you may well seek to exhaust my possible responses to his name, his picture, or to him, physically present as a stimulus object. Having worn yourself out you may not yet have discovered that he belongs to the class, member of Democratic-Farmer-Labor party, friend, nearsighted people who hate fat meats, or arbitrarily many other classes to which he may belong and of which I have knowledge and might admit him as an instance if you had asked me. Certainly, his membership in a class and my recognition of it is not contingent on my volunteering the information under some general set of instructions to respond. Indeed, I may recognize his membership in a class which had never before been defined for me if you create such a class in terms which I can understand (e.g., tank commanders of World War II who were wounded in the right knee in France in 1944).

My actual responses may further be positively misleading as to the relevance of the stimulus to some particular concept. In the course of responding to the stimulus of my colleague, it is quite likely that I would be led to name his wife and the art in his home which she collects. In the uninterpreted responses there is nothing to guide one as to the properties that he possesses and those possessed by his surroundings and thus "merely associated" with him. The brute fact is that until my responses are utilized or put to work in some as yet unspecified way I do not know what bearing they have on any concept. *Tables* are not *chairs* and *black* is not *white* yet these are strong bidirectional associates. Whether they are instances of the same concept depends on what concepts are employed. Then, depending on the task at hand, the observed behavioral relationship, i.e., the fact of their association, may be facilitating, interfering, or irrelevant. Associative networks provide an important part of the material on which other orderings and relationships can be imposed and against which requirements and specification may be checked. This does not mean that "checking" is easy. To see a stimulus as an instance of a particular concept or to see how it relates to a more general conceptual scheme may be a great intellectual feat or a trivial exercise akin to running a batch of cards through an IBM machine to pick off all that have a "9" in the second column. But, surely, it is not *merely* the latter.

Three Kinds of Concepts

Perhaps the orientation of this paper can be made clearer by considering concepts to belong to three general classes. The first class is that of concepts that depend on the isolation of some aspect (or set of aspects) of the stimuli which are instances of that concept. The second class is that of concepts that depend on community or agreement of particular responses to the stimuli. The third class is that of concepts that are constructs in general systems of relationships. Instances may be recognized by submitting them to some test procedure or set of procedures. Neither the test procedures nor the rules of the concept system may be clear to the subject who possesses the concept.

Consider the first class. At the first level, so to speak, we can talk of concepts that are dependent on shared characteristics of the physical stimulus. This kind of concept-formation study began to appear in the literature in the 1920's. Concepts of this class may be very complex in expression (as in taxonomic zoology) or very simple (as in the psychologists' concept identification experiments with children and animals). The important aspect for our purpose is that these concepts may be made *explicit* in the form of physical characteristics present in the stimulus display itself. Presumably, the subject needs to learn what to look for and where and how to look; in extreme cases he may even need an elaborate check list to work from and require special apparatus. But the psychological problem involved in such concept identification does not seem particularly deep. (The parallel "simple process" is presumably primary stimulus generalization.)

The second kind of concept is seen emerging in the literature in the late 1930's and early 1940's. This concept is defined in terms of a common response or set of responses which the subject makes to disparate physical stimuli. In this case the invariance is moved from the stimuli to the subject's behavior (and sometimes right out of sight). The simplest case is mediation through "naming" or "labeling" responses. The parallel simple process is secondary stimulus generalization.

The third kind of concept, and the one that I want to call to your attention, is that based on systematic relations; a concept that has its existence in a body of rules and that can be identified by testing procedures involving these rules in some fashion even though no simple labels or common features can be identified. Examples abound, I believe, for I think these are the most common of all concepts, but I must choose from those with which I am best acquainted. A very complex concept might be illustrated by the following:

S_1 The boy hit the ball
S_2 Elephants trumpet at midnight
S_3 of Soldiers the street down march

The first two stimuli exemplify a particular concept; the third does not. The first two are English sentences; the third is not. *Why* this is so is difficult to say, but *that* it is so is readily agreed. Any bypassing of the problem by saying the concept is simply a function of the tendency to label familiar sequences as English sentences can be refuted by "odd" sentences that we all agree are sentences but have low probability values (e.g., "The green cows on the cloud are eating pancakes") and relatively high probability sequences which are not (e.g., ". . . boy and girls are always doing what you please is a word of . . ."). Nor is it fruitful to say that the concept is the result of the common mediating response which one makes to these stimuli, e.g., "That is a sentence in English," since we cannot explain how that response comes to be made to an infinite variety of stimuli. The same argument holds for identification of parts of speech, sentence types, intersentential relations, awareness of underlying linguistic structure, perception of speech sounds, etc.

It must be clear that all three kinds of concepts are important (indeed, they are distinct kinds only for purposes of pedagogy). The first two are neither unnecessary or trivial though could be subsumed under the third kind. The first involves important orderings of the world and the second mediates many kinds of thinking and problem solving. But the time has come when we must seriously attend to the third kind of concept, difficult though it may be for present psychological theories. This kind of concept has precisely the same status as a construct in a scientific theory. It need not be immediately available, nor directly observable but may rest on an inferential base specified only by its systematic relationships.

Linguistic Concepts as Determiners of Meaningfulness

The notion of a concept as being identified by a set of rules can lead one to a rather interesting consequence. Although we must argue that concepts do not have meaningfulness as it is usually defined, conceptual systems may, nevertheless, play an important role in determining the meaningfulness of stimuli. This can be illustrated by examples from research on language.

The work that follows was performed in collaboration with Joseph H. Greenberg, the distinguished anthropologist-linguist whose penetrating insights into linguistic structure and indefatigable analytic zeal made these studies possible. The research began in 1958–1959 when Greenberg was concerned with the problem of the "virtual syllable." This is an old linguistic problem. When one has written the rules for syllable formation in a particular language one is always confronted with the fact that not all possible entries exist (or rather one usually does not know whether they exist or not; one must say he has not yet found them). This is not surprising to the psychologist but it is troublesome to the linguist since he cannot be sure he has written his rules "tightly" enough, unless he finds instances of everything that is possible. But this creates an interesting psychological problem—given that two sequences of sound are not English words, what meaning does it have to say that one of them *could* be and the other one *couldn't* be? Or given two sequences, neither of which could be English words, what does it mean to say that one of them violates fewer rules and thus is more like English than the other?

In the psychological literature, Ebbinghaus (1913) struggled with exactly the same problem (though he did not guess its linguistic foundation) as he studied the nonsense syllables he had invented.

". . . the homogeneity of the series of syllables falls considerably short of what might be expected of it. These series exhibit very important and almost incomprehensible variation as to ease or difficulty with which they are learned. It even appears from this point of view as if the differences between sense and nonsense material were not nearly so great as one would be inclined *a priori* to imagine" (Ebbinghaus, 1913, p. 23).

Greenberg's general hypothesis was that the variations in response to "the probability of something being a word" as well as the variations of meaningfulness of nonsense syllables were attributable to the degree to which the novel stimuli accorded with or departed from the rule structures of syllable and word formation in English.

In English, and probably in all languages, the sequences of phonemes (elementary speech sounds) which may occur are subject to powerful constraints. Let us suppose that we are playing a game, such as anagrams, where we draw at random a sequence of English phonemes. If we draw sets of six symbols and keep the order in which they are originally drawn, the overwhelming majority will not be existent English sequences. As an example, we might well draw a sequence as *g ʋ s u r s*. This is, of course, a nonexistent sequence in English. (It should be noted that this sequence is not "impossible" in any universal sense. It is, in fact, a word in Georgian.) Something further can be said, however, for in a certain sense it is an "impossible" combination. Thus we would not be tempted to look it up in a dictionary to discover whether it might be a rare word that we just happened not to know. We would, further, feel safe in predicting that no soap manufacturer would use it as a brand name for his product.

Let us draw a second time, this time taking three phonemes. Suppose that we draw *d i b* in that order. Let us further suppose that we are unacquainted with any word *dib*, just as was the case with *gʋsurs*. There will be this difference, however; in the case of *dib* we would be quite willing to look it up in the dictionary or assume its possible coinage as a brand name or slang expression in the future. Indeed, *The Oxford English Dictionary* does list a word *dib* meaning, among other things, a counter used in playing at cards as a substitute for money.

Let us now draw a third time, taking three phonemes. On this occasion we obtain the sounds that we would represent in spelling as *lut* or *lutt*. Surely we would be willing to look this up and would half expect to find it in a large dictionary. But even the unabridged Oxford dictionary in this case gives no such word. It seems, then, that some things which are not in English, such as *lut*, are more "possible" than others which are not, such as *gʋsurs*.

Linguists have established a set of rules regarding such possible combinations. These are rules of patterning for the English syllable which have been constructed on the basis of sequences found in existent forms.

Thus, *gʋsurs* would immediately be declared impossible, among other considerations, because all existent English syllables that begin with as many as three consonants (the upper limit) have an initial *s*, a medial unvoiced stop (*p, t*, or *k*) and final liquid or semivowel (*r, l, w*, or *y*). Thus another nonexistent sequence, such as *strab*, would not have been ruled out by these considerations because it contains an initial consonant sequence *str-* which conforms to this rule. In fact, *strab* obeys this and all other rules for the patterning of English syllables, though it, like *lut*, happens not to exist.

On the basis of the rule set we have a simple threefold division of sequences we might draw. Every sound sequence will be "possible" if it conforms to rules such as the above [which are to be found in Whorf (1956)] or "impossible" if not. Among the "possible" ones some will be found in a dictionary and some will not. Thus, we have (1) impossible sequences, (2) possible but not actual sequences, and (3) actual sequences. These are illustrated by *gʋsurs, strab*, and *struk* (struck), respectively.

But the situation is not merely one of such gross categorizations. Pursuing the same general line of attack we can discover still finer divisions which are reasonable. Going back to our game, let us suppose that we now draw *stwip*. Here the first consonant group, *stw*, conforms to the general rule for initial sequences described above; *s*, followed by unvoiced stop (in this case *t*), followed by liquid or semivowel (in this case *w*); yet in this instance we will in all probability not be tempted to look it up in a dictionary. This is because *stw* does not occur as an initial sequence in any English word whatsoever. It can, however, be educed by analogy from *skr: skw* : : *str* : ? , where *skr, skw*, and *str* all occur (e.g., in *script, square*, and *strap*). Here we evidently have a case which is, so to speak, not quite so possible as *strab* but certainly more possible than *gʋsurs*.

As these examples suggest, we can go on to construct a scale of "distance from English" depending on degree of conformity to permissible English sequences of sound structure. At one extreme we have sequences actually found in English and at the other those which we know deviate most drastically, with impermissible sounds and orders. Greenberg did exactly that, developing a 16-step scale by the systematic use of the common linguistic procedure of sound substitution. The linguistic details of the scale need not concern us here except to note that the scale was a rational one, developed from the logical base of the linguistic rules for syllable construction in English.

Following the development of the scale, Greenberg generated instances (i.e., particular monosyllables) at various points on the scale. We then tested these instances for perceived psychological distance from English as judged by native English speakers. The research, reported elsewhere (Greenberg & Jenkins, 1964), is a dramatic demonstration of the mapping of a psychological dimension (judged distance from English) by a logical-rational dimension. For every additional linguistic step away from English, the psychological distance increased by one unit as shown in Figure 1. It turned out, in addition, that this correspondence between psychological judgment and linguistic rationale was extraordinarily robust in terms of the kinds of psychological measurement employed, magnitude estimation, or category rating scales.

The results from the magnitude estimation experiments correlated +.94 with the linguistic scale whereas the results from the category scale correlated +.95 with the linguistic scale. The two psychological techniques correlated +.99.

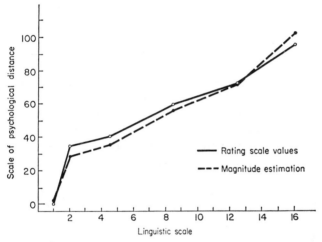

Figure 1   Relation between linguistic and psychological distance.

We then went on in a separate experiment to evaluate the meaningfulness of the test stimuli. We presented the stimuli in the same fashion as in the scaling experiment and allowed the subjects 15 seconds to write down associates to each stimulus. The median number of associates per syllable correlates with the magnitude estimation values—.84, with the rating scale values—.84, and with the linguistic scale itself—.75. In this case, then, meaningfulness appears to be a derived value that reflects how well a stimulus fits into the linguistic-conceptual-logical net which defines a syllable in English.

It should be noticed that this study reverses the usual psychological pattern. Rather than determining meaningfulness in order to structure a stimulus domain, it ordered a stimulus domain on extrapsychological grounds and then observed the resulting meaningfulness. Similarly, this study implies a change in emphasis in interpretation. Perhaps meaning-ful stimuli are not related to a host of concepts because they have many associates; the reverse may be true. Stimuli which are systematically re-lated to a host of concepts (i.e., which readily enter into the rule sets which define concepts) have more associates as a consequence.

Linguistic Analysis of Nonsense Syllables

But it may be argued that these experiments constitute special cases in which only a few stimuli are generated and that there may be all sorts of biases working in the generation and selection of instances which predetermine the outcome of the experiments. A much more gen-eral case is posed by the body of data existing on the set of all conso-nant-vowel-consonant "syllables" collected by psychologists as part of the operation of norming materials for learning experiments. These materi-als are, of course, biased in other directions: orthography has been allowed to determine what a vowel or a consonant is; not all combina-tions are actually used (e.g., syllables which begin and end with the same consonant are avoided and sometimes all real words are avoided); visual presentations are employed; etc. Nevertheless, if one is willing to make a set of simplifying assumptions, it is possible to arrange at least an approximate linguistic analysis of the data.

We began with the assumption that the subject applies normative rules to the orthographic stimulus to attempt pronunciation. If he can pro-nounce it, he checks it against his knowledge of English words. If it is an English word, he checks the spelling to make sure that it is accepta-ble. Thus when the subject sees *KOT* we assume that he attempts to pronounce it and comes up with "*k o t*" which he recognizes as an Eng-lish word (cot) but which he must also realize is incorrect orthographi-cally. When he sees *COT* we assume that he goes through the same op-erations but that the orthography conforms to the norm and thus the combination achieves a higher rating. Archer's norms (1960) show that *KOT* is judged meaningful by 86% whereas *COT* is judged meaningful by 100%. Proceeding in this fashion, we can readily recognize a four-step scale such as the following:

1. COT   pronounceable, an English word, spelled correctly
2. KOT   pronounceable, an English word, spelled incorrectly
3. BOD   pronounceable, not a word
4. XYM   not pronounceable

This almost seems to be what Archer had in mind when he instructed his subjects: "Is this a word? Does it sound like a word? Does it remind me of a word?"

This scale can be expanded by introducing an additional distinction for words that are analogically pronounceable (e.g., SAF can be pronounced but it has no strict parallel in written English since there are no CVCs which end in F). A five-step scale built on this simple model showed very convincing orderliness over the Archer data as Table I shows. Each linguistic class differs by a large amount in rated meaningfulness from the next and each decile of the Archer norms is distinct from the next in terms of mean linguistic scale value. There are no reversals in either set of means.

Table I
Relation between the Five-Step Scale and Archer's Norms for Association Value of CVCs

Mean Association Values for Linguistic Scale Classes

Linguistic Scale	Example	Mean Archer Value
Real English words	CAT	96.05
Pronounceable as words	KOT	72.19
Pronounceable but not words	BOD	50.22
Only analogically pronounceable	SAF	38.68
Unpronounceable	XYM	23.48

Mean Linguistic Scale Values for Association Scale Classes

Archer Deciles	Mean Linguistic Scale Value
1–10	4.63
11–20	4.27
21–30	4.00
31–40	3.82
41–50	3.46
51–60	3.10
61–70	2.87
71–80	2.62
81–90	2.31
91–100	1.81

Encouraged by these findings we went on to split apart the variables of pronunciability and identification with a meaningful word as being of particular interest. Pronunciability was developed as a substitution scale directly analogous to the scale described earlier. In essence it asked how the CVC had to be treated to make it pronounceable. Meaning was then treated by taking the closest target word in English and asking what one had to do to the orthography to achieve a match with the CVC. These procedures depended on the development of explicit pronunciation rules for CVCs; a standard for what counted as a word in English, and a scoring procedure to bridge the correspondence between the CVC with which one started and the specified English word. Although some of the

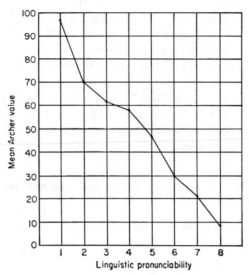

Figure 2   Relation between ease of pronunciability and Archer association values.

decisions that were made were arbitrary, particularly with respect to the weights given to spelling changes, the rules have been made clear and detailed and are completely objective (see Greenberg & Jenkins, forthcoming). The final product was two scales: one, ranging in value from 1

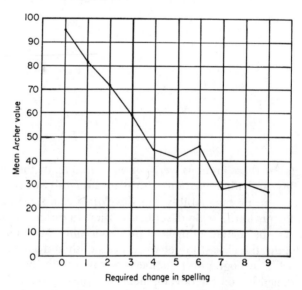

Figure 3   Relation between spelling change required and Archer association value.

to 8, specified the pronunciability of the CVC, the second, ranging from 0 to 9, evaluated the amount of change that was required to move from the CVC to the English orthography of the phonemically closest English word.

Figure 2 shows the mean Archer value for each value of the first variable, and Figure 3 shows the mean Archer value for each value of the second variable. Taken together in a multiple regression equation, the two variables correlate $+.857$ with the Archer values of each CVC. When correlated against Nobel's m' values (independent ratings of association for the nonsense syllables; 1961), the relation is virtually the same, $+.824$.

When one considers that our systematic procedures allow us no judgment about English words that are "known" versus those that are "unknown" by the subject and that we have taken no advantage of our knowledge of other sources of meaningfulness of these materials (XYZ is an outstanding example), it seems fair to claim an outstanding degree of success for a systematic linguistic approach to the meaningfulness of nonsense syllables.

Perhaps it is time to return to the main purpose of the paper, the relation between meaningfulness and concepts. The findings just reported can be used to support the notion that stimuli achieve meaningfulness through their relationship to powerful general conceptual systems which bestow meanings or provide routes to meanings for these previously unexperienced assemblies of elements.

The language case is a particularly fascinating one because at least part of the linguistic rules are known. Knowing the conceptual scheme suggests ways one can analyze performance on related materials and affords some insights as to the operation of the subject when he is called on to respond to or judge new material. In this important sense, studies of conceptual schemes may lead to better descriptions of behavior and more understanding of the nature of tasks than any particularistic exploration of the surface nature of the stimulus or the response. In the specific case of nonsense syllables, psychologists usually ask whether a complete account of association value could not be accomplished by an analysis of the letter frequencies involved, the subject's reading habits, etc. From our experience in the analysis of letter frequency data, it appears to us that this kind of approach is ineffective when taken by itself. Raw letter frequencies are of little predictive value in appraising nonsense syllable meaningfulness. They improve only as one tempers them with explicitly linguistic considerations, i.e., frequency counts become more closely related to judgments of meaningfulness as one counts frequency of a letter in syllable initial position, syllable final position, in conjunction with this particular vowel, etc. As a supplement to linguistic analysis it appears that frequency has some value (as, for example, in selecting words which are known as opposed to words which are un-known) but *what it is that one is to count* is a question that must be de-termined by systematic concerns related to conceptual systems; it does not emerge in any automatic fashion from the frequency notion itself.

Summary

This paper began by denying that meaningfulness was a property of concepts and ended by asserting that the meaningfulness of stimuli might be determined by the rules of the conceptual frameworks in which they could be imbedded. In between it was argued that some, if not most, concepts are not to be found in stimuli or even in responses but rather in sets of systematic relations or bodies of rules. An especially clear case involving the rules of language having to do with the forma-tion of syllables in English was chosen for elaboration. Experiments were discussed in which the set of rules provided a metric on which a psychological distance metric was found to depend. Further, the linguis-tic scale predicted meaningfulness of the stimuli concocted to test the theory. The more general case of accounting for the meaningfulness of CVC nonsense syllables was briefly treated and shown to be amenable to the same kind of analysis. The final thought was that meaningfulness of stimuli might be accounted for in terms of concepts but that concepts were not to be found in any simple way in the raw elements of the stim-uli or responses.

References

Archer, E. J. A re-evaluation of the meaningfulness of all possible CVC trigrams. *Psychol. Monogr.*, 1960, 74, No. 10 (Whole No. 497).

Ebbinghaus, H. *Memory: A contribution to experimental psychology.* Transl. by A. H. Ruger & C. E. Bussenius. New York: Columbia Univer. Teachers Coll., 1913.

Greenberg, J. H., & Jenkins, J. J. Studies in the psychological correlates of the sound sys-tem of American English. *Word*, 1964, 20, 157–177.

Noble, C. E. Measurements of association value (a), rated associations (a'), and scaled meaningfulness (*m'*) for the 2100 CVC combinations of the English alphabet. *Psy-chol. Rep.*, 1961, 8, 487–521.

Whorf, B. L. Linguistics as an exact science. *Technological Rev.*, 1940, 43, 61–63, 80–83. Reprinted in J. B. Carroll (Ed.), *Language, thought, and reality.* Cambridge, Mas-sachusetts: M.I.T. Press, 1956. Pp. 220–232.

19 WORDS, MEANINGS AND CONCEPTS
John B. Carroll

The teaching of words, and of the meanings and concepts they designate or convey, is one of the principal tasks of teachers at all levels of education. It is a concern of textbook writers and programmers of self-instructional materials as well. Students must be taught the meanings of unfamiliar words and idioms; they must be helped in recognizing unfamiliar ways in which familiar words may be used; and they must be made generally aware of the possibility of ambiguity in meaning and the role of context in resolving it. Often the task that presents itself to the teacher is not merely to explain a new word in familiar terms, but to shape an entirely new concept in the mind of the student.

Whether the teaching of words, meanings, and concepts is done by the teacher, the textbook writer, or the programmer, it is generally done in an intuitive, unanalytic way. The purpose of this article is to sketch, at least in a first approximation, a more analytical approach to this task. One would have thought that volumes would have been written on the subject, but apart from such brief treatments as those of Brownell and Hendrickson,[1] Serra,[2] Levit,[3] and Vinacke,[4] for example, one searches the literature in vain for any comprehensive treatment of concept teaching. One is reassured that there are gaps to be filled.

There is, in the first place, an unfortunate hiatus between the word "meaning" and the very word "concept" itself. *Meaning* and *concept* have usually been treated as quite separate things by different disciplines. *Meaning*, for example, has been considered the province of a somewhat nebulous and insecure branch of linguistics called *semantics*.[5]

[1] William A. Brownell and Gordon Hendrickson, "How Children Learn Information, Concepts, and Generalizations," *Forty-Ninth Yearbook, National Society for the Study of Education, Part I*, ed. N. B. Henry (Chicago: University of Chicago Press, 1950), 92 128.

[2] Mary C. Serra, "How to Develop Concepts and Their Verbal Representations," *Elem. Sch. I,* LIII (1953), 275–285.

[3] Martin Levit, "On the Psychology and Philosophy of Concept Formation," *Educ. Theory,* III (1953), 193–207.

[4] W. Edgar Vinacke, "Concept Formation in Children of School Ages," *Education,* LXXIV (1954), 527–534.

[5] Even if a technical science of "semantics" is a comparatively modern invention,— dating, say, from Bréal's article on the subject published in a classical journal in

SOURCE: John B. Carroll, "Words, Meanings and Concepts," *Harvard Educational Review*, 34 (Spring 1964), 178–202. Copyright © 1964 by President and Fellows of Harvard College. Reprinted by permission of the *Harvard Educational Review*.

Concept is almost anybody's oyster: it has continually been the concern of the philosopher, but has received generous attention from psychology. While the meanings of these two terms can be usefully distinguished in many contexts, it is also the case that a framework can be made for considering their intimate interconnections.

Second, there is a gap between the findings of psychologists on the conditions under which very simple "concepts" are learned in the psychological laboratory and the experiences of teachers in teaching the "for real" concepts that are contained in the curricula of the schools. It is not self-evident that there is any continuity at all between learning

---

1883,—the field might be said to have been thoroughly discussed. The classic work of Ogden and Richards (C. K. Ogden and I. A. Richards, *The Meaning of Meaning* [3rd ed.; New York: Harcourt, Brace, 1930].), the somewhat faddish writings stemming from Korzybski's doctrines of "general semantics" (A. Korzybski, *Science and Sanity; an Introduction to Non-Aristotelian Systems and General Semantics* [8th ed.; Lakeville, Conn.: 1948].), and the recent work in psychology of Osgood *et al.* (Charles E. Osgood, George J. Suci, and Percy Tannenbaum, *The Measurement of Meaning* [Urbana, Illinois: Univ. of Illinois Press, 1957].), Brown (Roger Brown, *Words and Things* [Glencoe, Illinois: The Free Press, 1958].), and Skinner (B. F. Skinner, *Verbal Behavior* [New York: Appleton-Century-Crofts, 1957].) might be said to have disposed of most of the general problems of a science of meaning. On the other hand, Stephen Ullmann's recent book (Stephen Ullmann, *Semantics, an Introduction to the Science of Meaning* [Oxford: Basil Blackwell, 1962].) claims only to be in the nature of a "progress report," pointing to the "revolution" that has taken place in modern linguistics and the "advances in philosophy, psychology, anthropology, communication engineering and other spheres" that have had "important repercussions in the study of meaning."

There has been a rash of papers on the implications of linguistics for the teaching of English, the teaching of reading, the teaching of foreign languages, and so on. In fact, the idea that linguistics has much to contribute to educational problems in the "language arts" has become almost embarrassingly fashionable. One's embarrassment comes from the fact that despite certain very definite and positive contributions that linguistics can make to these endeavors, these contributions are of relatively small extent. Once we accept such fundamental tenets of linguistics as the primacy of speech over writing, the structure of the language code as a patterning of distinctive communicative elements, and the arbitrariness of standards of usage, and work out their implications in detail, we find we are still faced with enormous problems of methodology in the teaching of such subjects as English, reading, and foreign languages. The position is particularly difficult in connection with the study of meaning, because most branches of linguistics have paid little attention to this study; some linguists have seemed to go out of their way to exclude the study of meaning from their concerns as linguists. Although there are recent attempts (Paul Ziff, *Semantic Analysis* [Ithaca, N. Y.: Cornell Univ. Press, 1960] and Jerrold J. Katz and Jerry A. Fodor, "The Structure of a Semantic Theory," *Language*, XXXIX [1963], 170–210.) to systematize semantic studies, these efforts may be less than completely successful if they fail to take account of the fundamentally psychological problem of how individuals attain concepts and how these individually-attained concepts are related to word meanings. The treatment of this problem offered in the present paper is exceedingly sketchy and must be regarded as only a first approximation.

"DAX" as the name of a certain geometrical shape of a certain color and learning the meaning of the word "longitude." Even if such a continuity exists, it is not clear how the relative difficulty or complexity of concepts can be assessed.

Third, a problem related to the second arises when we ask whether there is any continuity, with respect to psychological "processes," between the inductive, non-verbal type of learning studied in the psychological laboratory under the guise of "concept learning" and the usually more deductive, verbal-explanatory type of teaching used in the classroom and in typical text materials. Take, for example, the kind of concept learning that has been explored so fruitfully by Bruner and his associates.[6] The experimental setting they employed is essentially a game between the experimenter and the subject: the experimenter says he is thinking of a concept—and perhaps he shows an example of his "concept," whereupon the subject's task is to make guesses about other possible instances of the concept in such a way that he will eventually be able to recognize the concept as defined by the experimenter. But in every case, one feels that the experimenter could have "taught" the subject the concept by a very simple verbal communication like "three circles" (for a "conjunctive" concept in which two attributes must occur together) or "any card that has either redness or two borders" (for a "disjunctive" concept) or "any card with more figures than borders" (for a "relational" concept). Teaching a concept in school is usually not all that simple.

In an effort to fill these gaps, we will sketch out a framework for conceptualizing problems of Meaning and Concept. For reasons that will eventually become clear, we must start with the notion of Concept.

The Nature of Concepts

In a totally inorganic world there could be no concepts, but with the existence of organisms capable of complex perceptual responses, concepts become possible. In brief, concepts are properties of organismic experience—more particularly, they are the abstracted and often cognitively structured classes of "mental" experience learned by organisms in the course of their life histories. There is evidence that animals other than human beings behave with regard to concepts in this sense, but we shall confine our attention to human organisms. Because of the continuity of the physical, biological, and social environment in which human beings live, their concepts will show a high degree of similarity; and through language learning, many concepts (classes of experience) will

[6] Jerome S. Bruner, Jacqueline J. Goodnow, and George A. Austin, *A Study of Thinking* (New York: Wiley, 1956).

acquire names, that is, words or phrases in a particular language, partly because some classes of experience are so salient and obvious that nearly every person acquires them for himself, and partly because language makes possible the diffusion and sharing of concepts as classes of experience. We use the term "experience" in an extremely broad sense —defining it as any internal or perceptual response to stimulation. We can "have experience of" some aspect of the physical, biological, or social environment by either direct or indirect means; we can experience heat, or light, or odor directly, while our experiences of giraffes or atoms, say, may be characterized as being indirect, coming only through verbal descriptions or other patterns of stimuli (pointer readings, etc.) that evoke these concepts.

One necessary condition for the formation of a concept is that the individual must have a series of experiences that are in one or more respects similar; the constellation of "respects" in which they are similar constitutes the "concept" that underlies them. Experiences that embody this concept are "positive instances" of it; experiences that do not embody it may be called "negative instances." A further necessary condition for the formation of a concept is that the series of experiences embodying the concept must be preceded, interspersed, or followed by other experiences that constitute negative instances of the concept. As the complexity of the concepts increases (i.e., as there is an increase in the number of interrelations of the respects in which experiences must be similar in order to be positive instances), there is a greater necessity for an appropriate sequencing of positive and negative instances in order to insure adequate learning of the concept.[7] At least this is true when the concept has to be formed from *non-verbal* experiences only, i.e., from actual exemplars or referents of the concept as contrasted with non-exemplars. But concept learning from verbal explanation, as will be noted below, must, as it were, put the learner through a series of vicarious experiences of positive and negative instances. For example, in telling a child what a lion is, one must indicate the range of positive and negative instances—the range of variations that could be found in real lions and the critical respects in which other animals—tigers, leopards, etc.— differ from lions.

We have been describing what is often called the process of abstraction. We have given a number of *necessary* conditions for the formation of a concept; exactly what conditions are *sufficient* cannot yet be stated, but in all likelihood this will turn out to be a matter of (a) the number, sequencing, or timing of the instances presented to the individual, (b) the reinforcements given to the individual's responses, and (c) the individual's orientation to the task. The evidence suggests that the learner

[7] Earl B. Hunt, *Concept Learning: An Information Processing Problem* (New York: Wiley, 1962).

must be oriented to, and attending to, the relevant stimuli in order to form a concept. The public test of the formation of a concept is the ability to respond correctly and reliably to new positive and negative instances of it; we do not wish to imply, however, that a concept has not been formed until it is put to such a test.

The infant acquires "concepts" of many kinds even before he attains anything like language. One kind of concept that is acquired by an infant quite early is the concept embodied in the experience of a particular object—a favorite toy, for example. As the toy is introduced to the infant, it is experienced in different ways—it is seen at different angles, at different distances, and in different illuminations. It is felt in different positions and with different parts of the body, and experienced with still other sense-modalities—taste, smell. But underlying all these experiences are common elements sufficient for the infant to make an identifying response to the particular toy in question—perhaps to the point that he will accept only the particular specimen that is familiar with and reject another specimen that is in the least bit different. The acceptance or rejection of a specimen is the outward sign of the attainment of a concept—as constituted by the class of experiences associated with that particular specimen. The experiences themselves are sufficiently similar to be their own evidence that they constitute a class—a perceptual invariant, therefore, together with whatever affective elements that may be present to help reinforce the attainment of the concept (pleasure in the sight, taste, smell, and feel of the toy, for example).

Even the concept contained in a particular object represents a certain degree of generality—generality over the separate presentations of the object. But pre-verbal infants also attain concepts which from the standpoint of adult logic have even higher degrees of generality. A further stage of generality is reached when the infant comes to recognize successive samples of something—e.g., a particular kind of food—as equivalent, even though varying slightly in taste, color, temperature, etc. Because the different samples of food are about equally reinforcing, the infant gradually learns to overcome the initial tendency to reject a sample that is experienced as not quite the same as one previously experienced. That is, what seems to be initially a negative instance turns out to be a positive instance because it provides the same reinforcement as the earlier instance—the reinforcement being in this case a "sign" that the new experience is to be taken in the same class as former ones. An even higher stage of generality is achieved when the child will accept and make a common response to any one of a number of rather different stimuli—for example, any one of a number of different foods. In adult terms, he has attained the concept of "food" in some elementary sense. The explanation of this phenomenon may indeed draw upon the usual primary reinforcement theory (the equivalence of different foods in satisfying a hunger drive) but it also depends upon various secondary reinforcements, as when the parent punishes the child for eating something not considered "food," like ants or mud. This is an elementary case in which culture, as represented by parents, provides signs as to what the positive and negative instances of a concept are.

Direct experience, i.e., the recognition of experiences as identical or similar, allows the infant to attain concepts that in adult language have names such as redness, warmth, softness, heaviness, swiftness, sweetness, loudness, pain, etc. In some cases, the infant's concepts of sensory qualities may be rather undifferentiated. For example, because big things are generally experienced as heavy and strong, and small things are generally experienced as lightweight and weak, the infant's concept of size may not be adequately differentiated from his concepts of weight and strength. Without any social reinforcement to guide him, his concept of "redness" may range over a rather wide range of the color spectrum, and if he happens to have been born into a culture which pays little attention to the difference, say, between what we would call "red" and "orange," his concept of "redness" may remain relatively undifferentiated even after he has learned a language—just as it has been demonstrated that different varieties of blue are not well coded in everyday English.[8]

Furthermore, we can infer from various investigations of Piaget [9] that the child's concepts of size, weight, and other physical attributes of objects do not contain the notion of "conservation" that his later experiences will teach him. For all the infant or young child knows of the physical universe, objects can change in size, weight, etc., in quite arbitrary ways. It is only at a later stage, when the child has had an opportunity to form certain concepts about the nature of the physical universe that his concepts of size, weight, and number can incorporate the notion of constancy or conservation that mature thinking requires. Experience with objects that can expand or contract through stretching or shrinking gives the child a concept of size than can properly explain the fact that a balloon can be blown up to various sizes. Indeed, this explanation may involve the concepts of "expansion" and "contraction." At a still later stage, the child may learn enough about the relation of heat to expansion to explain why it is necessary to have seams in concrete roads, or why one allows for expansion in the building of large bridges. And it will be relatively unlikely that even as an adult he will learn enough about the concept of size to understand the concept of relativity—that the size of a body is relative to the speed at which it is traveling and the system in which it is measured.

[8] Roger W. Brown and Eric H. Lenneberg, "A Study in Language and Cognition," *J. Abnorm. Soc. Psychol.*, XLIX (1954), 454–462.

[9] John H. Flavell, *The Developmental Psychology of Jean Piaget* (Princeton: Van Nostrand, 1963).

Thus, concepts can in the course of a person's life become more complex, more loaded with significant aspects. Concepts are, after all, essentially idiosyncratic in the sense that they reside in particular individuals with particular histories of experiences that lead them to classify those experiences in particular ways. My concept of "stone" may not be precisely your concept of "stone" because my experiences with stones may have included work with pieces of a peculiar kind of vitreous rock that you have seldom seen. To a large extent, how I sort out my experiences is my own business and may not lead to the same sortings as yours.

Nevertheless, I can specify the way I sort out my experiences by noting the *critical attributes* that differentiate them. I can specify what sensory qualities and attributes are necessary before I will classify an experience as being an experience of what I call a stone. But it is not even necessary for a person to be able to specify such attributes. A child who has learned a certain concept—who has learned to recognize certain experiences as being similar—may not necessarily be able to verbalize what attributes make them similar; he may not even be aware of the fact that he has attained a certain concept, since it may be the case that only his behavior—the fact that he consistently makes a certain response to a certain class of stimuli—indicates that he has formed a concept. Such would be the case, for example, for the classic instance where the child is afraid of the barber because he wields instruments (scissors) that look like those of the doctor whom he has already learned to fear, and because he wears a similar white smock.

Indeed, this last instance exemplifies the fact that concepts may include affective components. Because concepts are embodied in classes of experiences they include all the elements of experiences that may occur in common—perceptual and cognitive elements as well as motivational and emotional elements. My concept of "stone" may reflect, let us say, my positive delight in collecting new varieties of minerals, whereas your concept may reflect the fact that you had unpleasant experiences with stones—having them thrown at you in a riot, or finding lots of them in your garden. Osgood's "semantic differential," [10] in which one is asked to rate one's concepts on scales such as good-bad, strong-weak, fast-slow, active-passive, light-heavy, pungent-bland, etc., is a way of indexing certain relatively universal cognitive and affective components of individual experiences as classed in concepts; it would perhaps more properly be called an "experiential differential" than a "semantic differential." The fact that fairly consistent results are obtained when concept ratings from different people are compared or averaged implies that people tend to have generally similar kinds of experiences, at least within a given culture.

[10] Charles E. Osgood, George J. Suci, and Percy H. Tannenbaum, *The Measurement of Meaning* (Urbana, Illinois: Univ. of Illinois Press, 1957).

It has already been suggested earlier that since man lives in an essentially homogeneous physical and biological environment and a partially homogeneous social environment, it is inevitable that a large number of concepts arrived at by individual people should be the same or at least so nearly indentical in their essential attributes as to be called the same; these concepts we may call *conceptual invariants*. We can be sure that throughout the world people have much the same concepts of *sun, man, day, animal, flower, walking, falling, softness*, etc. by whatever names they may be called. The fact that they have names is incidental; there are even certain concepts that for one reason or another (a taboo, for example) may remain nameless.

It is probably when we enter into the realms of science and technology and of social phenomena that the concepts attained by different people will differ most. In science and technology concepts vary chiefly because of differences, over the world, in the levels of scientific and technological knowledge reached; and in the social sphere they will differ chiefly because of the truly qualitative differences in the ways cultures are organized. Nevertheless, within a given community there will be a high degree of commonality in the concepts recognized and attained, in the sense that there will be relatively high agreement among people as to the attributes that are criterial for a given concept. For example, even though types of families vary widely over the world, the concept of *family* within a given culture is reasonably homogeneous. At the same time, differences in intellectual and educational levels will account for differences in the sheer number of concepts attained by individuals within a given culture.

Words and Their Meanings

In the learning of language, words (and other elements in a linguistic system, including phonemes, morphemes, and syntactical patterns) come to be perceived as distinct entities, and in this sense they form one class of perceptual invariants along with the perceptual invariants that represent common objects, feelings, and events. The child must learn to perceive the various instances of a given sound or word as similar, and eventually to differentiate the several contexts in which a given sound or sound pattern is used. (We know of an instance of a very young child who somehow learned to react violently to the word "no," but she would react just as violently to the word "know," even when it was embedded in a sentence. The processs of differentiation took a considerable time.)

Many words or higher units of the linguistic system come to stand for, or name, the concepts that have been learned pre-verbally. Certainly this is true for a long list of words that stand for particular things or classes of things, qualities, and events. For the English language, these categories correspond roughly to proper and common nouns; adjectives; and verbs of action, perception, and feeling. It is perhaps less clear that "function words" like prepositions and conjunctions, or grammatical markers like the past tense sign can represent concepts, but a case can be made for this. For example, prepositions like *in, to, above, below, beside, near* correspond to concepts of relative spatial position in a surprisingly complex and subtle way; and conjunctions like *and, but, however, or* correspond to concepts of logical inclusion and exclusion, similarity and difference of prepositions, etc.

The processes by which words come to "stand for" or correspond to concepts can best be described in psychological terms. Without going into the details here, we can only say that in every case there is some sort of reinforcing condition that brands a word as being associated with a given concept. This is true whether the word is learned as what Skinner [11] calls a *mand* (as when a child learns the meaning of *water* as a consequence of having water brought whenever he says "water") or as a *tact* (as where the child is praised or otherwise reinforced for saying "water" when he sees or experiences water), because in either case the word is paired contiguously with the concept *as an experience.* The connection between a word and the concept or experience with which it stands in relation must work in either direction: the word must evoke the concept and the concept must evoke the word.

As a physical symbol, a word is a cultural artifact that takes the same, or nearly the same, form throughout a speech community. It is a standardized product on which the speech community exercises a considerable degree of quality control. Not so with concepts, which as we have seen may vary to some extent with the individual, depending on his experiences of the referents of the words. Society does, however, maintain a degree of "quality control" on the referential meaning of words. The conditions under which the use of words is rewarded or not rewarded —either by successful or unsuccessful communication or by direct social approval or disapproval—can be looked upon as constituting the "rules of usage" of a word, and these rules of usage define the *denotative meaning* of a term. Thus, there is a rule of usage such that the noun *mother* can be used only for a certain kind of kinship relation. One thinks of denotative meaning as something that is socially prescribed. Connotative meaning, however, banks heavily on those aspects of concepts that are widely shared yet non-criterial and perhaps affective (emotional) in content. "Mother" as a noun might evoke various emotional feelings depending upon one's experience with mothers.

Perhaps it is useful to think of words, meanings, and concepts as form-

[11] B. F. Skinner, *Verbal Behavior* (New York: Appleton-Century, Crofts, 1957).

ing *three* somewhat independent series. The words in a language can be thought of as a series of physical entities—either spoken or written. Next, there exists a set of "meanings" which stand in complex relationships to the set of words. These relationships may be described by the rules of usage that have developed by the processes of socialization and communication. A "meaning" can be thought of as a standard of communicative behavior that is shared by those who speak a language. Finally, there exist "concepts"; the classes of experience formed in individuals either independently of language processes or in close dependence on language processes.

The interrelations found among these three series are complex: almost anyone can give instances where a word may have many "meanings," or in which a given "meaning" corresponds to several different words. The relationships between societally-standardized "meanings" and individully formed "concepts" are likewise complex, but of a somewhat different nature. It is a question of how well each individual has learned these relationships, and at least in the sphere of language and concepts, education is largely a process whereby the individual learns either to attach societally-standardized words and meanings to the concepts he has already formed, or to form new concepts that properly correspond to societally-standardized words and meanings. A "meaning" of a word is, therefore, a societally-standardized concept, and when we say that a word stands for or names a concept it is understood that we are speaking of concepts that are shared among the members of a speech community.

To the extent that individual concepts differ even though they possess shared elements, misunderstandings can arise. My concept of "several" may correspond to the range "approximately three to five," where yours may correspond to "approximately five to fifteen." Speech communities may differ, too, in the exact ranges in which they standardize meanings. The word *infant* seems to include a higher age range in Great Britain (in the phrase "infants' schools") than it does in the United States, and in legal contexts the word may even refer to anyone who has not attained some legal age like twenty-one years.

The fact that words vary in meaning according to context has given rise to one form of a "context theory of meaning" which seems to allege that the meaning of a word is to be found in its context; this is only true, however, in the sense that the context may provide a *clue* as to the particular meaning (or standardized concept) with which a word is intended to be associated. In fact, the clue usually takes the form of an indication of one or more elements of a concept. For example, in the phrase *A light load* the context suggests (though it does not determine absolutely) that *light* is to be taken as the opposite of heavy because loads vary more importantly in weight than in their color, whereas the context in *A light complexion* suggests the element of color because complexions can vary in color but only very improbably in weight. It is not surprising that normal language texts have been found to have redundancy, for the elements of concepts suggested by the words in a sentence are often overlapping.

Frequently context is the key to the fact that a word is being used in an archaic or unusual sense. A student who cannot square the usual meaning of *smug* with its use in the following lines from Shakespeare's *Henry IV(Part I)*:

> "And here the smug and silver Trent shall run
> In a new channel, fair and evenly"

had better resort to a dictionary, where he will find that an earlier meaning of *smug* is *trim, neat.* We cannot dwell here on the interesting ways in which words change in meaning historically, often in response to changes in emphasis given to the various criterial attributes embodied in the concepts corresponding to words. Just as one example, though, consider the historical change of meaning of "meat" from (originally), "any kind of food" to "edible part of animal body, flesh," where the criterial attribute "part of animal body" gradually came to be reinforced alongside the attribute "edible thing."

Definitions

What, by the way, is the function of a dictionary definition in the light of the system of ideas being presented here? Aside from the few instances where dictionary definitions present pictures or drawings of the items being defined, two main techniques are used in dictionary entries: (1) the use of verbal equivalents, and (2) the use of formal definition by stating *genus et differentia.* The use of verbal equivalents, as where we are told that *smug* can mean "trim, smooth, sleek," has the function of evoking either a (hopefully) previously known concept to which both the defined word and the defining word stand in the same relation, or a series of (hopefully) previously known concepts from whose common elements the reader can derive the concept to which the defined word properly stands in relation. The use of a formal definition, on the other hand, literally "marks off the boundaries of" the concept by first indicating what it has in common with other experiences (*genus*) and then indicating in what respects or attributes (*differentia*) it differs from other experiences. For example, if we are told that *tarn* is a small mountain lake or pool, we know that in many respects it is similar to other lakes or pools—that it is an enclosed, contained body of water, but that it is a special kind of lake of a given size and location. One could, therefore, presumably acquire the concept named *tarn* by learning to make this response only in connection with the criterial attributes defining it. What could be simpler, particularly if one is verbally told what the criterial attributes are? The only kind of intellectual mishap would occur, one would think, when one of the attributes is misunderstood or overlooked. Calling Lake George (in the Adirondacks) a *tarn* would be grossly to neglect or misunderstand the element of small size.

Concept Formation Research

We are now in a position to inquire into the possible relevance of concept formation research to the learning of the meanings and concepts associated with words in a language.

Practically all concept formation research since the days of Hull [12] has been concerned with essentially the following task: the subject is presented with a series of instances which are differentiated in some way; either the task is finding out in what way the several instances match up with one of a small number of names, or (in the simpler case) it is one of discovering why some instances are "positive" (i.e., instances of the "concept" the experimenter has in mind) or "negative" (not instances of the "concept"). Typically the stimulus material consists of simple visual material characterized by a number of clearly salient dimensions—e.g., the color of the figures, the geometrical shape of the figures, the number of figures, the number of borders, the color of the background, etc. Occasionally the critical characteristics of the concept are not clearly in view—as in Hull's experiment where the critical stroke elements of Chinese characters tended to be masked by the rest of the figures, or as in Bouthilet's [13] experiment where the critical feature was the inclusion of letters found in the stimulus word. Sometimes the critical elements are semantic elements of words, as in Freedman and Mednick's experiment [14] in which the task was to find the common semantic element in a series of words such as *gnat, needle, stone,* and *canary.*

Thus, there are two elements to be studied in any concept-formation task: (1) the attributes which are criterial to the concept—their nature and number, the number of values each attribute has and the discriminability of these values, and the salience of the attributes themselves—that is, whether the attributes command attention and are readily per-

---

[12] C. L. Hull, "Quantitative Aspects of the Evolution of Concepts," *Psychol. Monogr.*, No. 123, (1920).

[13] L. Bouthilet, "The Measurement of Intuitive Thinking" (unpublished Ph.D. Thesis, Univ. of Chicago, 1948).

[14] J. L. Freedman and S. A. Mednick, "Ease of Attainment of Concepts as a Function of Response Dominance Variance," *J. Exp. Psychol.*, LV (1958), 463–466.

ceivable, and (2) the information-handling task required of the subject in view of the order in which positive and negative instances are presented and the amount of information concerning the concept that is furnished by each presentation. Most of what we know about this kind of concept attainment task can be summarized in the following statements:

1. Concept attainment becomes more difficult as the number of relevant attributes increases, the number of values of attributes increases, and the salience of the attributes decreases.

2. Concept attainment becomes more difficult as the information load that must be handled by the subject in order to solve the concept increases, and as the information is increasingly carried by negative rather than positive instances.

3. Various strategies for handling the information load are possible, and some are in the long run more successful than others.

Concept Learning in School

I suspect that anyone who has examined the concept formation literature with the hope of finding something of value for the teaching of concepts in school has had cause for some puzzlement and disappointment, because however fascinating this literature may be, as it wends its way through the detailed problems posed by the methodology itself, its relevance to the learning of concepts in the various school subjects is a bit obscure.

Let us look at the major differences between concept learning in school and in the laboratory.

(1) One of the major differences is in the nature of the concepts themselves. A new concept learned in school is usually a genuinely "new" concept rather than an artificial combination of familiar attributes (like the concept "three blue squares" such as might be taught in a psychological experiment).

(2) New concepts learned in school depend on attributes which themselves represent difficult concepts. In more general terms, concepts learned in school often depend upon a network of related or prerequisite concepts. One cannot very well learn the concept of derivative, in the calculus, until one has mastered a rather elaborate structure of prerequisite concepts (e.g., slope, change of slope, algebraic function, etc.). Further, the attributes on which school-learned concepts depend are frequently verbal, depending on elements of meaning that cannot easily be represented in terms of simple sensory qualities as used in concept formation experiments.

(3) Many of the more difficult concepts of school learning are of a re-

lational rather than a conjunctive character; they deal with the relations among attributes rather than their combined presence or absence. Concept formation experiments have thus far revealed little about the acquisition of relational concepts.

(4) An important element in school learning is the memory problem involved in the proper matching of words and concepts. Thus, the problems of paired-associate memory are added to those of concept learning itself. For example, a student in biology or social studies has to learn not only a large number of new concepts, but also a large number of unfamiliar, strange-looking words to be attached to these concepts. The rate at which new concepts can be introduced is probably limited, just as the rate at which foreign language words can be acquired is limited.

(5) The most critical difference between school concept learning and concept learning in psychological experiments is that the former is for the most part deductive and the latter is generally inductive. It would be relatively rare to find a concept taught in school by the procedure of showing a student a series of positive and negative instances, labeled as such, and asking him to induce the nature of the concept with no further aid. Such instances could be found, of course; perhaps they would exemplify a pure "discovery method," and perhaps there should be more use of this method than is the case. The fact is that a pure discovery method is seldom used, because it is rather slow and inefficient. Even if a teaching procedure incorporates "discovery" elements, it is likely to be combined with deductive elements. The concept to be taught is described verbally—perhaps by a rule or definition—and the student is expected to attain the concept by learning to make correct identification of positive and negative instances. For example, he is told what an "indirect object" is and then is given practice in identifying the indirect objects (positive instances) among other words (negative instances). Many simple concepts can be taught by a wholly deductive procedure. For most students, the dictionary definition of *tarn* will be a sufficient stimulus for attainment of the concept. On the other hand, it is well known that purely deductive, verbal procedures are frequently insufficient to help learners attain concepts. Concept formation experimentation would be more relevant to school learning problems if it could give more attention to examining the role of verbalization and other deductive procedures in concept attainment.

Nevertheless, there are certain similarities between concept attainment in school and concept formation in psychological experiments. These arise chiefly from the fact that not every concept is learned *solely* in a formalized, prearranged school setting. The school environment is in many ways continuous with the out-of-school environment; concepts are learned partly in school, partly out of school. The process whereby the elementary concepts of a language are learned closely parallels that of the psychological concept formation experiment. A child learns the concept "dog" not by having the concept described to him but by learning to restrict his usage of the word *dog* to instances regarded as positive by the speech community. In this process there are many false responses—either false positives (calling a non-dog a dog) or false negatives (believing a dog to be a non-instance), before an appropriate series of reinforcements produces correct concept attainment. Similar phenomena occur with concepts in the school curriculum. A child who has been told that his cousins visiting him from Peoria are "tourists" may not realize that tourists do not need to be relatives, and when he is told that the Germans who have settled in his town are "immigrants," he may believe that all foreigners visiting his town are immigrants. Concept formation experiments yield information as to the range and variety of instances that have to be furnished for efficient and correct concept formation in the absence of formal instruction.

But if the foregoing statement is true, concept formation studies should also yield insights as to what information has to be furnished for *deductive* concept formation, e.g., from a formal definition. Obviously, a formal definition is successful only to the extent that it correctly identifies and describes all the criterial attributes that are likely to be relevant for a concept, and to the extent that it communicates the proper values and relationships of these to the learner. The burden is both on the definition itself and on the learner. A student may fail to learn the concept *tarn* from the definition previously cited either because it omits some essential criterial attribute (e.g., that a tarn must contain *water* rather than, say, *oil* or *lava*), or because the student fails to comprehend the meaning of its elements (for example, how small is "small"?).

What is actually going on in most school learning of concepts is a process that combines in some way deductive and inductive features.

Descriptions and definitions provide the deductive elements of the process. The several parts of a description of definition specify the attributes and relationships that are criterial for the concept. The order in which these specifications are arranged in the description and presented to the student may have something to do with the ease of concept attainment, particularly in the case of complex concepts with many attributes and complex interrelationships like the case of *tort* discussed below). As yet we have no well-founded generalizations about the order in which the criterial attributes for a concept should be presented.

At the same time, inductive procedures entail the citing of positive and negative instances of the concept. We know from concept attainment research that learning is facilitated more by positive than by negative instances, even though the "information" conveyed by these instances is the same in a given experimental context. But in real-life concept learning, the number of dimensions that may possibly be relevant is less limited; the function of positive instances is as much to show *which* dimensions are relevant as it is to show what values of them are critical. We may speculate that the real value of what we are calling inductive procedures in concept learning is to afford the learner an opportunity to test his understanding of and memory for the elements of verbal descriptions and definitions. This testing may even involve the construction and testing of alternative hypotheses.

For example, consider the following verbal statement of what a "paradigm" (for research on teaching) is:

> "Paradigms are methods, patterns, or schemata. Paradigms are not theories; they are rather ways of thinking or patterns for research that, when carried out, can lead to the development of theory." [15]

As a verbal statement, this is hardly adequate; fortunately, Gage proceeds to exhibit a number of positive instances of "paradigms" by which his readers can test out their notions of what this concept might be. Many readers will still have difficulty, however, because he fails to exhibit *negative* instances of paradigms.

What is needed, eventually, is a scientific "rhetoric" for the teaching of concepts—assembled not only from the traditional rhetoric of exposition but also from whatever scientific experiments on concept teaching can tell us. We will be better off, however, if concept-attainment studies begin to give attention to the manner in which real-life, non-artificial concepts can be taught most efficiently—presumably by combination of both deductive and inductive procedures.

Illustrations of Concept Teaching Problems

To suggest the kinds of problems that arise in the teaching of concepts or that might be investigated through formal research, I propose to analyze a small number of concepts of various types, at several levels of difficulty.

TOURIST VS. IMMIGRANT

A fourth grade teacher reported difficulty in getting her pupils to understand and contrast the meanings of the words *tourist* and *immigrant*. Neither word appears in Dale and Eichholz's [16] list of words known by at least sixty-seven percent of children in the fourth grade, although *tour* (as a sight-seeing trip) was known by seventy percent. In the sixth-grade

---

[15] N. L. Gage, "Paradigms for Research on Teaching," *Handbook of Research on Teaching*, ed. N. L. Gage (Chicago: Rand McNally, 1963), 94–141.

[16] Edgar Dale and Gerhard Eichholz, *Children's Knowledge of Words* (Columbus: Bureau of Educational Research and Service, Ohio State University, 1960).

list, *immigrant* was known by seventy percent and *tourist* by seventy-seven percent; the figures are ninety-seven percent (for *immigration*) and ninety-six percent (for *tourist*) in the 8th-grade list.

To an adult, the differentiation between the concepts designated by *tourist* and *immigrant* looks almost trivially simple. Aside from the sheer memory problem in learning and differentiating the words themselves, what are the sources of confusion for the child? In specific cases, a tourist and an immigrant might have many common characteristics: both might be from a foreign country, or at least from some distance away from the local community; both might be of obviously non-native culture because of dress, complexion, speech, and behavior; both might be doing what would appear to be "sight-seeing," though possibly for different purposes. The differences between a tourist and an immigrant might not be very apparent, being primarily differences of motivation. Indeed, a tourist might become an immigrant overnight, just by deciding to be one.

As we have seen, there is a sense in which the concept-attainment experimental literature is relevant to the child's problem in learning the meanings of the words *tourist* and *immigrant*. If the child is presented with various instances of people who are either tourists or immigrants, properly labeled as such, but with no further explanation, it will be the child's task to figure out what attributes or characteristics are relevant to the differentiation of these concepts. This might occur either in school or outside of school. Most likely the instances of tourists and immigrants will be relatively sporadic over time, and the instances may not vary in such a way as to show what attributes are truly relevant. For example, all the tourists may be obviously American whereas all the immigrants may be obviously Mexican, let us say. The tourists may all be well-dressed, the immigrants poorly dressed, and so on. If the natural environment is like a grand concept-formation experiment, it may take the child a long time to attain the concepts *tourist* and *immigrant*; indeed, the environment may not be as informative as the usual experimenter, since the child may not always be informed, or reliably informed, as to the correctness of his guesses. No wonder a child might form the concept that a tourist is any well-dressed person who drives a station-wagon with an out-of-state license plate!

The purpose of teaching is to short-cut this capricious process of concept attainment within the natural environment. Through the use of language, there should be relatively little difficulty in explaining to a child that an immigrant is one who moves from one country or region to another in order to change his permanent residence, while a tourist is one who travels around for pleasure without changing his permanent residence. One can use simple explanations like: "He's going to stay here, have his home here . . ." or "He's just traveling around for the fun of it while he's on vacation, and someday he'll get back home." There should be no difficulty, at any rate, if the child has already mastered certain prerequisite concepts. Among these prerequisite concepts would be: the concept of home or permanent residence and all that it implies; the concept of the division of world territory into different countries and those in turn into regions; and the concept of traveling for pleasure or curiosity. It is very likely that the child who is having trouble understanding the concept of tourist vs. the concept of immigrant has not got clearly in mind these prerequisite notions that constitute, in fact, the criterial attributes upon which the distinction hangs.

Alternatively, a child might be having trouble because he has not dispensed with irrelevant aspects of these concepts: he might think that a tourist has to be always an American, whereas an immigrant must be a foreigner, because he has seen *American* tourists and *foreign* immigrants, no *American* immigrants nor *foreign* tourists. The ingenious teacher will think of the possible misunderstandings that could arise through the influence or irrelevant attributes of tourists and immigrants.

TIME

K. C. Friedman [17] pointed out that elementary school children have much trouble with various time concepts. A child sees no incongruity, for example, in saying, "My older brother was born a long time ago." According to Friedman, it was not until Grade VI that all children in his school could state the date or list the months in perfect order. They had difficulty, he reports, in forming a concept of the "time line" and then in recognizing the placement of various historical events on such a time line. It is easy to see why the child would have these difficulties; even as adults it is difficult for us to appreciate the significance of the fantastically long periods implied by geological time. It should be noted that our concept of a time line is essentially a *spatial* concept whereby we translate temporal succession in terms of spatial order and distances. For a child, times does not flow in a straight line nor in any other particular direction, unless it is around the clock, in a circular or spiral dimension! How can the child form a concept of time and its units? Is time a class of experiences? Does it have criterial attributes? The paradigms of concept-formation experiments do not seem to apply here readily. But let us examine the situation more closely. How can the child have experiences of time and generate the concept of a time line? Certainly there can be experiences of intervals of time—watching a second hand of a clock move through the second-markings, or experiencing the succession of night and day, noticing the change of seasons or waiting for the end of the school year. Moving from one time period to another

[17] Kopple C. Friedman, "Time Concepts of Elementary-school Children," *Elem. Sch. J.,* XLIV (1944), 337–342.

could be likened to moving from one square of a sidewalk to the next. It should be an easy transition to thinking of the time line as a sidewalk of infinite extent in both directions—toward the past and toward the future. Marking off the days on the calendar and naming the days and months should help to reinforce this cognitive structure. Extrapolation of the time line is like generalizing these time experiences to all possible such experiences.

One of the difficulties comes, presumably, from the fact that the far reaches of the past and the future cannot be immediately experienced, and one immediately has trouble if one attempts to show a time line that includes historical events in the distant past along with a representation of the relationship between today, yesterday, and the day before yesterday. (Incidentally, it is hard to believe Pistor's [18] claim that young children cannot tell the difference between the present and the past, in view of the fact that they can correctly use the present tenses of verbs in simple situations.) Time lines of different scales must be used, and the concept of scale will itself be hard for children to understand unless it is carefully explained—perhaps by showing maps of the immediate environment in different scales. Only after such ideas have been mastered will it be possible for the child to have any appreciation of such concepts as *year, century, 1492* (as a date), *B.C., generation. Generation* and *eon*, by the way, would have to be introduced as somewhat flexible, arbitrary units of time, as contrasted with fixed, measurable units such as *year* and *century.*

QUANTITATIVE EXPRESSIONS LIKE "MANY," "FEW," "AVERAGE"

Ernest Horn [19] pointed out that certain quantitative concepts like *many, few,* and *average* are often so difficult that children do not give reasonable interpretations of them. It is very likely that the source of the difficulty is that children tend not to be able to think in relative terms. Children (and perhaps their teachers) would like to be able to assign definite ranges of numbers for such words as *many, few, average, a sizable amount*, etc., when actually they are all relative terms. There has even been a psychological experiment to demonstrate this: Helson, Dworkin, and Michels [20] showed that adult subjects will consistently give different meanings to a word like "few" when it is put in different contexts. For example, "few" meant about twelve percent on the aver-

---

[18] Frederick Pistor, "Measuring the Time Concepts of Children," *J. Educ. Res.*, XXX (1939), 293–300.

[19] Ernest Horn, *Methods of Instruction in Social Studies* (New York: Scribner, 1937).

[20] Harry Helson, Robert S. Dworkin and Walter C. Michels, "Quantitative Denotations of Common Terms as a Function of Background," *Amer. J. Psychol.*, LXIX (1956), 194–208.

age, in relation to 100 people, whereas it meant four percent, on the average, in relation to 1,728,583 people.

In teaching a child these relational concepts the problem would be to exhibit or describe numerous instances in which the absolute base varies but in which the actual numbers of quantities meant would at the same time vary sufficiently to give the impression that these words do not indicate anything like exact amounts. It should be pointed out that 100 things might be "many" in some situations and "few" in others. The use of "average" in such a context as "There was an average number of people in church today" can be taught by drawing attention to its relation to the probable extremes of the numbers of people that might be in church, generalizing the concept to other situations like "I caught an average number of fish today." This might lead to the introduction of the average as a statistic or number that gives information about the "central tendency" of some frequency distribution. It may help to use an unfamiliar or unusual context to bring out this concept in sharp relief. For example, I like to illustrate the utility of the statistical mean or arithmetic average by asking students to imagine that the first space men to reach Mars discover human-like creatures there whose average height is —and this is where the mean becomes really informative—3 inches!

The basic concept of the mean arises in the context of experiences in which there is a plurality of objects measured in some common way. As a first approximation, as far as a child is concerned, the average is a number that is roughly halfway between the highest and lowest measurements encountered, and in some way "typical" of these measurements. Only at some later stage does the child need to learn that the mean is a number that can be computed by a formula and that it has certain properties.

LONGITUDE

It is difficult to understand why E. B. Wesley [21] says that concepts related to the sphericity of the earth, like latitude and longitude, are not easily taught to the average child before Grades VI and VII. Wesley was writing before the advent of the space age when every child knows about space capsules traveling around the globe. Though it may still be difficult to get a child to see how the flatness of his immediate environment is only apparent and that the immediate environment corresponds to just a small area on the globe, it can certainly be done, well before Grade VI, through suitable demonstrational techniques. Having established the sphericity of the earth, one should be able to teach latitude and longitude as concepts involved in specifying locations on the globe. Their introduction should properly be preceded by simpler cases in

[21] E. B. Wesley and Mary A. Adams, *Teaching Social Studies in Elementary Schools* (Rev. ed.: Boston: D. C. Heath, 1952), p. 307.

which one uses a system of coordinates to specify location—e.g., equally spaced and numbered horizontal and vertical lines drawn on a blackboard with a game to locate letters placed at intersection of lines, a map of one's town or city in which marginal coordinates are given to help locate given streets or places of interest, and finally a Mercator projection map of the world with coordinates of latitude and longitude. Children exposed to the "new math" with its number lines and coordinates should have no trouble with this. Then let us show children by easy stages how a Mercator projection corresponds to the surface of the Earth (certainly an actual globe marked off with latitude and longitude should be used), then how it is necessary to select a particular line (that passes through the Greenwich Observatory) as the vertical coordinate from which to measure, and how the circumference of the earth is marked off in degrees—180° West and 180° East from Greenwich meridian.

The object is to build for the child a vivid experience of the framework or cognitive structure within which the concept of longitude is defined. The further complications introduced by the use of other kinds of world projections or by the use of regional or even local maps could then be explored. Easily-obtained U.S. Geological Survey maps of one's locality would concretize the meanings of further concepts, e.g., the division of degrees into minutes and seconds, and the fact that a degree of longitude will gradually shrink in length as one moves northward from the equator.

TORT

The concept of *tort* is very likely to be unfamiliar or at least vague to the average reader. Even a dictionary definition [22] may not help much in deciding whether arson, breach of contract, malicious prosecution, or libel are positive instances of torts. The case method used in many law schools, whereby students examine many positive and negative instances of torts in order to learn what they are, is somewhat analogous to a concept formation experiment of the purely inductive variety.

A study [23] of the various laws and decisions relating to torts yields the following approximate and tentative characterization of the concept as having both conjunctive and disjunctive aspects:

$$\text{TORT} = (A+B+C+D+E+F+G+H) \ (I+J) \ (K) \ (-L) \ (-M)$$
$$(-N) \ (-O) \ \text{where}$$

[22] The *American College Dictionary* defines *tort* as "a civil wrong (other than a breach of contract or trust) such as the law requires compensation for in damages; typically, a willful or negligent injury to a plaintiff's person, property, or reputation."

[23] For helping me in my treatment of the concepts of *tort* and *mass* I am indebted to my student, Mr. Edward A. Dubois.

A = battery
B = false imprisonment
C = malicious prosecution
D = trespass to land
E = interference to chattels
F = interference with advantageous relations
G = misrepresentation
H = defamation
I = malicious intent
J = negligence
K = causal nexus
L = consent
M = privilege
N = reasonable risk by plaintiff
O = breach of contract

Within a parenthesis, terms joined by the sign + are mutually disjunctive attributes; a minus sign (−) within a parenthesis signifies "absence of"; the full content of each parenthesis is conjunctive with the content of every other parenthesis. Thus, we can read the formula as follows: "A tort is a battery, a false imprisonment, a malicious prosecution, a trespass to land, . . . , or a defamatory act which is done either with malicious intent or negligently, which exhibits a causal nexus with the injury claimed by the plaintiff, *and* which is done without the plaintiff's consent, *or* without privilege on the part of the defendant, *or* without a reasonable risk by the plaintiff, *or* which is not a breach of contract."

Thus, *tort* turns out to be a concept very much on the same order as *tourist*—a collocation of criterial attributes with both conjunctive and disjunctive features. Deciding whether an act is a tort requires that one check each feature of a situation against what can be put in the form of a formula (as done above). Presumably, a person presented with a properly organized series of positive and negative instances of torts could induce the concept, provided he also understood such prerequisite concepts as *battery*, *misrepresentation*, etc.

MASS VS. WEIGHT

One of the more difficult concepts to teach in elementary physics is that of *mass*. What kind of concept is it and how can one learn it and experience it? How can it be distinguished from the concept of weight? Actually, if we ignore certain subtle questions about mass, such as that of whether inertial and gravitational mass are demonstrably identical, the concept of mass is not as difficult as it might seem; the real difficulty is to teach the sense in which it is different from weight. In fact, weight is perhaps the more difficult concept, because the weight of an object can vary to the point that it can become "weightless."

The concept of mass, one would think, ought to develop for the learner (be he a child or an adult) in much the same way that concepts of other properties of the physical world develop—analogously, that is, to concepts of color, number, and volume. For mass is a property of objects that differentiates them in our experience: there are objects with great mass (like the earth, or a large boulder) and there are objects with small mass (like a feather or a pin or the air in a small bottle), and our experiences of objects with respect to mass can differ enormously, particularly in our proprioceptive senses. Further, mass is a property of objects that is *conserved* regardless of whether the object is in motion or at rest; conservation of mass is learned through experience just as conservation of other properties is learned. Even the physical definition of mass as that property of things which accounts for the relative amount of force which has to be applied to produce a certain amount of acceleration is perceived in common-sense terms as the property of objects that determines the amount of force or effort that one would have to exert to move or lift it. The well-known "size-weight" illusion (in which, for example, we exert an undue amount of effort to lift or push some large but relatively light object) illustrates the fact that our perceptions of an object typically include some impression of its mass. The physical operation of measuring mass by determining the ratio of force to acceleration is an operational extension of the kind of behavior we exhibit when we see how much force it will take to move a heavy trunk.

The real trouble comes in the fact that we are too prone to equate mass with weight, mainly because equal masses also have equal weights when compared by means of a balance, or when measured with a spring balance at the same point on the earth's surface (at least, at the same distance from the earth's center). If we were more easily able to experience the fact that the weight of an object of given mass changes as acceleration due to gravity changes—for example by going to the moon and observing the "weight" of objects there, or by experiencing "weightlessness" in an orbital flight around the earth, weight and mass might be just as easy to distinguish as size and mass. Since such experiences would be rather hard to come by, to put it mildly, we have to be content with the imaginal representation of weight as a *variable* property of objects that really depends upon a relation between the gravitational force exerted on an object and its mass (actually, the product of these two). A child might be made to understand how objects of different masses could have equal "weight"—a relatively large object on the moon and a relatively small one on the earth, for example, as measured by a spring balance which is sensitive to the pull of gravity; or how an object of constant mass would have different weights at different distances from the earth (the pull of gravity thus varying). We would have to conclude that weight, properly speaking, is a relational concept that can only be understood when the total framework in which weight can be defined is described. Mass, on the other hand, is a concept that corresponds much more directly to immediate perceptions of reality.

It will be noted that the teaching of mass and weight concepts involves several prerequisite concepts—e.g., the pull of gravity, the relation between the mass of an object like the earth or the moon and the gravitational force it exerts, and the concept of acceleration. The pull exerted by a magnet could be used for illustrating certain aspects of the concept of gravitational force; a large magnet and a small magnet could represent the respective gravitational pulls of earth and moon; the concept of acceleration can be introduced verbally as "how fast something gets started" and later as an accelerating curve of velocity.

Without really meaning to do so, this discussion of mass and weight has turned out to be a consideration of how such concepts might be taught at relatively early stages—say, somewhere in the elementary school. Nevertheless, some of the same teaching techniques might not be amiss even at high school or college levels. At these levels the chief problem is to give meaning to mathematical formulas such as

$$\text{mass} = \frac{\text{force}}{\text{acceleration}}$$

The implication of this formula, that mass is constant for a given object, can be illustrated by showing with actual physical materials that as force is increased, acceleration is increased proportionately. The effect of increasing mass could be shown by demonstrating that acceleration (roughly indicated by distance traveled against friction) under a constant force diminishes. To a large extent, such experiments can be considered as yielding in precise mathematical terms the relationships that are perceived in every-day experience and that lead to our intuitive understanding of such a concept as mass.

Above all, it should be noted that *mass* is a relational concept, a constant property of objects that reveals itself through the relation between the forces applied to the object and the resultant acceleration. Negative instances can only be properties of objects like weight, size, etc., that are not revealed in this way.

Summary

The basic concern of this paper has been with the teaching of concepts and the relevance of psychological and psycholinguistic theory and experimentation in guiding such teaching.

It has been necessary, first, to point out that concepts are essentially nonlinguistic (or perhaps better, *a*linguistic) because they are classes of experience which the individual comes to recognize as such, whether or not he is prompted or directed by symbolic language phenomena. Because the experiences of individuals tend to be in many respects similar, their concepts are also similar, and through various processes of learning and socialization these concepts come to be associated with words. The "meanings" of words are the socially-standardized concepts with which they are associated. One of the problems in teaching concepts is that of teaching the associations between words and concepts, and this is analogous to a paired-associate learning task.

At the same time, new concepts can be taught. One procedure can be called inductive: it consists of presenting an individual with an appropriate series of positive and negative instances of a concept, labeled as such, and allowing him to infer the nature of the concept by noticing invariant features or attributes. This is the procedure followed in the usual concept formation experiment: although our present knowledge allows us to specify several *necessary* conditions for the formation of a concept, we still do not know what conditions are *sufficient*.

Another procedure for concept teaching may be called deductive, and it tends to be the favored procedure in school learning (and, in fact, in all expository prose). It is the technique of presenting concepts by verbal definition or description. This technique has received relatively little attention in psychological experimentation, but it seems to parallel inductive concept attainment in the sense that verbal descriptions are specifications of criterial attributes that can enable the individual to shortcut the process of hypothesis, discovery, and testing that typically occurs in the inductive concept-attainment procedure. Nevertheless, it is not known how relevant our knowledge of critical factors in inductive concept formation is for the guidance of deductive teaching procedures.

It is pointed out, however, that the efficient learning of concepts in school probably involves both inductive and deductive procedures. An analysis of typical concepts of the sort taught in school shows that they do indeed follow the models studied in psychological experimentation, but that they are more likely to involve complex relationships among prerequisite concepts. The difficulties that learners have in attaining a concept are likely to be due to their inadequate mastery of prerequisite concepts and to errors made by the teacher in presenting in proper sequence the information intrinsic to the definition of the concept.

20 THE ACQUISITION OF KNOWLEDGE [1]
Robert M. Gagné

The growing interest in autoinstructional devices and their component learning programs has had the effect of focusing attention on what may be called "productive learning." By this phrase is meant the kind of change in human behavior which permits the individual to perform successfully on an entire *class* of specific tasks, rather than simply on one member of the class. Self-instructional programs are designed to ensure the acquisition of capabilities of performing classes of tasks implied by names like "binary numbers," "musical notation," "solving linear equations" rather than tasks requiring the reproduction of particular responses.

When viewed in this manner, learning programming is not seen simply as a technological development incorporating previously established learning principles, but rather as one particular form of the ordering of stimulus and response events designed to bring about productive learning. It should be possible to study such learning, and the conditions which affect it, by the use of any of a variety of teaching machines, although there are few studies of this sort in the current literature (cf. Lumsdaine & Glaser, 1960). In the laboratory, the usual form taken by studies of productive learning has been primarily that of the effects of instructions and pretraining on problem solving (e.g., Hilgard, Irvine, & Whipple, 1953; Katona, 1940; Maltzman, Eisman, Brooks, & Smith, 1956).

When an individual is subjected to the situation represented by a learning program, his performance may change, and the experimenter then infers that he has acquired a new capability. It would not be adequate to say merely that he has acquired new "responses," since one cannot identify the specific responses involved. (Adding fractions, for example, could be represented by any of an infinite number of distinguishable stimulus situations, and an equal number of responses.) Since we need to have a term by means of which to refer to what is acquired as a result of responding correctly to a learning program, we may as

[1] This study was made possible in part by funds granted by the Carnegie Corporation of New York. The opinions expressed are those of the author, and do not necessarily reflect the views of that Corporation.

SOURCE: Robert M. Gagné, "The Acquisition of Knowledge," *Psychological Review*, 69, no. 4 (July 1962), 355–65. Copyright © 1962 by the American Psychological Association. Reprinted by permission of the publisher.

well use the term "knowledge." By definition, "knowledge" is that inferred capability which makes possible the successful performance of a *class of tasks* that could not be performed before the learning was undertaken.

SOME INITIAL OBSERVATIONS

In a previous study of programmed learning (Gagné & Brown, 1961) several kinds of learning programs were used in the attempt to establish the performance, in high school boys, of deriving formulas for the sum of n terms in a number series. Additional observations with this material led us to the following formulation: In productive learning, we are dealing with two major categories of variables. The first of these is knowledge, that is, the capabilities the individual possesses at any given stage in the learning; while the second is instructions, the content of the communications presented within the frames of a learning program.

In considering further the knowledge category, it has been found possible to identify this class of variable more comprehensively in the following way: Beginning with the final task, the question is asked, What kind of capability would an individual have to possess if he were able to perform this task successfully, were we to give him only instructions? The answer to this question, it turns out, identifies a new class of task which appears to have several important characteristics. Although it is conceived as an internal "disposition," it is directly measurable as a performance. Yet it is *not the same* performance as the final task from which it was derived. It is in some sense *simpler,* and it is also *more general.* In other words, it appears that what we have defined by this procedure is an entity of "subordinate knowledge" which is essential to the performance of the more specific final task.

Having done this, it was natural to think next of repeating the procedure with this newly defined entity (task). What would the individual have to know in order to be capable of doing *this* task without undertaking any learning, but given only some instructions? This time it seemed evident that there were two entities of subordinate knowledge which combined in support of the task. Continuing to follow this procedure, we found that what we were defining was a *hierarchy* of subordinate knowledges, growing increasingly "simple," and at the same time increasingly general as the defining process continued.

By means of this systematic analysis, it was possible to identify nine separate entities of subordinate knowledge, arranged in hierarchical fashion (see Figure 1). Generally stated, our hypothesis was that (a) no individual could perform the final task without having these subordinate capabilities (i.e., without being able to perform these simpler and more general tasks); and (b) that any superordinate task in the hierarchy could be performed by an individual provided suitable instructions were given, and provided the relevant subordinate knowledges could be recalled by him.

It may be noted that there are some possible resemblances between the entities of such a knowledge hierarchy and the hypothetical constructs described by three other writers. First are the habit-family hierarchies of Maltzman (1955), which are conceived to mediate problem solving, and are aroused by instructions (Maltzman et al., 1956). The second are the "organizations" proposed by Katona (1940), which are considered to be combined by the learner into new knowledge after receiving certain kinds of instructions, without repetitive practice. The third is Harlow's (1949) concept of learning set. Harlow's monkeys acquired a general capability of successfully performing a class of tasks, such as oddity problems, and accordingly are said to have acquired a learning set. There is also the suggestion in one of Harlow's (Harlow & Harlow, 1949) reports that there may be a hierarchical arrangement of tasks more complex than oddity problems which monkeys can successfully perform. Since we think it important to imply a continuity between the relatively complex performances described here and the simpler ones performed by monkeys, we are inclined to refer to these subordinate capabilities as "learning sets."

Requirements of Theory

If there is to be a theory of productive learning, it evidently must deal with the independent variables that can be identified in the two major categories of instructions and subordinate capabilities, as well as with their interactions, in bringing about changes in human performance.

INSTRUCTIONS

Within a learning program, instructions generally take the form of sentences which communicate something to the learner. It seems possible to think of such "communication" as being carried out with animals lower than man, by means of quite a different set of experimental operations. Because of these communications, the human learner progresses from a point in the learning sequence at which he can perform one set of tasks to a point at which he achieves, for the first time, a higher level learning set (class of tasks). What functions must a theory of knowledge acquisition account for, if it is to encompass the effects of instructions? The following paragraphs will attempt to describe these functions, not necessarily in order of importance.

First, instructions make it possible for the learner to *identify the required terminal performance* (for any given learning set). In educational terms, it might be said that they "define the goal." For example, if the task is adding fractions, it may be necessary for the learner to identify $15\frac{3}{4}$ as an adequate answer, and $6\frac{3}{4}$ as an inadequate one.

Second, instructions bring about proper *identifications of the elements of the stimulus situation.* For example, suppose that problems are to be presented using the word "fraction." The learner must be able to identify $\frac{2}{5}$ as a fraction and $.4$ as not a fraction. Or, he may have to identify Σ as "sum of," and n as "number." Usually, instructions establish such identifications in a very few repetitions, and sometimes in a single trial. If there are many of them, differentiation may require several repetitions involving contrasting feedback for right and wrong responses.

A third function of instructions is to establish *high recallability* of learning sets. The most obviously manipulable way to do this is by repetition. However it should be noted that repetition has a particular meaning in this context. It is not exact repetition of a stimulus situation (as in reproductive learning), but rather the presentation of additional examples of a class of tasks. Typically, within a learning program, a task representing a particular learning set is achieved once, for the first time. This may then be followed by instructions which present one or more additional examples of this same class of task. "Variety" in such repetition (meaning variety in the stimulus context) may be an important subvariable in affecting recallability. Instructions having the function of establishing high recallability for learning sets may demand "recall," as in the instances cited, or they may on other occasions attempt to achieve this effect by "recognition" (i.e., not requiring the learner to produce an answer).

The fourth function of instructions is perhaps the most interesting from the standpoint of the questions it raises for research. This is the "guidance of thinking," concerning whose operation there is only a small amount of evidence (cf. Duncan, 1959). Once the subordinate learning sets have been recalled, instructions are used to promote their application to (or perhaps "integration into") the performance of a task that is entirely new so far as the learner is concerned. At a minimum, this function of instructions may be provided by a statement like "Now put these ideas together to solve this problem"; possibly this amounts to an attempt to establish a *set*. Beyond this, thinking may be guided by suggestions which progressively limit the range of hypotheses entertained by the learner, in such a way as to decrease the number of incorrect solutions he considers (cf. Gagné & Brown, 1961; Katona, 1940). Within a typical learning program, guidance of thinking is employed after identification of terminal performance and of stimulus elements have been completed, and after high recallability of relevant learning sets has been ensured. In common sense terms, the purpose of these instructions is to suggest to the learner "how to approach the solution of a new task" without, however, "telling him the answer."

Obviously, much more is needed to be known about the effects of this variable, if indeed it is a single variable. Initially, it might be noted that guidance of thinking can vary in *amount;* that is, one can design a set of instructions which say no more than "now do this new task" (a minimal amount); or, at the other end of the scale, a set of instructions which in

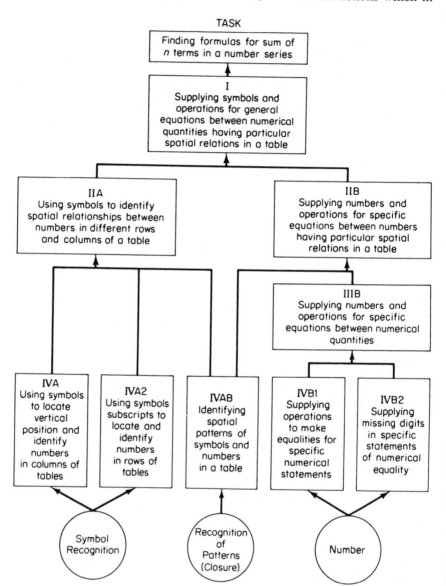

Figure 1 Hierarchy of knowledge for the task of finding formulas for the sum of *n* terms in a number series.

effect suggest a step-by-step procedure for using previously acquired learning sets in a new situation.

SUBORDINATE CAPABILITIES: LEARNING SETS

When one begins with the performance of a particular class of tasks as a criterion of terminal behavior, it is possible to identify the subordinate learning sets required by means of the procedure previously described. The question may be stated more exactly as, "What would the individual have to be able to do in order that he can attain successful performance on this task, provided he is given only instructions?" This question is then applied successively to the subordinate classes of tasks identified by the answer. "What he would have to be able to do" is in each case one or more performances which constitute the denotative definitions of learning sets for particular classes of tasks, and totally for the entire knowledge hierarchy.

A theory of knowledge acquisition must propose some manner of functioning for the learning sets in a hierarchy. A good possibility seems to be that they are mediators of positive transfer from lower-level learning sets to higher-level tasks. The hypothesis is proposed that specific transfer from one learning set to another standing above it in the hierarchy will be zero if the lower one cannot be recalled, and will range up to 100% if it can be.

In narrative form, the action of the two classes of variables in the acquisition of knowledge is conceived in the following way. A human learner begins the acquisition of the capability of performing a particular class of tasks with an individual array of relevant learning sets, previously acquired. He then acquires new learning sets at progressively higher levels of the knowledge hierarchy until the final class of tasks is achieved. Attaining each new learning set depends upon a process of positive transfer, which is dependent upon (a) the recall of relevant subordinate learning sets, and upon (b) the effects of instructions.

Experimental Predictions and Results [2]

Using the procedure described, we derived the knowledge hierarchy depicted in Figure 1 for the final task of "deriving formulas for the sum of n terms in number series."

As mentioned previously, it contained nine hypothesized learning sets. (The final row of circled entities will be discussed later.) Each of these

[2] The author [Robert Gagné] is grateful to Bert Zippel, Jr., for assistance in the preparation of learning program materials and in the collection of a portion of the data.

subordinate knowledges can be represented as a class of task to be performed.

MEASURING INITIAL PATTERNS OF LEARNING SETS

It is predicted that the presence of different patterns of learning sets can be determined for individuals who are unable to perform a final task such as the one under consideration. To test this, we administered a series of test items to a number of ninth-grade boys. These items were presented on 4" x 6" cards, and the answers were written on specially prepared answer sheets. This particular method was used in order to make testing continuous with the administration of a learning program to be described hereafter. Each test item was carefully prepared to include instructions having the function of identification of terminal performance and of elements of the stimulus situation.

Beginning with the final task, the items were arranged to be presented in the order I, IIA, IVA, IVA$_2$, IVAB, IIB, IIIB, IVBI, and IVB$_2$. For any given subject, the sequence of testing temporarily stopped at the level at which successful performance was first reached, and a learning program designed to foster achievement at the next higher level (previously failed) was administered. This program and its results will shortly be described. Following this, testing on the remaining learning set tasks was undertaken in the order given. The possibility of effects of the learning program on the performance of these lower-level learning sets (not specifically practiced in the learning) is of course recognized, but not further considered in the present discussion.

A particular time limit was set for each test item, at the expiration of which the item was scored as failed. If a wrong answer was given before this time limit, the subject was told it was wrong, and encouraged to try again; if the correct answer was supplied within the time limit, the item was scored as passed. It is emphasized that these time limits, which were based on preliminary observations on other subjects with these tasks, were *not* designed to put "time pressure" on the subjects, nor did they appear to do so.

The patterns of success achieved on the final task and all subordinate learning set tasks, by all seven subjects, are shown in Table 1. The subjects have been arranged in accordance with their degree of success with all tasks, beginning with one who failed the final task but succeded at all the rest. Several things are apparent from these data. First of all, it is quite evident that there are quite different "patterns of capability" with which individuals approach the task set by the study. Some are unable to do a task like IIA (see Figure 1), others to do a task like IIB which is of course quite different. Still others are unable to do either of these, and in fact cannot perform successfully a task like IIIB. All seven of these subjects were able to perform IV-level tasks successfully, although in preliminary observations on similar tasks we found some ninth-grade boys who could not.

Table 1
Pattern of Success on Learning Set Tasks Related to the Final Number Series Task for Seven Ninth Grade Boys

Subject						Task				
	Final	I	IIA	IIB	IIIB	IVA1	IVA2	IVAB	IVB1	IVB2
WW	−	+	+	+	+	+	+	+	+	+
WC	−	+	+	+	+	+	+	+	+	+
PM	−	−	−	+	+	+	+	+	+	+
GR	−	−	−	+	+	+	+	+	+	+
DJ	−	−	−	−	+	+	+	+	+	+
JR	−	−	−	−	−	+	+	+	+	+
RH	−	−	−	−	−	+	+	+	+	+

Note. − + = Pass; − = Fail.

Second, the patterns of pass and fail on these tasks have the relationships predicted by the previous discussion. There are no instances, for example, of an individual who is able to perform what has been identified as a "higher-level" learning set, and who then shows himself to be unable to perform a "lower-level" learning set related to it.

If learning sets are indeed essential for positive transfer, the following consequences should ensue:

1. If a higher-level learning set is passed (+), *all* related lower-level tasks must have been passed (+).

2. If *one or more* lower-level tasks have been failed (−), the related higher-level tasks must be failed (−).

3. If a higher-level task is passed (+), *no* related lower-level tasks must have been failed (−).

4. If a higher-level task has been failed (−), related lower-level tasks may have been passed (+). The absence of positive transfer in this case would be attributable to a deficiency in instructions, and does not contradict the notion that lower-level sets are essential to the achievement of higher-level ones.

The relationships found to exist in these seven subjects are summarized in Table 2, where each possible higher–lower-level task relationship possible of testing is listed in the left-hand column. It will be noted that there are several relationships of the type higher (−), lower (+), as listed in Column 5. These provided no test of the hypothesis regarding hierarchical relations among learning sets. The instances in the remaining columns do, however. The + + and − − instances are verifying, whereas + − instances would be nonverifying. As the final column indicates, the percentage of verifying instances is in all cases 100%.

Table 2
Pass-Fail Relationship between Related Adjacent Higher- and Lower-Level Learning Sets for a Group of Seven Ninth-Grade Boys

| | Number of Cases with Relationship | | | | Test of Relationships | |
Relationship Examined	Higher + Lower +	Higher − Lower −	Higher + Lower −	Higher − Lower +	N (1+2+3)	Proportion (1+2), (1+2+3)
Final Task: I	0	6	0	1	6	1.00
I: IIA, IIB	1	5	0	1	6	1.00
IIA: IVA1, IVA2, IVAB	2	0	0	5	2	1.00
IIB: IIIB	3	2	0	2	5	1.00
IIIB: IVAB, IVB1, IVB2	5	0	0	2	5	1.00

Note.— + =Pass; − = Fail.

EFFECTS OF LEARNING PROGRAM ADMINISTRATION

If the characteristics of instructions as previously described are correct, it should be possible to construct a learning program which can be begun for each individual at the point of his lowest successful learning set achievement, and bring him to successful achievement of the final class of tasks. Briefly, its method should be to include frames which have the functions of (a) insuring high recallability of relevant learning sets on which achievement has been demonstrated; (b) making possible identifications of expected performance and of new stimuli, for each newly presented task; and (c) guiding thinking so as to suggest proper directions for hypotheses associating subordinate learning sets with each new one.

A program of this sort was administered to each of the seven ninth-grade boys, beginning at the level at which he first attained success on learning set tasks (Table 1). This was done by means of a simple teaching machine consisting of a visible card file clipped to a board mounted at a 40° angle to the learner's table, and containing material typed on 4" x 6" cards. He wrote his answer to successive frames on a numbered answer sheet, then flipped over the card to see the correct answer on the back. He was instructed that if his answer was wrong, he should flip the card back, and read the frame again until he could "see" what the right answer was.

After completing the instructional portion of the program for each learning set, the learner was again presented with the identical test-item problem he had tried previously and failed. If he was now able to do it correctly, he was given five additional items of the same sort to perform, and then taken on by instructions to another learning set in either a co-ordinate or higher-level position in the hierarchy. This process was continued through the performance of the final task.

The data collected in this way yield pass-fail scores on each test item (representing a particular member of a class of tasks) *before* the administration of the learning program, and similar scores on the same item *after* learning. It is recognized that for certain experimental purposes, one would wish to have a different, matched, task for the test given after learning, to control for the effects of "acquaintance" during the first test. Since this study had an exploratory character, such a control was not used this time. However, it should be clearly understood that the first experience with these test items in question, for these subjects, involved only activity terminating in failure to achieve solution. No information about the correct solutions was given.

A striking number of instances of success in achieving correct solutions to learning set tasks was found following learning as compared with before. These results are summarized in Table 3. Although for

Table 3
Number of Instances of Passing and Failing Final Task and Subordinate Learning Set Tasks Before and After Administration of an Adaptive Learning Program, in a Group of Seven Ninth-Grade Boys

Task	Number Failing before Learning	Number of these Passing after Learning	Percentage Success
Final Task	7	6	86
I	5	4	80
II	5	5	100
IIB	2	1	50
IIIB	2	2	100
Total	21	18	86

learning set IIB the percentage of success was only 50% (with two cases), there were two learning sets for which 100% success was achieved, and the percentage for all instances combined was 86%. These results provide additional evidence compatible with the idea of the knowledge hierarchy.

The learner in such a program does not "practice the final task"; he acquires specifically identified capabilities in a specified order. In as many as six out of seven cases, we were able by this means to bring learners from various levels of competence all the way to final task achievement. (It is perhaps important that the exception was JR, one of two who had most to learn.) Of course, it must be recognized that two separable causes contribute to the effects of the learning program in this study: (*a*) the correctness of the learning set analysis; and (*b*) the specific effectiveness of the instructions contained in the learning program.

Implications for Individual Differences Measurement

It is evident that learning sets, as conceived in this paper, operate as "individual differences" variables, which, when suitably manipulated, also become "experimental" variables. There are some additional implications which need to be pointed out regarding the functioning of learning sets in the determination of measured individual differences.

As the process of identification of subordinate learning sets is progressively continued, one arrives at some learning sets which are very simple and general, and likely to be widespread within the population of learners for which the task is designed. Consider, for example, learning set IVB (Figure 1), which is represented by a task such as $4 \times 2 = 5 + ?$ If one makes a further analysis to identify a subordinate learning set for this task, the answer appears to be, "adding, subtracting, multiplying, and dividing one- and two-place numbers." It is interesting to note that this is exactly the task provided by a set of factor reference tests (French, 1954) called Number. In a similar manner, the other two circled entities in the last row of Figure 1 were identified. One is Symbol Recognition (called Associative Memory by the factor researchers), and Recognition of Patterns (called Flexibility of Closure). The implication is, therefore, that these simplest tasks, identified by factor analysis techniques as common to a great variety of human performances, also function as learning sets.

The hypothesis has been proposed that learning sets mediate positive transfer to higher-level tasks. Very often, if not usually, the measurement of transfer of training implies that a second task is learned *more* rapidly when preceded by the learning of an initial task, than when not so preceded. Accordingly, it seems necessary to distinguish between expected correlations of these basic factors (at the bottom of the hierarchy) with rate of attainment of higher-level learning sets on the one hand, and correlations of these same factors with achievement of higher-level learning sets on the other.

The implications of this line of reasoning would seem to be somewhat as follows: Factors which are found by the kind of psychological analysis previously described to lie at the bottom of the knowledge hierarchy should exhibit certain predictable patterns of correlation with higher-level learning sets. They should correlate most highly with rate of attainment of the learning sets in the next higher level to which they are related, and progressively less as one progresses upwards in the hierarchy. The reason for this is simply that the rate of attainment of learning sets in a hierarchy comes to depend to an increasing extent on the learning sets which have just previously been acquired and accordingly to a decreasing extent upon a basic factor or ability. Some analogy may be drawn here with the findings of Fleishman and Hempel (1954) on motor tasks.

The expected relationships between factor test scores and achievement scores (passing or failing learning sets) throughout such hierarchies seem to require a somewhat more complex derivation. First of all, such relationships will depend upon the effectiveness of a learning program, or perhaps on the effectiveness of previous learning. If the learning program is perfectly effective, for example, and if differences in rate of attainment are ignored, everyone will pass all the learning set tasks, and the variance will accordingly be reduced to zero. Under these circumstances, then, one may expect all correlations with basic factors to be zero. However, one must consider the case in which the learning program is not perfectly effective. In such a case, the probability that an individual will acquire a new learning set, as opposed to not acquiring it, will presumably be increased to the extent that he scores high on tests of related basic abilities. If one continues to collect scores on learning set tasks of both successful achievers and those who fail, the result will presumably be an increasing degree of correlation between basic ability scores and learning set tasks as one progresses upwards in the hierarchy. The reason for this is that the size of the correlation comes to depend more and more upon variance contributed by those individuals who are successful, and less and less on that contributed by those who effectively "drop out."

The difference in expectation between the increasing pattern of correlation with achievement scores, and the decreasing pattern with measures of rate of attainment, is considered to be of rather general importance for the area of individual differences measurement. Confirmatory results have been obtained in a recent study (Gagné & Paradise, 1961) concerned with the class of tasks "solving linear algebraic equations."

Discussion

The general view of productive learning implied in this paper is that it is a matter of transfer of training from component learning sets to a new activity which incorporates these previously acquired capabilities. This new activity so produced is qualitatively different from the tasks which correspond to the "old" learning sets; that is, it must be described by a different set of operations, rather than simply being "more difficult." The characteristics of tasks which make achievement of one class of task the required precursor of achievement in another, and not vice versa, are yet to be discovered. Sufficient examples exist of this phenomenon to convince one of its reality (Gagné, Mayor, Garstens, & Paradise, 1962; Gagné & Paradise, 1961). What remains to be done, presumably, is to begin with extremely simple levels of task, such as discriminations, and investigate transfer of training to tasks of greater and greater degrees of complexity, or perhaps abstractness, thus determining the dimensions which make transfer possible.

The path to research on the characteristics of instructions appears more straightforward, at least at first glance. The establishment of identifications is a matter which has been investigated extensively with the use of paired associates. The employment of instructions for this purpose may need to take into consideration the necessity for learning differentiations among the stimulus items to be identified, as well as other variables suggested by verbal learning studies. The function of inducing high recallability would seem to be a matter related to repetition of learning set tasks, and may in addition be related to time variables such as those involved in distribution of practice. As for guidance of thinking, the distinguishing of this function from others performed by instructions should at least make possible the design of more highly analytical studies than have been possible in the past.

In the meantime, the approach employed in the experiment reported here, of proceeding backwards by analysis of an already existing task, has much to recommend it as a way of understanding the learning of school subjects like mathematics and science, and perhaps others also. Naturally, every human task yields a different hierarchy of learning sets when this method of analysis is applied. Often, the relationship of higher to lower learning sets is more complex than that exhibited in Figure 1. It should be possible, beginning with any existing class of tasks, to investigate the effects of various instruction variables within the framework of suitably designed learning programs.

The major methodological implication of this paper is to the effect that investigations of productive learning must deal intensively with the kinds of variables usually classified as "individual differences." One cannot depend upon a measurement of *general* proficiency or aptitude to reveal much of the important variability in the capabilities people bring with them to a given task. Consider, for example, the seven ninth-grade boys in our study. Each of them had "had" algebra, and each of them had "had" arithmetic. There was no particularly striking relationship between their ultimate performance and their previous grades in algebra (although there is no doubt some correlation), nor between this performance and "general intelligence." But the measurement of their learning sets, as illustrated in Table 1, revealed a great deal about how they would behave when confronted with the learning program and the final task. For some, instructions had to begin, in effect, "lower down" than for others. Some could do Task 1 right away, while others could not, but could do it equally well provided they learned other things first. The methodological point is simply this: if one wants to investigate the effects of an experimental treatment on the behavior of individuals or groups who start from the same point, he would be well advised to measure and map out for each individual the learning sets relevant to the experimental task. In this way he can have some assurance of the extent to which his subjects are equivalent.

References

Duncan, C. P. Recent research on human problem solving. *Psychol. Bull.*, 1959, 56, 397–429.

Fleishman, E. A., & Hempel, W. E. Changes in factor structure of a complex psychomotor test as a function of practice. *Psychometrika*, 1954, 19, 239–252.

French, J. W. (Ed.) *Kit of selected tests for reference aptitude and achievement factors.* Princeton, N. J.: Educational Testing Service, 1954.

Gagné, R. M., & Brown, L. T. Some factors in the programming of conceptual learning. *J. exp. Psychol.*, 1961, 62, 313–321.

Gagné, R. M., Mayor, J. R., Garstens, H. L., & Paradise, N. E. Factors in acquiring knowledge of a mathematical task. *Psychol. Monogr.*, 1962, 76 (7, Whole No. 526).

Gagné, R. M., & Paradise, N. E. Abilities and learning sets in knowledge acquisition. *Psychol. Monogr.*, 1961, 75 (14, Whole No. 518).

Harlow, H. F. The formation of learning sets. *Psychol. Rev.*, 1949, 56, 51–65.

Harlow, H. F., & Harlow, M. K. Learning to think. *Scient. American*, 1949, 181, 36–39.

Hilgard, E. R., Irvine, R. P., & Whipple, J. E. Rote memorization, understanding, and transfer: An extension of Katona's card-trick experiments. *J. exp. Psychol.*, 1953, 46, 288–292.

Katona, G. *Organizing and memorizing.* New York: Columbia Univer. Press, 1940.

Lumsdaine, A. A., & Glaser, R. *Teaching machines and programmed learning.* Washington, D.C.: National Education Association, 1960.

Maltzman, I. Thinking: From a behavioristic point of view. *Psychol. Rev.*, 1955, 62, 275–286.

Maltzman, I., Eisman, E., Brooks, L. O., & Smith, W. M. Task instructions for anagrams following different task instructions and training. *J. exp. Psychol.*, 1956, 51, 418–420.

21 SOME PSYCHOLOGICAL ASPECTS OF THE STRUCTURE OF KNOWLEDGE
David P. Ausubel

Introduction

In the light of Professor Schwab's opening remarks yesterday, I suppose that I am guilty of considerable temerity in even venturing to appear at this symposium to discuss some psychological aspects of the structure of knowledge. You will recall that the second sentence of his paper read as follows: "We have had more than enough scrutiny, discussion, and debate about the learning process, thanks to the popularity of psychological investigations." And now, in the face of this sober pronouncement, I propose to add another hour's worth of psychological discussion to the existing sickening surfeit.

Strangely enough, I agree for the most part with Professor Schwab's appraisal. I would put it somewhat differently, however. Instead of saying that we have had more than enough scrutiny and discussion of the learning process, I would say that insofar as the learning of subject-matter knowledge is concerned, we have more than enough wild and naive extrapolation of evidence and theory from rote, motor, animal, short-term, and stimulus-response learning. I still cling to the opinion that psychological processes are implicated in the individual acquisition of a body of knowledge and that it is important for teachers and curriculum-builders to understand the nature of these processes. The task that lies ahead, then, demands *not* that we dismiss the relevance of learning processes for the activities involved in transmitting and acquiring subject-matter knowledge, but rather that we formulate and test theories of learning that are relevant for the kinds of meaningful ideational learning that take place in school and similar learning environments.

The major portion of this symposium is rightly concerned with various problems associated with the logical structure of knowledge in general and with the logical structure of knowledge in particular subject-matter fields. It should not be forgotten, however, that in addition to organized bodies of knowledge that represent the collective recorded wisdom of recognized scholars in particular fields of inquiry, there are correspond-

SOURCE: Ausubel, David P., "Some Psychological Aspects of the Structure of Knowledge," in *Education and the Structure of Knowledge*, S. Elam, ed. (New York: Rand McNally, 1964), pp. 221–62.

ing psychological structures of knowledge as represented by the organization of internalized ideas and information in the minds of individual students of varying degrees of both cognitive maturity and subject-matter sophistication in these same disciplines. I am making a distinction, in other words, between the formal organization of the subject-matter content of a given discipline, as set forth in authoritative statements in generally accepted textbooks and monographs, on the one hand, and the organized, internalized representation of this knowledge in the memory structures of particular individuals, especially students, on the other.

This paper will be devoted to these latter psychological aspects of the structure of knowledge. After a preliminary general inquiry into the relationship between the logical and the psychological structure of knowledge, I propose to suggest some principles of accretion, organization, and retention that apply to the psychological structure of knowledge, to examine some variables influencing these processes, and to discuss some pedagogic implications arising from these various psychological considerations.

Relationship Between the Logical and the Psychological Structure of Knowledge

In some ways the logical and psychological structures of knowledge are quite similar, and in some ways they are very different. These similarities and differences can be demonstrated most conveniently, in my opinion, by comparing the two structures of knowledge with respect to four of their principal attributes: (a) meaning, (b) process of organization, (c) arrangement of component elements, and (d) cognitive maturity of content.

MEANING

Corresponding to the distinction between the logical and the psychological structure of knowledge is an equally important distinction between logical and psychological meaning. Actual phenomenological meaning, I submit, is an idiosyncratic psychological experience. Subject-matter content can at best have logical or potential meaning. Potential meaning becomes converted into actual meaning when a *particular* individual, employing a meaningful learning set, incorporates a potentially meaningful proposition or unit of information within his cognitive structure.

Subject-matter material possesses logical or potential meaning if it consists of possible and nonarbitrary relationships that are relatable on a nonarbitrary, substantive basis to a hypothetical human cognitive structure exhibiting, in general, the necessary ideational background and cognitive maturity. This criterion of logical meaning applies primarily to the attributes of the learning material itself. If the material manifests the characteristics of nonarbitrariness, lucidity, and plausibility, then it is by definition also relatable to the aforementioned hypothetical cognitive structure. Obviously excluded, therefore, from the domain of logical meaning is the vast majority of the almost infinite number of possible relationships between concepts that can be formulated on the basis of purely random pairings. This does not mean that all propositions with logical meaning are necessarily valid or even logically correct. The questions of substantive and logical validity are issues that simply do not enter into the determination of logical meaning. Propositions based on unvalidated premises or on faulty logic may conceivably abound in logical or potential meaning.

It is nonarbitrary subsumability of logically meaningful propositions within a *particular* cognitive structure that creates the possibility of transforming logical into psychological meaning. Hence the emergence of psychological meaning depends not only on the learner's possession of the requisite intellectual capacities and ideational background, but also on his *particular* ideational content. When an individual learns logically meaningful propositions, therefore, he does not learn their logical meaning but the meaning they have for him. Psychological meaning is always an idiosyncratic phenomenon. The idiosyncratic nature of psychological meaning, however, does not rule out the possibility of social or shared meanings. The various individual meanings possessed by members of a given culture are ordinarily sufficiently similar to permit interpersonal communication and understanding. This intracultural homogeneity of shared meanings reflects both the same logical meaning inherent in potentially meaningful propositions and the interindividual commonality of ideational background.

PROCESS OF ORGANIZATION

The logical and psychological structures of knowledge obviously differ in terms of the kinds of processes that enter into their organization. From a process standpoint the laws applying to the psychological organization of knowledge are the laws of meaningful learning and retention, whereas the laws governing the logical organization of knowledge are derived from the logic of classification. Nevertheless these two sets of process laws overlap to the extent that the meaningful learning of new ideas conforms to principles of logical classification insofar as it may be described as a process of subsumption under those relevant existing ideas in cognitive structure which exhibit a higher order of generality and inclusiveness. Thus not only do both kinds of organizational processes rely on the logic of classification, but they also employ the same principle of structuring knowledge in terms of unifying elements which manifest the greatest generality, inclusiveness, and explanatory power, and which are capable of relating and integrating the widest possible array of subject matter.

The difference between the two kinds of organizational processes stems from two facts: (a) that the psychological structure of knowledge is subject throughout its development to systematic decrement resulting from the gradual loss of the identity and availability of subsumed materials as their distinctive import is assimilated by the more general meaning of their more inclusive and established subsumers; and (b) that both the learning of new ideas and their memorial resistance to the aforementioned decremental processes are largely a function of such properties of existing cognitive structure as the availability of relevant subsumers, the stability and clarity of these subsumers, and their discriminability from the new learning material. These two limiting conditions obviously do not apply to the logical structure of knowledge.

The psychological, unlike the logical structure of knowledge, therefore, is in a very real sense both an organized residue of inclusive subsumers and those elements of related subsumed materials that have managed to resist the process of memorial reduction or assimilation, plus the residual products of forgetting, namely, the original subsuming ideas which have completely assimilated their subsumed materials.

ARRANGEMENT OF COMPONENT ELEMENTS

It is also reasonable to assume that the psychological and logical structures of knowledge differ with respect to the sequential placement, ordering, and arrangement of component elements. The kinds of processes involved in the psychological organization of knowledge, i.e., in meaningful learning and retention, imply a hierarchical type of structure which is progressively differentiated in terms of degree of generality and inclusiveness. This is the kind of structure which obviously results when new learning materials are subsumed under relevant, more inclusive concepts in existing cognitive structure. The logical structure of knowledge, on the other hand, although using general and inclusive ideas as organizing elements, strives for topical relatedness and homogeneity rather than progressive differentiation in the sequential arrangement of subject matter. Psychologically, however, this kind of structure is not approached until the terminal stages of subject-matter sophistication. Only after an individual develops mature cognitive capacities and acquires an expert, specialized knowledge of a subject does his psychological structure of knowledge in that discipline correspond (although in somewhat less systematized form) to the logical structure of knowledge in the same discipline; in any case he can at this stage easily reorganize this psychological structure in terms of the topically most homogeneous and systematic ordering of relationships between component facts, concepts, and propositions. This degree of parallelism between the logical and the psychological structure of knowledge does not exist during earlier stages of intellectual development and subject-matter sophistication.

It is apparent from the previous discussion that the logical structure of a subject is necessarily dependent on and a product of human cognitive processes. Only human beings who possess mature cognitive capacities and whose psychological structure of knowledge in a given discipline is highly sophisticated can structure this field of knowledge in a logically satisfactory fashion.[1] It is evident therefore that the following degree of interdependence prevails between the logical and the psychological structure of knowledge: on the one hand, the psychological structure of knowledge is a derivative of subject-matter content abstracted from the logical structure of knowledge, and psychological meaning is an idiosyncratic elaboration of logical meaning; on the other hand, the logical structure of knowledge is a topically systematized reorganization of the psychological structure of knowledge as it exists in mature scholars in a particular discipline.

COGNITIVE MATURITY OF CONTENT

Just as level of subject-matter sophistication determines the sequential arrangement of the psychological structure of knowledge, general level of cognitive maturity, particularly along the concrete-abstract dimension of intellectual functioning, determines the cognitive maturity of the content contained in this structure. The logical structure of subject matter, on the other hand, does not manifest any developmental variability in cognitive maturity of content. Whereas the level of abstraction, generality, explicitness, and precision characteristic of the logical structure of subject-matter content is invariably and necessarily high, being the product of sophisticated scholars, the same high level of maturity in these cognitive attributes of content is found in the psychological structure of knowledge only when the individual is in the terminal stages of intellectual development.

During the elementary school period, for example, when the child is in the stage of concrete logical operations (10), he is dependent upon current or recently prior concrete-empirical experience for the understanding or manipulation of relationships between abstractions or ideas about ideas. When such experience is not available he finds abstract propositions unrelatable to cognitive structure and hence devoid of meaning. This dependence upon concrete-empirical props self-evidently limits his ability meaningfully to grasp and manipulate relationships between abstractions, since he can only acquire those understandings and

[1] This does not necessarily imply, of course, that the logical validity of a particular organization of subject-matter relationships is dependent on human ability to appreciate these relationships or to execute logical operations.

perform those logical operations which do not go beyond the concrete and particularized representation of ideas implicit in his use of props. Thus where complex abstract concepts and propositions are involved, he is largely restricted to a concrete or intuitive level of cognitive functioning, a level that falls far short of the clarity, precision, explicitness, and generality associated with the more advanced stage of intellectual development.

Beginning in the junior high school period, however, children become increasingly less dependent upon the availability of concrete-empirical experience in meaningfully relating complex abstract propositions to cognitive structure. Eventually, after sufficient gradual change in this direction, a qualitatively new capacity emerges: the intellectually mature individual becomes capable of understanding and manipulating relationships between abstractions without any reference whatsoever to concrete, empirical reality. Instead of reasoning directly from a particular set of data, he uses indirect, second-order abstractions for structuring the data; instead of merely grouping data into classes or arranging them serially in terms of a given variable, he deals with all possible or hypothetical relations between ideas. He can now transcend the previously achieved level of intuitive thought and understanding, and formulate general laws relating general categories of variables that are divorced from the concrete-empirical data at hand. His concepts and generalizations, therefore, tend more to be second-order constructs derived from relationships between previously established abstractions already one step removed from the data itself.

Relative level of abstraction of subject-matter content becomes an important pedagogic consideration in determining the order in which pupils should be introduced to the different scientific disciplines. On strictly logical grounds one might argue that the various disciplines should be introduced in the order of their relative phenomenological complexity, i.e., that the phenomenologically more fundamental and simple laws of physics and chemistry should be mastered before the phenomenologically more complex and variable data of biology are studied. Psychologically, however, the logically simple laws of physics and chemistry are more abstract and difficult than the logically complex laws of biology which are both more descriptive in nature and closer to everyday, concrete experience.

The Psychological Accretion and Organization of Knowledge

The principle of subsumption, in my opinion, provides a key to understanding the processes underlying the psychological accretion and organization of knowledge. The human nervous system as a data processing and storing mechanism is so constructed that new ideas and information can be meaningfully learned and retained only to the extent that more inclusive and appropriately relevant concepts are already available in cognitive structure to serve a subsuming role or to provide ideational anchorage. Thus subsumption accounts for accretion to the psychological structure of knowledge by determining the acquisition of new meanings, their retention or resistance to assimilation, and the forgetting process itself; and over a period of time the nature and outcome of this accretion process, i.e., the cumulative residue of what is meaningfully learned, retained, and forgotten, determines how knowledge is psychologically organized. The subsumption process, therefore, also ultimately explains why an individual's organization of the content of a particular subject-matter discipline in his own mind consists of a hierarchical structure in which the most inclusive concepts occupy a position at the apex of the structure and subsume progressively less inclusive and more highly differentiated subconcepts and factual data.

LEARNING

Meaningful reception learning occurs as potentially meaningful material enters the cognitive field and interacts with and is appropriately subsumed under a relevant and more inclusive conceptual system. The very fact that such material is subsumable in nonarbitrary, substantive fashion accounts for its potential meaningulness and makes possible the emergence of phenomenological meaning. If it were not subsumable it would form discrete and relatively isolated traces.

The initial effects of subsumption, therefore, may be described as facilitation of both learning and retention. Only orienting, relational, and cataloguing operations are involved at first. These preliminary operations are obviously essential for meaningful learning and retention, since the hierarchical incorporation of new material into existing cognitive structure is both the basis for the emergence of new meaning and must also necessarily conform to the prevailing principle of cognitive organization. Furthermore, subsumption of the traces of the learning task by an established ideational system provides anchorage for the new material, and thus constitutes the most orderly, efficient, and stable way of retaining it for future availability. Hence, for a variable period of time, the recently catalogued subconcepts and informational data can be dissociated from their subsuming concepts and are reproducible as individually identifiable entities.

RETENTION AND FORGETTING

Although the stability of meaningful material is initially enhanced by anchorage to relevant conceptual foci in the learner's cognitive structure, such material is gradually subjected to the erosive influence of the reductionist trend in cognitive organization. Because it is more economical and less burdensome to retain a single inclusive concept than to remember a large number of more specific items, the import of the latter tends to be incorporated by the generalized meaning of the former. When the second or obliterative stage of subsumption begins, the specific items become progressively less dissociable as entities in their own right until they are no longer available and are said to be forgotten. Thus the same subsumability that is necessary for meaningful reception learning somewhat paradoxically provides the basis for later forgetting.

This process of memorial reduction to the least common denominator capable of representing cumulative prior experience is very similar to the reduction process characterizing concept formation. A single abstract concept is more manipulable for cognitive purposes than the dozen diverse instances from which its commonality is abstracted; and similarly, the memorial residue of ideational experience is also more functional for future learning and problem-solving occasions when stripped of its tangential modifiers, particularized connotations, and less clear and discriminable implications. Hence, barring repetition or some other special reason (e.g., primacy, uniqueness, enhanced discriminability, or the availability of a specially relevant and stable subsumer) for the perpetuation of dissociability, specific items of meaningful experience that are supportive of or correlative to an established conceptual entity tend gradually to undergo obliterative subsumption.

Unfortunately, however, the advantages of obliterative subsumption are gained at the expense of losing the differentiated body of detailed propositions and specific information that constitute the flesh if not the skeleton of any body of knowledge. The main problem of acquiring a firm grasp of any academic discipline, therefore, is counteracting the inevitable process of obliterative subsumption that characterizes all meaningful learning.

LEARNING VERSUS RETENTION

In reception learning the distinctive attribute of both learning and retention is a change in the availability of the meanings derived from the subsumed learning material. Learning refers to the process of acquiring meanings from the potential meanings presented in the learning material and of making them more available. It represents an increment in the availability of new meanings, i.e., the situation that prevails when they emerge or are first established, or when their dissociability strength is increased by repetition or by conditions increasing discriminability. Retention, on the other hand, refers to the process of maintaining the availability of a replica of the acquired new meanings. Thus forgetting represents a decrement in availability, i.e., the situation that prevails between the establishment of a meaning and its reproduction, or between two presentations of the learning material. Retention, therefore, is largely a later temporal phase and diminished aspect of the same phenomenon or functional capacity involved in learning itself. Later availability is always at least in part a function of initial availability.

DERIVATIVE VERSUS CORRELATIVE SUBSUMPTION

It is important to distinguish between two basically different kinds of subsumption that occur in the course of meaningful learning and retention. *Derivative* subsumption takes place when the learning material constitutes a specific example of an established concept in cognitive structure, or is supportive or illustrative of a previously learned general proposition. In either case the material to be learned is directly and self-evidently derivable from or implicit in an already established and more inclusive concept or proposition in cognitive structure. Under these circumstances the meaning of the derivative material emerges quickly and effortlessly, and unless greatly overlearned tends to undergo obliterative subsumption very rapidly. If such data are needed, however, they can easily be synthesized or reconstructed by appropriately manipulating specific elements of past and present experience so that they exemplify the desired concept or proposition.

More typically, however, new subject matter is learned by a process of *correlative* subsumption. The new learning material in this case is an extension, elaboration, or qualification of previously learned propositions. It is incorporated by and interacts with relevant and more inclusive subsumers in cognitive structure, but its meaning is not implicit in and cannot be represented by these latter subsumers. Nevertheless, in the interests of economy of cognitive organization and of reducing the burden of memory, the same trend toward obliterative subsumption occurs. But in this instance the consequences of obliterative subsumption are not as innocuous as in the case of derivative subsumption. When correlative propositions lose their identifiability and can no longer be dissociated from their subsumers, a genuine loss of knowledge occurs. The subsumers cannot adequately represent the meaning of the propositions in question, and hence the availability of the subsumers in memory does not make possible a reconstruction of the forgotten material.

The problem of acquiring a body of knowledge, therefore, is largely concerned with counteracting the trend toward obliterative subsumption in retaining correlative materials. Bruner's exclusive emphasis on "generic learning" or acquiring "generic coding systems" (5, 6, 7) as a means of facilitating school learning is unrealistic because it focuses on derivative aspects of subsumption which are atypical both of the subsumption process in general and of most instances of incorporating new subject matter. It is true, as he asserts, that most specific content aspects of sub-

ject matter can be forgotten with impunity as long as they are derivable
or can be reconstructed when needed from those generic concepts or
formulae which are worth remembering. But the analogous forgetting of
correlative content results in a loss of knowledge that cannot be regen-
erated from residual generic concepts. The conceptualizing trend in
memorial reduction (i.e., obliterative subsumption), which is functional
or at the very worst innocuous in the case of derivative material, constitutes the principal difficulty in acquiring a body of knowledge in the more
typical context of learning correlative propositions. Hence the problem of
meaningful learning and retention cannot ordinarily be solved by incorporating "a representation of the criterial characteristics of [a] situation,
[or] a contentless depiction of the ideal case" (7), and then ignoring the
loss of specific content that occurs. The main purpose of learning generic
concepts and propositions is not so much to make possible the reconstruction of forgotten derivative instances as to provide stable anchorage
for correlative material; and it is the inhibition of the rate of obliterative
subsumption in relation to this material that is the major problem con-
fronting teachers in transmitting subject-matter content.

Factors Influencing Meaningful Learning and Retention

It follows from the very nature of accretion to the psychological structure of knowledge through the subsumption process that existing
cognitive structure—an individual's organization, stability, and clarity
of knowledge in a particular subject-matter field at any given time—is
the major factor influencing the learning and retention of meaningful
new material in this same field. Since potentially meaningful material is
always learned in relation to an existing background of relevant concepts, principles, and information, which provide a framework for its reception and make possible the emergence of new meanings, it is evident
that the stability, clarity, and organizational properties of this background crucially affect both the accuracy and the clarity of these
emerging new meanings and their immediate and long-term retrievabil-
ity. If cognitive structure is stable, clear, and suitably organized, accurate and unambiguous meanings emerge and tend to retain their dissociability strength or availability. If, on the other hand, cognitive structure
is unstable, ambiguous, disorganized, or chaotically organized, it tends
to inhibit meaningful learning and retention. Hence it is largely by
strengthening relevant aspects of cognitive structure that new learning
and retention can be facilitated. Thus it is a commonplace that the details of a given discipline are learned as rapidly as they can be fitted
into a contextual framework consisting of a stable and appropriate body

of general concepts and principles. When we deliberately attempt to influence cognitive structure so as to maximize meaningful learning and retention we come to the heart of the educative process.

In my opinion, the most significant advances that have occurred in recent years in the teaching of such subjects as mathematics, chemistry, physics, and biology have been predicated on the assumption that efficient learning and functional retention of ideas and information are largely dependent upon the adequacy of cognitive structure. And inasmuch as existing cognitive structure reflects the outcome of all previous subsumption processes, it in turn can be influenced substantively by the inclusiveness and integrative properties of the particular unifying and explanatory principles used in a given discipline, and programmatically by methods of presenting, arranging, and ordering learning materials and practice trials.

COGNITIVE STRUCTURE AND TRANSFER

I have just hypothesized that past experience influences or has positive or negative effects on new meaningful learning and retention by virtue of its impact on relevant properties of cognitive structure. If this is true, all meaningful learning necessarily involves transfer because it is impossible to conceive of any instance of such learning that is not affected in some way by existing cognitive structure; and this learning experience, in turn, results in new transfer by modifying cognitive structure. In meaningful learning, therefore, cognitive structure is always a relevant and crucial variable, even if it is not deliberately influenced or manipulated so as to ascertain its effect on new learning—as for example, in those short-term learning situations where just a single unit of material is learned and transfer to new learning units is not measured. A single practice trial both reflects the influence of existing cognitive structure and induces modification of that structure.

Much more saliently than in laboratory types of learning situations, school learning requires the incorporation of new concepts and information into an existing and established cognitive framework with particular organizational properties. The transfer paradigm still applies here, and transfer still refers to the impact of prior experience upon current learning. But prior experience in this case is conceptualized as a cumulatively acquired, hierarchically organized, and established body of knowledge which is organically relatable to the new learning task, rather than a recently experienced constellation of stimulus-response connections influencing the learning of another discrete set of such connections. Furthermore, the relevant aspects of past experience in this type of transfer paradigm are such organizational properties of the learner's subject-matter knowledge as clarity, stability, generalizability, inclusiveness, cohesiveness, and discriminability—not degree of similarity between stimuli and responses in the two learning tasks; and recent prior experience is not regarded as influencing current learning by interacting *directly* with the stimulus-response components of the new learning task, but only insofar as it modifies significant relevant attributes of cognitive structure.

Because training and criterion tasks in laboratory studies of transfer have usually been separate and discrete, we have tended to think in terms of how prior task *A* influences performance on criterion task *B*. If performance has been facilitated, in comparison with that of a control group which had not been exposed to task *A*, we say that positive transfer has occurred. Actually, however, in typical classroom situations, *A* and *B* are not discrete but continuous. *A* is a preparatory stage of *B* and a precursive aspect of the same learning process; *B* is not learned discretely but in relation to *A*. Hence in school learning we deal not so much with transfer in the literal sense of the term as with the influence of prior knowledge on new learning in a continuous sequential context. This latter learning context also typically involves correlative subsumption. Hence, as pointed out above, the relevant transfer effect with which we are usually concerned is not the ability to reconstruct forgotten details from generic principles or to recognize new phenomena as specific variants of these principles, but rather enhanced ability to learn and *retain* the more detailed correlative material.

Moreover, unlike the kind of transfer Bruner calls nonspecific (7), the kind of transfer just described is not restricted to those instances in which "a general idea . . . can be used as a basis for recognizing subsequent problems as special cases of the ideas originally mastered." Actually, the principal effect of existing cognitive structure on new cognitive performance is on the learning and retention of newly presented materials where potential meanings are given—not on the solution of problems requiring the application and reorganization of cognitive structure to new ends. Thus a transfer situation exists whenever existing cognitive structure influences new cognitive functioning, irrespective of whether it is in regard to reception learning or problem-solving.

PRINCIPAL COGNITIVE STRUCTURE VARIABLES

The learner's acquisition of a clear, stable, and organized body of knowledge constitutes more than just the major longterm objective of classroom learning activity or the principal *dependent* variable (or criterion) to be used in evaluating the impact of all factors impinging on learning and retention. Cognitive structure is *also* in its own right the most significant *independent* variable influencing the learner's capacity for acquiring more new knowledge in the same field. The importance of cognitive structure variables, however, has been generally underestimated in the past because preoccupation with noncognitive, rote, and motor kinds of learning has tended to focus attention on such situational and intrapersonal factors as practice, drive, incentive, and reinforcement variables. But in searching for knowledge about the processes underlying meaningful reception learning and retention, it is not enough to stress the importance of relevant antecedent experience that is represented in existing cognitive structure. Before fruitful experimentation can be attempted it is necessary to specify and conceptualize those properties (variables) of cognitive structure that influence new learning and retention.

In the more general and long-term sense, cognitive structure variables refer to significant organizational properties of the learner's *total* knowledge in a given subject-matter field and their influence on his future academic performance in the same area of knowledge. In the more specific and short-term sense, cognitive structure variables refer to the organizational properties of just the *immediately* or proximately relevant concepts within a particular subject-matter field and their effects on the learning and retention of small units of related subject matter.

One important variable affecting the incorporability of new meaningful material is the availability in cognitive organization of relevant subsuming concepts at an appropriate level of inclusiveness to provide optimal anchorage. The appropriate level of inclusiveness may be defined as that level which is as proximate as possible to the degree of conceptualization of the learning task—considered, of course, in relation to the existing degree of differentiation of the subject as a whole in the learner's cognitive background. Thus, the more unfamiliar the learning task, i.e., the more undifferentiated the learner's background of relevant concepts, the more inclusive or highly generalized the subsuming concepts must be in order to be proximate.

What happens if an appropriate relevant subsumer is not available in cognitive structure when new potentially meaningful material is presented to a learner? If some existing though not entirely relevant and appropriate concept cannot be utilized for subsuming purposes, the only alternative is rote learning. More typically, however, some tangentially relevant subsumer is pressed into serivce. This type of subsumer obviously cannot provide very adequate or efficient anchorage, thereby giving rise to unclear, unstable, and ambiguous meanings with little longevity. The same outcome may also result when appropriate relevant subsumers *are* available, if their relevance is not recognized. For both reasons, therefore, in meaningful learning situations, it is preferable to introduce suitable organizers whose relevance is made explicit rather than to rely on the spontaneous availability of appropriate subsumers.

A second important factor presumably affecting the retention of a potentially meaningful learning task is the extent to which it is discriminable from the established conceptual systems that subsume it. A reasonable assumption here, borne out by preliminary investigation, is that if the new concepts are not originally salient and clearly discriminable from established subsuming foci, they can be adequately represented by the latter for memorial purposes, and would not persist as dissociable entities in their own right. In other words, only discriminable categorical variants of more inclusive concepts have long-term retention value.

Lastly, the learning and longevity of new meaningful material in memory are a function of the stability and clarity of its subsumers. Ambiguous and unstable subsumers not only provide weak anchorage for related new materials, but also cannot be easily discriminated from them.

Implications for Teaching

What are some of the pedagogic implications both of the foregoing model of the psychological structure of knowledge and of the factors that influence its accretion and organization? The major implication for teaching perhaps is that control over the accuracy, clarity, longevity in memory, and transferability of a given body of knowledge can be most effectively exercised by attempting to influence the crucial variables of cognitive structure. This can be done both substantively and programatically: (a) by using for organizational and integrative purposes those unifying concepts and propositions in a given discipline that have the widest explanatory power, inclusiveness, generalizability, and relatability to the subject-matter content of that discipline; and (b) by employing suitable programatic principles of ordering the sequence of subject matter, constructing its internal logic and organization, and arranging practice trials.

The principal strategy advocated in this paper for deliberately manipulating cognitive structure so as to enhance proactive facilitation or minimize proactive inhibition involves the use of appropriately relevant and inclusive introductory materials (i.e., organizers) that are maximally clear and stable. These organizers are introduced in advance of the learning material itself, and are also presented at a higher level of abstraction, generality, and inclusiveness; and since the substantive content of a given organizer or series of organizers is selected on the basis of their appropriateness for explaining, integrating, and interrelating the material they precede, this strategy simultaneously satisfies the substantive as well as the programing criteria specified above for enhancing the organizational strength of cognitive structure. Summaries and overviews, on the other hand, are ordinarily presented at the same level of abstraction, generality, and inclusiveness as the learning material itself. They simply emphasize the salient points of the material by omitting less important information, and largely achieve their result by repetition.

The function of the organizer is to provide ideational scaffolding for the stable incorporation and retention of the more detailed and differentiated material that follows in the learning passage, as well as to increase discriminability between the latter and related interfering concepts in cognitive structure. In the case of completely unfamiliar material, an "expository" organizer is used to provide relevant proximate subsumers. These subsumers primarily furnish ideational anchorage in terms that are already familiar to the learner. In the case of relatively familiar material, a "comparative" organizer is used both to integrate new concepts with basically similar concepts in cognitive structure, as well as to increase discriminability between new and existing ideas which are essentially different but confusable.

PROGRESSIVE DIFFERENTIATION OF LEARNING TASKS

When subject matter is programed in accordance with the principle of progressive differentiation, the most general and inclusive ideas of the discipline are presented first and are then progressively differentiated in terms of detail and specificity. This order of presentation presumably corresponds to the postulated way in which knowledge is represented, organized, and stored in the human nervous system, and recognizes that new ideas and information can be meaningfully learned and retained only to the extent that more inclusive and appropriately relevant concepts are already available in cognitive structure to play a subsuming role or to furnish ideational anchorage.

But even though this principle seems rather self-evident, it is rarely followed in actual teaching procedures or in the organization of most textbooks. The more typical practice is to segregate topically homogeneous materials into separate chapters, and to present them throughout at an undifferentiated level of conceptualization in accordance with a logical outline of subject-matter organization. This practice, of course, although logically sound is psychologically incongruous with the postulated process whereby meaningful learning occurs, i.e., with the mechanism of accretion through a process of progressive differentiation of an undifferentiated field. Thus, in most instances, students are required to learn the details of new and unfamiliar disciplines before they have acquired an adequate body of relevant subsumers at an appropriate level of inclusiveness.

As a result of this latter practice, students and teachers are coerced into treating meaningful materials as if they were rote in character, and consequently experience unnecessary difficulty and little success in both learning and retention. The teaching of mathematics and science, for example, still relies heavily on rote learning of formulas and procedural steps, on recognition of stereotyped "type problems," and on mechanical manipulation of symbols. In the absence of clear and stable concepts which can serve as anchoring points and organizing foci for the incorporation of new potentially meaningful material, students have little choice but rotely to memorize learning tasks for examination purposes.

Progressive differentiation in the programing of subject matter is accomplished by using a hierarchical series of organizers (in descending order of inclusiveness), each organizer preceding its corresponding unit of detailed, differentiated material. In this way not only is an appropriately relevant and inclusive subsumer made available to provide ideational scaffolding for each component unit of differentiated subject matter, but the various units in relation to each other are also progressively differentiated, i.e., organized in descending order of inclusiveness. The initial organizers, therefore, furnish anchorage at a global level before the learner is confronted with *any* of the new material. Hence, for example, a generalized model of class relationships is first provided as a general subsumer for *all* new classes, subclasses, and species before more limited subsumers are provided for the particular subclasses or species they encompass.

Thus when undergraduates are first exposed to organizers presenting relevant and appropriately inclusive subsuming principles they are better able to learn and retain completely unfamiliar ideational material (1). Differential analysis in another similar study showed that the facilitating effect of organizers occurs only for those individuals who have relatively poor verbal ability, and who therefore tend spontaneously to structure such material less effectively (3). The greater retention by pro-Southern than by pro-Northern students of a controversial passage presenting the Southern point of view on the Civil War can also be explained in terms of the relative availability of appropriate subsuming ideas (9). The pro-Northern students lack relevant subsumers to which the pro-Southern passage can be functionally related. The material therefore cannot be clearly and securely anchored to cognitive structure, concepts with existing meanings, and is consequently ambiguous and subject to rapid forgetting. The pro-Southern students, on the other hand, possess relevant subsuming concepts; hence the material can be readily anchored to cognitive structure and is less ambiguous and subject to forgetting.

In sequential school learning, knowledge of earlier appearing material in the sequence plays much the same role as an organizer in relation to later appearing material in the sequence: it constitutes relevant ideational scaffolding and hence a crucial limiting condition for learning the latter material. One of the principal advantages of programed instruction is its careful sequential arrangement and gradation of difficulty which insure that each attained increment in learning serves as an appropriate foundation and anchoring post for the learning and retention of subsequent items in the ordered sequence.

CONSOLIDATION

By insisting on consolidation or mastery of ongoing lessons before new material is introduced, we make sure of continued readiness and success in sequentially organized learning. This kind of learning presupposes, of course, that the preceding step is always clear, stable, and well organized. If it is not, the learning of all subsequent steps is jeopardized. Hence new material in the sequence should never be introduced until all previous steps are thoroughly mastered. This principle also applies to those kinds of intra-task learning in which each component task (as well as entire bodies of subject matter) tends to be compound in content and to manifest an internal organization of its own.

Abundant experimental research (e.g., 8, 11) has confirmed the proposition that prior learnings are not transferable to new learning tasks until they are first overlearned. Overlearning, in turn, requires an adequate number of adequately spaced repetitions and reviews, sufficient intra-task repetitiveness prior to intra- and inter-task diversification, and opportunity for differential practice of the more difficult components of a task. Frequent testing and provision of feedback, especially with test items demanding fine discrimination among alternatives varying in degree of correctness, also enhances consolidation by confirming, clarifying, and correcting previous learnings.

The stability and clarity of existing cognitive structure are important both for the depth of anchorage they provide for related new learning tasks as well as for their effects on the discriminability of these new tasks. The discriminability of new learning material is in large measure a function of the clarity and stability of existing concepts in the learner's cognitive structure to which it is relatable. In learning an unfamiliar passage about Buddhism, for example, subjects with greater knowledge of Christianity make significantly higher scores on the Buddhism retention test than do subjects with less knowledge of Christianity (2, 4). This significantly positive relationship between Christianity and Buddhism scores holds up even when the effect of verbal ability is statistically controlled. When a parallelly organized passage about Zen Buddhism is introduced after the Buddhism passage, knowledge of Buddhism similarly facilitates the learning of Zen Buddhism when verbal ability is held constant (4). In more directly sequential tasks, where the learning of Part II materials presupposes understanding of Part I materials, the stability and clarity of the antecedent material crucially affects the learning and retention of the later-appearing material (3). Even in the learning of controversial ideas contrary to prevailing belief (e.g., the learning by Illinois students of the Southern point of view about the Civil War), the more knowledgeable students, namely, those who know more about the Civil War period, are better able to learn and remember the "other side" arguments (9), presumably because they find them more discriminable from established ideas than do less knowledgeable subjects. Thus, much of the effect of overlearning—both on retaining a given unit of material and on learning related new material—is probably a reflection of enhanced discriminability, which can be accomplished by increasing the clarity and stability of either the learning material itself or of its subsumers.

Perhaps the most important feature of automated instruction insofar as the facilitation of meaningful learning and retention is concerned is not the incentive and drive-reducing effects of immediate feedback, but the extent to which such instruction influences learning by enhancing the stability and clarity of cognitive structure. By deferring the introduction of new material until prior material in the learning sequence is consolidated, it maximizes the effect of stability of cognitive structure on new learning; and by supplying immediate feedback, it rules out and corrects alternative wrong meanings, misinterpretations, ambiguities, and misconceptions before they have an opportunity to impair the clarity of cognitive structure and thereby inhibit the learning of new material.

INTEGRATIVE RECONCILIATION

The principle of integrative reconciliation in programing instructional material can be best described as antithetical in spirit and approach to the ubiquitous practice among textbook writers of compartmentalizing and segregating particular ideas or topics within their respective chapters or subchapters. Implicit in this latter practice is the assumption (perhaps logically valid, but certainly psychologically untenable) that pedagogic considerations are adequately served if overlapping topics are handled in self-contained fashion, so that each topic is presented in only *one* of the several possible places where treatment is relevant and warranted, i.e., the assumption that all necessary cross-referencing of related ideas can be satisfactorily performed, and customarily is, by students. Hence little serious effort is made explicitly to explore relationships between these ideas, to point out significant similarities and differences, and to reconcile real or apparent inconsistencies. Some of the undesirable consequences of this approach are that multiple terms are used to represent concepts which are intrinsically equivalent except for contextual reference, thereby generating incalculable cognitive strain and confusion, as well as encouraging rote learning; that artificial barriers are erected between related topics, obscuring important common features, and thus rendering impossible the acquisition of insights dependent upon recognition of these commonalities; that adequate use is not made of relevant, previously learned ideas as a basis for subsuming and incorporating related new information; and that since significant differences between apparently similar concepts are not made clear and explicit, these concepts are often perceived and retained as identical.

The principle of integrative reconciliation also applies when subject matter is organized along parallel lines, that is, when related materials are presented in serial fashion but there is no *intrinsic* sequential dependence from one topic to the next. Unlike the case in sequentially organized subject matter, successive learning tasks are inherently independent of each other in the sense that understanding of Part II material does not presuppose understanding of Part I material. Each set of material is logically self-contained and can be adequately learned by itself without any reference to the other; order of presentation is therefore immaterial. This situation, for example, prevails in presenting alternative theoretical positions in ethics, religion, and epistemology; opposing theories of biological evolution; and different systems of learning and personality theory.

Nevertheless, although successive learning tasks of parallelly organized material are not intrinsically dependent on each other, much cognitive interaction obviously occurs between them. Earlier learned elements of a parallel sequence serve an orienting and subsuming role in relation to later-presented elements. The latter are comprehended and interpreted in terms of existing understandings and paradigms provided by analogous, familiar, previously learned, and already established concepts in cognitive structure. Hence for learning of the unfamiliar new ideas to take place, they must be adequately discriminable from the established familiar ideas; otherwise the new meanings are so permeated with ambiguities, misconceptions, and confusions as to be partially or completely nonexistent in their own right. If, for example, the learner cannot discriminate between new idea A^1 and old idea A, A^1 does not really exist for him, it is phenomenologically the same as A. Furthermore, even if the learner can discriminate between A and A^1 at the moment of learning, unless the discrimination is sharp and free from ambiguity and confusion, there will be a tendency over time for A^1 to be remembered as A as the two ideas interact during the retention interval.

In some instances of meaningful learning and retention, the principal difficulty is not one of discriminability but of apparent contradiction between established ideas in cognitive structure and new propositions in the learning material. Under these conditions the learner may dismiss the new propositions as invalid, may try to compartmentalize them as isolated entities apart from previously learned knowledge, or may attempt integrative reconciliation under a more inclusive subsumer. Compartmentalization, of course, may be considered a common defense against forgetting. By arbitrarily isolating concepts and information, one prevents interaction with and obliterative subsumption by relevant concepts in cognitive structure. This is a modified variety of rote learning in which new learning material is allowed to interact with only certain of several potential subsumers. Through overlearning, relatively stable subsumption may be achieved, but the fabric of knowledge as a whole is unintegrated and full of internal contradictions.

Organizers may also be expressly designed to further the principle of integrative reconciliation. They do this by explicitly pointing out in what ways previously learned, related concepts in cognitive structure are either basically similar to or essentially different from new ideas in the learning task. Hence, on the one hand, organizers explicitly draw upon and mobilize all available concepts in cognitive structure that are relevant for and can play a subsuming role in relation to the new learning material. This maneuver effects great economy of learning effort, avoids the isolation of essentially similar concepts in separate, noncommunicable compartments, and discourages the confusing proliferation of multiple terms to represent ostensibly different but essentially equivalent ideas. On the other hand, organizers increase the discriminability of genuine differences between the new learning materials and analogous but often conflicting ideas in the learner's cognitive structure. Comparative organizers, for example, have been successfully used in facilitating the meaningful learning and retention of an unfamiliar passage dealing with Buddhism (2, 4), and of a controversial passage presenting the Southern point of view about the Civil War (9).

INTERNAL LOGIC OF LEARNING MATERIAL

The internal logic of the learning task is obviously relevant for meaningful learning and retention outcomes since the existence of logical or potential meaning within the material (i.e., its relatability to a hypothetical human cognitive structure with the necessary background knowledge) is a prerequisite for the emergence of psychological (phenomenological) meaning. Logical meaning, as previously pointed out, is a function of the plausibility, lucidity, and nonarbitrariness of the material rather than of its logical or substantive validity. Hence "internal logic" is used somewhat idiosyncratically here to designate those properties of the material that enhance these latter criteria of logical meaning.

At least four aspects of the internal logic of material affect the extent to which it is endowed with potential meaning: (a) adequacy of definition and diction (i.e., precise, consistent, and unambiguous use of terms; definition of all new terms prior to use; and the use of the simplest and least technical language that is compatible with conveying precise meanings); (b) the use of concrete-empirical data and of relevant analogies when developmentally warranted or otherwise helpful in the acquisition, clarification, or dramatization of meanings; (c) encouragement of an active, critical, reflective, and analytic approach on the part of the learner by requiring him to reformulate the material in terms of his own vocabulary, experiential background, and structure of ideas; and (d) explicit delineation of the distinctive logic and philosophy of each subject-matter discipline (i.e., its implicit epistemological assumptions; general problems of causality, categorization, inquiry, and measurement that are specific to the discipline; and the distinctive strategy of learning how to learn the particular subject matter of the discipline).

As Professor Phenix has so succinctly expressed it, "it is difficult to imagine how any effective learning could take place without regard for the inherent patterns of what is to be learned." Yet he was careful to point out that "attention to the structure of knowledge in the disciplines is certainly not a *sufficient* condition for learning to occur. Aptitude, maturation, and motivation are other important factors in learning." In this paper I have also stressed the importance of such cognitive structure variables as the availability of relevant subsumers, the stability and clarity of these subsumers, and their discriminability from the learning material. Finally, I have tried to show how these variables can be most advantageously manipulated for purposes of facilitating meaningful learning and retention by following the principles of progressive differentiation and integrative reconciliation in programing learning materials; by emphasizing sequential organization and prior consolidation of subject-matter content; by using advance organizers; and by employing for organizational and integrative purposes those unifying concepts and propositions in a given discipline that have the widest explanatory power, generalizability, and relatability to the subject-matter content of that discipline.

References

1. Ausubel, D. P. "The Use of Advance Organizers in the Learning and Retention of Meaningful Verbal Material," *Journal of Educational Psychology*, LI (1960), 267–72.
2. Ausubel, D. P., and Fitzgerald, D. "The Role of Discriminability in Meaningful Verbal Learning and Retention," *Journal of Educational Psychology*, LII (1961), 266–74.
3. Ausubel, D. P., and Fitzgerald, D. "Organizer, General Background, and Antecedent Learning Conditions in Sequential Verbal Learning," *Journal of Educational Psychology*, LIII (1962), 243–49.
4. Ausubel, D. P., and Yousef, M. "The Role of Discriminability in Meaningful Parallel Learning," *Journal of Educational Psychology*, in press.
5. Bruner, J. S. Going beyond the information given. In *Contemporary approaches to cognition*. Cambridge, Mass.: Harvard Univ. Press, 1957.
6. Bruner, J. S. "Learning and Thinking," *Harvard Educational Review*, XXIX (1959), 84–92.

7. Bruner, J. S. *The process of education*. Cambridge, Mass.: Harvard Univ. Press, 1960.

8. Duncan, C. P. "Transfer after Training with Single versus Multiple Tasks," *Journal of Experimental Psychology*, LV (1959), 63–72.

9. Fitzgerald, D., and Ausubel, D. P. "Cognitive versus Affective Factors in the Learning and Retention of Controversial Material," *Journal of Educational Psychology*, LIV (1963), 73–84.

10. Inhelder, Barbel, & Piaget, J. *The growth of logical thinking from childhood to adolescence*. New York: Basic Books, 1958.

11. Morrisett, L., and Hovland, C. I. "A Comparison of Three Varieties of Training in Human Problem Solving," *Journal of Experimental Psychology*, LVIII (1959), 52–55.

PART V   POTPOURRI: TOWARD A PSYCHOLOGY OF SCHOOL LEARNING

School learning, as stated earlier, is a process whereby the mechanisms of learning are engaged within the context of schooling. Once these mechanisms are adequately understood, prescriptive statements can be written for the conditions under which behavioral change can be accomplished most efficiently. Carroll provides a model for the general process of school learning that may help structure future research and practice.

Bruner's article illustrates categories for prescriptive statements. It provides a glimpse of the kinds of questions that must be answered in order to formulate an adequate theory of instruction. The article by Groen and Atkinson (although at points quite technical) then provides examples of prescriptive statements based on current principles of psychology.

Models for school learning and rules for writing principles of instruction must eventually be incorporated into any satisfactory theory of instruction. Until such time as we have adequate descriptions of school learning, however, we must rely on the intuition of men such as Carroll and Bruner for approximations to principles of instruction. These principles which are based on a knowledge of psychology can help to clarify, and make more effective, principles of practice formulated by the teacher, counselor, and parent.

22　A MODEL OF SCHOOL LEARNING
John B. Carroll

The primary job of the educational psychologist is to develop and apply knowledge concerning why pupils succeed or fail in their learning at school, and to assist in the prevention and remediation of learning difficulties.

This job is inherently difficult because behavior is complex and has a multiplicity of causes. To deal with it, educational psychologists have evolved a number of concepts which they find useful in classifying the phenomena of behavior. Textbooks in the field are commonly organized around such concepts as maturation, individual differences, learning, thinking, motivation, and social development. These are useful categories, but because they overlap or refer to different levels of organization in the subject matter, it is difficult to build them into an integrated account of the process of school learning. What is needed is a schematic design or conceptual model of factors affecting success in school learning and of the way they interact. Such a model should use a very small number of simplifying concepts, conceptually independent of one another and referring to phenomena at the same level of discourse. It should suggest new and interesting research questions and aid in the solution of practical educational problems. With the aid of such a framework, the often conflicting results of different research studies might be seen to fall into a unified pattern.

Many such formulations, perhaps, are possible. A conceptual model will be presented here that seems to have the advantage of comprehensiveness combined with relative simplicity. The model is amenable to elaboration, but for our immediate purposes, we will leave aside any such elaborations.

Scope of the Model

We need first to define *learning task*. The learner's task of going from ignorance of some specified fact or concept to knowledge or understanding of it, or of proceeding from incapability of performing some specified act to capability of performing it, is a learning task. To call it a task does not necessarily imply that the learner must be aware *that* he is supposed to learn or be aware of *what* he is supposed to learn, although in

SOURCE: John B. Carroll, "A Model of School Learning," *Teachers College Record*, 64, no. 8 (May 1963), 723–33. Reprinted by permission of the author and publisher.

most cases it happens that such awarenesses on the part of the learner are desirable.

Most, but not all, goals of the school can be expressed in the form of learning tasks or a series of such tasks. Teaching the child to read, for example, means to teach him to perform certain acts in response to written or printed language. Examples of other learning tasks taught in the schools can be multiplied at will: learning to spell all the words in common use, learning to perform certain operations with numbers, learning to explain or otherwise demonstrate an understanding of the subject matter of biology, learning to speak a foreign language, learning to perform in competitive sports, and learning to carry out certain responsibilities of a citizen. Some of these tasks are very broadly defined, such as learning to read printed English, but we can also consider narrowly defined tasks like mastering the content of Lesson 20 in a certain textbook of French, or even mastering a certain grammatical construction covered in that lesson. The model presented here is intended to apply equally well to all such tasks, no matter how broad or narrow. It is required, however, that the task can be unequivocally described and that means can be found for making a valid judgment as to when the learner has accomplished the learning task—that is, has achieved the learning goal which has been set for him.

It will be seen that as many as possible of the basic concepts in the model are defined so that they can be measured in terms of *time* in order to capitalize on the advantages of a scale with a meaningful zero point and equal units of measurement. An effort is made to provide for a mathematical description of the degree to which a learning task is achieved. Although the model applies only to one learning task at a time, it should be possible in principle to describe the pupil's success in learning a series of tasks (*e.g.*, all the work of the fifth grade) by summating the results of applying the model successively to each component task.

The model is admittedly oversimplified. The assumption that the work of the school can be broken down into a series of learning tasks can be called into question. In actual school practice, the various tasks to be learned are not necessarily treated as separate and distinct, and the process of teaching is often organized (whether rightly so or not) so that learnings will take place "incidentally" and in the course of other activities. Nevertheless, a conceptual model requires certain simplifying assumptions, and the assumption of discrete learning tasks is a useful one to make.

The model can be regarded as applying even to those educational goals ordinarily formulated in terms of "transfer"—that is, the ability to apply in a "new" situation something learned previously. The concept of the learning task is defined to include the attainment of that degree of competence which will make "transfer" essentially as automatic as demonstration of performance in the original setting. "Transfer," correctly viewed, is a term in a metalanguage which states the conditions under which particular learnings occur or manifest themselves. Thus, when we say that "learning which occurred in situation A transfers to situation B," we are really saying that "something learned in situation A also manifested itself in situation B, there being sufficient commonality between the two situations to elicit the learned performance in both."

The model is not intended to apply, however, to those goals of the school which do not lend themselves to being considered as learning tasks. Such, for example, are those goals having to do with attitudes and dispositions. Educating a child so that he has tolerance for persons of other races or creeds, respect for parental or legal authority, or attitudes of fair play, is thought to be largely a matter of emotional conditioning or of the acquisition of values and drives. Learning tasks may indeed be involved in the cognitive support of such attitudes (as where the child learns facts about different races or creeds), but the acquisition of attitudes is postulated to follow a different paradigm from that involved in learning tasks. Perhaps the distinctions made by Skinner (6) are of use in this connection: We could say that whereas learning tasks typically involve "operants," the attitudinal goals of education typically involve "respondents."

Overview of the Model

Briefly, our model says that the learner will succeed in learning a given task to the extent that he spends the amount of time that he *needs* to learn the task. The terms of this statement, however, require special definition, explication, and interpretation if the statement is to be properly understood.

First, it should be understood that "spending time" means *actually spending time on the act of learning.* "Time" is therefore not "elapsed time" but the time during which the person is oriented to the learning task and actively engaged in learning. In common parlance, it is the time during which he is "paying attention" and "trying to learn."

Second, there are certain factors which determine how much time the learner *spends* actively engaged in learning.

Third, there are certain factors which determine how much time a person *needs to spend* in order to learn the task. These factors may or may not be the same as, or associated with, those which influence how much time he spends in learning.

The major part of this article is devoted to a presentation of the factors conceived as determining the times needed or actually spent in the course of a learning task and the way in which these factors interact to result in various degrees of success in learning. Four of these factors are convenient intervening variables or constructs which may, in turn, be regarded as functions of still other factors or variables; one, however, is in principle a directly manipulable and measurable factor ("opportunity").

This model of school learning should not be confused with what is ordinarily called "learning theory," that is, with the exact scientific analysis of the essential conditions of learning and the development of systematic theory about this process. Rather, the model may be thought of as a description of the "economics" of the school learning process; it takes the fact of learning for granted.

The five factors or variables in the model will be presented under two headings: (1) determinants of time needed for learning, and (2) determinants of time spent in learning.

Time Needed in Learning

Aptitude. Suppose that a randomly selected group of children is taught a certain learning task by a teacher (or teaching device) with the best possible teaching techniques. Suppose further that each child is willing to stick attentively with the learning task for the number of minutes, hours, or days required for him to learn it to the specified criterion of success, and that each child is in fact given the opportunity to do this. Common experience, as well as abundant research evidence, suggests that the amounts of time needed by the children even under these ideal conditions will differ widely. Let us think, then, of the amount of time the pupil will need to learn the task under these conditions as the primary measure of a variable which we shall call his *aptitude for learning this task.* In ordinary parlance, learners who need only a small amount of time are said to have high aptitude; learners who need a large amount of time are said to have low aptitude. Some learners, it may be, will never learn even under these optimal conditions; we may say that these learners would need an indefinitely large (or an infinite) amount of time to learn the task.

It will be noted that this variable is measured in the opposite direction from the usual way of measuring aptitude—the shorter the time needed for learning, the higher the aptitude.

Furthermore, it will be noted that the measure of aptitude is specific to the task under consideration. Aptitude may be regarded as a function of numerous other variables. For one thing, it may depend upon the amount of prior learning which may be relevant to the task under consideration. A learner who has already progressed far towards the mastery of a task may not need much time to complete his learning. On the other hand, aptitude may also depend upon a series of traits or characteristics of the learner which enter into a wide variety of tasks; whether these traits can be accounted for solely on the basis of generalized prior learnings, or whether they reflect genetically determined individual characteristics, is of no immediate concern here. It may be useful, however, to conceive that a learner's estimated needed time, a_t, for learning a given task, t, may be written as a mathematical function of a series of basic aptitudes, symbolized with Greek letters and subscripts, minus the amount of time, s_t, saved by virtue of prior learnings relevant to the task. Thus:

$$a_t = f(\alpha_1, \alpha_2, \ldots, \alpha_n) - s_t$$

The exact form of this formula would vary for different tasks. Presumably, the basic aptitudes $\alpha_1, \alpha_2, \ldots, \alpha_n$ could be measured with considerable exactitude by appropriate tests.

Ability to understand instruction. We find it useful to postulate as a variable separate from those we consider under "aptitude" the ability to understand instruction, since this variable (in contrast to pure aptitude variables) is thought of as interacting with the method of instruction in a special and interesting way. The ability to understand instruction could be measured, one would suppose, as some combination of "general intelligence" and "verbal ability"; the former of these two would come into play in instructional situations where the learner is left to infer for himself the concepts and relationships inherent in the material to be learned, rather than having them carefully spelled out for him, while the latter would come into play whenever the instruction utilized language beyond the grasp of the learner. The way in which ability to understand instruction is postulated to interact with the type of instruction will be explained after we introduce a third variable affecting time needed for learning, the *quality of instruction.*

Quality of instruction. One job of the teacher (or any person who prepares the materials of instruction) is to organize and present the task to be learned in such a way that the learner can learn it as rapidly and as efficiently as he is able. This means, first, that the learner must be told, in words that he can understand, what he is to learn and how he is to learn it. It means that the learner must be put into adequate sensory contact with the material to be learned (for example, one must insure that the learner will adequately see or hear the materials of instruction). It also means that the various aspects of the learning task must be presented in such an order and with such detail that, as far as possible, every step of the learning is adequately prepared for by a previous step. It may also mean that the instruction must be adapted for the special needs and characteristics of the learner, including his stage of learning. All these things may be summarized in what we call *quality of instruction*. This variable applies not only to the performance of a teacher but also to the characteristics of textbooks, workbooks, films, teaching-machine programs, etc.

Now, if the quality of instruction is anything less than optimal, it is possible that the learner will need more time to learn the task than he would otherwise need. Some learners will be more handicapped by poor instruction than others. The extent of this handicap is conceived to be a function of the learner's *ability to understand instruction*. Learners with high ability in this respect will be able to figure out for themselves what the learning task is and how they can go about learning it; they will be able to overcome the difficulties presented by poor quality of instruction by perceiving concepts and relationships in the teaching materials which will not be grasped by those with lesser ability.

For the purposes of this conceptual model, we shall say that the amount of time actually needed by a person to learn a given task satisfactorily is a function not only of aptitude (as defined previously), but also of the quality of instruction in so far as it is less than optimal. And the amount of additional time he will need is an inverse function of his ability to understand instruction.

We could, of course, apply Occam's razor and get rid of both of the two preceding variables by conceiving that a change in the quality of instruction causes an essential change in the learning task itself. In this case, we would deal only with a learner's aptitude for learning a given task, subscripted with the quality of instruction attached to it. Such a modification of our model seems undesirable, however, for one would tend to lose sight of instructional quality as one of the important manipulable variables in educational psychology.

Time Spent in Learning

Time allowed for learning ("opportunity"). It may come as a surprise to some to be told that the schools may allow less than adequate time for learning any task, but second thought will make one realize that this is very often the case. It is partly a consequence of the very large amount of material that the schools are expected to teach; the available time must somehow be distributed among many things. And it is partly a consequence of the very great variation that exists in the amounts of time that children *need* for learning, even under a good quality of instruction, and particularly when the instructional quality is such that many children of lower ability to understand instruction require much more time than they might otherwise need.

The school responds to differences in learning rates (for that is what differences in aptitude are) in many ways. Sometimes the policy of the school is, in effect, to ignore these differences; a certain amount of time is provided for everybody to learn, and no more. (For example, at some military academies, study time is prescribed and scheduled uniformly for all cadets.) At the opposite extreme is the case where each student is allowed to proceed exactly at his own rate; private instruction in music or foreign languages and self-instruction by teaching machine or other means are approximations to this case. The middle position is occupied by learning situations in which there is some kind of "ability grouping": Pupils are assigned to different groups, classes, or curricula on the basis of estimated learning rates.

Even when there is some constraint upon the amount of time "officially" provided for learning, teachers and instructional programs vary in the amount of time they allow for learning. Some programs present material at such a rapid pace that most students are kept under continual pressure; only the apter students can keep up with this instruction, while the others fall back or out, sometimes never to get caught up. In other programs, the instruction is paced for the benefit of the slower student. The faster student is fortunate if the teacher takes appropriate steps to "enrich" his instructional content; but this will not always happen, and it is undoubtedly the case that many fast learners lose some of their motivation for learning when they feel that their time is being wasted or when they are not kept at the edge of challenge.

Perseverance

Obviously, failure to allow enough time for learning produces incomplete learning. If a person needs two hours to learn something and is allowed only one hour, and if we assume that learning proceeds linearly with time, the degree of learning is only 50 per cent. Probably one of the most aversive things which a school can do is not to allow sufficient time for a well-motivated child to master a given learning task before the next is taken up. Children meet such frustrations by indifference or the more extreme avoidance reactions and are, in any case, handicapped in undertaking the next task.

The time the learner is willing to spend in learning ("perseverance"). The term *perseverance* is used here, rather than persistence, because of the somewhat pejorative connotations of the latter. Nevertheless, the concept is similar to what Paul Brandwein describes in the following passage:

> The characteristics grouped under the Predisposing Factor . . . include a spectrum of traits which the writer places under the head of *Persist-*

ence. This is defined as consisting of three attitudes. (1) A marked willingness to spend time, beyond the ordinary schedule, in a given task (this includes the willingness to set one's own time schedules, to labor beyond a prescribed time, such as nine to five). (2) A willingness to withstand discomfort. This includes adjusting to shortened lunch hours, or no lunch hours, working without holidays, etc. It includes withstanding fatigue and strain and working even through minor illness, such as a cold or a headache. (3) A willingness to face failure. With this comes a realization that patient work may lead to successful termination of the task at hand (1, pp. 9–10).

But the variable of perseverance applies not only in the case of the "gifted student" and not only in the case of long durations of effort, but also to all other learners and also to learning tasks which require only short times for mastery. That is, in the general case, a learner who (in view of his aptitude, the quality of the instruction, and his ability to understand the instruction) needs a certain amount of time to learn a task may or may not be willing to persevere for that amount of time in trying to learn. It is not a matter of his predicting how long he will be willing to learn: we simply postulate that there is a certain time over and above which he will not continue active learning of a task, and this time may lie anywhere on the scale from zero to infinity. The learner may not be motivated to learn at all, or he may regard the task as something too difficult for him to learn; in either case, he may spend no time at all in trying to learn. He may start to learn and later become distracted or bored, or he may lose confidence in his ability. He may go far toward mastery and then overestimate his achievement, thus prematurely terminating his efforts to learn. He may, of course, be so highly motivated that he would be willing to spend more time than he needs in order to reach a specified criterion of mastery. Nevertheless, for the purposes of our conceptual model, it will be assumed that the learner will never actually spend more time than he needs to master the task as defined, that is, that he will stop learning as soon as he has mastered the learning task. (In this way we avoid, for the present, the necessity of incorporating a concept of "overlearning" in the model.)

This variable, which may be called *perseverance-in-learning-to-criterion,* is thus measured in terms of time, and if it is not sufficiently great to allow the learner to attain mastery, it operates in our conceptual model to reduce the degree of learning. Assume, as before, that learning proceeds as a linear function of time. Then if a child needs two hours to learn something, is allowed one hour, but will persevere only thirty minutes, the degree of learning is only 25 per cent. Perseverance-in-learning is measured only in terms of the amount of time the child is actively engaged in learning; a child who is actively engaged in learning for various periods totaling only thirty minutes during an hour is presumably not paying attention to learning for the other thirty minutes, and this time is not counted.

Perseverance-in-learning is itself a function of many other variables which will not be separately treated in this conceptual model. It is a function partly of what is ordinarily called "motivation" or desire to learn. But there are many reasons for desiring to learn a given thing: To please the teacher, to please one's parents or friends, to get good grades or other external rewards, to achieve self-confidence in one's learning ability, to feed one's self-esteem, to avoid disapproval—all these can operate *in place of* or *in addition to* any incentives for learning which may derive from the intrinsic interest or perceived utility of the thing being learned. And there are probably just as many reasons which one may adopt (consciously or unconsciously) for *not* learning: to avoid the responsibilities which learning brings, to avoid the exertion of learning, to behave consistently with one's image of oneself as a non-learner, or to avoid wasting time on learning tasks of no perceived importance.

Perseverance-in-learning may also be a function of what are ordinarily called emotional variables. One may desire to learn but be unable to endure frustrations caused by difficulties in the learning task or distractions from external circumstances. It may also interact with the quality of instruction; poor quality of instruction may reduce perseverance-in-learning even beyond the toll it takes in wasted minutes or even weeks.

The Complete Model

It will be noticed that the model involves five elements—three residing in the individual and two stemming from external conditions. Factors in the individual are (1) aptitude—the amount of time needed to learn the task under optimal instructional conditions, (2) ability to understand instruction, and (3) perseverance—the amount of time the learner is willing to engage actively in learning. Factors in external conditions are (4) opportunity—time allowed for learning, and (5) the quality of instruction—a measure of the degree to which instruction is presented so that it will not require additional time for mastery beyond that required in view of aptitude.

Three of the factors are expressed purely in terms of time. If ability to understand instruction corresponds to a combination of general and verbal intelligence, it can be assessed in relative terms by currently available measuring devices. The most elusive quantity in this model is that called *quality of instruction*, but both it and the ability to understand instruction are interconnected with temporally measurable variables in such a way that by appropriate experimental manipulations, they could eventually be indexed in terms of time. Temporarily, let us put quality of instruction on a scale from 0 (poor) to 1 (optimal), and ability to understand instruction on a standard score scale with mean=0 and $\sigma=1$.

The five factors can be worked into a tentative formula which expresses the degree of learning, for the ith individual and the tth task, as a function of the ratio of the amount of time the learner actually spends on the learning task to the total amount he needs. Thus:

$$Degree\ of\ learning = f\left(\frac{time\ actually\ spent}{time\ needed}\right)$$

The numerator of this fraction will be equal to the *smallest* of the following three quantities: (1) opportunity—the time allowed for learning, (2) perseverance—the amount of time the learner is willing to engage actively in learning, and (3) aptitude—the amount of time needed to learn, increased by whatever amount necessary in view of poor quality of instruction and lack of ability to understand less than optimal instruction. This last quantity (time needed to learn after adjustment for quality of instruction and ability to understand instruction) is also the denominator of the fraction. It is not necessary or worthwhile here, however, to pursue the detailed mathematical formulation, which has been given elsewhere (3).

As an illustration of the usefulness of this model in clarifying other educational concepts, let us see how it provides a framework for interpreting the notion of "underachievement" as criticized by Henry Dyer (4). While we are at it, let us also look at the notion of "overachievement." It is our contention that these terms are useful and salvageable if properly defined.

Underachievement and overachievement, like underweight and overweight, are ordinarily taken with reference to some norm or baseline of expectation. The underachiever does poorer than we expect him to, and the overachiever does better than we expect him to. The issue is this: Upon what do we base our expectation? The approved manner of doing this is to make predictions from those tests or other measurements which in fact yield the best predictions of success, and statistical theory tells us how to make best use of these predictors (*i.e.*, by making our predictions along a regression line). There is, however, a paradox here. Suppose our predictions were perfect: Then there would be no "underachievers" and no "overachievers." An unlikely eventuality to be sure! Nevertheless, our intuitive rejection of the case of perfect prediction lends credence to the following analysis of what we mean by "underachievement": Underachievement is a situation in which there is a discrepancy between actual achievement and that expected on the basis of a certain *kind* of evidence—evidence concerning the "capacity" or "aptitude" of the individual to achieve in a particular context. Such evidence is recognized as being quite distinct from evidence concerning other factors in achievement, *e.g.*, "motivation," "opportunity for learning," etc., and these latter factors would not figure in forming our expectations. Instead, we would hope to gather as much evidence as possible concerning the "capacity" or "aptitude" of the individual, defined as his learning rate when all other factors are optimal.

Achievement and Expectancy

With reference to the conceptual model presented earlier, our expectation of an individual's achievement in a given learning task would in the strictest sense be that which he would attain when he spends all the time he needs—that is, when the ratio of the time spent to the time needed is unity. Anything less than this is, to some degree, underachievement. From this point of view, *all* learners are underachievers unless they are superhuman beings in an ideal world. Perseverance sometimes flags; the quality of instruction is seldom optimal, and time allowed for learning is not always sufficient.

Let us, therefore, strike some sort of average for perseverance, instructional quality, and opportunity for learning. Our expectation of the degree of learning will be somewhat less than unity because, on the average, individuals will spend less time in learning than they need. And we may gauge underachievement and overachievement with reference to this expectation. In effect, this is what we do by the customary regression techniques based on aptitude measures, although in a less precise way than might be done if we were able to measure each of the components of achievement as stated by the model. In the framework of the model, however, underachievement is now seen to be a state of affairs which results whenever perseverance is less than some "reasonable value," whenever the quality of instruction is poor, whenever time allowed for learning has not been sufficient, or whenever some combination of these conditions has occurred. "Overachievement," contrariwise, may occur when there is an especially favorable combination of attendant events: high perseverance, instruction of high quality, or ample opportunity for learning.

We have a feeling about the relative amenability of different factors in achievement to manipulation or treatment: "Aptitude" is regarded as relatively resistant to change, whereas it is the hope of the psychologist that he can readily intervene to modify "perseverance," "quality of instruction," or "opportunity for learning." To some extent, this feeling is justified not only by logic but also by research findings—by the research on the apparent constancy of the IQ, on the effect of various instructional variables, etc. On the other hand, if aptitude is largely a matter of prior learnings, it may be more modifiable than we think, whereas, conversely, some kinds of clinical findings suggest that motivational characteristics of the individual may be much harder to change than one might think. These considerations, however, need not detract from the basic utility of the concepts of underachievement and overachievement. The concept of "underachievement" does not automatically imply the possibility of remediation any more than the concept of illness does. Some patients never get well, and some underachievers remain underachievers.

Babies and Bathwater

Henry Dyer (4) has drawn attention to possible dangers in the concept of underachievement—for example, the dangers of making predictions from unreliable or invalid predictors, of assuming that ability is innate or fixed, of making unwarranted inferences from school marks, and of overlooking determinants of school performance which are external to the pupil. Nevertheless, in suggesting that we kill the notion of underachievement, it would seem that he wants to throw out the proverbial baby with the bathwater. The concepts of underachievement and of overachievement are meaningful from both a statistical and a clinical point of view, as shown by the many fruitful studies of "underachieving" groups of students (e.g., 5). Careful attention to the elements of the conceptual model presented here will afford a safeguard against misuse of the concepts: Aptitude must be estimated by relevant and reliable measures (in actuality, all of them measures of past performance); the degree of learning must be accurately appraised, and the possible role of instructional variables must be considered. Above all, the variable which we have called *perseverance* must be validly assessed; the most direct evidence concerning it, our model would suggest, would come from observations of the amount of time the pupil actively engages in learning.

Before leaving this topic, let us consider another way in which the term "overachievement" is sometimes used. When a person is designated as an overachiever, it is often implied that his achievements derive more from his perseverance than from his aptitude or his intelligence. In terms of our model, this can occur when the learning task can be broken down into a series of subtasks of varying difficulty with difficulty roughly gauged in terms of average learning time. Because of his great perseverance, the overachiever masters to a criterion more of the *easy* tasks—tasks which are within the compass of his aptitude—than the student of average perseverance. While he may fail to learn some of the more difficult tasks, the net result may be a high score on an achievement test—a score considerably higher than predicted from aptitude measures. This concept of overachievement is distinctly different from the concept of overachievement suggested previously; responsible users of the term must clearly state which of these meanings they intend.

Future Research

Our conceptual model could lead, it would seem, to almost endless possibilities for research. It should provoke renewed effort to develop measures of each of the basic variables included in the model. The measurement of *aptitudes* is a fairly well advanced art, although the exact ways in which these aptitudes are relevant to school learning tasks remain to be worked out. The same remark may be made about the measurement of *ability to understand instruction.* But measurements of *perseverance* and of *instructional quality* are practically nonexistent. It should be intriguing to attempt to provide a general way of measuring *opportunity to learn,* that is, the actual time available to individual students to learn in view of the pacing of instruction; for it is our hypothesis that variations in the pacing of instruction have remained largely unrecognized in pedagogical discussions.

Research is also needed on the interactions of the several variables in the model. Is the model correctly put together? To what extent are the variables interdependent? For example, how does instructional quality affect perseverance? In what way is the degree of learning a function of the ratio of the amount of time spent in learning to the amount of time needed? Are we correct in postulating an interaction between instructional quality and ability to understand instruction such that pupils low in latter ability suffer most from poor instructional quality?

One of the most exciting possibilities suggested by the model is that of being able to state parameters for different types of learning by learners of varying characteristics under stated instructional conditions. Perhaps ultimately such parameters could be tied back to the data of pure learning theory. One of the bolder hypotheses implicit in the model is that the degree of learning, other things being equal, is a simple function of the amount of time during which the pupil engages actively in learning. Psychologists have paid little attention to this variable of pure time in human learning. A recent experiment by Bugelski (2) is one of the few to consider time factors in the field of paired-associated learning; and interestingly enough, it supports the hypothesis that more parsimonious descriptions of learning may be obtained by use of time as a variable rather than, say, number of trials.

What is important to emphasize is that this conceptual model probably contains, at least at a superordinate level, every element required to account for an individual's success or failure in school learning (at least in the learning tasks to which the model applies). The explication and refinement of these factors and the exploration of their interactions constitute a major task of educational psychology. Its other major task is to account for those types of school learning (*e.g.*, attitudinal and emotional conditioning) to which the present model is not intended to apply and for which a separate model might well be constructed.

References

1. Brandwein, P. F. *The gifted student as future scientist.* New York: Harcourt Brace, 1955.
2. Bugelski, B. R. Presentation time, total time, and mediation in paired-associate learning. *J. exper. Psychol.,* 1962, *63,* 409–412.
3. Carroll, J. B. The prediction of success in intensive language training. In Glaser, R. (Ed.) *Training research and education.* Pittsburgh: Univ. Pittsburgh Press, 1962. Pp. 87–136.
4. Dyer, H. S. A psychometrician views human ability. *Teach. Coll. Rec.,* 1960, *61,* 394–403.
5. Goldberg, Miriam, *et al.* A three-year experimental program at DeWitt Clinton High School to help bright underachievers. *High Points,* 1959, *41,* 5–35.
6. Skinner, B. F. *Science and human behavior.* New York: Macmillan, 1953.

23 NOTES ON A THEORY OF INSTRUCTION
Jerome S. Bruner

In this essay I shall attempt to develop a few simple theorems about the nature of instruction. I shall try to illustrate them by reference to the teaching and learning of mathematics. The choice of mathematics as a mode of illustration is not premised on the typicality of mathematics, for mathematics is restricted to well-formed problems and does not concern itself with empirical proof by either experiment or observation. Nor is this an attempt to elucidate mathematical teaching as such, for that would be beyond my competence. Rather, mathematics offers an accessible and simple example for what, perforce, will be a simplified set of

SOURCE: Jerome S. Bruner, *Toward a Theory of Instruction* (Cambridge: The Belknap Press of Harvard University Press, 1966), ch. 3, pp. 39–72. Copyright © 1966 by the President and Fellows of Harvard College. Reprinted by permission of the Harvard University Press.

propositions about teaching and learning. And there are data available from mathematics learning that have some bearing on our problem.

The plan is as follows. First some characteristics of a theory of instruction will be set forth, followed by a statement of some highly general theorems about the instructional process. I shall then attempt, in the light of specific observations of mathematics learning, to convert these general propositions into workable hypotheses. In conclusion, some remarks will be made on the nature of research in support of curriculum making.

The Nature of a Theory of Instruction

A theory of instruction is *prescriptive* in the sense that it sets forth rules concerning the most effective way of achieving knowledge or skill. By the same token, it provides a yardstick for criticizing or evaluating any particular way of teaching or learning.

A theory of instruction is a *normative* theory. It sets up criteria and states the conditions for meeting them. The criteria must have a high degree of generality: for example, a theory of instruction should not specify in *ad hoc* fashion the conditions for efficient learning of third-grade arithmetic; such conditions should be derivable from a more general view of mathematics learning.

One might ask why a theory of instruction is needed, since psychology already contains theories of learning and of development. But theories of learning and of development are descriptive rather than prescriptive. They tell us what happened after the fact: for example, that most children of six do not yet possess the notion of reversibility. A theory of instruction, on the other hand, might attempt to set forth the best means of leading the child toward the notion of reversibility. A theory of instruction, in short, is concerned with how what one wishes to teach can best be learned, with improving rather than describing learning.

This is not to say that learning and developmental theories are irrelevant to a theory of instruction. In fact, a theory of instruction must be concerned with both learning and development and must be congruent with those theories of learning and development to which it subscribes.

A theory of instruction has four major features.

First, a theory of instruction should specify the experiences which most effectively implant in the individual a predisposition toward learning—learning in general or a particular type of learning. For example, what sorts of relationships with people and things in the preschool environment will tend to make the child willing and able to learn when he enters school?

Second, a theory of instruction must specify the ways in which a body of knowledge should be structured so that it can be most readily grasped by the learner. "Optimal structure" refers to a set of propositions from which a larger body of knowledge can be generated, and it is characteristic that the formulation of such structure depends upon the state of advance of a particular field of knowledge. The nature of different optimal structures will be considered in more detail shortly. Here it suffices to say that since the merit of a structure depends upon its power for *simplifying information,* for *generating new propositions,* and for *increasing the manipulability of a body of knowledge,* structure must always be related to the status and gifts of the learner. Viewed in this way, the optimal structure of a body of knowledge is not absolute but relative.

Third, a theory of instruction should specify the most effective sequences in which to present the materials to be learned. Given, for example, that one wishes to teach the structure of modern physical theory, how does one proceed? Does one present concrete materials first in such a way as to elicit questions about recurrent regularities? Or does one begin with a formalized mathematical notation that makes it simpler to represent regularities later encountered? What results are in fact produced by each method? And how describe the ideal mix? The question of sequence will be treated in more detail later.

Finally, a theory of instruction should specify the nature and pacing of rewards and punishments in the process of learning and teaching. Intuitively it seems quite clear that as learning progresses there is a point at which it is better to shift away from extrinsic rewards, such as a teacher's praise, toward the intrinsic rewards inherent in solving a complex problem for oneself. So, too, there is a point at which immediate reward for performance should be replaced by deferred reward. The timing of the shift from extrinsic to intrinsic and from immediate to deferred reward is poorly understood and obviously important. Is it the case, for example, that wherever learning involves the integration of a long sequence of acts, the shift should be made as early as possible from immediate to deferred reward and from extrinsic to intrinsic reward?

It would be beyond the scope of a single essay to pursue in any detail all the four aspects of a theory of instruction set forth above. What I shall attempt to do here is to explore a major theorem concerning each of the four. The object is not comprehensiveness but illustration.

Predispositions

It has been customary, in discussing predispositions to learn, to focus upon cultural, motivational, and personal factors affecting the desire to learn and to undertake problem solving. For such factors are of deep importance. There is, for example, the relation of instructor to student —whatever the formal status of the instructor may be, whether teacher or parent. Since this is a relation between one who possesses something and one who does not, there is always a special problem of authority involved in the instructional situation. The regulation of this authority relationship affects the nature of the learning that occurs, the degree to which a learner develops an independent skill, the degree to which he is confident of his ability to perform on his own, and so on. The relations between one who instructs and one who is instructed is never indifferent in its effect upon learning. And since the instructional process is essentially social—particularly in its early stages when it involves at least a teacher and a pupil—it is clear that the child, especially if he is to cope with school, must have minimal mastery of the social skills necessary for engaging in the instructional process.

There are differing attitudes toward intellectual activity in different social classes, the two sexes, different age groups, and different ethnic groupings. These culturally transmitted attitudes also pattern the use of mind. Some cultural traditions are, by count, more successful than others in the production of scientists, scholars, and artists. Anthropology and psychology investigate the ways a "tradition" or "role" affects attitudes toward the use of mind. A theory of instruction concerns itself, rather, with the issue of how best to utilize a given cultural pattern in achieving particular instructional ends.

Indeed, such factors are of enormous importance. But we shall concentrate here on a more cognitive illustration: upon the predisposition to explore alternatives.

Since learning and problem solving depend upon the exploration of alternatives, instruction must facilitate and regulate the exploration of alternatives on the part of the learner.

There are three aspects to the exploration of alternatives, each of them related to the regulation of search behavior. They can be described in shorthand terms as *activation, maintenance,* and *direction.* To put it another way, exploration of alternatives requires something to get it started, something to keep it going, and something to keep it from being random.

The major condition for activating exploration of alternatives in a task is the presence of some optimal level of uncertainty. Curiosity, it has been persuasively argued,[1] is a response to uncertainty and ambiguity. A cut-and-dried routine task provokes little exploration; one that is too uncertain may arouse confusion and anxiety, with the effect of reducing exploration.

The maintenance of exploration, once it has been activated, requires

[1] D. E. Berlyne, *Conflict, Arousal, and Curiosity* (New York: McGraw-Hill, 1960).

that the benefits from exploring alternatives exceed the risks incurred. Learning something with the aid of an instructor should, if instruction is effective, be less dangerous or risky or painful than learning on one's own. That is to say, the consequences of error, of exploring wrong alternatives, should be rendered less grave under a regimen of instruction, and the yield from the exploration of correct alternatives should be correspondingly greater.

The appropriate direction of exploration depends upon two interacting considerations: a sense of the goal of a task and a knowledge of the relevance of tested alternatives to the achievement of that goal. For exploration to have direction, in short, the goal of the task must be known in some approximate fashion, and the testing of alternatives must yield information as to where one stands with respect to it. Put in briefest form, direction depends upon knowledge of the results of one's tests, and instruction should have an edge over "spontaneous" learning in providing more of such knowledge.

Structure and the Form of Knowledge

Any idea or problem or body of knowledge can be presented in a form simple enough so that any particular learner can understand it in a recognizable form.

The structure of any domain of knowledge may be characterized in three ways, each affecting the ability of any learner to master it: the *mode of representation* in which it is put, its *economy,* and its effective *power.* Mode, economy, and power vary in relation to different ages, to different "styles" among learners, and to different subject matters.

Any domain of knowledge (or any problem within that domain of knowledge) can be represented in three ways: by a set of actions appropriate for achieving a certain result (enactive representation); by a set of summary images or graphics that stand for a concept without defining it fully (iconic representation); and by a set of symbolic or logical propositions drawn from a symbolic system that is governed by rules or laws for forming and transforming propositions (symbolic representation). The distinction can most conveniently be made concretely in terms of a balance beam, for we shall have occasion later to consider the use of such an implement in teaching children quadratic functions. A quite young child can plainly act on the basis of the "principles" of a balance beam, and indicates that he can do so by being able to handle himself on a see-saw. He knows that to get his side to go down farther he has to move out farther from the center. A somewhat older child can represent the balance beam to himself either by a model on which rings can be hung and balanced or by a drawing. The "image" of the balance beam can be varyingly refined, with fewer and fewer irrelevant details present, as in the typical diagrams in an introductory textbook in physics. Finally, a balance beam can be described in ordinary English, without diagrammatic aids, or it can be even better described mathematically by reference to Newton's Law of Moments in inertial physics. Needless to say, actions, pictures, and symbols vary in difficulty and utility for people of different ages, different backgrounds, different styles. Moreover, a problem in the law would be hard to diagram; one in geography lends itself to imagery. Many subjects, such as mathematics, have alternative modes of representation.

Economy in representing a domain of knowledge relates to the amount of information that must be held in mind and processed to achieve comprehension. The more items of information one must carry to understand something or deal with a problem, the more successive steps one must take in processing that information to achieve a conclusion, and the less the economy. For any domain of knowledge, one can rank summaries of it in terms of their economy. It is more economical (though less powerful) to summarize the American Civil War as a "battle over slavery" than as "a struggle between an expanding industrial region and one built upon a class society for control of federal economic policy." It is more economical to summarize the characteristics of free-falling bodies by the formula $S = \frac{1}{2}gt^2$ than to put a series of numbers into tabular form summarizing a vast set of observations made on different bodies dropped different distances in different gravitational fields. The matter is perhaps best epitomized by two ways of imparting information, one requiring carriage of much information, the other more a pay-as-you-go type of information processing. A highly imbedded sentence is an example of the former (This is the squirrel that the dog that the girl that the man loved fed chased); the contrast case is more economical (This is the man that loved the girl that fed the dog that chased the squirrel).

Economy, as we shall see, varies with mode of representation. But economy is also a function of the sequence in which material is presented or the manner in which it is learned. The case can be exemplified as follows (I am indebted to Dr. J. Richard Hayes for this example). Suppose the domain of knowledge consists of available plane service within a twelve-hour period between five cities in the Northeast—Concord, New Hampshire, Albany, New York, Danbury, Connecticut, Elmira, New York, and Boston, Massachusetts. One of the ways in which the knowledge can be imparted is by asking the student to memorize the following list of connections:

> Boston to Concord
> Danbury to Concord

Albany to Boston
Concord to Elmira
Albany to Elmira
Concord to Danbury
Boston to Albany
Concord to Albany

Now we ask "What is the shortest way to make a round trip from Albany to Danbury?" The amount of information processing required to answer this question under such conditions is considerable. We increase economy by "simplifying terms" in certain characteristic ways. One is to introduce an arbitrary but learned order—in this case, an alphabetical one. We rewrite the list:

Albany to Boston
Albany to Elmira
Boston to Albany
Boston to Concord
Concord to Albany
Concord to Danbury
Concord to Elmira
Danbury to Concord

Search then becomes easier, but there is still a somewhat trying sequential property to the task. Economy is further increased by using a diagrammatic notation, and again there are varying degrees of economy in such recourse to the iconic mode. Compare the diagram on the left and the one on the right.

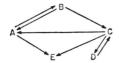 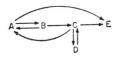

The latter contains at a glance the information that there is only one way from Albany to Danbury and return, that Elmira is a "trap," and so on. What a difference between this diagram and the first list!

The effective power of any particular way of structuring a domain of knowledge for a particular learner refers to the generative value of *his* set of learned propositions. In the last paragraph, rote learning of a set of connections between cities resulted in a rather inert structure from which it was difficult to generate pathways through the set of cities. Or, to take an example from a recent work,[2] children who are told that

[2] Margaret Donaldson, *A Study of Children's Thinking* (London: Tavistock Publications, 1963).

"Mary is taller than Jane, and Betty is shorter than Jane" are often unable to say whether Mary is taller than Betty. One can perfectly well remark that the answer is "there" in the logic of transitivity. But to say this is to miss the psychological point. Effective power will, to be sure, never exceed the inherent logical generativeness of a subject—although this is an admittedly difficult statement from the point of view of epistemology. In commonsense terms, it amounts to the banality that grasp of a field of knowledge will never be better than the best that can be done with that field of knowledge. The effective power within a particular learner's grasp is what one seeks to discover by close analysis of how in fact he is going about his task of learning. Much of Piaget's research [3] seeks to discover just this property about children's learning and thinking. There is an interesting relation between economy and power. Theoretically, the two are independent: indeed, it is clear that a structure may be economical but powerless. But it is rare for a powerful structuring technique in any field to be uneconomical. This is what leads to the canon of parsimony and the faith shared by many scientists that nature is simple: perhaps it is only when nature can be made reasonably simple that it can be understood. The power of a representation can also be described as its capacity, in the hands of a learner, to connect matters that, on the surface, seem quite separate. This is especially crucial in mathematics, and we shall return to the matter later.

Sequence and Its Uses

Instruction consists of leading the learner through a sequence of statements and restatements of a problem or body of knowledge that increase the learner's ability to grasp, transform, and transfer what he is learning. In short, the sequence in which a learner encounters materials within a domain of knowledge affects the difficulty he will have in achieving mastery.

There are usually various sequences that are equivalent in their ease and difficulty for learners. There is no unique sequence for all learners, and the optimum in any particular case will depend upon a variety of factors, including past learning, stage of development, nature of the material, and individual differences.

If it is true that the usual course of intellectual development moves from enactive through iconic to symbolic representation of the world,[4] it is likely that an optimum sequence will progress in the same direction.

[3] Jean Piaget, *The Child's Conception of Number* (New York: Humanities Press, 1952).

[4] Jerome S. Bruner, "The Course of Cognitive Growth," *American Psychologist*, 19: 1–15 (January 1964).

Obviously, this is a conservative doctrine. For when the learner has a well-developed symbolic system, it may be possible to by-pass the first two stages. But one does so with the risk that the learner may not possess the imagery to fall back on when his symbolic transformations fail to achieve a goal in problem solving.

Exploration of alternatives will necessarily be affected by the sequence in which material to be learned becomes available to the learner. When the learner should be encouraged to explore alternatives widely and when he should be encouraged to concentrate on the implications of a single alternative hypothesis is an empirical question, to which we shall return.

Reverting to the earlier discussion of activation and the maintenance of interest, it is necessary to specify in any sequences the level of uncertainty and tension that must be present to initiate problem-solving behavior, and what conditions are required to keep active problem solving going. This again is an empirical question.

Optimal sequences, as already stated, cannot be specified independently of the criterion in terms of which final learning is to be judged. A classification of such criteria will include at least the following: speed of learning; resistance to forgetting; transferability of what has been learned to new instances; form of representation in terms of which what has been learned is to be expressed; economy of what has been learned in terms of cognitive strain imposed; effective power of what has been learned in terms of its generativeness of new hypotheses and combinations. Achieving one of these goals does not necessarily bring one closer to others; speed of learning, for example, is sometimes antithetical to transfer or to economy.

The Form and Pacing of Reinforcement

Learning depends upon knowledge of results at a time when and at a place where the knowledge can be used for correction. Instruction increases the appropriate timing and placing of corrective knowledge.

"Knowledge of results" is useful or not depending upon when and where the learner receives the corrective information, under what conditions such corrective information can be used, even assuming appropriateness of time and place of receipt, and the form in which the corrective information is received.

Learning and problem solving are divisible into phases. These have been described in various ways by different writers. But all the descriptions agree on one essential feature: that there is a cycle involving the formulation of a testing procedure or trial, the operation of this testing procedure, and the comparison of the results of the test with some criterion. It has variously been called trial-and-error, means-end testing, trial-and-check, discrepancy reduction, test-operate-test-exit (TOTE), hypothesis testing, and so on. These "units," moreover, can readily be characterized as hierarchically organized: we seek to cancel the unknowns in an equation in order to simplify the expression in order to solve the equation in order to get through the course in order to get our degree in order to get a decent job in order to lead the good life. Knowledge of results should come at that point in a problem-solving episode when the person is comparing the results of his try-out with some criterion of what he seeks to achieve. Knowledge of results given before this point either cannot be understood or must be carried as extra freight in immediate memory. Knowledge given after this point may be too late to guide the choice of a next hypothesis or trial. But knowledge of results must, to be useful, provide information not only on whether or not one's particular act produced success but also on whether the act is in fact leading one through the hierarchy of goals one is seeking to achieve. This is not to say that when we cancel the term in that equation we need to know whether it will all lead eventually to the good life. Yet there should at least be some "lead notice" available as to whether or not cancelation is on the right general track. It is here that the tutor has a special role. For most learning starts off rather piecemeal without the integration of component acts or elements. Usually the learner can tell whether a particular cycle of activity has worked—feedback from specific events is fairly simple—but often he cannot tell whether this completed cycle is leading to the eventual goal. It is interesting that one of the nonrigorous short cuts to problem solution, basic rules of "heuristic," stated in Polya's noted book [5] has to do with defining the overall problem. To sum up, then, instruction uniquely provides information to the learner about the higher-order relevance of his efforts. In time, to be sure, the learner must develop techniques for obtaining such higher-order corrective information on his own, for instruction and its aids must eventually come to an end. And, finally, if the problem solver is to take over this function, it is necessary for him to learn to recognize when he does not comprehend and, as Roger Brown [6] has suggested, to signal incomprehension to the tutor so that he can be helped. In time, the signaling of incomprehension becomes a self-signaling and equivalent to a temporary stop order.

The ability of problem solvers to use information correctively is known to vary as a function of their internal state. One state in which information is least useful is that of strong drive and anxiety. There is a sufficient body of research to establish this point beyond reasonable

[5] Gyorgy Polya, *How To Solve It,* 2nd ed. (New York: Doubleday, 1957).

[6] Roger Brown, *Social Psychology* (New York: Free Press of Glencoe, 1965), chapter 7, "From Codability to Coding Ability."

doubt.[7] Another such state has been referred to as "functional fixedness" —a problem solver is, in effect, using corrective information exclusively for the evaluation of one single hypothesis that happens to be wrong. The usual example is treating an object in terms of its conventional significance when it must be treated in a new context—we fail to use a hammer as a bob for a pendulum because it is "fixed" in our thinking as a hammer. Numerous studies point to the fact that during such a period there is a remarkable intractability or even incorrigibility to problem solving. There is some evidence to indicate that high drive and anxiety lead one to be more prone to functional fixedness. It is obvious that corrective information of the usual type, straight feedback, is least useful during such states, and that an adequate instructional strategy aims at terminating the interfering state by special means before continuing with the usual provision of correction. In such cases, instruction verges on a kind of therapy, and it is perhaps because of this therapeutic need that one often finds therapylike advice in lists of aids for problem solvers, like the suggestion of George Humphrey [8] that one turn away from the problem when it is proving too difficult.

If information is to be used effectively, it must be translated into the learner's way of attempting to solve a problem. If such translatability is not present, then the information is simply useless. Telling a neophyte skier to "shift to his uphill edges" when he cannot distinguish which edges he is traveling on provides no help, whereas simply telling him to lean into the hill may succeed. Or, in the cognitive sphere, there is by now an impressive body of evidence that indicates that "negative information"—information about what something is *not*—is peculiarly unhelpful to a person seeking to master a concept. Though it is logically usable, it is psychologically useless. Translatability of corrective information can in principle also be applied to the form of representation and its economy. If learning or problem solving is proceeding in one mode—enactive, iconic or symbolic—corrective information must be provided either in the same mode or in one that translates into it. Corrective information that exceeds the information-processing capacities of a learner is obviously wasteful.

Finally, it is necessary to reiterate one general point already made in passing. Instruction is a provisional state that has as its object to make the learner or problem solver self-sufficient. Any regimen of correction carries the danger that the learner may become permanently dependent upon the tutor's correction. The tutor must correct the learner in a fash-

[7] For full documentation, see Jerome S. Bruner, "Some Theorems on Instruction Illustrated with Reference to Mathematics," *Sixty-third Yearbook of the National Society for the Study of Education*, Part I (Chicago: University of Chicago Press, 1964), pp. 306–335.
[8] George Humphrey, *Directed Thinking* (New York: Dodd, Mead, 1948).

ion that eventually makes it possible for the learner to take over the corrective function himself. Otherwise the result of instruction is to create a form of mastery that is contingent upon the perpetual presence of a teacher.

Selected Illustrations from Mathematics

Before turning to the task of illustrating some of the points raised, a word is in order about what is intended by such illustration. During the last decade much work has gone into the mathematics curriculum. One need only mention the curriculum projects that are better known to appreciate the magnitude of the effort—the School Mathematics Study Group, the University of Illinois Committee on School Mathematics, the several projects of Educational Services Incorporated, the Madison Project, the African Mathematics Project, the University of Maryland Mathematics Project, the University of Illinois Arithmetic Project, and the Stanford Project. From this activity, it would be possible to choose illustrations for many purposes. Illustration in such a context in no sense constitutes evidence.

For the fact of the matter is that the evidence available on factors affecting the learning of mathematics is still very sparse. Research on the instructional process—in mathematics as in all disciplines—has not been carried out in connection with the building of curricula. As noted, psychologists have come upon the scene, armed with evaluative devices, only after a curriculum has already been put into operation. Surely it would be more efficient and more useful if embryonic instructional materials could be tried out under experimental conditions so that revision and correction could be based upon immediate knowledge of results.

By means of systematic observational studies—work close in spirit to that of Piaget and of ethologists like Tinbergen [9]—investigators could obtain information sufficiently detailed to allow them to discern how the student grasps what has been presented, what his systematic errors are, and how these are overcome. Insofar as one is able to formalize, in terms of a theory of learning or concept attainment, the nature of the systematic errors and the strategies of correction employed, one is thereby enabled to vary systematically the conditions that may be affecting learning and to build these factors directly into one's curriculum practice. Nor need such studies remain purely observational. Often it is possible to build one's mathematics materials into a programmed form and obtain a detailed behavioral record for analysis.

To make clear what is intended by a detailed analysis of the process

[9] Nikolaas Tinbergen, *Social Behavior in Animals* (New York: John Wiley & Sons, 1953).

of learning, an example from the work of Patrick Suppes[10] will be helpful. He has observed, for example, that the form $3+x=8$ is easier for children to deal with than the form $x+3=8$, and while the finding may on the surface seem trivial, closer inspection shows that it is not. Does the difficulty come in dealing with an unknown at the beginning of an expression or from the transfer of linguistic habits from ordinary English, where sentences are easier to complete when a term is deleted from the middle than from beginning of the sentence? The issue of where uncertainty can best be tolerated and the issue of the possible interference between linguistic habits and mathematical habits are certainly worthy of careful and detailed study.

Let me turn now to some illustrations from mathematics that have the effect of pointing up problems raised in the theorems and hypotheses earlier presented. They are not evidence of anything, only ways of locating what might be worth closer study.[11]

Rather than presenting observations drawn from different contexts, I shall confine the discussion to one particular study carried out on a small group of children.[12] The observations to be reported were made on four eight-year-old children, two boys and two girls, who were given an hour of daily instruction in mathematics four times a week for six weeks. The children were in the IQ range of 120–130, and they were all enrolled in the third grade of a private school that emphasized instruction designed to foster independent problem solving. They were all from middle-class professional homes. The "teacher" of the class was a well-known research mathematician (Z. P. Dienes), his assistant a professor of psychology at Harvard who has worked long and hard on human thought processes.

Each child worked at a corner table in a generous-sized room. Next to each child sat a tutor-observer, trained in psychology and with sufficient background in college mathematics to understand the underlying mathe-

[10] Patrick Suppes, "Towards a Behavioral Psychology of Mathematics Thinking," in J. Bruner, ed., *Learning about Learning*, U.S. Office of Education monograph, in press.

[11] For a closer discussion of some of the observations mentioned in what follows, the reader is referred to Bruner, "The Course of Cognitive Growth," and to Jerome S. Bruner and Helen Kenney, "Representation and Mathematic Learning," in L. Morrisett and J. Vinsonhaler, eds., *Mathematical Learning*, Monographs of the Society for Research in Child Development, 30 (University of Chicago Press, 1965), pp. 50–59. The general "bias" on which these observations are based is contained in Jerome S. Bruner, *The Process of Education* (Cambridge: Harvard University Press, 1960), and in J. S. Bruner, J. J. Goodnow, and G. A. Austin, *A Study of Thinking* (New York: John Wiley & Sons, 1956).

[12] I am grateful to Z. P. Dienes, Samuel Anderson, Eleanor Duckworth, and Joan Rigney Hornsby for their help in designing and carrying out this study. Dr. Dienes particularly formed our thinking about the mode of presenting the mathematical materials.

matics being taught. In the middle of the room was a large table with a supply of blocks and balance beams and cups and beans and chalk that served as instructional aids. In the course of the six weeks, the children were given instruction in factoring, in the distributive and commutative properties of addition and multiplication, and finally in quadratic functions.

Each child had available a series of graded problem cards which he could go through at his own pace. The cards gave directions for different kinds of exercises, using the materials mentioned above. The instructor and his assistant circulated from table to table helping as needed, and each tutor-observer similarly assisted as needed. The problem sequences were designed to provide, first, an appreciation of mathematical ideas through concrete constructions involving materials of various kinds. From such constructions, the child was encouraged to form perceptual images of the mathematical idea in terms of the forms that had been constructed. The child was then further encouraged to develop or adopt a notation for describing his construction. After such a cycle, a child moved on to the construction of a further embodiment of the idea on which he was working, one that was mathematically isomorphic with what he had learned, though expressed in different materials and with altered appearance. When such a new topic was introduced, the children were given a chance to discover its connection with what had gone before and shown how to extend the notational system used before. Careful minute-by-minute records were kept of the proceedings, along with photographs of the children's constructions.

In no sense can the children, the teachers, the classroom, or the mathematics be said to be typical of what occurs in third grade. Four children rarely have six teachers, nor do eight-year-olds ordinarily get into quadratic functions. But our concern is with the processes involved in mathematical learning, and not with typicality. It seems quite reasonable to suppose that the thought processes that were going on in the children are quite ordinary among eight-year-old human beings.

Activating Problem Solving

One of the first tasks faced in this study was to gain and hold the child's interest and to lead him to problem-solving activity. At the same time, there was a specific objective to be achieved—to teach the children factoring in such a way that they would have this component skill in an accessible form to use in the solution of problems. It is impossible to say on the basis of our experience whether the method we employed was the best one, but in any case it appeared to work.

A considerable part of the job of activation had already been done before ever we saw the children. They had working models of exploratory adults in their teachers and their parents. They had no particular resistance to trying out and rejecting hypotheses. The principal problem we faced as teachers who outnumbered the students was to keep the children from converting the task into one where they would become dependent upon us. All of us had had the experience of working with children from less intellectually stimulating backgrounds where there had been less emphasis upon intellectual autonomy, and the contrast was appreciable. Indeed, I can only repeat that where predisposition to learning was concerned, the children in the study were almost specifically trained for the kind of approach we were about to use—an approach with strong emphasis on independence, on self-pacing, on reflectiveness. Had we used a more authoritarian, more mnemonic approach with our group, we would have had to prepare the ground. As it was, the task had already been well begun.

The first learning task introduced was one having to do with the different ways in which a set of cubic blocks could be arranged as "flats" (laid out in rectangular forms on the table, not more than one cube high) and in "walls" and "buildings." The problem has an interesting uncertainty to it, and the children were challenged to determine whether they had exhausted all the possible ways of laying things out. Unquestionably they picked up some zest from the evident curiosity of their teachers as well. After a certain amount of time, the children were encouraged to start keeping a written record of the different shapes they could make, and what their dimensions were. Certain numbers of cubes proved intractable to re-forming (the primes, of course), and others proved combinable in interesting ways—three rows of three cubes made nine, three layers of these nine "flats" had the dimensions of 3 x 3 x 3, and so on. The idea of factoring was soon grasped, and with very little guidance the children went on to interesting conjectures about distributiveness. The task had its own direction built into it in the sense that it had a clear terminus: how arrange a set of cubes in regular two- or three-dimensional forms? It also had the added feature that the idea of alternatives was built in: what are the different ways of achieving such regularity? As the children gained in skill, they shifted to other ways of laying out cubes—in pyramids, in triangles where the cubes were treated as "diamonds," and so on. At this stage of the game, it was necessary to judge in each case whether the child should be let alone to discover on his own.

We shall see, when we come to discuss the balance beam, that the idea of factoring was further deepened by being applied to a "new" problem. I mention the point here because it relates to the importance of *maintaining* a problem-solving set that runs in a continuous direction. It is often the case that novelty must be introduced in order that the enterprise be continued. In the case of the balance beam, the task was to discover the different combinations of rings that could be put on one side of the balance beam to balance a single ring placed on hook 9. In effect, this is the same problem as asking the different ways in which nine blocks can be arranged. But it is in a different guise, and the new embodiment seems capable of stimulating interest even though it is isomorphic with something else that has been explored to the border of satiety.

Structure and Sequence

We can best illustrate the points made at the outset by reference to our teaching of quadratic equations to the four children we studied. Each child was provided with building materials. These were large flat squares made of wood whose dimensions were unspecified and described simply as "unknown, or x long and x wide." There were also a large number of strips of wood that were as long as the sides of the square and were described arbitrarily as having a width of "1" or simply as "1 by x." And there was a supply of little squares with sides equal to the width "1" of the strips, thus "1 by 1." The reader should be warned that the presentation of these materials is not as simple as all that. To begin with, it is necessary to convince the children that we really do not know and do not *care* what the metric size of the big square is, that rulers are of no interest. A certain humor helps establish in the pupils a proper contempt for measuring in this context, and the snob appeal of simply calling an unknown by the name "x" is very great. From there on, the children readily discover for themselves that the long strips are x long—by correspondence. They take on faith (as they should) that the narrow dimension is "1," but that they grasp its arbitrariness is clear from one child's declaration of the number of such "1" widths that made an x. As for "1 by 1" little squares, that too is established by simple correspondence with the narrow dimension of the "1 by x" strips. It is horseback method, but quite good mathematics.

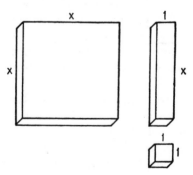

The child is asked whether he can make a square bigger than the x by x square, using the materials at hand. He very quickly builds squares with designs like those illustrated below. We ask him to record how much wood is needed for each larger square and how long and wide each square is.

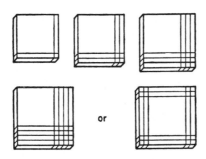

or

He describes one of his constructed squares: very concretely the pieces are counted out: "an x-square, two x-strips, and a one square," or "an x-square, four x-strips, and four ones," or "an x-square, six x-strips and nine ones," and so forth. We help him with language and show him a way to write it down. The big square is an "$x^\square$," the long strips are "$1x$" or simply "x," and the little squares are "one squares" or "one by one" or, better still, simply "1." And the expression "and" can be shortened to $+$. And so he can write out the recipe for a constructed square as $x^\square + 4x + 4$. At this stage, these are merely names put together in little sentences. How wide and long is the square in question? This the child can readily measure off—an x and 2, or $x+2$, and so the whole thing is $(x+2)^\square$. Brackets are not so easily grasped. But soon the child is able to put down his first equality: $(x+2)^\square = x^\square + 4x + 4$. Virtually everything has a referent that can be pointed to with a finger. He has a notational system into which he can translate the image he has constructed.

Now we go on to making bigger squares, and each square the child makes he is to describe in terms of what wood went into it and how wide and how long it is. It takes some ruled sheets to get the child to keep his record so that he can go back and inspect it for what it may reveal, and he is encouraged to go back and look at the record and at the constructions they stand for.

Imagine now a list such as the following, again a product of the child's own constructing:

$$x^\square + 2x + 1 \text{ is } x+1 \text{ by } x+1$$
$$x^\square + 4x + 4 \text{ is } x+2 \text{ by } x+2$$
$$x^\square + 6x + 9 \text{ is } x+3 \text{ by } x+3$$
$$x^\square + 8x + 16 \text{ is } x+4 \text{ by } x+4$$

It is almost impossible for him not to make some discoveries about the numbers: that the x values go up 2, 4, 6, 8, and the units values go up 1, 4, 9, 16, and the dimensions increase by additions to x of 1, 2, 3, 4. The syntactical insights about regularity in notation are matched by perceptual-manipulative insights about the material referents.

After a while, some new manipulations occur that provide the child with a further basis for notational progress. He takes the square $(x+2)^2$ and reconstructs it in a new way. One may ask whether this is constructive manipulation, and whether it is proper factoring. But the child is learning that the same amount of wood can build quite strikingly different patterns and remain the same amount of wood—even though it also has a different notational expression. Where does the language begin and the manipulation of materials stop? The interplay is continuous. We shall return to this same example later.

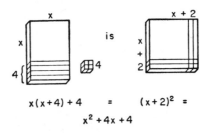

$$x(x+4) + 4 \quad = \quad (x+2)^2 \; =$$
$$x^2 + 4x + 4$$

What is now a problem is how to "detach" the notation that the child has learned from the concrete, visible, manipulable embodiment to which it refers—the wood. For if the child is to deal with mathematical properties he will have to deal with symbols per se, else he will be limited to the narrow and rather trivial range of symbolism that can be given direct (and only partial) visual embodiment. Concepts such as x^2 and x^3 may be given a visualizable referent, but what of x^n?

How do children wean themselves from the perceptual embodiment to the symbolic notation? Perhaps it is partly explained in the nature of variation and contrast.

The child is shown the balance beam again and told: "Choose any hook on one side and put the same number of rings on it as the number the hook is away from the middle. Now balance it with rings placed on the other side. Keep a record." Recall that the balance beam is familiar from work on factoring and that the child knows that 2 rings on 9 balances 9 on 2 or m rings on n balances n on m. He is back to construction. Can anything be constructed on the balance beam that is like the squares? With little effort, the following translation is made. Suppose x is 5. Then 5 rings on hook 5 is x^2, 5 rings on hook 4 is $4x$, and 4 rings on hook 1 is 4: x^2+4x+4. How can we find whether this is like a square that is $x+2$ wide by $x+2$ long, as before? Well, if x is 5, then $x+2$ is 7, and so 7 rings on hook 7. And nature obliges—the beam balances. One notation works for two strikingly different constructions and perceptual events. Notation, with its broader equivalency, is clearly more economical than reference to embodiments. There is little resistance to using this more convenient language. And now construction can begin—commutative and distributive properties of equations can be explored: $x(x+4)+4=x^2+4x+4$, so that $x+4$ rings on hook x plus 4 rings on hook 1 will also balance. The child if he wishes can also go back to the wood and find that the same materials can make the designs illustrated earlier.

Contrast is the vehicle by which the obvious that is too obvious to be appreciated can be made noticeable again. A discovery by an eight-year-old girl illustrates the matter. "Yes, 4×6 equals 6×4 in numbers, like in one way six eskimos in each of four igloos is the same as four in

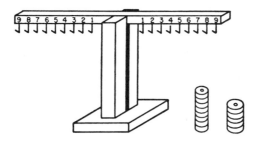

each of six igloos. But a venetian blind *isn't* the same as a blind Venetian." By recognizing the noncommutative property of much of our ordinary language, the commutative property of a mathematical language can be partly grasped. But it is still only a partial insight into commutativity and noncommutativity. Had we wished to develop the distinction more deeply we might have proceeded concretely to a contrast between sets of operations that can be carried out in any sequence—like the order in which letters are put in a post box or in which we see different movies—and operations that have a noncommutative order—like putting on shoes and socks—where one must precede the other. The child could be taken from there to a more general idea of commutative and noncommutative cases and to ways of dealing with a notation for them, perhaps by identical sets and ordered identical sets.

We need not reiterate what must be obvious from this sequence. The object was to begin with an enactive representation of quadratics—something that could literally be "done" or built—and to move from there to an iconic representation, however restricted. Along the way, notation was developed and, by the use of variation and contrast, converted into a properly symbolic system. Again, the object was to start with as economical a representation as possible and to increase complexity only when there was some way for the child to relate the complex instance to something simpler that had gone before.

What was so striking in the performance of the children was their initial inability to represent things to themselves in a way that transcended immediate perceptual grasp. The achievement of more comprehensive insight requires, we think, the building of a mediating representational structure that transcends such immediate imagery, that renders a sequence of acts and images unitary and simultaneous. The children always began by constructing an embodiment of some concept, building a concrete model for purposes of operational definition. The fruit of the construction was an image and some operations that "stood for" the concept. From there on, the task was to provide means of representation that were free of particular manipulations and specific images. Only symbolic operations provide the means of representing an idea in this way. But consider this matter for a moment.

We have already remarked that by giving the child multiple embodiments of the same general idea expressed in a common notation we lead him to "empty" the concept of specific sensory properties until he is able to grasp its abstract properties. But surely this is not the best way of describing the child's increasing development of insight. The growth of such abstractions is important. But what struck us about the children as we observed them is that they not only understood the abstractions they had learned but also had a store of concrete images that served to exemplify the abstractions. When they searched for a way to deal with new problems, the task was usually carried out not simply by abstract means but also by "matching up" images. An example will help here. In going from the woodblocks embodiment of the quadratic to the balance-beam embodiment, it was interesting that the children would "equate" concrete features of one with concrete features of another. One side of the balance beam "stood for" the amount of wood, the other side for the sides of the square. These were important concrete props on which they leaned. We have been told by research mathematicians that the same use of props—heuristics—holds for them, that they have preferred ways of imaging certain problems while other problems are handled silently or in terms of an imagery of the symbolism on a page.

We reached the tentative conclusion that it was probably necessary for a child, learning mathematics, to have not only a firm sense of the abstraction underlying what he was working on, but also a good stock of visual images for embodying them. For without the latter it is difficult to track correspondences and to check what one is doing symbolically. We had occasion, again with the help of Dr. Dienes, to teach a group of ten nine-year-olds the elements of group theory. To embody the idea of a mathematical group initially, we gave them the example of a four-group made up of the following four maneuvers. A book was the vehicle, a

book with an arrow up the middle of its front cover. The four maneuvers were rotating the book a quarter turn to the left, rotating it a quarter turn to the right, rotating it a half turn (without regard to direction
of rotation), and letting it stay in the position it was in. They were
quick to grasp the important property of such a mathematical group:
that any sequence of maneuvers made could be reproduced from the
starting position by a single move. This is not the usual way in which
this property is described mathematically, but it served well for the children. We contrasted this elegant property with a series of our moves
that did *not* constitute a mathematical group—indeed, they provided
the counter example themselves by proposing a one-third turn left, one-
third turn right, half turn either way, and stay. It was soon apparent
that it did not work. We set the children the task of making games of
four maneuvers, six maneuvers, and so on, that had the property of a
"closed" game, as we call it—one in which the result of any combination
of moves can be achieved by a single move. They were, of course, highly
ingenious. But what soon became apparent was that they needed some
aid in imagery—in this case an imagery notation—that would allow
them to keep track and then to discover whether some new game was
an isomorph of one they had already developed. The prop in this case
was, of course, the matrix, listing the moves possible across the top and
then listing them down the side, thus making it easily possible to check
whether each combination of pairs of moves could be reproduced by a
single move. The matrix in this case is a crutch or heuristic and as such
has nothing to do with the abstraction of the mathematical group, yet it
was enormously useful to them not only for keeping track but also for
comparing one group with another for correspondence. The matrix with
which they started looked like this:

	s	a	b	c	
	s	a	b	c	s = stay
s	s	a	b	c	a = quarter-turn left
a	a	c	s	b	b = quarter-turn right
b	b	s	c	a	c = half-turn
c	c	b	a	s	

Are there any four-groups with a different structure? It is extremely difficult to deal with such a question without the aid of this housekeeping
matrix as a vehicle for spotting correspondence. What about a game in
which a cube can be left where it is, rotated 180° on its vertical axis, rotated 180° on its horizontal axis, and rotated 180° on each of its four
cubic diagonals? Is it a group? Can it be simplified to a smaller number
of maneuvers? Does it contain the group described above?

In sum, then, while the development of insight into mathematics in
our group of children depended upon their development of "example-

free" abstractions, this did not lead them to give up their imagery. Quite to the contrary, we had the impression that their enriched imagery was very useful to them in dealing with new problems.

We would suggest that learning mathematics reflects a good deal about intellectual development. It begins with instrumental activity, a kind of definition of things by doing them. Such operations become represented and summarized in the form of particular images. Finally, and with the help of a symbolic notation that remains invariant across transformations in imagery, the learner comes to grasp the formal or abstract properties of the things he is dealing with. But while, once abstraction is achieved, the learner becomes free in a certain measure of the surface appearance of things, he nonetheless continues to rely upon the stock of imagery he has built en route to abstract mastery. It is this stock of imagery that permits him to work at the level of heuristic, through convenient and nonrigorous means of exploring problems and relating them to problems already mastered.

Reinforcement and Feedback

With respect to corrective information, there is something particularly happy about the exercises we chose to use. In learning quadratics by the use of our blocks and then by the aid of the balance beam, children were enabled by immediate test to determine whether they had "got there." A collection of square pieces of wood is aggregated in a form that either makes a square or doesn't, and the child can see it immediately. So too with a balance beam: it either balances or it does not. There is no instructor intervening between the learner and the materials.

But note well that the instructor had to enter in several ways. In the first place, he determined within quite constrained limits the nature of the sequences, so that the children would have the greatest chance of seeing the relation of what went before to what was up now. Whether we succeeded well in these sequences we do not know—save that the children learned some elegant mathematics in a fairly short time. What guided us was some sort of psychological-mathematical intuition, and while that may be satisfactory for such engineering as we did, it is certainly not satisfactory from the point of view of understanding how to do it better.

We failed on several occasions, as judged by the lagging interest of a particular child, when we wanted to be sure that the child had really understood something. Our most glaring failure was in trying to get across in symbolic form (probably too early) the idea of distributiveness —that $a+(b+c)$ and $(a+b)+c$ could be treated as equivalent. One of our cleverest young pupils commented at the beginning of an hour, with a groan, "Oh, they're distributing the distributive law again." In fact, our difficulty came from a misjudgment of the importance of giving them a symbolic mode for correcting iconic constructions. We were too eager to be sure that they sensed the notational analogue of the factoring constructions they had been making and which they understood at the iconic level so well that further construction was proving a bore.

We have few fresh observations to report on the matter of overdrive and anxiety. One of our pupils had a rather strong push about mathematics from his father at home. He was the child who, on the first day, had to demonstrate his prowess by multiplying two large and ugly numbers on the board, announcing the while, "I know a lot of math." He was probably our best student, but he made no progress until he got over the idea that what was needed was hard computation. It was he, too, who complained that the blocks used for quadratics *had* to have *some* size. But once he was willing to play with unknowns as "x" he showed considerable power. His father was his unwilling ally at this point, for he told him that "x's" were from algebra, which was a subject most children took in high school.

Perhaps the greatest problem one has in an experiment of this sort is to keep out of the way, to prevent oneself from becoming a perennial source of information, interfering with the child's ability to take over the role of being his own corrector. But each classroom situation is unique in this way, and each dyad of teacher and pupil. Some of the teacher-pupil pairs became quite charged with dependency; in others the child or the teacher resisted. But that is another story.

Some Conclusions

A first and obvious conclusion is that one must take into account the issues of predisposition, structure, sequence, and reinforcement in preparing curriculum materials—whether one is concerned with writing a textbook, a lesson plan, a unit of instruction, a program, or, indeed, a conversation with didactic ends in view. But this obvious conclusion suggests some rather nonobvious implications.

The type of supporting research that permits one to assess how well one is succeeding in the management of relevant instructional variables requires a constant and close collaboration of teacher, subject-matter specialist, and psychologist. As intimated earlier, a curriculum should be prepared jointly by the subject-matter expert, the teacher, and the psychologist, with due regard for the inherent structure of the material, its sequencing, the psychological pacing of reinforcement, and the building and maintaining of predispositions to problem solving. As the curriculum is being built, it must be tested in detail by close observational and experimental methods to assess not simply whether children are "achieving" but rather what they are making of the material and how they are organizing it. It is on the basis of "testing as you go" that revision is made. It is this procedure that puts the evaluation process at a time when and place where its results can be used for correction while the curriculum is being constructed.

Only passing reference has been made to the issue of individual differences. Quite plainly, they exist in massive degree—in the extent to which children have problem-solving predispositions, in the degree of their interest, in the skills that they bring to any concrete task, in their preferred mode of representing things, in their ability to move easily through any particular sequence, and in the degree to which they are initially dependent upon extrinsic reinforcement from the teacher. The fact of individual differences argues for pluralism and for an enlightened opportunism in the materials and methods of instruction. Earlier we asserted, rather off-handedly, that no single ideal sequence exists for any group of children. The conclusion to be drawn from that assertion is not that it is impossible to put together a curriculum that would satisfy a group of children or a cross-section of children. Rather, it is that if a curriculum is to be effective in the classroom it must contain different ways of activating children, different ways of presenting sequences, different opportunities for some children to "skip" parts while others work their way through, different ways of putting things. A curriculum, in short, must contain many tracks leading to the same general goal.

Our illustrations have been taken from mathematics, but there are some generalizations that go beyond to other fields. The first is that it took the efforts of many highly talented mathematicians to discern the underlying structure of the mathematics that was to be taught. That is to say, the simplicity of a mathematics curriculum rests upon the history and development of mathematics itself. But even so glorious an intellectual tradition as that of mathematics was not enough. For while many virtues have been discovered for numbers to the base 10, students cannot appreciate such virtues until they recognize that the base 10 was not handed down from the mountain by some mathematical God. It is when the student learns to work in different number bases that the base 10 is recognized for the achievement that it is.

Finally, a theory of instruction seeks to take account of the fact that a curriculum reflects not only the nature of knowledge itself but also the nature of the knower and of the knowledge-getting process. It is the enterprise par excellence where the line between subject matter and method grows necessarily indistinct. A body of knowledge, enshrined in a university faculty and embodied in a series of authoritative volumes, is the result of much prior intellectual activity. To instruct someone in these disciplines is not a matter of getting him to commit results to mind. Rather, it is to teach him to participate in the process that makes possible the establishment of knowledge. We teach a subject not to produce little living libraries on that subject, but rather to get a student to think mathematically for himself, to consider matters as an historian does, to take part in the process of knowledge-getting. Knowing is a process, not a product.

24 MODELS FOR OPTIMIZING THE LEARNING PROCESS [1]
G. J. Groen and R. C. Atkinson

Although the experimental work in the field of programmed instruction has been quite extensive, it has not yielded much in the way of unequivocal results. For example, Silberman (1962), in a summary of 80 studies dealing with experimental manipulations of instructional programs, found that 48 failed to obtain a significant difference among treatment comparisons. When significant differences were obtained, they seldom agreed with findings of other studies on the same problem. The equivocal nature of these results is symptomatic of a deeper problem that exists not only in the field of programmed instruction but in other areas of educational research.

An instructional program is usually devised in the hope that it optimizes learning according to some suitable criterion. However, in the absence of a well-defined theory, grave difficulties exist in interpreting the results of experiments designed to evaluate the program. Usually the only hypothesis tested is that the program is better than programs with different characteristics. In the absence of a theoretical notion of why the program tested should be optimal, it is almost impossible to formulate alternative hypotheses in the face of inconclusive or contradictory results. Another consequence of an atheoretical approach is that it is difficult to predict the magnitude of the difference between two experimental treatments. If the difference is small, then it may not turn out to be

[1] Support for this research was provided by the National Aeronautics and Space Administration, Grant No. NGR-05-020-036, and by the Office of Education, Grant No. OE5-10-050.
SOURCE: G. J. Groen and R. C. Atkinson, "Models for Optimizing the Learning Process," *Psychological Bulletin*, 66, no. 4 (October 1966), 309–20. Copyright © 1966 by the American Psychological Association. Reprinted by permission of the publisher.

significant when a statistical test is applied. However, as Lumsdaine (1963) has pointed out, lack of significance is often interpreted as negative evidence.

What appears to be missing, then, is a theory that will predict the conditions under which an instructional procedure optimizes learning. A theory of this type has recently come to be called a *theory of instruction*. It has been pointed out by several authors (e.g., articles in Gage, 1963, and Hilgard, 1964), that one of the chief problems in educational research has been a lack of theories of instruction. Bruner (1964) has characterized a theory of instruction as a theory that sets forth rules concerning the most efficient way of achieving knowledge or skill; these rules should be derivable from a more general view of learning. However, Bruner made a sharp distinction between a theory of learning and a theory of instruction. A theory of learning is concerned with *describing* learning. A theory of instruction is concerned with *prescribing* how learning can be improved. Among other things, it prescribes the most effective sequence in which to present the materials to be learned and the nature and pacing of reinforcement.

While the notion of a theory of instruction is relatively new, optimization problems exist in many other areas and have been extensively studied in a mathematical fashion. Within psychology, the most prominent example is the work of Cronbach and Gleser (1965) on the problem of optimal test selection for personnel decisions. Outside psychology, optimization problems occupy an important place in areas as diverse as physics, electrical engineering, economics, and operations research. Despite the fact that the specific problems vary widely from one field to another, several mathematical techniques have been developed that can be applied to a broad variety of optimization problems.

The purpose of this paper is to indicate how one of these techniques, dynamic programming, can be utilized in the development of theories of instruction. Dynamic programming was developed by Bellman and his associates (Bellman, 1957, 1961, 1965; Bellman & Dreyfus, 1962) for the solution of a class of problems called multistage decision processes. Broadly speaking, these are processes in which decisions are made sequentially, and decisions made early in the process affect decisions made subsequently.

We will begin by formalizing the notion of a theory of instruction and indicating how it can be viewed as a multistage decision process. This formalization will allow us to give a precise definition of the optimization problem that arises. We will then consider in a general fashion how dynamic programming techniques can be used to solve this problem. Although we will use some specific optimization models as illustrations, our main aim will be to outline some of the obstacles that stand in the way of the development of a quantitative theory of instruction and indicate how they might be overcome.

Multistage Instructional Models

The type of multistage process of greatest relevance to the purposes of this paper is the so-called discrete N-stage process. This process is concerned with the behavior of a system that can be characterized at any given time as being in State w. This state may be univariate but is more generally multivariate and hence is often called a state vector (the two terms will be used interchangeably). The state of this system is determined by a set of decisions. In particular, every time a decision d (which may also be multivariate) is made, the state of the system is transformed. The new state is determined by both d and w and will be denoted by $T(w,d)$. The process consists of N successive stages. At each of the first $N-1$ stages, a decision d is made. The last stage is a terminal stage in which no decision is made. The process can be viewed as proceeding in the following fashion: Assume that, at the beginning of the first stage, the system is in state w_1. An initial decision d_1 is made. The result is a new state w_2 given by the relation:

$$w_2 = T(w_2,d_1).$$

We are now in the second stage of the process, so a second decision d_2 is made, resulting in a new state w_3 determined by the relation

$$w_3 = T(w_2,d_2).$$

The process continues in this way until finally:

$$w_N = T(w_{N-1},d_{N-1}).$$

If each choice of d determines a unique new state, $T(w,d)$, then the process is deterministic. It is possible, however, that the new state is probabilistically related to the previous state. In this nondeterministic case, it is also necessary to specify for each Stage i a probability distribution $Pr(w_i w_{i-1},d_{i-1})$.

In a deterministic process, each sequence of decisions d_1, $d_2, \ldots d_{N-1}$ and states $w_1, w_2, \ldots, w_N$ has associated with it a function that has been termed the criterion or return function. This function can be viewed as defining the utility of the sequence of decisions. The optimization problem one must solve is to find a sequence of decisions

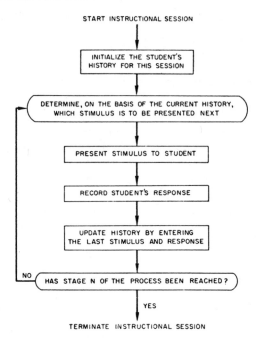

Figure 1   Flow diagram for an instructional system.

that maximizes their criterion function. The optimization problem for a nondeterministic process is similar except that the return function is some suitable type of expectation.

In order to indicate how an instructional process can be considered as an N-stage decision process, a fairly general instructional paradigm will be introduced. This paradigm is based on the type of process that is encountered in computer-based instruction (Atkinson & Hansen, 1967). In instruction of this type, a computer is programmed to decide what will be presented to the student next. The decision procedure, which is given in diagrammatic form in Figure 1, is based on the past stimulus-response history of the student. It should be noted that this paradigm contains, as special cases, all other programmed instructional techniques currently in vogue. It may also correspond to the behavior of a teacher making use of a well-defined decision procedure.

It will be assumed that the objective of the instructional procedure is to teach a set of concepts and that the instructional system has available to it a set of stimulus materials regarding these concepts. A stage of the process will be defined as being initiated when a decision is made regarding which concept is to be presented and terminated when the history file is updated with the outcome of the decision. In order to completely define the instructional system we need to define:

1. The set S of all possible stimulus presentations.
2. The set A of all possible responses that can be made by the student.
3. The set H of histories. An element of H need not be a complete history of the student's behavior. It may only be a summary.
4. A function δ of H onto S. This defines the decision procedure used by the system to determine the stimulus presentation on the basis of the history.
5. A function μ of $S \times A \times H$ onto H. This function updates the history.

Thus, at the beginning of Stage i, the history can be viewed as being in State h_i. A decision is then made to present $s_i = \delta(h_i)$, a response a_i is made to s_i and the state of the system is updated to $h_{i+1} = \mu(s_i, a_i, h_i)$.

In a system such as this, the stimulus set S is generally predetermined by the objectives of one's instructional procedure. For example, if the objective is to teach a foreign language vocabulary, then S might consist of a set of words from the language. The response set A is, to a great extent, similarly predetermined. Although there may be some choice regarding the actual response mode utilized (e.g., multiple choice vs. constructed response), this problem will not be considered here. The objectives of the instructional procedure also determine some criterion of optimality. For example, in our vocabulary example this might be the student's performance on a test given at the end of a learning session. The optimization problem that is the main concern of this paper is to find a suitable decision procedure for deciding which stimulus s to present at each stage of the process, given that S, A, and the optimality criterion are specified in advance. Such a decision procedure is called a *strategy*. It is determined by the set of possible histories H, the decision function δ, and the updating function μ.

For a particular student, the stimulus presented at a given stage and the response the student makes to that stimulus can be viewed as the observable outcome of that stage of the process. For an N-stage process, the sequence $(s_1, a_1, s_2, a_2, \ldots, s_{N-1}, a_{N-1})$ of outcomes at each stage can be viewed as the outcome of the process. The set of all possible outcomes of an instructional procedure can be represented as a tree with branch points occurring at each stage for each possible stimulus presentation and each possible response to a stimulus. An example of such a tree is given in Figure 2 for the first two stages of a process with stimulus presentations, s, s' and two responses a, a'.

The most complete history would contain, at the beginning of each stage, a complete account of the outcome of the procedure up to that stage. Thus, h_i would consist of some sequence $(s_1, a_1, s_2, a_2, \ldots, s_{i-1}, a_{i-1})$. Ideally, one could then construct a decision function δ which spec-

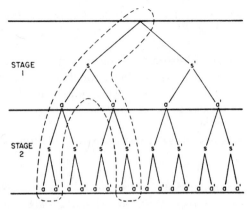

Figure 2   Tree diagram for the first two stages of a process with two stimuli s and s', and two responses a and a'. (The dotted lines enclose the subtree generated by a possible response sensitive strategy.)

ified, for each possible outcome, the appropriate stimulus presentation s_i. However, two problems emerge. The first is that the number of outcomes increases rapidly as a function of the number of stages. For example, at the tenth stage of a process such as that outlined in Figure 2, we would have 4^{10} outcomes. The specification of a unique decision for each outcome would clearly be a prohibitively lengthy procedure. As a result, any practical procedure must classify the possible outcomes in such a way as to reduce the size of the history space. Apart from the problem of the large number of possible outcomes, one is also faced with the problem that many procedures do not store as much information as others. For example, in a linear program in which all students are run in lockstep, it is not possible to make use of information regarding the student's responses.

In general, instructional systems may be classified into two types: those that make use of the student's response history in their stage-by-stage decisions, and those that do not. The resulting strategies may be termed *response insensitive* and *response sensitive*. A response insensitive strategy can be specified by a sequence of stimulus presentations $(s_1, s_2, \ldots, s_{n-1})$. A response sensitive strategy can be represented by a subtree of the tree of possible outcomes. An example is given in Figure 2. There are two chief reasons for making this distinction. The first is that response insensitive strategies are less complicated to derive. The second is that response insensitive strategies can be completely specified in advance and so do not require a system capable of branching during an actual instructional session.

While this broad classification will be useful in the ensuing discussion, it is important to note that several types of history spaces are possible within each class of strategy. Even if the physical constraints of the system are such that only response insensitive strategies can be considered, it is possible to define many ways of "counting" stimulus presentations. The most obvious way is to define the history at Stage i as the number of times each stimulus has been presented. A more complicated procedure (which might be important in cases where stimuli were easily forgotten) would be to also count for each stimulus the number of other items that had been presented since its most recent presentation.

The discussion up to this point has been concerned mainly with the canonical representation of an instructional system, and a deliberate effort has been made to avoid theoretical assumptions. While this leads to some insight into the nature of the optimization problem involved, the multistage process cannot be sufficiently well-defined to yield a solution to the optimization problem without imposing theoretical assumptions. It will be recalled that, in order to define a multistage process, it is necessary to specify a transformation $w_{i+1} = T(w_i, d_i)$ given the state and decision at Stage i. In order to optimize the process, it is also necessary to be able to state at each stage the effect of a decision upon the criterion function. The simplest criterion function to use is one which depends only on the final state of the system. This function will be called the *terminal return function* and denoted $\phi(w_N)$. An intuitive interpretation of $\phi(w_N)$ is the score on a final test.

If the transformation T were deterministic, then the sequence of optimum decisions could be determined by enumerating in a tree diagram all possible outcomes and computing $\phi(w_N)$ for each path. A path that maximized $\phi(w_N)$ would yield a sequence of decisions corresponding to appropriate nodes of the tree. If T were nondeterministic, then a strategy would yield a tree. Each tree would define a probability distribution over the w and thus an expected terminal return

$$E(\phi(w_N)|\sigma) = \sum_{w_N \, \epsilon W} \phi(w_N) P(w_N|\sigma) \qquad [1]$$

could be computed for each strategy σ. In either case, this process of simple enumeration of the possible branches of a tree is impossible in any practical situation since too many alternative paths exist, even for a reasonably small N. The problem of developing a feasible computational procedure will be discussed in the next section. The problem of immediate concern is the most satisfactory way of defining the state space W and the transformations $T(w_i, d_i)$.

At first sight, it would seem that w_i could be defined as the history at Stage i and $T(w_i, d_i)$ as the history updating rule. However, while this might be feasible in cases where the history space is either specified in advance or subject to major constraints, it has the severe disadvantage that it necessitates an ad hoc choice of histories and, without the addition of theoretical assumptions, it is impossible to compare the effectiveness of different histories. Even if the history space is predetermined, such as might be the case in a simple linear program where all a history can do is "count" the occurrences of each stimulus item, it is necessary to make some theoretical assumption regarding the precise form of $\phi(w_N)$.

One way to avoid problems such as this is to introduce theoretical assumptions regarding the learning process explicitly in the form of a mathematical model. In the context of an N-stage process, a learning model consists of: (a) a set of learning states Y; (b) a usually nondeterministic response rule which gives (for each state of learning) the probability of a correct response to a given stimulus; and (c) an updating rule which provides a means of determining the new learning state (or distribution of states) that results from the presentation of a stimulus, the response the student makes, and the reinforcement he receives. At the beginning of Stage i of the process, the student's state is denoted by y_i. After Stimulus s_i is presented, the student makes a response a_i, the probability of which is determined by s_i and y_i. The learning state of the student then changes to $y_{i+1} = T(y_i, s_i)$. Models of this type have been found to provide satisfactory descriptions for a variety of learning phenomena in areas such as paired-associate learning and concept formation. Detailed accounts of these models and their fit to empirical phenomena are to be found in Atkinson, Bower, and Crothers (1965), Atkinson and Estes (1963), and Sternberg (1963).

In the example of the learning of a list of vocabulary items, the two simplest models that might provide an adequate description of the student's learning process are the single-operator linear model (Bush & Sternberg, 1959) and the one-element model (Bower, 1961; Estes, 1960). In the single-operator linear model, the set Y is the closed unit interval $[0,1]$. The states are values of response probabilities. Although these probabilities can be estimated from group data, they are unobservable when individual subjects are considered. If, for a particular stimulus j, $q_i^{(j)}$ is the probability of an error at the start of Stage i and that item is presented, then the new state (i.e., the response probability) is given by

$$q_{i+1}^{(j)} = \alpha q_i^{(j)} \quad (0 < \alpha \leqslant 1). \qquad [2]$$

If $q_1^{(j)}$ is the error probability at the beginning of the first stage, then it is easily shown that

$$q_i^{(j)} = q_1^{(j)} \alpha^{n_i^{(j)}} \qquad [3]$$

where $n^{i(j)}$ is the number of times Item j has been presented and reinforced prior to Stage i. The response rule is simply that if a subject is in state q_i with respect to a stimulus and that stimulus is presented, then he makes an error with probability q_i. This model has two important properties. The first is that, although the response rule is nondeterministic, the state transformation that occurs as the result of an item presentation is deterministic. The second is that the model is response insensitive since the same transformation is applied to the state whether a correct or incorrect response occurs. The only information that can be used to predict the state is the number of times an item has been presented.

In the one-element model, an item can be in one of two states: a learned state L and an unlearned state $\bar{L}$. If an item is in State L, it is always responded to correctly. If it is in State $\bar{L}$, it is responded to correctly with probability g. The rule giving the state transformation is nondeterministic. If an item is in State $\bar{L}$ at the beginning of a stage and is presented, then it changes its state to L with probability c (where c remains constant throughout the procedure). Unlike the linear model, the one-element model is response sensitive. If an error is made in response to an item then that item was in State $\bar{L}$ at the time that the response was made. To see how this fact influences the response probability, it is convenient to introduce the following random variable:

$$X_n^{(j)} = \begin{cases} 1, & \text{if an error occurs on the } n\text{th presentation of Item } j \\ 0, & \text{if a success occurs on the } n\text{th presentation of Item } j \end{cases}$$

Then

$$Pr(X_n^{(j)} = 1) = (1-g)(1-c)^{n-1}, \quad [4]$$

but

$$Pr(X_n^{(j)} = 1 \mid X_{n-1}^{(j)} = 1) = (1-g)(1-c). \quad [5]$$

In contrast, for the single-operator linear model

$$Pr(X_n^{(j)} = 1) = Pr(X_n^{(j)} = 1 \mid X_{n-1}^{(j)} = 1) = q_1^{(j)} \alpha^{n-1}. \quad [6]$$

Although these two models cannot be expected to provide the same optimization scheme in general, they are equivalent when only response-insensitive strategies are considered. This is due to the fact that if α is set equal to $1-c$ and $q_1^{(j)}$ to $1-g$ then identical expressions for $Pr(x_n^{(j)} = 1)$ result for both models.

With the introduction of models such as these, the state space W and the transformation T can be defined in terms of some "learning state" of the student. For example, in the case of the linear model and a list of m stimulus items, we can define the state of the student at State i as the m-tuple

$$q = (q^{(1)}, q^{(2)}, \ldots, q^m) \qquad [7]$$

where $q^{(j)}$ denotes the current probability of making an error to item s_j and define $T(q,s_j)$ as the vector obtained by replacing $q^{(j)}$ with $\alpha_q^{(j)}$. This notation is illustrated in Figure 3. If the behavioral optimization criterion were a test on the m items administered immediately after Stage N of the process, then the return function would be the expectation of the test score, that is,

$$\sum_{j=1}^{m} \{1 - q_N^{(j)}\}$$

where $1 - q_N^{(j)}$ is the probability of a correct response at the end of the instructional process. It is not necessary, however, that W be the actual state space of the model. It may, instead, be more convenient to define w_i as some function of the parameters of the model. For example, if the process of learning a list of simple items can be described by a one-element model, then w_i can be defined as the n-tuple whose j^{th} element is either L or $\bar{L}$. However, if one is interested in some criterion that can be expressed in terms of probabilities of the items being in State L, then it may be computationally more convenient to consider w_i as an n-tuple whose j^{th} element is the probability that stimulus s^j is in State L at the beginning of Stage i.

It is clear from these examples that a learning model can impose a severe constraint upon the history space in the sense that information regarding observable outcomes is rendered redundant. For example, if $q_1^{(j)}$ is known on a priori grounds (for each j), then the linear model renders the entire response history redundant. This is because the response probability of each item is completely determined by the number of

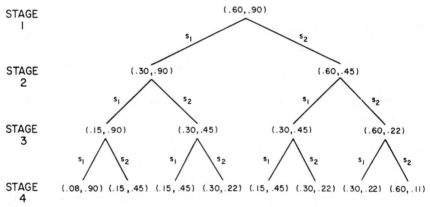

Figure 3   Outcome tree of response probabilities for linear model with $a = .5$, $q_1^{(1)} = .6$, $q_1^{(2)} = .9$.

times it has been presented. With the one-element model, the nature of the constraint on the history is not immediately clear.

In general, the problem of deciding on an appropriate history, h_i, is similar to the problem of finding an observable statistic that provides an adequate basis for inferring the properties of the distribution of states. A desirable property for such a history would be for it to summarize all information concerning the state so that no other history would provide additional information. A history with this property can be called a *sufficient history*. The most appropriate sufficient history to use would be that which was the most concise.

In the theory of statistical inference, a statistic with an analogous property is called a sufficient statistic. Since w_i is a function of the parameters of the model, it would seem reasonable to expect that if a sufficient statistic exists for these parameters, then a sufficient history would be some function of the sufficient statistic. For a general discussion of the role of sufficient statistics in reducing the number of paths that must be considered in trees resulting from processes similar to those considered here, the reader is referred to Raiffa and Schlaiffer (1961).

Optimization Techniques

Up to now, the only technique we have considered that enables us to find an optimal strategy is to enumerate every path of the tree generated by the N-stage process. Although the systematic use of learning models can serve to reduce the number of paths that must be considered, much too large a number of paths still remains in most problems where a large number of different stimuli are used. The main success with a direct approach has been in the case of response insensitive strategies (Crothers, 1965; Dear, 1964; Dear & Atkinson, 1962; Suppes, 1964). In these cases, either the number of stimulus types is drastically limited or the problem is of a type where the history can be simplified on a priori grounds. The techniques used in these approaches are too closely connected with the specific problem treated and the models used for any general discussion of their merits.

The theory of dynamic programming provides a set of techniques that reduce the portion of a tree that must be searched. These techniques have the merit of being model-free. Moreover, they provide a computational algorithm that may be used to discover optimal strategies by numerical methods in cases where analytic methods are too complicated. The first application of dynamic programming to the design of optimal instructional systems was due to Smallwood (1962). Since then, several other investigators have applied dynamic programming techniques to instructional problems of various types (Dear, 1964; Karush & Dear, 1966;

Matheson, 1964). The results obtained by these investigators are too specific to be reviewed in detail. The main aim in this section is to indicate the nature of the techniques and how they can be applied to instructional problems.

Broadly speaking, dynamic programming is a method for finding an optimal strategy by systematically varying the number of stages and obtaining an expression which gives the return for a process with N stages as a function of the return from a process with $N-1$ stages. In order to see how this is done, it is necessary to impose a restriction on the return function and define a property of optimal policies. Following Bellman (1961, p. 54), a return function is Markovian if, for any $K < N$, the effect of the remaining $N - K$ stages of the N-stage process upon the return depends only upon: (a) the state of the system at the end of the Kth decision, and (b) whatever subsequent decisions are made. It is clear that the return function $\phi(w_N)$ possesses this property. Another type of return function that possesses this property is one of the form:

$$g(w_1,d_1) + g(w_2,d_2) + \ldots + g(w_{N-1}, d_{N-1}) + \phi(w_N).$$

A return function of this latter form may be important when cost as well as final test performance is an important criterion in designing the system. For example, in a computer-based system, $g(w_i, d)$ might be the cost of using the computer for the amount of time required to make Decision d_i and present the appropriate stimulus. Since the expressions resulting from a function of this form are somewhat more complicated, we will limit our attention to return functions of the form $\phi(w_N)$. However, it should be borne in mind that essentially the same basic procedures can be used with the more complicated return function.

If a deterministic decision process has this Markovian property, then an optimal strategy will have the property expressed by Bellman (1961, p. 57) in his optimality principle: *whatever the initial state and the initial decision are, the remaining decisions constitute an optimal policy with regard to the state resulting from the first decision*. To see how this principle can be utilized, let $f(w)$ denote the return from an N-stage process with initial state w if an optimal strategy is used throughout, and let us assume that T is deterministic and W is discrete. Since the process is deterministic, the final state is completely determined by the initial state w and the sequence of decisions $d_1, d_2, \ldots, d_{N-1}$ (it should be recalled that no decision takes place during the last stage). If D_N denotes an arbitrary sequence of $N-1$ successive decisions (D_1 being the empty set), then the final state resulting from w and D_N can be written as $w'(D_N, w)$. The problem that must be solved is to find the sequence D_N which maximizes $\phi[w'(D_N, w)]$. If such a sequence exists, then

$$f_N(w) = \max_\phi \left[w'(D_N, w) \right]. \qquad [8]$$

While the solution of such a problem can be extremely complicated for an arbitrary N, it is easily shown that for $N = 1$

$$f_1(w) = \phi(w). \qquad [9]$$

As a result, if a relation can be found that connects $f_i(w)$ with $f_{i-1}(w)$ for each $i \leq N$ then $f_N(w)$ can be evaluated recursively by evaluating $f_i(w)$ for each i. Suppose that, in an i-stage process, an initial decision d is made. Then w is transformed into a new state, $T(w,d)$, and the decisions that remain can be viewed as forming an $(i-1)$-stage process with initial state $T(w,d)$. The optimality principle implies that the maximum return from the last $i-1$ stages will be $f_{i-1}[T(w,d)]$. Moreover, if $D_i = (d, d_2, \ldots, d_{i-1})$ and $D_{i-1} = (d_2, d_3, \ldots, d_{i-1})$ then

$$\phi[w'(D_i, w)] = \phi[w'(D_{i-1}, T(w,d))]. \qquad [10]$$

Suppose that D_{i-1} is the optimal strategy for the $i-1$ stage process. Then the right-hand side of this equation is equal to $f_{i-1}[T(w,d)]$. An optimal choice of d is one which maximizes this function. As a result, the following basic recurrence relation holds:

$$f_n(w) = \max_d f_{n-1}[T(w,d)] \quad (2 \leq n \leq N) \qquad [11]$$

$$f_1(w) = \phi(w). \qquad [12]$$

Equations 11 and 12 relate the optimal return from an n-stage process with the optimal return from a process with only $n-1$ stages. Formally, n may be viewed as indexing a sequence of processes. Thus, the solution of these equations provides us with a maximum return function $f_n(w)$ for each process and (also for each process) an initial decision d which ensures that this maximum will be attained if optimal decisions are made thereafter. It is important to note that both d and $f_n(w)$ are functions of w and that w should, in general, range over all values in the state space W. In particular, the initial state and initial decision of a typical member of the sequence of processes we are considering should not be confused with the initial state and initial decisions of the N-stage process we are trying to optimize. In fact, the initial decision of the two-stage process corresponds to the last decision d_{N-1} of the N-stage process; the initial decision of the three-stage process corresponds to the next-to-last decision d_{N-2} of the N-stage process, and so on.

The linear model of Equation 2 with the state space defined in Equation 7 provides an example of a deterministic process. The use of Equations 11 and 12 to find an optimal strategy for the special case of a four-state process with two items is illustrated in Table 1. The state at the beginning of Stage i is defined by the vector $(q_i^{(1)}, q_i^{(2)})$. The optimization criterion is the score on a test administered at the end of the instructional process. Since Item j will be responded to correctly with probability $1 - q_N^{(j)}$, the terminal return function for an N-stage process is $2 - (q_N^{(1)} + q_N^{(2)})$. The calculation is begun by viewing the fourth stage as a one-stage process and obtaining the return for each possible state by means of Equation 12. The possible states at this fourth stage are obtained from Figure 3. The third and fourth stages are then viewed as a two-stage process and Equation 11 is used to determine the return that results from presenting each item for every possible state that can occur in Stage 3, the previously computed result for a one-stage process being used to complete the computations. For each state, the item with the maximum return represents the optimal decision to make at Stage 3. The three-stage process beginning at Stage 2 is analyzed in the same way, using the previously computed results for the last two stages. The result is an optimal decision at Stage 2 for each possible state, assuming optimal decisions thereafter. Finally, the procedure is repeated for the four-stage process beginning at Stage 1. The optimal strategies of item presentation that result from this procedure are given at the bottom of Table 1.

With a nondeterministic process, the situation is considerably more complicated. The transformation T is some type of probability distribution and the final return is a mathematical expectation. While arguments based on the optimality principle allow one to obtain recursive equations similar in form to Equations 11 and 12, both the arguments used to obtain the equations and the methods used to solve them can contain many subtle features. A general review of the problems encountered in this type of process was given by Bellman (1961), and some methods of solution were discussed by Bellman and Dreyfus (1962). For the case where the transformation defines a Markov process with observable states, Howard (1960) has derived a set of equations together with an iterative technique of solution which has quite general applicability. However, in the case of instructional processes, it has so far tended to be the case that either the learning model used has unobservable states or that the process can be reduced to a more deterministic one (as is the case with the linear model discussed in the example above).

A response insensitive process can often be viewed as a deterministic process. This is not, in general, possible with a response sensitive process. The only process of this type that has been extensively analyzed is that in which a list of stimulus-response items is to be learned, the re-

Table 1
Calculation of Optimal Strategy for Example of Figure 3 Using Dynamic Programming

Number of Stages in Process N	Initial State w	Initial Decision d	Next State $T(w,d)$	Final Return of optimal $N-1$ Stage Process $f_{N-1}[T(w,d)]$	Optimal Decision
1	(.08, .90)			1.02	
	(.15, .45)			1.40	
	(.30, .22)			1.48	
	(.60, .11)			1.29	
2	(.15, .90)	1	(.08, .90)	1.02	2
		2	(.15, .45)	1.40	
	(.30, .45)	1	(.15, .45)	1.40	2
		2	(.30, .22)	1.48	
	(.60, .22)	1	(.30, .22)	1.48	1
		2	(.60, .11)	1.29	
3	(.30, .90)	1	(.15, .90)	1.40	2
		2	(.30, .45)	1.48	
	(.60, .45)	1	(.30, .45)	1.48	1 or 2
		2	(.60, .22)	1.48	
4	(.60, .90)	1	(.30, .90)	1.48	1 or 2
		2	(.60, .45)	1.48	

Optimal Strategies

Stage 1	Stage 2	Stage 3
Item 1	Item 2	Item 2
Item 2	Item 1	Item 2
Item 2	Item 2	Item 1

turn function is the score on the test administered at the end of the process, and the learning of each item is assumed to occur independently and obey the assumptions of the one-element model. An attempt to solve this problem by means of a direct extension of Howard's techniques to Markov processes with unobservable states has been made by Matheson (1964). However, this approach appears to lead to somewhat cumbersome equations that are impossible to solve in any nontrivial case. A more promising approach has been devised by Karush and Dear (1966). As in our example of the linear model, the states of the process are defined in terms of the current probability that an item is in the conditioned state and a similar (though somewhat more general) return function is assumed. An expression relating the return from an $N-1$ stage process to the return from an N-stage process is then derived. The main complication in deriving this expression results from the fact that the outcome tree is more complicated, the subject's responses having to be explicitly considered. Karush and Dear proceeded to derive certain properties of the return function and proved that in an N-trial experiment[2] with items $s_1, s_2, \ldots, s_m$ (where $N > m$) and arbitrary *initial* conditioning probabilities $(\lambda^{(1)}, \lambda^{(2)}, \ldots, \lambda_m)$, an optimal strategy is given by presenting at any trial an item for which the *current* conditioning probability is least. In most applications, the initial probabilities $\lambda^{(j)}$ can be assumed to be zero. In this case, an observable sufficient history can be defined in terms of a counting process. An optimal strategy is initiated by presenting the m items in any order on the first m trials, and a continuation of this strategy is optimal if and only if it conforms to the following rules:

1. For every item set the count at 0 at the beginning of Trial $m+1$.

2. Present an item at a given trial if and only if its count is *least* among the counts for all items at the beginning of the trial.

4. Following a trial, increase the count for the presented item by 1 if the response was correct but set it at 0 if the response was incorrect.

Discussion

In this paper we have attempted to achieve two main goals. The first has been to provide an explicit statement of the problems of optimal instruction in the framework of multistage decision theory. The main reason for introducing a somewhat elaborate notational system was the need for a clear distinction between the optimization problem, the learning process that the student is assumed to follow, and the method of solving the optimization problem. The second goal has been to indicate, using dynamic programming as an example, how optimization problems can be solved in practice. Again, it should be emphasized that dynamic programming is not the only technique that can be used to solve optimization problems. Many response-insensitive problems are solvable by more simple, though highly specific, techniques. However, dynamic programming is the only technique that has so far proved useful in the derivation of response sensitive strategies. In describing dynamic programming, an attempt has been made to emphasize two basic features: the optimality principle, and the backward-induction procedure by means of which an optimal strategy is obtained by starting, in effect, at the last stage. It should be noted that these can be used independently. For example, it is possible to combine the optimality principle with a forward induction procedure which starts at the first stage of the process.

---

[2] Here the term N-trial experiment refers to an anticipatory paired-associate procedure which involves N presentations. To each stimulus presentation, the subject makes a response and then is told the correct answer for that stimulus.

In any attempt to apply an optimization theory in practice, one must ask the question; how can it be tested experimentally? In principle, it is easy to formulate such an experiment. A number of strategies are compared—some theoretically optimal, others theoretically suboptimal. A test is administered at the end of the process that is designed to be some observable function of the final return. However, the only experiment that has been explicitly designed to test an optimization theory is that by Dear, Silberman, Estavan, and Atkinson (1965), although in the case of response insensitive theories, it is often possible to find experiments in the psychological literature which provide indirect support.

The experiment reported by Dear et al. was concerned with testing the strategy proposed by Karush and Dear (1966) for the case outlined in the preceding section. The major modification of this strategy was to prohibit repeated presentations of the same item by forcing separations of several trials between presentations of individual items.[3] Each subject was presented with two sets of paired-associate items. The first set of items was presented according to the optimization algorithm. Items in the second set were presented an equal number of times in a suitable random order. (It will be recalled that this strategy is optimal if the linear model is assumed.) It was found that while the acquisition data (e.g., rate of learning) tended to favor items in the first set, no significant difference was found in posttest scores between items of the two sets.

It follows from the result of this experiment that, even for a simple problem such as this, an optimization theory is needed that assumes a more complicated learning model. At least one reason for this is that, in simple paired-associate experiments that result in data which is fitted by the one-element model, any systematic effects of stimulus-presentation sequences are usually eliminated by presenting different subjects with different random sequences of stimuli. When a specific strategy is used, it may be the case·that either the assumption of a forgetting process or of some short-term memory state becomes important in accounting for the data (Atkinson & Shiffrin, 1965).

Unfortunately, the analytic study of the optimization properties of more complex models, at least by dynamic programming techniques, is difficult. The only major extension of response sensitive models has been a result of Karush and Dear (1965) which shows that the optimal strategy for the one-element model is also optimal if it is assumed that the probability of a correct response in the conditioned state L is less than one. However, there are ways by means of which good approximations to optimal strategies might be achieved, even in the case of extremely complex models. Moreover, in many practical applications one is not

---

[3] This modification was necessary because it has been shown experimentally that if the same item is presented on immediately successive trials then the subject's response is affected by considerations of short-term memory.

really critically concerned about solving for an optimal procedure, but would instead be willing to use an easily determined procedure that closely approximates the return of the optimum procedure. The main means of achieving a good approximation is by analyzing the problem numerically, computing the optimal strategy for a large number of special cases. A useful general algorithm for doing this is the backward induction procedure described in the preceding section. Table 1 illustrates how this algorithm can be used to find an optimal strategy for one particular case. Dear (1964) discussed the use of this algorithm in other response insensitive problems.

The chief disadvantage of the backward induction algorithm is that it can only be used for optimal strategy problems involving a fairly small number of stages. Although its use can eliminate the need to search every branch of a tree, the computation time still increases as a function of the number of possible final states that can result from a given initial state. However, a backward induction solution for even a small number of stages would provide a locally optimal policy for a process with a large number of stages, and this locally optimal strategy might provide a good approximation to an optimal strategy. To decide how "good" an approximation such a strategy provided, its return could be evaluated and this could be compared with the returns of alternative strategies.

References

Atkinson, R. C., Bower, G. H., & Crothers, E. J. *An introduction to mathematical learning theory.* New York: Wiley, 1965.

Atkinson, R. C., & Estes, W. K. Stimulus sampling theory. In R. D. Luce, R. R. Bush, & E. Galanter (Eds.), *Handbook of mathematical psychology.* Vol. 2. New York: Wiley, 1963. Pp. 121–268.

Atkinson, R. C., & Hansen, D. N. Computer-assisted instruction in initial reading: The Stanford Project. *Reading Research Quarterly,* 1967, in press.

Atkinson, R. C., & Shiffrin, R. M. Mathematical models for memory and learning. Technical Report 79, Institute for Mathematical Studies in the Social Sciences, Stanford University, 1965. (To be published in D. P. Kimble, Ed., *Proceedings of the Third Conference on Learning, Remembering, and Forgetting.* New York: New York Academy of Sciences, 1966, in press.)

Bellman, R. *Dynamic programming.* Princeton: Princeton University Press, 1957.

Bellman, R. *Adaptive control processes.* Princeton: Princeton University Press, 1961.

Bellman, R. Functional equations. In R. D. Luce, R. R. Bush, & E. Galanter (Eds.), *Handbook of mathematical psychology.* Vol. 3. New York: Wiley, 1965. Pp. 487–513.

Bellman, R., & Dreyfus, S. E. *Applied dynamic programming.* Princeton: Princeton University Press, 1962.

Bower, G. H. Application of a model to paired-associate learning. *Psychometrika,* 1961, 26, 255–280.

Bruner, J. S. Some theorems on instruction stated with reference to mathematics. In E. R. Hilgard (Ed.), *Theories of learning and theories of instruction.* (63rd National

Society for the Study of Education Yearbook, Part 1) Chicago: University of Chicago Press, 1964. Pp. 306–335.

Bush, R. R., & Sternberg, S. H. A single operator model. In R. R. Bush & W. K. Estes (Eds.), *Studies in mathematical learning theory*. Stanford: Stanford University Press, 1959. Pp. 204–214.

Cronbach, L. J., & Gleser, G. *Psychological tests and personnel decisions*. Urbana: University of Illinois Press, 1965.

Crothers, E. J. Learning model solution to a problem in constrained optimization. *Journal of Mathematical Psychology*, 1965, 2, 19–25.

Dear, R. E. Solutions for optimal designs of stochastic learning experiments. Technical Report SP-1765/000/00. Santa Monica: System Development Corporation, 1964.

Dear, R. E., & Atkinson, R. C. Optimal allocation of items in a simple, two-concept automated teaching model. In J. E. Coulson (Ed.), *Programmed learning and computer-based instruction*. New York: Wiley, 1962. Pp. 25–45.

Dear, R. E., Silberman, H. F., Estavan, D. P., & Atkinson, R. C. An optimal strategy for the presentation of paired-associate items. Technical Memorandum TM-1935/101/00. Santa Monica: System Development Corporation, 1965.

Estes, W. K. Learning theory and the new mental chemistry. *Psychological Review*, 1960, 67, 207–223.

Gage, N. L. (Ed.) *Handbook of research on teaching*. Chicago: Rand McNally, 1963.

Hilgard, E. R. (Ed.) *Theories of learning and theories of instruction*. (63rd National Society for the Study of Education Yearbook, Part 1) Chicago: University of Chicago Press, 1964.

Howard, R. A. *Dynamic programming and Markov processes*. New York: Wiley, 1960.

Karush, W., & Dear, R. E. Optimal procedure for an N-state testing and learning process —II. Technical Report SP-1922/001-00. Santa Monica: System Development Corporation, 1965.

Karush, W., & Dear, R. E. Optimal stimulus presentation strategy for a stimulus sampling model of learning. *Journal of Mathematical Psychology*, 1966, 3, 19–47.

Lumsdaine, A. A. Instruments and media of instruction. In N. L. Gage (Ed.), *Handbook of research on teaching*. Chicago: Rand McNally, 1963. Pp. 583–683.

Matheson, J. Optimum teaching procedures derived from mathematical learning models. Unpublished doctoral dissertation, Stanford University, 1964.

Raiffa, H., & Schlaiffer, R. *Applied statistical decision theory*. Cambridge, Mass.: Harvard University, Graduate School of Business Administration, 1961.

Silberman, H. F. Characteristics of some recent studies of instructional methods. In J. E. Coulson (Ed.), *Programmed learning and computer-based instruction*. New York: Wiley, 1962. Pp. 13–24.

Smallwood, R. D. *A decision structure for teaching machines*. Cambridge, Mass.: MIT Press, 1962.

Sternberg, S. H. Stochastic learning theory. In R. D. Luce, R. R. Bush, & E. Galanter (Eds.), *Handbook of mathematical psychology*. Vol. 2. New York: Wiley, 1963. Pp. 1–120.

Suppes, P. Problems of optimization in learning a list of simple items. In M. W. Shelly, II, & G. L. Bryan (Eds.), *Human judgment and optimality*. New York: Wiley, 1964. Pp. 116–126.

EPILOGUE

A final word is in order concerning the view of educational psychology represented by the selections in this book.

Early psychologists such as James and Thorndike were genuinely interested in problems of education. Moreover, both these individuals and others like them were sensitive to the problems of understanding behavior in the context of the school. As psychology developed, however, the attempt to understand behavior was gradually replaced by an emphasis on establishing precise relationships between stimuli and responses.

At the same time as psychology moved away from a concern with knowing and teaching, educational psychology appeared (the first issue of the *Journal of Educational Psychology* was published in 1910). While psychologists and educational psychologists continued to write on the problems of subject matter learning (e.g., Judd, 1915; Thorndike, 1932), the focus of empirical concern within education gradually shifted to measurement and methods studies (for summary of early methods research especially in the sciences, see Curtis, 1931, 1939).

The emphasis on measurement was not surprising given the work of Galton and the success of Binet. And, comparing different methods of instruction was a natural enough outcome of an interest in helping to make the classroom a more effective place in which to learn. The net result of the emphasis on methods studies and measurement was, however, that the "educationist" and educational psychologist left theorizing about human behavior largely to the experimental psychologist. Moreover, while progress has been made in some areas of mental measurement (e.g., Merwin, 1969) little if any progress can be claimed for almost a half a century of methods research (for a summary and critique of early as well as recent studies in this area see Stephens, 1967).

It is an underlying assumption of this book that one reason for the general lack of progress in methods research is the poverty of theories and models for knowledge. Without such theories and models as sources of independent and dependent variables, we have no way of deciding what our experiments shall be about. There are innumerable things to look at in schooling, and without some systematic way of talking about these phenomena we have no way of defining variables for experimentation. Even in the area of measurement where we have advanced more rapidly, we have reached a point where descriptions of knowledge would make a substantial contribution.

To disparage the lack of theory is one thing, but to suggest fruitful theoretical activity is quite another. For as Deese (1969) has recently argued, we have the era of learning theories such as those of Tolman, Hull, and Guthrie to point to as instances of premature, and on occasion fruitless activity. If, then, premature theories can be as bad as no theories at all, what are we to do?

In one sense, any empirical investigation presupposes some theory even if it is unarticulated. Our choice of variables is based on assumptions about the nature of behavior as well as its major determinants. We must at least make the assumptions that underlie our work explicit. Having done this, we must then relate them to the assumptions of others in both experimental psychology and educational psychology.

In another sense, however, we can ask whether educational psychology should not be looking at a particular set of problems, namely, the conditions of knowledge acquisition. To be sure, these problems are not the exclusive property of the educational psychologist, and we can profit from an examination of the models constructed by the experimental psychologist. On the other hand, describing knowledge in the context of schooling may be uniquely accomplished within the "discipline" of education.

It may help to clarify our thinking if we consider the idea of macroscopic variables (Kepes, 1965). By macroscopic we mean variables on a more general level than those usually chosen by the laboratory investigator. Examples of such variables and their role in the description of phenomena can be found in the physical sciences. For example, a gas may be described in terms of pressure, volume, and temperature (macroscopic variables). The same gas may also be described in terms of the masses and velocities of hypothetical particles (the kinetic theory of gases). Both descriptions lead to the same predictions about the behavior of a gas and if they did not, it would be the description in terms of the kinetic theory that would have to be changed—barring a revolution in scientific thinking (Kuhn, 1962).

When we want to control the behavior of a gas, we manipulate its pressure, volume, and temperature. The kinetic theory of gases does not give us variables we can manipulate directly, but rather enables us to understand the changes we observe. We are successful in controlling the behavior of gases, not because of the kinetic theory, but because we have macroscopic variables.

The point of this analogy for educational psychology is that we need to work systematically on two levels. On the level of practice, we need to describe the variables of schooling so that we can predict and control its outcomes. And, on a more fine-grained level, we should have models and theories to explain the effects we produce. The way a practitioner can benefit from a description of school learning in terms of macroscopic variables is obvious. It is perhaps less clear how theories of school learning based on hypothetical models of behavior can have practical value.

The role of building models for school learning may become more apparent if we remind ourselves that theories and models give us ways of thinking about behavior so that we need not rely on trial and error when principles based on intuition and experience break down. The contribution of science to practice is to enlarge the evidence that must be taken into account before forming our own opinions.

References

Curtis, Francis D., *Second Digest of Investigations in the Teaching of Science* (Philadelphia: P. Blakiston's Son & Co., 1931).

Curtis, Francis D., *Third Digest of Investigations in the Teaching of Science* (Philadelphia: P. Blakiston's Son & Co., 1939).

Deese, James, "Behavior and Fact," *American Psychologist*, vol. 24 (May, 1969), 515–22.

Judd, C. H., *Psychology of High School Subjects* (Boston: Ginn and Co., 1915).

Kepes, Gyorgy, ed., *Structure in Art and in Science* (New York: George Braziller Inc., 1965).

Kuhn, T., *Structure of Scientific Revolutions* (Chicago: University of Chicago Press, 1962).

Merwin, Jack C., "Historical Review of Changing Concepts of Education," *Sixty-eighth Yearbook of the National Society for the Study of Education* (Chicago: University of Chicago Press, 1969), pp. 6–25.

Stephens, J. M., *The Process of Schooling: A Psychological Examination* (New York: Holt, Rinehart & Winston, 1967).

Thorndike, E. L., *The Psychology of Algebra* (New York: The Macmillan Co., 1932).